A

First

Introduction

to

Husserl's Phenomenology

A

First

Introduction

to

Husserl's Phenomenology

by

JOSEPH J. KOCKELMANS, PH.D.

DUQUESNE UNIVERSITY PRESS
Editions E. Nauwelaerts, Louvain

Other works by Joseph J. Kockelmans

Edmund Husserl's Phenomenological Psychology. *A Historico-Critical Study.* 358 pages. Price: $7.95.

Phenomenology and Physical Science. 208 pages. Price: $6.95.

Martin Heidegger. A First Introduction to His Philosophy. 190 pages. Price: $3.75.

by others

MANFRED S. FRINGS—*Max Scheler. A Concise Introduction into the World of a Great Thinker.* 223 pages. Price: $6.50.

HENRY J. KOREN—*Research in Philosophy. A Bibliographical Introduction to Philosophy and a Few Suggestions for Dissertations.*

Library of Congress Catalog Card Number 67-27996
Printed in the United States of America

PREFACE

In principle this book delivers the text which constituted the background for a series of lectures I gave on several different occasions. My audiences each time were made up of graduate students in philosophy and psychology. The content and framework of this book has been determined partly by the character of those audiences.

The purpose of these lectures was to give the students a *first* introduction to Husserl's phenomenology in which, as far as Husserl himself is concerned, nothing was presupposed. In lieu of discussing the insights of the most important commentators, I have tried here to allow Husserl to explain again his own ideas. And as the main intention of my lectures was to present only an introduction to Husserl's thought, I did not dwell on special phenomenological analyses concerning such topics as the 'world', nature, space, time, man, language, the human body, and so on, because I felt that in an introduction the question of what phenomenology itself is must occupy the central place. It was for this reason that I tried to describe the genesis of Husserl's phenomenology and to explain the most important aspects of its content and method, both of which, otherwise, are *essentially* correlated. But although it is true that one of the intentions of this study is to describe the development which Husserl underwent in regard to his own view on phenomenology, since 1906 especially, the stress in the different chapters is placed nonetheless on the doctrinal and methodological aspects of Husserl's thought. This is why I have felt free not to respect the chronological order of Husserl's works in a strict way.

Each chapter deals with one or another aspect which in Husserl's own view is essential to his phenomenological philosophy. In addition to the most relevant historical remarks, each chapter contains a paraphrase or brief summary of a few sections of one of Husserl's own publications, followed by certain surveying, critical, and concluding remarks inasfar as these appeared to be in keeping with the main intention of this study. The reason I have chosen to adhere rather closely to Husserl's own text in the body of each chapter lies in the fact that Husserl uses an analyzing and describing style. Although it is true that one can easily give a brief survey of the results of an analysis, the analyses and descriptions themselves, which generally are more important than the isolated results, cannot be maintained in their richness except by 'repeating' them in one way or another. Furthermore as it is well-known that Husserl's style of writing makes a literal translation very difficult, if not sometimes even impossible,[1] I have for the most part given preference to summaries or to a free paraphrasis rather than to a literal translation. Only in crucial sentences have I followed Husserl's text as closely as possible, but even then I have tried to strip Husserl's overcrowded sentences of all non-vital elements. It will be obvious that in composing these summaries and paraphrases I have employed also the existing translations of Gibson, Cairns, Lauer, Alston, and Nakhnikian. As far as terminology is concerned I have generally followed the list of phenomenological terms proposed by Spiegelberg in the second volume of *The Phenomenological Movement*. Grateful acknowledgment must therefore be made to the following publishers for their permission to use the translations of Husserl's works in the sense indicated: Martinus Nijhoff, The Hague, Netherlands; Harper & Row, Publishers, New York; and The Macmillan Company, New York.

This book does not deliver a complete picture of Husserl's work. For a first introduction, however, this fact should not inspire serious objections, for it does give a relatively clear and concise overall picture of the most essential themes and topics of Husserl's phenomenological philosophy. Neither is this study original; it does not offer new ideas concerning Husserl's philosophy. I have tried only to help the reader to become conversant with the major topics of Husserl's phenomenology and the extensive literature on the subject. That is why I wish also explicitly to acknowledge that I have used throughout the book the excellent commentaries of Fink, Landgrebe, Biemel, De Waelhens, Van Breda, Ricoeur, Gurwitsch, and Diemer to which I have nevertheless seldom explicitly referred as they are not yet available in English. Also I owe very much to the works of Spiegelberg, Farber, and Lauer, whose

---

1. Quentin Lauer, ed., *Edmund Husserl: Phenomenology and the Crisis of Philosophy*. Translated with an Introduction by Quentin Lauer (New York: Harper and Row, 1965), p. 1.

publications I have quoted many times in the historical sections of this study.

I am deeply indebted to Father Henry J. Koren, S. T. D., who worked extensively with the first draft of this book and later gave his painstaking attention to its final draft.

Pittsburgh, Pennsylvania
December 15, 1965

JOSEPH J. KOCKELMANS

TABLE OF CONTENTS

Table of Contents

A First Introduction to Husserl's Phenomenology

LIST OF ABBREVIATIONS

References to Husserl's publications are all to the German edition of his works as indicated in this list. However, references have also been made to translations wherever that was possible. The translations used are listed below. References to translations are always put between brackets.

Phil. d. Arithm.	*Philosophie der Arithmetik. Psychologische und logische Untersuchungen.* Erster Band (Halle a.S.: C.E.M. Pfeffer, 1891).
L. U.	*Logische Untersuchungen,* 3 vols. (Halle a.S.: Max Niemeyer, 1921-1922).
Die Idee	*Die Idee der Phänomenologie. Fünf Vorlesungen* (1907). Herausgegeben und eingeleitet von Walter Biemel, Husserliana, Band II (The Hague: Martinus Nijhoff, 1950).
	The Idea of Phenomenology. Trans. William P. Alston and George Nakhnikian. (The Hague: Martinus Nijhoff, 1964).
Phil. str. W.	"Philosophie als strenge Wissenschaft", *Logos,* 1 (1910-1911) 289-341.
	"Philosphy as Rigorous Science", in Quentin Lauer, *Edmund Husserl: Phenomenology and the Crisis of Philosophy* (New York: Harper and Row, 1965), pp. 69-147. See also: *Cross Currents,* 6 (1956), pp. 228-246, 324-344.
Ideen	*Ideen zu einer reinen Phänomenologie und phänomenologischen Philosophie.*
Ideen I	*Erstes Buch: Allgemeine Einführung in die reine Phänomenologie.* Herausgegeben von Walter Biemel, Husserliana, Band III (The Hague: Martinus Nijhoff, 1950).
	Ideas. General Introduction to Pure Phenomenology. Trans. W. R. Boyce Gibson (New York: Collier Books, 1962).
Ideen II	*Zweites Buch: Phänomenologische Untersuchungen zur Konstitution.* Herausgegeben von Marley Biemel, Husserliana, Band IV (The Hague: Martinus Nijhoff, 1952).

Ideen III   *Drittes Buch: Die Phänomenologie und die Fundamente der Wissenschaften.* Herausgegeben von Marley Biemel, Husserliana, Band V (The Hague: Martinus Nijhoff, 1952).

Erste Philos.   *Erste Philosophie. Erster Teil: Kritische Ideengeschichte* (1923-1924). Herausgegeben von Rudolf Boehm, Husserliana, Band VII (The Hague: Martinus Nijhoff, 1956).

    Zweiter Teil: Theorie der phänomenologischen Reduktion (1923-1924). Herausgegeben von Rudolf Boehm, Husserliana, Band VIII (The Hague: Martinus Nijhoff, 1959).

Phän. Psych.   *Phänomenologische Psychologie* (1925). Herausgegeben von Walter Biemel, Husserliana, Band IX (The Hague: Martinus Nijhoff, 1962).

Phenomenology   "Phenomenology", in *Encyclopaedia Britannica,* 14th edition. London, 1927, vol. 17, col. 699-702.

F. tr. L.   *Formale und transzendentale Logik. Versuch einer Kritik der logischen Vernunft* (Halle a.S.: Max Niemeyer, 1929).

Cart. Med.   *Cartenianische Meditationen und Pariser Vorträge.* Herausgegeben und eingeleitet von Prof. S. Strasser, Husserliana, Band I (The Hague: Martinus Nijhoff, 1950).

    Cartesian Meditations. An Introduction to Phenomenology. Trans. Dorion Cairns (The Hague: Martinus Nijhoff, 1960).

Krisis   *Die Krisis der europäischen Wissenschaften und die transzendentale Phänomenologie. Eine Einleitung in die phänomenologische Philosophie.* Herausgegeben von Walter Biemel, Husserliana, Band VI (The Hague: Martinus Nijhoff, 1954).

Erf. u. Urt.   *Erfahrung und Urteil. Untersuchungen zur Genealogie der Logik* Redigiert und herausgegeben von Ludwig Landgrebe, (Hamburg: Claassen, 1954).

INTRODUCTION

Biographical Notes

Prossnitz, Moravia is the birthplace of *Edmund Gustav Albrecht Husserl*. He was born on April 8, 1859 when Moravia was part of the Austrian Empire. It had previously been under Hapsburg rule and later became part of the Czechoslovakian republic, but its situation at the time of Husserl's birth makes him an Austrian.

Husserl finished his elementary education at the age of ten and went to Vienna to enter secondary school. He completed his studies at the *Realgymnasium* there and at the *Staatsgymnasium* in Olmütz, and then entered college. When he arrived at the University of Leipzig in 1876 he was without much promise, for his scholastic record at Olmütz had not been outstanding. With the exception of mathematics and physics for which he showed considerable enthusiasm, he had little interest in his courses.

Husserl did study astronomy along with mathematics and physics at Leipzig from 1876 to 1878. During this time he was also attending lectures in philosophy given by Wilhelm Wundt, but even this prominent phychologist and philosopher could not stimulate his interest in the study of philosophy. In 1878 Husserl left Leipzig and went to Friedrich Wilhelm University in Berlin.

In Berlin he met three of the leading mathematicians of the era: Kronecker, Kummer and Weierstrass who taught him a rigorous and disciplined way of thinking. The influence of these three scholars led Husserl to develop a keen interest in the philosophy of mathematics. Weierstrass and Kronecker claimed that the concept of space is not the last foundation of mathematics, but that the concept of integral numbers is basic to this science. While pondering such problems as these Husserl was beginning also to feel a profound interest in philosophy as such. The lectures of Friedrich Paulsen contributed greatly to this interest. Paulsen recognized Husserl's reflective capacity and sought to channel his thinking in ways which were later to prove productive of revolutionary insights.

In 1881 Husserl transferred to the University of Vienna to finish his mathematical studies although he had become more and more interested in philosophy. He received his degree of doctor of philosophy in 1883, having studied under Königsberger and written a dissertation entitled *Beiträge zur Theorie der Variationsrechnung* (Contributions to the Theory of the Calculus of Variations).

In 1883 Husserl was summoned to Berlin by Weierstrass to work as the latter's assistant. He accepted the call although he would have preferred to stay in Vienna to study philosophy. When subsequently Weierstrass became ill and unable to lecture, Husserl returned to Vienna to continue his philosophical studies, having decided definitely by this time to dedicate himself entirely to the cause of philosophy. For the next two years he attended the lectures of Franz Brentano. Husserl was impressed by the way in which Brentano presented the philosophy of Hume and Mill, and especially by his lectures on psychology, ethics, and logic. Husserl is indebted to Brentano for his thinking on the subject of intentionality, although from the very beginning there was some disagreement between the two on this topic. In the years which followed Brentano directed Husserl in the study of Bolzano's *Wissenschaftslehre* (Doctrine of Science), the importance of which became clear to Husserl after he later studied Lotze's *Logic*.

In addition to being impressed by Bolzano as introduced to him by Brentano, Husserl was particularly struck by the way in which Brentano himself linked philosophy and science. Brentano held that philosophy above all must be 'scientific', which Husserl understood as meaning that all philosophers must recognize the necessity of rigorous methods of investigation. Whereas Paulsen and Wundt had emphasized the biological sciences when dealing with the relationship between science and philosophy, Brentano stressed psychology and logic in this context. Seeing the fact that Husserl, under the influence of Mill, more or less identified psychology with philosophy, it is understandable why he became interested in investigations into the function of 'philosophy', taken as a 'strict and rigorous science', in the realm of logic.

In 1886 Brentano advised Husserl to go to the University of Halle as Stumpf's assistant in order to obtain a thorough grounding in psychology. One year later Husserl was made a *Privatdozent* under Stumpf and became a member of the philosophy faculty at Halle. Here in 1891 he published his *Philosophy of Arithmetic.* Influenced by Frege's critique of this book as well as by certain other factors, Husserl abandoned the psychologism of his first work in later publications. In Part One of his *Logical Investigations,* viz., *Prolegomena to Pure Logic,* he explicitly rejected all forms of psychologism in logic. This work was well received by many of the great scholars of the time and definitely established Husserl as a philosopher.

Husserl went to Göttingen as "extraordinarius professor" of philosophy in 1901 and remained there until 1916. During this period he wrote extensively, including *Lectures on Phenomenology, The Idea of Phenomenology,* the famous *Logos* article entitled *Philosophy as a Rigorous Science,* and the first part of his *Ideas;* of these writings only the two latter were published. These works reflect the influence of Descartes and Kant on Husserl's thinking.

In 1916 Husserl was called to Freiburg as a full professor. There he completed the last two parts of *Ideas,* his *First Philosophy, Phenomenological Psychology,* and *Formal and Transcendental Logic,* the last of which was the only book published during his lifetime. Husserl stayed at Freiburg until 1929 when he applied for superannuation. Thereafter and until 1937 he worked feverishly on several major works from which he later published only the *Cartesian Meditations* and the first part of *Crisis.*

Husserl, originally of the Jewish faith, converted to Lutheranism in 1886. He is said to have been sympathetic to Catholicism toward the end of his life, but did not convert a second time. He died in 1938 after a long and painful struggle with pleurisy.[1]

---

1. See for these bibliographical notes in general, Andrew D. Osborn, *The Philosophy of Edmund Husserl in Its Development from His Mathematical Interest to His First Conception of Phenomenology in 'Logical Investigations'* (New York: International Press, 1934). Marvin Farber, *The Foundation of Phenomenology. Edmund Husserl and the Quest for a Rigorous Science of Philosophy* (Cambridge: Harvard University Press, 1940). E. Parl Welch, *The Philosophy of Edmund Husserl. The Origin and Development of His Phenomenology.* (New York: Octagon Books, Inc., 1965). Herbert Spiegelberg, *The Phenomenological Movement. A Historical Introduction,* 2 vols. (The Hague: Martinus Nijhoff, 1960), vol. I, pp. 73-163. *Edmund Husserl. 1859-1959.* Récueil coménoratif publié à l'occasion du Centenaire de la naissance du Philosophie, H. L. Van Breda et J. Taminiaux ed. (The Hague: Martinus Nijhoff, 1959).

The Husserl Archives[2]

In 1938 Herman L. Van Breda, O.F.M., went to Freiburg in Breisgau to prepare his doctoral dissertation on the phenomenology of Husserl. There he learned that the Nazis were undoubtedly intending to destroy Husserl's manuscripts. After consultation with Husserl's widow, Mrs. Malvina Husserl, he began immediately to take the necessary measures to safeguard the extremely valuable collection. After many difficulties and various detours via Berlin and Brussels, the manuscripts finally arrived in Louvain, Belgium.

Presently the Husserl Archives contain not only Husserl's manuscripts, but also his philosophical library, his letters and numerous rewritings in longhand of manuscripts previously written in shorthand. Among the some 8,000 works kept at Louvain there are many reprints dedicated to Husserl by several renowned philosophers. One can find annotations made by Husserl himself in the margins of many of these books and essays. One of the most remarkable items in this philosophical collection is a copy of the first edition of *Sein und Zeit* by Heidegger containing a lengthy hand-written dedication by its author to his master. This copy, too, is full of marginal philosophical remarks by Husserl; they gradually reveal his disappointment in noticing how his beloved pupil grew further and further away from him. After having read the book he wrote on the title page: "Amicus Plato, magis amica veritas".

Almost all of the unpublished manuscripts which Husserl left behind at his death have been stored at Louvain; they comprise about 40,000 pages in 8°, practically all of which were written in the Gabelberg shorthand system. These manuscripts have proven to be of inestimable value for the understanding of Husserl's philosophical evolution, for they contain the result of his philosophical explorations in his later and still fruitful years. Study of his latest manuscripts has brought to light the

---

2. See for the following H. L. Van Breda, "Le sauvetage de l'héritage husserlien et la fondation des Archives-Husserl", *Husserl et la Pensée moderne.* Actes du deuxième Colloque International de Phénoménologie. Krefeld, 1-3 novembre, 1956, édités par les soins de H. L. Van Breda et J. Taminiaux (The Hague: Martinus Nijhoff, 1959), pp. 1-77. See also Joseph J. Kockelmans, *Edmund Husserl. Een inleiding tot zijn fenomenologie* (The Hague: Lannoo, 1963), pp. 14-16.

fact that his unpublished works are probably in a sense even more important than the books which Husserl himself published.

In addition to an extensive collection of letters and diaries, the Archives contain also about 7,000 pages of longhand transcriptions of original shorthand Husserl texts; his assistants Edith Stein, Ludwig Landgrebe, and Eugen Fink are responsible for this work. Most of these pages have been scrutinized, annotated and sometimes even reworked by Husserl. As early as 1916 Edith Stein had started a systematic transcription which was later continued by Fink and Landgrebe. Multiple transcriptions exist for some of the lecture series and books; these make it possible to decipher Husserl's handwriting with greater ease and to test the accuracy of the copyists. In 1939 the most difficult job in this regard still remained to be done.

In 1935 at Freiburg, Fink and Landgrebe undertook a first classification of the shorthand manuscripts following a system which Husserl had checked and endorsed. This system was made still more complete at Louvain. Subsequently all manuscripts were grouped in packages of approximately 80 pages each.

Since 1939 various scholars have been engaged in the systematic deciphering of Husserl's writings with the intention of preparing the most important texts for publication. In 1939 Fink and Landgrebe came to Louvain to start the transcription of still unstudied manuscripts. From 1942 until 1947 Professor Strasser continued this labor of patience and endurance; from 1945 on Walter and Marley Biemel cooperated in this work for more than ten years, and since 1951 Rudolph Boehm has been carrying the lion's share. During this time more than 60% of the manuscripts have been typed in five-fold. Cards are made from the transcribed texts and these provide a chronological and systematic survey of Husserl's work. Transcriptions and cards are forwarded to the four cooperating centers in Paris, Buffalo, Cologne and Freiburg; in these locations the texts are studied further and, in consultation with Louvain, prepared for publication.

As a preparation for the publication of Husserl's complete philosophical works, a basic text is selected at first which is then complemented and illustrated by additional smaller texts. Eleven volumes with a total of about 5,000 pages have already been published in the Husserliana series which is being published with the purpose of providing a surveyable and systematically ordered whole of the complete philosophical work which Husserl left behind.

A supplement to these publications has existed since 1950. It is called *Phaenomenologica* and consists of philosophical studies by scholars who think along phenomenological lines. Within the span of three years, nine works of this latter series have been published; in 1965 this series comprised nineteen volumes.

The administration of the Husserl Archives anticipates that it will take another fifteen years for the transcription, scientific elaboration and, insofar as possible, the publication of all the manuscripts which Husserl has left us.

In connection with the Husserl movement and stimulated by the active director of the Husserl Archives, Father Herman Leo Van Breda, three international congresses have been held thus far, namely, at Brussels in 1951, at Krefeld, Germany in 1956 and at Royaumont, near Paris, in 1957. The proceedings of these congresses have been published each time in book form. Since then additional conferences have been held in Bologna and Mexico City.

Periodizations of Husserl's Development

A number of suggestions have been proposed in connection with the periodizations of Husserl's philosophical development. Eugen Fink, Husserl's assistant in Freiburg, is responsible for the most familiar of these. He divides the development of Husserl's phenomenology into three stages which correspond to his years in Halle, Göttingen and Freiburg as private teacher, "extraordinarius professor," and full professor respectively. These phases comprise the periods of psychologism, simple descriptive phenomenology, and transcendental phenomenology. Husserl's *Logical Investigations* and *Ideas* are the works which mark the passing from periods one and two to the final phase. It is the first two periods which from the viewpoint of the later transcendental phenomenology are to be seen as stages on the road to the realm of philosophy accessible only through the phenomenological reduction. Accordingly it is possible to speak also of two major periods in Husserl's development, namely pre-transcendental and transcendental philosophy.[3]

The above classification is useful in that it directs attention in each successive period to the trend toward a deeper and more general level of analysis. Spiegelberg, however, seems to distinguish the phases in a more comprehensive and more appropriate was.[4] He also divides Husserl's philosophical development into three periods: (1) the pre-phenomenological period, covering most of the Halle years and corresponding to this thinking in the first volume of *Logical Investigations* (1894-1900); (2) the stage of phenomenology as a limited epistemological enterprise, corresponding to Husserl's first years in Göttingen (1901-1906) and including the second volume of *Logical Investigations;* (3) the period of pure phenomenology as the universal foundation of philosophy and science, which began in 1906 and led to a new transcendentalism as well as a characteristic phenomenological idealism whose increasing radicalization provides the theme for Husserl's Freiburg period (1906-1938).

Spiegelberg holds that this developmental schema is analogous to a spiral. The pre-phenomenological period begins with the attempt to interpret mathematics via a psychology starting in the subject. When this is a partial failure Husserl is led to the formulation of an 'objectivistic' pure logic devoid of psychologism. Then the initial stages of phenomenology show equal stress on both the subjective and objective aspects of experience in their necessary correlation. In the further development of phenomenology once again the subjective is stressed as the source of all objectivities, but now conceived as on a higher, transcendental level, beyond descriptive psychology. It is proposed that the course of this curvilinear development could account for the alternate attraction and repulsion which Husserl's philosophy exerted on the minds of those whose development might be characterized as more rectilinear.[5]

---

3. Herbert Spiegelberg, *op. cit.,* vol. I, p. 74.
4. *Ibid.,* p. 74.
5. *Ibid.,* pp. 74-75.

A First Introduction to Husserl's Phenomenology

Intention and Plan of This Book

The fact that Husserl's thinking underwent many important shifts even after he had reached the final conception of phenomenology raises the question of how far it will be possible to present his philosophy as a systematic whole. In my opinion such an enterprise is unrealizable since Husserl's thinking underwent *essential* shifts, especially around 1894 and 1906. This is why I wish to confine myself to Husserl's full-fledged phemenology as it was explained between 1906 and 1938.

Because even in this period Husserl's thinking underwent important shifts, it will be necessary in describing his main ideas about phenomenology and phenomenological philosophy to attempt to combine a historical and a thematic approach. The frame of this exposition will be a very rough picture of Husserl's philosophical development between 1891 and 1938. Space limitations preclude more than a brief reference to Husserl's first period, but this material can be found in the excellent study of Marvin Farber entitled *The Foundation of Phenomenology,* and in Andrew D. Osborn's book, *The Philosophy of Edmund Husserl in Its Development From His Mathematical Interest to His First Conception of Phenomenology in 'Logical Investigations.'* Into the frame mentioned I shall insert more detailed accounts of Husserl's most important doctrines, following Husserl's own texts, inasfar as an introduction to his philosophy allows this.

According to Eugen Fink, Husserl declared explicitly several times that he had tried to describe four different roads to phenomenology. The first starts in logic; taking one's departure from a phenomenology of logic one can try to find the way to a universal phenomenology; this way is described in its several phases in Husserl's *Logical Investigations, Formal and transcendental Logic,* and *Experience and Judgment.* The second road departs from psychology; this is explained by Husserl in his *Logos* article, in his lecture course *Phenomenological Psychology,* and especially in his last book *Crisis.* The third road takes its starting point in the *Lebenswelt;* this is the main theme of his *Crisis* and innumerable manuscripts of the last decade of his life. The final road is the way of Descartes' *Meditationes de prima philosophia* as found in

Husserl's *The Idea of Phenomenology, Ideas,* and *Cartesian Meditations.*[6]

In this book I shall try to describe the latter way as it was preferred by Husserl in the most fruitful years of his life (1906-1929) and because it is presupposed in the other approaches. However, inasfar as it is possible I shall try also to indicate the main lines of the course of the other three. In this connection particular attention will be given to the psychological approach because it has aroused such great interest in contemporary psychology. For this reason, too, a special chapter appears which deals with the relations between phenomenological psychology and transcendental phenomenology.

---

6. See the remarks made by Eugen Fink in the discussion following Walter Biemel's paper: "Les phases décisives dans le développement de la philosophie de Husserl", *Husserl.* Cahiers de Royaumont: Philosophie, no. III (Paris: Minuit, 1959), pp. 32-71, p. 65. See also Edmund Husserl, *Erste Philosophie:* Einleitung des Herausgebers (Rudolf Boehm), pp. *xxxi-xlii* of the second volume.

CHAPTER ONE

THE ORIGIN OF HUSSERL'S PHENOMENOLOGY

1. *Phenomenology as a Descriptive Psychology*

The term 'Phenomenology'

It was in 1900 that the forty-one year old Husserl first began to use the term 'phenomenology'. There is no doubt that Husserl was quite aware of the various ways in which it had been used both in science and philosophy, nor is there doubts that he chose initially to use the term in the way Ernst Mach had intended.[1]

To understand this way one must know that Mach, in an address given in 1894,[2] spoke of a *'general physical phenomenology'* conceived as extending to all the areas of physics and having the aim of ultimately yielding the most abstract concepts of physical research. As Mach proposed it, 'physical phenomenology' was to begin in descriptions and proceed to its end result by means of comparing with each other different phenomena from the several branches of physics. In 1895 in *The Contrast Between Mechanical and Phenomenological Physics,*[3] Mach pointed to what he saw as the common aim for both Newton's method and his own phenomenological approach; each attempted to eliminate unnecessary additions in physics and particularly to extirpate the metaphysical. Phenomenological physics then was actually a coming-true of the old program of 'thought economy'. That Husserl was familiar with such a use of the term 'phenomenology' is evident in his review of Mach's first address in his *Report Concerning German Publications on Logic.*[4]

The term first appeared in Husserl's own work in a footnote. This was in 1900 and in connection with the first edition of his *Logical Investigations,* wherein he speaks specifically of 'descriptive pheno-

1. Herbert Spiegelberg, *op. cit.,* vol. I, p. 103.
2. *Ibid.,* p. 9.
3. *Ibid.*
4. *Ibid.*

menology of inner experience' as a basis for both empirical psychology and epistemology. When the second volume of *Logical Investigation* appeared in 1901 the term 'phenomenology' could be found in the introduction as pertaining to a new and important philosophical discipline. At this point, however, Husserl referred to it erroneously as *'descriptive psychology'* using this term in the manner of Brentano.[5]

After 1903, however, Husserl began to realize that his new philosophical discipline was completely different from Brentano's descriptive psychology. He saw in fact that this new discipline would have to be the absolute foundation for the whole of philosophy. Under the influence of a rather profound study of Kant, Husserl henceforth characterized his new philosophical discipline, to distinguish it from phenomenology as a descriptive psychology, as *'transcendental phenomenology'*. In a series of lectures, given at the university of Göttingen in 1907 under the title *The Idea of Phenomenology,* he even spoke of phenomenology as a 'Critique of Pure Reason'.[6] It may be interesting to consider Husserl's first characterizations of his phenomenology more thoroughly.

'Philosophy of Arithmetic'

According to Walter Biemel we must go back to 1887 if we want to understand Husserl's philosophical development and the genesis of his phenomenology.[7] At this time Husserl was working on the first draft of his *Philosophy of Arithmetic.* In this work Husserl tried to base his investigations concerning the concept of number upon the logical and psychological ideas of his time. This attempt was in harmony with the special studies he had made of mathematics, logic, and psychology. As we have seen in the *Introduction,* Husserl had received his doctor's degree in mathematics. His study under Weierstrass had given him a firm basis for his later logical work, and Brentano had made him enthusiastic for the purely descriptive type of investigation in empirical psychology. The fusion of these apparently diverse streams of scholar-

---

5. *Ibid.,* pp. 103-104.
6. Edmund Husserl, *Die Idee:* Einleitung des Herausgebers (Walter Biemel), pp. *vii-xi.*
7. Walter Biemel, "Les phases décisives dans le développement de la philosophie de Husserl", *Husserl,* pp. 32-71, p. 35.

ship in the realm of mathematics set the stage for his later career. As we shall see, the important changes in Husserl's development are to be explained to a large extent by the difficulties he encountered in his attempts to integrate these different elements within a 'really' philosophical horizon.[8]

As early as his *Philosophy of Arithmetic* we find in Husserl's work several elements of his later phenomenology. For instance, he constantly speaks in terms of 'achievement', reflection, and the method of disclosing the essences of things by going back to the origin of their meaning in consciousness and to the description of this origin. In these elements we may see the first indications of his later ideas about constitution, reduction, intentional analysis, and eidetic intuition. On the other hand, however, in his *Philosohy of Arithmetic* Husserl remained within the horizon of psychologism, although he tried to find completely new ways by *starting form* the psychological investigations of Brentano and Stumpf.[9]

For this reason a first point to be considered here is Husserl's initial training as a mathematician under Karl Weierstrass and Leopold Kronecker. Husserl's mathematical studies at the universities of Leipzig, Berlin and Vienna between 1876 and 1881 were concluded with a thesis on the calculus of variations. Then, from 1884 till 1886, after returning to Vienna, he audited Franz Brentano's lectures. This philosopher and psychologist lectured on philosophy, elementary logic and its necessary reforms, and also on selected psychological questions. Husserl himself was still in doubt whether he would devote himself to philosophy or remain in mathematics, but Brentano's lectures decided his final choice. His motivation for attending Brentano's lectures was partly curiosity, for Brentano was much discussed in Vienna, partly the advice of his friend Masaryk, who became later President of Czechoslovakia.

Despite his initial prejudices, Husserl did not resist the power of Brentano's personality very long. Brentano soon aroused Husserl's interest in philosophy and also in his new descriptive psychology, although

---

8. Marvin Farber, *op. cit.,* p. 15.
9. Walter Biemel, *loc. cit.,* p. 39.

Husserl's own questions were still restricted to the realm of mathematics, and in particular the theory of numbers, which was of little interest to Brentano's own philosophy. The most important point, however, is that these lectures convinced Husserl that philosophy is a serious undertaking which can be pursued in the spirit of the most rigorous science. This conviction led him to dedicate his life to philosophy.[10]

Thus, when Husserl finally decided to accept a university position in philosophy at Halle under the direction of Brentano's former student Carl Stumpf, he wrote his 'probationary thesis' *On the Concept of Number*. Its subtitle was 'Psychological Analyses'. Subsequently also his first book, Volume One of his unfinished *Philosophy of Arithmetic* (1891), dedicated to Brentano, was described as 'Psychological and Logical Studies'.

In this book it was not Husserl's intention to construct a system of arithmetic but merely to lay the scientific basis for a future system by means of a series of psychological and logical investigations, in which both criticism and positive developments should be included. The objective of these studies in the philosophy of mathematics was to derive the fundamental concepts of arithmetic, and later also of Euclidean geometry, from certain psychological acts. For this purpose these acts had to be traced in rigorous detail. The first part of his *Philosophy of Arithmetic* studies the main psychological questions connected with the analysis of the concepts of plurality, unity, and number, insofar as they are given to us really and not through indirect symbolization. The second part considers the symbolic concepts of plurality and number, and attempts to show how the fact that we are almost entirely limited to symbolic concepts of number determines the meaning and purpose of the theory of numbers.

The tools for all these attempts were taken from Brentano, Locke, Hume and Berkeley. These thinkers had been Husserl's introductory readings in philosophy and remained of basic importance to him throughout his later development. For all practical purposes, however, Husserl

---

10. Marvin Farber, *op. cit.*, pp. 8-9. Herbert Spiegelberg, *op. cit.*, vol. I, pp. 91-92.

borrowed most of his tools from John Stuart Mill, whose *System of Logic* he had studied intensively.[11]

Philosophy as a Radical Study of the Essences of Beings

In his *Philosophy of Arithmetic* Husserl attempts to develop a philosophy of numbers. According to him, this philosophy is a study of the psychological sources from which our number concepts are derived. The first intention of this work, however, is not to determine the nature of the psychological functions which are at the source of numeration, but to understand number itself, precisely as that which has been achieved by consciousness in its perception of numerable objects. It stands to reason that numbers as such cannot be perceived, but a certain mode of perceiving is connected with the operation of numbering the various numerable objects which results in numbers. It is also evident, according to Husserl, that a study of the numerable objects themselves does not enable us to determine what a number really is. To understand the essence of number, an accurate study must be made of the concepts which consciousness has constituted in itself; by numbering different numerable things, our consciousness imposes a determinate number upon them, and this number as such is constituted in consciousness by virtue of the data given in original perception.

Husserl was deeply aware of the fact that many thinkers before him had considered numbers to be mental constructs. But for him this point was only the beginning. The problem that remained was to explain how exactly numbers are constituted by consciousness and what the fundamental meaning is of these constitutive activities of consciousness. Moreover, if it is possible to arrive at the essence of numbers by analyzing the concept of number itself, why is it not possible to attain the essence of anything else simply by examining the concept of the object known? For, the intelligibility of the things themselves must be limited, it seems, to that which can be conceptualized.

If this supposition is correct, our first task will be to determine exactly what is meant by concepts and especially what is meant by con-

---

11. Marvin Farber, *op. cit.*, pp. 25-26. Herbert Spiegelberg, *op. cit.*, vol. I, pp. 92-93.

sciousness, which is at the source of all our concepts. However, if consciousness is what psychology claims, namely, nothing but a describable function, then, Husserl says, consciousness itself simply belongs to the class of things or facts. But if consciousness is only a thing, then concepts and ideas which are the results of the various activities of consciousness, likewise can only be things. Ideas, however, that are mere things are simply contingent facts; hence the possibility of knowledge, in any intelligible sense of the term, seems to be lost. In this supposition, therefore, skepticism will inevitably result, since to deny the necessary character of knowledge is to deny its very possibility. Skepticism, however, is completely inadmissible because it is self-contradictory. But if it is absolutely certain that there must be knowledge, then it is equally certain that knowledge is possible only on the condition that we are able to eliminate contingency in any form. Now, to eliminate the contingent is to eliminate the factual from our considerations. Thus, consciousness can be the seat of knowledge only if it belongs to a world completely separated from the world of facts. If it is possible to purify consciousness of everything factual, so that its content can truly be called knowledge in the proper sense of this term, then the objects of consciousness will be necessary objects and, therefore, *beings* in the full sense of the term. But to grasp beings in the full sense of the term is to grasp beings as absolutely necessary, and to grasp beings as absolutely necessary is to grasp the very essences of those beings. This, then, is for Husserl what philosophy must be: a radical and essential study of beings, that is to say, a radical study of the very essences of beings.[12]

These ideas, which were only latently present in Husserl's *Philosophy of Arithmetic,* implicitly contradicted the psychologism which his book explicitly tried to defend. Probably they were among the most important reasons why in the following years Husserl's ideas underwent a radical change with respect to the importance of psychology for mathematics and logic. Another factor in the reorientation of his thought was his exchange of ideas with Gottlob Frege. Long before Husserl,

---

12. Quentin Lauer, *The Triumph of Subjectivity* (New York: Fordham University Press, 1958), pp. 22-24. Marvin Farber, *op. cit.,* pp. 58-60; see also *ibid.,* pp. 25-60 (passim).

Frege had contended that logic and psychology are fundamentally different studies. He had done so again with great clarity in his critique of Husserl's *Philosophy of Arithmetic*. Paul Natorp's critique of psychologism also influenced Husserl's development in this matter. In any case, around 1894 Husserl's lectures began to develop a rigorous critique of psychologism. Published in 1900 as *Prolegomena to Pure Logic* (the first volume of *Logical Investigations*), this critique immediately stirred up interest and even excitement among logicians and psychologists.[13]

Psychologism. Reactions

As Spiegelberg mentions, the term 'psychologism' existed already before Husserl used it. Husserl himself credited it to Stumpf, who had used it as early as 1891 and who mentioned as its source the Hegelian historian Johann Eduard Erdmann. Compared with Stumpf's wider use, Husserl's was more specific, since at that time he was oriented to problems of mathematics and logic only. Husserl defined psychologism as the view that the theorectical foundation of mathematics and logic is supplied by psychology only, and especially by the psychology of knowledge. According to Husserl, therefore, psychologism is the view that psychology is both the necessary and the sufficient foundation of mathematics and logic, a point of view that, for logic, was defended by John Stuart Mill, Wundt, Sigwart, and Lipps.[14]

One of the first reactions against psychologism was the critique of Carl Stumpf. Stumpf admitted a more or less determined distinction but no real separation between the different sciences, especially not between philosophy and the empirical sciences. According to him, 'the prescription of blinkers' fails wherever empirical connections are involved and deductive insights are impossible. He opposed, for instance, the anti-psychologistic position of the neo-Kantians who, as we shall see later, in the name of critical philosophy wanted to remove all psychological foundations from philosophy. On the other hand, however,

---

13. Walter Biemel, *loc. cit.*, pp. 41-44. Marvin Farber, *op. cit.*, pp. 4-7, 37-38, 57-58. Herbert Spiegelberg, *op. cit.*, vol. I, p. 93.
14. Herbert Spiegelberg, *ibid.*, p. 94. Marvin Farber, *ibid.*, pp. 4-5.

Stumpf opposed also 'psychologism', understanding by this term the reduction of *all* philosophical problems and especially of *all* epistemological issues to psychological questions.[15]

Natorp's Critique of Psychologism

We find an analogous critique of psychologism in Paul Natorp's review of Theodor Lipps' *Basic Facts of Mental Life*. Lipps, following Stuart Mill, regarded psychology as the basis of philosophy, whereas Natorp doubted the possibility of basing logic and epistemology upon psychology. According to Lipps, the genetic derivation of the basic laws of knowledge from original facts of psychic life is identical with their epistemological foundation; the theory of knowledge, therefore, is a branch of psychology.

Natorp pointed out that psychical facts, indeed, are represented in the laws of knowledge and that these facts, as psychical, are also an object investigated by psychology. But it is not correct, he argued, to conclude from this that the axioms and statements of the different sciences are merely psychological laws. On the contrary, our consciousness of truth is independent of any genetic explanation by means of general psychological bonds. If we want to explain scientific data as they manifest themselves to us, we must admit that the principles of knowledge and truth have an independent objective foundation. Hence it is not correct to reduce epistemology to psychology, for the critique of knowledge and the psychology of knowledge require and condition each other.

In another paper Natorp argued that either logic is not founded or it must be constructed entirely on its own ground and not borrow its foundations from any other science. Those who make of logic a branch of psychology assume that psychology is the basic science and that logic is at best an application of psychology. Natorp asserted that not only the meaning of logic but the meaning of any objective science is denied and almost perverted into its very opposite if we make the objective truth of knowledge dependent upon subjective experiences.

---

15. Herbert Spiegelberg, *ibid.*, pp. 56-57.

To base logic upon subjective grounds would be to abolish it as an independent theory regarding the objective validity of knowledge.[16]

Frege's Critique

According to Frege, Husserl also had become a victim of the widespread philosophical disease known as 'psychologism'. For in his *Philosophy of Arithmetic* Husserl had tried to explain the essence of numbers by means of the psychological acts of consciousness themselves. In Frege's opinion, the mixture of psychology and logic is merely a means of avoiding difficulties. Frege did not deny that it is possible to study arithmetic from a psychological point of view but, according to him, we must clearly distinguish a number as a 'representation' from the objective meaning of that number. In the second part of Husserl's book, however, Frege concedes, there are indications that its author recognizes that our primary concern is with the things themselves of which we make representations and not with these representations themselves. The 'numbers in themselves' are objective in character and independent of our thinking. But, Frege argues, if our representations of a number is not the number itself, then the very foundation of the psychological viewpoint collapses insofar as the investigation of the essence of numbers is concerned.[17]

Husserl's Refutation of Psychologism

Studying those criticisms of psychologism, Husserl did not admit that all of them were valid for his *Philosophy of Arithmetic*. On the other hand, he realized that he had made several mistakes. In an intensive study concerning the relation between psychology and logic he came to the conclusion that psychologism really is untenable, and that, therefore, he should try to express what he really wanted to say, in a more accurate way. In the decade following the year 1891 he came gradually to a strikingly new point of view, which for the first time was published in his *Logical Investigations* (1900-1901). The first volume, entitled

---

16. Marvin Farber, *op. cit.*, pp. 5-6.
17. *Ibid.*, pp. 57-58.

Prolegomena to Pure Logic, contains, as is mentioned above, a detailed statement and critique of psychologism. It is characterized by thoroughness as well as by fairness to the authors examined. Husserl's critique was intended also as a correction of his earlier viewpoint as is evidenced by his quotation of Goethe's saying that man is never more severe than with errors recently renounced.[18]

In formulating his criticism of logical psychologism, Husserl extensively explains the absurdity of the consequences to which it leads and then assails the underlying biases. One of the prime consequences with which Husserl is concerned here is psychologism's claim that the validity of logical axioms and principles depends ultimately on psychological laws. As one might expect it was not too difficult a task for Husserl to show that it is impossible to interpret logical principles as psychological laws based only on our way of thinking.

A second consequence to which Husserl turns his attention in this context is the fact that psychologism leads to skeptical relativism. If the logical principles are made to depend upon the psychological characteristics of the logician, then they are concomitantly relativized in relation to this thinker; as a consequence man in all his instability then becomes the standard against which everything else is to be measured. Relativism, however, Husserl holds, is self-contradictory in that it negates the possibility of all knowledge and, at the same time, maintains that its own statements must be true.

Next, Husserl focuses his attention on the biases of psychologism themselves. Among other matters, he points out, psychologism posits that the subject matter of logic consists only in psychological phenomena. In dealing with this prejudice Husserl makes a comparison between logic and mathematics. Mathematics is not concerned with our operations of counting, but with numbers themselves. Similarly, the subject matter of logic is not constituted by the operations by which we form concepts, judgments, and inferences, but with the products of these operations, namely, 'ideal' concepts, propositions, and conclusions.

The criticism of psychologism's biases contains at the same time a first analysis and description of the logical realm as a domain of entities

---

18. *Ibid.,* p. 99.

sui generis. Once he has dispensed with the idea that psychology can be of any help here, Husserl goes on to develop his own view on 'pure' logic free from every form of psychologism. But the details of this investigation need not engage our attention at this point.[19]

Husserl's 'Conversion'

When the first volume of *Logical Investigations* appeared, most of Husserl's readers regarded him as a protagonist of realistic objectivism or perhaps even of Platonism. For, his *Prolegomena to Pure Logic* clearly explain that mathematical and logical principles are true, regardless of whether or not they have ever been thought of by man. These truths must be independent of man who thinks them, and, therefore, they must have a 'Being' which is independent of the factual functioning of consciousness. To be sure, there is no thought without man to think it, but it is only the *factual appearing* of this thought which depends on man's thinking; the *validity* of what is thought, however, is entirely independent of any psychic activity on the part of man. And, moreover, if the concepts which are in man's consciousness are independent of its psychic functions, then consciousness itself must transcend the sphere of these psychic functions, too.

Logical or mathematical propositions are true, not because man's thinking functions properly in formulating them; if they are true, it is because those propositions have validity in themselves. The laws of mathematics and logic are not concerned with our thinking as such but with our thoughts. They do not determine whether our mind is thinking properly, but rather whether our thoughts are true. Thus we must conclude that mathematics and logic are 'pure' if and only if they are independent of man's factual thinking. That is why it is impossible to reduce them to a study of mental processes.

As Husserl sees it, the fundamental mistake of psychologism is that it not only has 'naturalized' our ideas but also consciousness itself. In so doing it did not see the necessity of making a clear distinction between the world of consciousness and the world of factual facts. What is true

---

19. Herbert Spiegelberg, *op. cit.,* vol. I, pp. 94-5.

can possess validity, even though it is impossible to explain the correspondence between this truth and our thinking as a concrete event happening in a 'real' world. Its 'Being' as an object of thought is somehow other than the Being characteristic of our acts of thinking as concrete events. Its very transcendence as an object lies in this that it transcends the thinking which, psychologically speaking, 'produced' it. However, in Husserl's earlier works it is not very clear what validity our thoughts precisely possess and what kind of Being can be ascribed to truth.[20]

Phenomenoloy as a Descriptive Psychology

In the first part of the *Logical Investigations* Husserl looked for a universe of ideal objects, such as the world of numbers, geometrical entities, logical generalities, the validity of which is independent of the psychical activities by which the apprehension of these ideal objects is effected. But at the same time he had to solve the problem of how exactly these ideal objects are given to consciousness, how they reach the state of 'being given'.

In a manuscript of this period Husserl argues as follows. We may manage to show in a fully evident way that ideal objects, although they take shape in consciousness, have a Being of their own, a Being in themselves. But even then an important task is left, namely, to explain the typical correlation between these ideal objects belonging to the sphere of pure logic, and our subjective, psychical, lived experiences as the activities which 'constitute' them. For, we must keep in mind that the performance of certain psychical activities, which evidently are activities of a fully determined order, results in the successive formation and constitution of meanings and that the different ideal objects appear necessarily as products of these activities.[21] This text clearly indi-

---

20. Quentin Lauer, *op. cit.*, pp. 26-27. L. Dupré, "The Concept of Truth in Husserl's Logical Investigation", *Philosophy and Phenomenological Research,* 24(1963-1964) 345-354.

21. Edmund Husserl, *Ms.* F I 36, p. 19, quoted by Walter Biemel, *loc. cit.,* p. 45.

cates what already then was Husserl's concern and what was to constitute the characteristic theme of his later phenomenology.[22]

Be this as it may, for anyone who on the basis of the first volume of the *Logical Investigations* had looked forward to a systematic development of the idea of a pure logic, it was a great surprise when the second volume appeared in 1901 under the title *Elements of a Phenomenological Elucidation of Knowledge*. For this volume contained six essays, four shorter ones about matters of immediate interest to pure logic, and two longer explanations bearing the strange titles "Intentional Experiences and Their Contests", and "Elements of a Phenomenological Elucidation of Knowledge". Especially the last two essays gave the impression of being relevant to psychology rather than to pure logic. Many readers thought therefore that Husserl had returned to the very psychologism which he had rejected in the first volume of the *Logical Investigations*. However, to understand the reason of this seeming renewal of psychologism is to see the fundamental reasons which were to lead Husserl to his later phenomenology.[23]

The idea of a pure logic has sometimes been represented as an attempt to divorce logic completely from every kind of psychology. Husserl's standpoint, however, in the second volume of his *Logical Investigations* precisely is that such a separation is inadmissible and even impossible. In a manuscript written after 1920 he points out that the main problem discussed in the *Logical Investigations* is the following. Hidden 'lived experiences' are connected with every ideal entity. These experiences must be in harmony with corresponding fully determined productions. How, then, must they manifest and present themselves in order that the subject will be able to be conscious of these ideal entities as objects in an, at least ultimately, evident act of knowledge?[24] For even ideal logical entities are given to us only in and through experience, even if this be an experience of a very special kind. No philosophical and critical logic, therefore, can ignore them.

---

22. Walter Biemel, *loc. cit.,* pp. 44-45.
23. Herbert Spiegelberg, *op. cit.,* vol. I, p. 101.
24. Edmund Husserl, *Ms.* F I 36 p. 19 b, quoted by Biemel, *loc. cit.,* p. 47.

But if this is true, then Husserl still seems to imply that a certain 'psychology of thinking' must underlie a philosophical study concerning the foundations of logic. The psychology which prevailed in Husserl's days, however, was unequal to the demands of the new logic. All that Husserl wanted was a descriptive study of the processes by which the entities studied in pure logic are 'constituted'.[25]

With respect to the meaning of the term 'constitution' in this context, we must observe that the thinking subject is not able arbitrarily to constitute any meaning he wants, because the constitutive acts depend on the essences of the objects in question. In a letter to Hocking, dated January 25, 1903, Husserl explains that in the *Logical Investigations* the expression "the objects constitute themselves in the different acts of consciousness" refers solely to that characteristic of an act by means of which it makes an object 'representable', and that there is no question here of constitution in the proper sense of the term.[26] In one of the following chapters we shall deal with the problem concerning the meaning of the term 'constitution' in Husserl's later publications.

At any rate, in the introduction to the second volume of the *Logical Investigations,* Husserl in passing refers to the new study, now called 'phenomenology' taken as a 'decriptive psychology', using this latter term in the sense which was given to it by Brentano. He mentions here discussions of the most general kind, which belong to the wider sphere of an 'objective' theory of knowledge, or "to a purely descriptive phenomenology of experiences of thought and knowledge". This entire sphere must be investigated in an epistemological preparation and clarification of pure logic.[27]

In another passage he specifies that it is not psychology as a complete science that is to be the foundation of pure logic. Certain types of description constitute a preliminary stage for the theoretical investigations of pure logic. These types describe empirical objects whose genetic connections psychology has to trace and which, at the same time, form the basis for those fundamental abstractions in which the logician grasps

---

25. Herbert Spiegelberg, *op. cit.,* vol. I, p. 102.
26. Walter Biemel, *loc. cit.,* pp. 45-46.
27. Edmund Husserl, *L. U.* (1900-1901), vol. I, p. 4.

the essences of his ideal objects and their connections with evidence. "Epistemologically it is of very great importance to separate the purely descriptive investigation of experiences of knowledge, which is not concerned with any question of interest to theoretical psychology, from the investigations which are really psychological and aim at empirical explanation and genesis. For this reason we shall do well to speak of phenomenology rather than of descriptive psychology."[28]

However, already in 1903 it was clear to Husserl that he had made several mistakes in his characterization of his new phenomenology. For, in a manner similar to any other descriptive science, descriptive psychology as such is only interested in man's experiences as they can be observed in concrete and individual cases. What Husserl wanted, however, was a description of the ideal types of logical experiences in their correspondence to ideal logical laws. He was especially interested in descriptive analyses of the various kinds of thinking, modes of intuitive consciousness, and forms of symbolic representation which seem to be paramount for a radical foundation of the laws of pure logic.

This study of the pure essences of these experiences must evidently divorce itself completely from that which happens in concrete and individual cases. The experiences as real events and everything which happens in them belong to the domain of empirical psychology. The new phenomenology, instead, is to study essential relationships which as such are independent of concrete experiences. Only with such a study will philosophy be able to bring to light the ultimate foundations of our knowledge of logical entities and laws.[29]

For this reason the second edition of Husserl's *Logical Investigations* which appeared after the publication of his *Ideas* in 1913, characterized 'the purely descriptive phenomenology' in the following way. This new discipline, like the pure phenomenology of experience in general described in the *Ideas*, "is concerned with the experiences that can be grasped and analyzed intuitively in their essential generality, but not with empirically apperceived experiences as real occurrences, as experiences of experiencing people or animals in the appearing world,

---

28. *Ibid.*, p. 18. See also: Marvin Farber, *op. cit.*, pp. 198-199.
29. Herbert Spiegelberg, *op. cit.*, vol. I, pp. 102-103.

posited as real facts of natural experience. The essences directly grasped in essential intuition, and the connections based solely upon these essences, are expressed *descriptively* in concepts of essences and logically correct statements about essences. Every such statement is an *a priori* statement in the best sense of the term."[30]

What has just been said concerning the relationship between pure logic and phenomenology, understood here in a limited sense as a special study of the experiences which correspond to the logical entities, contains an idea which in Husserl's later philosophy as a whole is of the greatest importance, namely his view on 'intentionality'. According to this idea the structures of the subjective act parallel those of its objective correlate. This parallelism constitutes the basis for investigations in which both these aspects of any 'phenomenon' must be described in connection with each other. It leads to artificial abstractions if one tries to study one aspect without the other. Although there might be some value in such a 'separate' study, it requires a reintegration of the aspects which in this way are brought to the fore, into the original phenomenon from which they have been drawn.[31]

Empirical and Phenomenological or Descriptive Psychology

In this historical sketch of the evolution undergone by Husserl's thinking between 1887 and 1903, one point is of great importance for our understanding of his later phenomenological philosophy. It is concerned with the question of what exactly is to be understood by phenomenology as a descriptive psychology and what its relation is to empirical psychology.

As we have explained in the preceding pages, in the second volume of the *Logical Investigations* Husserl tried to present an epistemological preparation for and clarification of pure logic. In the first volume of this work he had already explained that it is absolutely impossible to find this epistemological foundation in traditional empirical and experimental psychology. At first, Husserl thought that a descriptive psy-

---

30. Edmund Husserl, *L. U.* (1921-1922), vol. II, p. 2.
31. Herbert Spiegelberg, *op. cit.*, vol. I, p. 103.

chology in Brentano's style could provide such an explanation. As soon, however, as the second volume of the *Logical Investigations* which explained this idea, was published, Husserl realized its deficiency. It became evident to him that, although such a descriptive psychology is an important psychological discipline, it never will be able to provide a radical foundation for the epistemological aspects of our knowledge, for, to obtain such a foundation for the epistemological aspects of our knowledge we must eliminate all transcendent interpretations of immanent data, including the 'psychological activities and conditions' of real egos, physical things, and the experience of other persons.[32]

Moreover, it was never Husserl's intention to reject empirical psychology as such; he was simply opposed to those trends in psychology which he called 'naturalistic' or 'objectivistic'. On the basis of this it became evident to him that one has to make a sharp distinction between empirical psychology, descriptive or phenomenological psychology, and phenomenological philosophy, the latter understood as a *radical* study of consciousness. The role of phenomenological psychology simply is to fill the gap between the best possible type of empirical psychology and phenomenological philosophy. These insights are already implicity present in Husserl's article *Philosophy as a Rigorous Science* (1911) and explicitly formulated in his *Ideas* (1913).[33]

In 1903, however, Husserl did not yet have a clear idea about this phenomenological psychology as distinguished from phenomenological philosophy and about its concrete relations to empirical psychology. Later he describes it, in line with his tentative views of 1903,[34] as an *a priori* psychological discipline capable of providing the only secure basis for a strong empirical psychology. The task of this phenomenological psychology lies in a systematic examination of the types and forms of intentional experience as such, and the reduction of their structures to 'prime intentions', in order in this way to discover the nature of the 'psychical' as such and comprehend the very essence of

---

32. Marvin Farber, *op. cit.*, p. 199.
33. Herbert Spiegelberg, *op. cit.*, vol. I, pp. 149-150.
34. Edmund Husserl, "Phenomenology", pp. 699-702 (passim).

17

the soul. A phenomenological psychologist will pay attention only to internal experiences which are to be described as 'phenomena', that is, exactly as they appear to consciousness. This reduction to the phenomena themselves, to the purely psychical, requires two steps:

1. The systematic and radical inhibition or *epochē* of every objectifying position in every concrete experience.

2. The recognition, comprehension, and description of the very essence of that which no longer appears as an object, but only as a 'unity of meaning'. This phenomenological description itself comprises two phases: the description of the noetic aspect of the phenomena (the experiences), and the description of their noematic aspect (the experienced objects as such).

In this way, phenomenological psychology can be purified of every empirical and psycho-physical element; but, as purified in this way, it cannot deal with concrete matters of fact. However, Husserl claims, any closed field can be considered with respect to its essence and we may disregard the factual side of the phenomena by using them as 'examples' only. Thus we can ignore individual souls and societies to learn their *a priori*, their essential structures.

Psychology in general, in both its empirical and its phenomenological branches, is a *positive* science, since it remains within the realm of our 'natural attitude'. Taking our starting point in phenomenological psychology, however, we need only to use again the formal method of reduction in order to disclose the 'transcendental' phenomena of transcendental-phenomenological philosophy. For this reason phenomenological psychology is an excellent introduction to phenomenological philosophy, although transcendental phenomenology can also be developed independently of any psychology, Husserl remarks.

At any rate, just as the psychical experiences of phenomenological psychology are purged by a certain reduction, so the transcendental experiences of transcendental philosophy are to be purged by a new kind of reduction. This transcendental reduction may be regarded as a certain further purification of what interests phenomenological psychology. The reduction includes here not only the world, but also my soul and our souls. The psychologist reduces the everyday world to a subjectivity of souls which are a part of the real world in which they dwell. Next, the transcendental phenomenologist reduces this psychologically purified subjectivity to 'transcendental subjectivity'.

In the foregoing pages we have anticipated somewhat Husserl's development, but in the following chapters we will return to these topics. For the present we can confine ourselves to the remark that the descriptive psychology of the *Logical Investigations* is identical with that which Husserl later will call 'phenomenological psychology'.[35] Since this phenomenological psychology is still a natural and positive science, it is unable to present us with a *radical* foundation of pure logic. Such a foundation can only be given by phenomenological philosophy.

2. *Phenomenology as a Critique of Pure Reason*

'The Idea of Phenomenology'. Its Origin

As we have mentioned, in his *Logical Investigations* Husserl spoke of a kind of phenomenology which was to be understood there as a descriptive psychology. Around 1903, however, it had become clear to him, that a transcendental phenomenology must be admitted alongside the descriptive psychology pursued in the second volume of the first edition of the *Logical Investigations*. A rather profound study of the first two of Descartes' *Meditations of First Philosophy* and of Kant's *Critique of Pure Reason* had made this evident to Husserl.

A first systematic development of this new idea of phenomenology, whose main lines Husserl would always continue to maintain, was given in a series of five lectures at the University of Göttingen in 1907. These lectures were entitled *The Idea of Phenomenology*. Husserl intended them to be an introduction to a series of courses, 'Chapters of Phenomenology as a Critique of Pure Reason', which he had started as early as 1904 with his famous *Lectures on the Phenomenology of Internal Time Consciousness*. Since the genesis of *The Idea of Phenomenology*

---

35. Edmund Husserl, *L. U.*, vol. II, pp. 347-348.

is of importance for our understanding of Husserl's philosophical development, we must dwell upon it for a while.[36]

Five years after he had published the first volume of his *Logical Investigations* Husserl's philosophical evolution had come to a crisis. Husserl realized that in his philosophical investigations concerning the foundation of pure logic he had discovered a new philosophical discipline which perhaps could lead to a completely new ideal of philosophy itself. But at the same time he realized that he had not yet discovered the right way to explain his new ideas. In 1906 the Board of Education of the University of Göttingen had proposed him as a full professor, but the University itself had explicitly rejected this proposal. In the summer of 1906 Husserl began to seriously doubt himself and to wonder whether it would not be better to abandon his philosiphical career. On September 25, 1906, he noted in his diary: "In the first place there is the general problem which is to be solved if I wish to call myself a philosopher; I mean a critique of reason, a critique of logical, practical, and valuing reason. If, in general lines at least, I cannot clear up the important questions about meaning, essence, method, and other fundamental viewpoints of a *Critique of Pure Reason,* and if I should not be able to project, determine and provide a foundation for my ideas regarding these problems, it will be impossible for me to live truly as a philosopher."[37]

By the end 1906 Husserl thought that he had already found the right approach to a transcendental philosophy under the influence of Kant's *Critique of Pure Reason.* It seemed possible to him to go beyond phenomenology as the descriptive psychology used in his *Logical Investigations* and arrive at a transcendental phenomenology. This transcendental phenomenology would be able to give philosophy an absolute foundation by means of a wholly new process, which he would later call 'phenomenological reduction'. These main ideas were communicated for

---

36. Walter Biemel, *loc. cit.,* pp. 46-52.
37. Edmund Husserl, *Ms.* X x 5, pp. 17-18, quoted by Walter Biemel, ed., Edmund Husserl, *Die Idee,* pp. *vii-viii.*

the first time in 1907 in the above mentioned series of lectures, entitled *The Idea of Phenomenology*.[38]

The Natural Attitude

In these lectures Husserl points out that there is a profound difference between the 'natural' and the 'philosophical' sciences, and that this difference is ultimately based upon the essential difference between the 'natural' and the 'philosophical' attitudes. The characteristic of the 'natural' attitude consists in this that one who assumes it is not interested in the critical problem with which philosophy has struggled since the time of Descartes. The best way to make clear what is meant by this natural attitude, is to perform a few simple 'meditations', Husserl says.[39] The essence of his meditations seems to consist in the following.[40]

I am aware of a world which is spread out in space endlessly and which evolves endlessly in time. That I am aware of this world means, first of all, that I discover it immediately, intuitively, that I experience it. Through sight, touch, hearing, according to the various modes of sense perception, bodily beings which somehow are spatially distributed are for me simply there, they are 'present' to me, whether or not I pay special attention to them by occupying myself with them. Things, animals, and perhaps also men are immediately there for me; I see them, I hear them, I grasp them by the hand. When I speak with my fellow men, I understand immediately what they are perceiving and thinking, what they are feeling and willing. They are present as realities in my field of experience, even when I pay no attention to them.

However, it is not necessary that they and other objects should be present precisely in my field of perception. Real objects are there for me, they are definite, more or less familiar objects that agree with what I actually perceive, even though they themselves are now not perceived or immediately present to me. I can let my attention wander from the desk I have just been looking at to unseen parts of the room behind my back, to the porch, the garden, the children playing there in my im-

---

38. Edmund Husserl, *Die Idee:* Einleitung des Herausgebers, pp. *vii-xi*.
39. Edmund Husserl, *Die Idee*, pp. 17-19 (13-14).
40. Edmund Husserl, *Ideen I*, pp. 57-62 (91-96).

mediate co-perceived surroundings. This knowledge is not at all like conceptual thinking and becomes clear intuition only when I pay attention to it. Even then this intuition is only partial and to a large extent very imperfect.

However, not even the added reach of this intuitively distinct or indistinct co-present margin, which continuously surrounds my actual field of perception, exhausts the world that in every waking moment is in some conscious way present to me. On the contrary, this world extends in a fixed order toward a limitless horizon. That which is actually perceived and that which is more or less clearly co-present and determinate are partly permeated with, and partly surrounded by, a dimly apprehended margin of indeterminate reality. An empty haze of obscure indeterminacy is studded with possibilities of intuitive acts and with presumed present things, and only the general form of the world as world is foreshadowed. Moreover, the zone of indeterminacy is infinite. There always remains a vague horizon that can never be completely delineated.

What has been said about the world in as far as it presents itself to me as being spatially ordered, applies also to the world in that it manifests itself to me as being ordered in the succesion of time. This world that is present to me now, and the same holds true for every 'waking now', has also a temporal horizon. This horizon is infinite in both directions, in its known and unknown 'parts', in its intimately lived as well as in its not lived past and future. Moving freely within the moment of experience which brings what is present into my intuitive grasp, I can trace these connections of the reality which immediately surrounds me. I can change my standpoint in space and time, look in this direction or in that one, turn forward or backward in time; I can provide myself with constantly new, more or less clear images, in which I make intuitable to myself whatever can possibly exist, either really or supposedly, in the fixed order of time and space.

In this way, when I am consciously awake, I find myself always and invariably in relation to a world which, despite its constant changes, remains one and always the same. It is always 'present' to me, and I myself am a part of it. Therefore, this world is not there for me merely as a world of facts, states of affairs and things, but, equiprimordially, as a world of values, a world of goods, a practical world. Without making any further efforts, I find that the things before me have not only the qualities demanded by their positive nature, but also value: they are beautiful, ugly, agreeable or disagreeable, pleasant or unpleasant. In their immediacy things are there as objects to be used: the desk with its books, the glass to drink from, the vase with its flowers, the piano. These values and practical characteristics also belong to the constitution of the 'actually present' objects as such, whether or not I pay attention to these or to other objects. These considerations apply not only to mere things, but also to the animals and men in my surroundings.

Summarizing, we may say that the 'natural world' which is immediately present to me, is constituted by perceived objects, their co-perceived immediate surroundings, a dimly apprehended horizon. This horizon is not only ordered in a spatial but also in a temporal manner. Whenever I am conscious I always find myself related to this world, which is there not only as world of facts, matters of facts, and things, but also as a practical world of values.

According to Husserl's description, it is to this world, the world in which I find myself, that are related the complex forms of my spontaneous acts of consciousness as well as the various acts and states of emotion and will. The former are in general the theorizing activity of my consciousness, such as observing, conceptualizing, meaning through description, collecting and counting, presupposing and inferring. Examples of acts of emotion and will are approval and disapproval, joy and sorrow, desire and aversion, hope and fear, decision and action. All these acts and states, together with the pure acts of the ego in which I become acquainted with the world as immediately given to me, are included in the one Cartesian *cogito*. In my natural life I live constantly in this fundamental form of 'wakeful' living, regardless of whether I do or do not positively assert the *cogito,* and whether or not I am reflectively concerned with the ego and my thinking.

A First Introduction to Husserl's Phenomenology

I am constantly present to myself as someone who perceives, represents, thinks, feels, desires. Most of the time I find myself related in my present experiences to the real world around me. However, I am not always related in this fashion, and not every 'lived' *cogito* has as its *cogitatum* things, men, or objects belonging to this 'real' world. I may be occupied also with pure numbers and the laws which govern them; yet such numbers and laws are not present in the world around me, in the world of 'real' facts. Nevertheless, this world of numbers also is there-for-me, as the field of objects with which I am occupied in arithmetic. Obviously, this being-there-for-me is very different from the being-there of the natural world, for the arithmetical world is there-for-me only when and as long as I occupy the arithmetical standpoint.

The *natural* world, however, the world in the ordinary sense of the term, is constantly there for me, so long as I live naturally and look in its direction. I am then at the 'natural standpoint'. There is no need to modify this statement regarding the natural world when I appropriate the arithmetical world or any other similar 'world' by assuming a corresponding standpoint. The natural world still remains 'present', I am still in the natural standpoint, and in this respect I remain unchanged by adopting new standpoints. If my *cogito* is active only in and with respect to the world corresponding to the *new* standpoint, the natural world, indeed, remains unconsidered. In that case it is only the background for my consciousness as act, but it is not the horizon within which the arithmetical world finds its proper place. The two worlds are present together but remain disconnected, save insofar as both are related to the ego. By virtue of this disconnection I can freely direct my attention to either the one or the other.

Furthermore, I know that what applies to me personally, also applies to all other men whom I find present in my world-around-me. I experience them as men and thereby understand and take them as ego-subjects similar to myself and related to their natural surroundings. In this experience I apprehend the world-around-them and the world-around-me as objectively the same world, which differs only insofar as it affects the consciousness of each ego-subject in a different way. Each subject has his own place from which he sees the things that are present, and that is why to each subject things appear differently. For each also the actually present fields of perception and memory are different. Moreover, even that which in these fields is intersubjectively known in common is known and apprehended in different ways and with different grades of clarity. Yet, despite all these differences, we understand our neighbors and organize together an objective spatio-temporal real world as the world-around-us that is there for all of us and to which we ourselves nonetheless belong.

Briefly put, the various forms of my theorizing consciousness as well as my manifold emotions and acts of will put me into relation with the real world around me. All these acts are included in the 'Cartesian' *cogito*. My *cogitatum*, however, need not be taken from the real world as such, but can also be something ideal, such as pure numbers. When I consider something of the ideal world, the natural world remains present to me as a background of my actual consciousness, but it is not directly connected with the ideal world which I consider. The natural world is also intersubjective. Although each subject apprehends the real world in his own way, all human beings are in principle able to understand each other and to organize together one objective spatio-temporal world as the world-around-them.

The preceding sketch, characterizing both that which is given from the natural standpoint and our natural standpoint itself, Husserl continues, is a pure description prior to any theorizing, because we precisely intended to keep away from all theories and from any preconceived idea. It is only as facts of our own environment, and not as instruments for combining facts into a valid system, that theories concern us here at all. However, we do not intend to continue this pure description and make it a systematically all-inclusive and exhaustive characterization of the data that can be discovered from the natural standpoint. True, this task can and must be undertaken, for it is a scientific task of the utmost importance, which until the present has scarcely been touched. However, we do not have to attempt it here.

All we want to do here, Husserl says, is emphasize again a most important point. It is this: I find continually present to me and 'standing over against me' the one spatio-temporal real world, the fact-world to which I myself belong and all other men found in this world and related to it in the same way. This fact-world I find to be 'out there' and I take it just as it gives itself to me as something existing 'out there'. *This general thesis of the natural standpoint* is and remains untouched by any possible doubt or rejection of the data of the natural world. 'The' world is a fact-world that is always there. True, it may happen that at some particular points it is 'other' than I suppose; this or that particular point may be an illusion or hallucination that must be eliminated from it. But 'it itself' always remains as a world that is 'out there'. To know it more comprehensively, more reliably, more perfectly than our naïve knowledge is able to do, and to solve all the problems of scientific knowledge which present themselves in the natural world, is the goal pursued by the sciences of the natural standpoint.

In other words, from the natural standpoint the possibility of human knowledge is a self-evident fact. Because of the success attained by the sciences of the natural standpoint, no need was felt to raise the question concerning the possibility of human knowledge. Evidently, from the natural standpoint it is also possible to make inquiries about human knowledge; for, first, whatever is can be an object of scientific investigation, and, secondly, human knowledge itself is a 'fact of nature', a psychological fact, to be considered in psychology.

There it becomes clear that knowledge essentially is knowledge of an object, and that it is this because of a meaning which is inherent to it and through which it necessarily refers to objectivity. This relation itself may be considered also by the sciences of the natural standpoint, but in so doing one always remains, as a matter of principle, within the natural attitude. Even ontologies can be built on this basis; e.g. with regard to nature, it will be possible to distinguish certain 'regions' and to determine their essences. This applies also to living beings, the social order, and the arts. But even in these 'regional ontologies' one remains within the limits of the natural standpoint.[41]

Philosophical Attitude. Epistemology

It is also possible to assume a completely different attitude with regard to things and our knowledge of them. We may say, for instance,

---

41. Edmund Husserl, *Die Idee,* p. 19 (14), and p. 79-80.

that our knowledge is a psychological experience of a certain subject. The question then arises: How can this subject be certain that his knowledge agrees with these objects? The self-evident givenness of the objects of our natural attitude becomes problematic here. How do I, the subject, know that my subjective experience is not all that exists? How do I know that there are real things, independent of my experience? How can I be sure, that through my knowledge I know things as they are in themselves? Evidently, to those questions we can answer that, indeed, only phenomena are given to me; it is possible to say that only I myself am real and that the non-ego merely is a phenomenon.

Instead of this solipsism, it is perhaps also possible to say with Hume that every transcendent objectivity is only a human fiction for which psychology can give an explanation. When we reflect on this standpoint, it becomes evident that sooner or later it will lead to contradictions, and that this viewpoint is, therefore, unacceptable.

However, even when it is evident to me that such a standpoint is unacceptable, I have not yet found a convincing and positive answer to the above-mentioned problem. After all, what is the use of making an appeal to the impossibility of contradiction, if even logic has become problematic since it too is a natural science? No matter how we try to approach it, within the domain of the natural attitude the problem about the possibility of human knowledge cannot be solved. Despite all the successes of the sciences of the natural standpoint, our whole knowledge ends in skepticism and therefore in nonsense so long as we do not find a convincing answer to the question about the possibility of knowledge.[42]

The point now where all problems about this possibility of knowledge and the age-old disputes around it converge is found in the theory of knowledge or epistemology and in the ontology that is connected with it. Epistemology then has a double task:

1. It has to show that the errors into which a natural reflection about the relation between knowledge and the objects known must almost necessarily fall, are in reality avoidable and that therfore no skeptical theory about the essence of human knowledge is acceptable.

---

42. *Ibid.*, pp. 19-21 (14-16) and pp. 81-82.

2. By accurately investigating the very essence of knowledge, epistemology must try to find a solution for the problems concerning the real relations between knowledge, the meaning of knowledge, and the objects known.

By attempting to solve these questions, epistemology is a critique of our natural knowledge and of all the sciences of the natural standpoint. for it enables us to arrive at an exact interpretation of the onological value proper to the results of the natural sciences. At last, therefore, it will put an end to the arbitrary interpretations of those sciences in a materialistic, spiritualistic, dualistic, psychomonistic, positivistic, or scientistic fashion. Epistemology, in which the difference between philosophy and science reveals itself, must show that the natural sciences cannot pronounce definitive judgments about Being and that such judgments require a metaphysics emanating from the critique of the natural sciences.[43]

Phenomenology as Epistemology of Knowledge. Philosophy and Science

If epistemology has to explicitate the essence of knowledge and of the cognitive objects we may say that epistemology and phenomenology of knowledge are identical and also that epistemology, as described above, is the fundamental part of the whole of phenomenology. In other words, phenomenology, which we must circumscribe here more exactly, is a complex of philosophical disciplines, of which the phenomenology of knowledge or epistemology constitutes the foundation. Phenomenology, however, is primarily a method, that is to say, the specifically philosophical way of thinking.[44]

Many philosophers are of the opinion that philosophy can lay claim to a scientific character only if it adopts the method of the physical sciences. Some people even believe in a harmonious unity of all the sciences, even with respect to their method. This conception is in perfect agreement with the ideal of philosophy proposed in the seventeenth century. At that time everyone believed that the success of philosophy depended

---

43. *Ibid.,* pp. 21-23 (16-18).
44. *Ibid.,* p. 23 (18-19).

on the acceptance of the methods used in the exact sciences and especially in mathematics and mathematical physics. This methodological equalization implies that philosophy is to be placed on the same level as the other sciences.

Many contemporary philosophers continue to think that philosophy is not only of necessity concerned with the other sciences, but also that it must be based on their results. However, as will become more manifest later, such a positivistic and scientistic view is completely unacceptable, because it is rooted in arbitrary preconceptions. Although one physical science may presuppose another within certain limits determined by the very nature of their respective objects, philosophy cannot do so. Philosophy lies in a completely new dimension and it needs wholly new starting points and a wholly new method, through which it is perfectly distinguished from the other sciences.

Thus, Husserl concludes here, it necessarily follows that the logical and methodological processes of the physical sciences are completely different from the method of philosophy, and that philosophy cannot presuppose any of them. For it is not conceivable that our 'natural' knowledge and its results could help us find a solution for the fundamental critical problem. When the sense and the value of our natural knowledge becomes problematic in all its methodological processes and in all its exact foundations, then it has, neither as a starting point nor as a methodological idea, any importance for epistemology and for the metaphysics which is based on epistemology.[45]

Accordingly, we have to admit a radical distinction between philosophy and science. This distinction is based upon the radical distinction between the natural and the philosophical attitudes. We have explained what we must understand by the natural and by the philosophical standpoints. We must now ask the question: How is man, who naturally always lives in the natural attitude, able to assume the philosophical viewpoint? It is Husserl's opinion that this is possible only by means of a special phenomenological process which he called 'phenomenological reduction'.

---

45. *Ibid.,* pp. 23-26 (18-21).

A First Introduction to Husserl's Phenomenology

Phenomenological Reduction

In the foregoing we have already seen that according to Husserl a certain kind of epistemology is the necessary condition of the possibility of any metaphysics whatsoever. Phenomenology as the general doctrine of essences is supposed to deliver the method of such an epistemology.

Every form, then, of epistemology must initially deal with the question of to which extent such a science is possible. For, if it questions man's knowledge as such and, therefore, all concrete forms of cognition, the science seems to be unable to find a legitimate starting point, since every cognition chosen as a starting point is supposed to be subject to reasonable doubt. In Husserl's view, however, this problem is not a serious one, for by calling cognition into question we do not disavow it nor consider it as doubtful in every sense. Descartes has shown us how one can find a legitimate starting point in epistemology. In applying his methodical doubt properly it becomes evident that there are certain cogitations which can be legitimately accepted as absolute data and, therefore, as a valid starting point for epistemological investigations.

A second question which epistomology has to consider refers to the problem concerning the distinction between the apodicticity of man's knowledge as such and the uncertainty found in so many concrete instances of his cognition. Why do we find in the history of philosophy a rather strong tendency toward skepticism as soon as the question of how man's knowledge can reach reality is asked? Some philosophers try to solve the problem by making a distinction between immanent and transcendent cognition. They explain the apodicticity of the *cogito* as such by pointing to its immanence, and the doubtfulness of concrete instances of cognition by referring to their transcendence. According to them one can and, therefore, must ask the question of how our knowledge can reach a being which is not to be found within the realm of consciousness itself, but it is without meaning to ask the same question for the intuitive cognition which confines itself to the *cogito* as such.

The Origin of Husserl's Phenomenology

In Husserl's view, however, it is impossible to solve the problem under consideration in this way, because the terms 'immanence' and 'transcendence' are ambiguous. These terms are very often understood in the sense of 'inside' and 'outside' of consciousness. But it will be evident that this means that every object of cognition whatsoever has to be immanent, especially if we take immanence here in a psychological sense, as immanence in something real. If, however, we take the term 'immanent' to mean the adequately self-given, then it will be clear that the genuinely immanent can be accepted as the indubitable because it points to nothing outside itself, and what is intended here is adequately given in itself. If one adopts this point of view one may conclude at once that the genuinely immanent is beyond all epistemological questions, but the transcendent, in the sense of the not genuinely immanent, cannot be used in epistemology without further investigation. Adopting this point of view amounts, therefore, to performing a 'phenomenological reduction' by means of which all that is not genuinely immanent is excluded from the sphere of 'absolute' data. Such a reduction implies that henceforth in epistemology all so-called realities are accepted exclusively as *phenomena* only and, furthermore, that in epistemology we can no longer appeal to the sciences of the natural attitude inasfar as they intend to deal with real things.

Thus in epistemology only 'pure phenomena' can be accepted as truly absolute data. Therefore, even the psychological ego and man's mental activities as the activities of such ego are not absolute data either, so that in epistemology we have to abandon also the point of view of empirical psychology and even that of descriptive psychology. Once we have performed the phenomenological reduction in a radical way, it will become clear that our leading problem does not consist in the question of how man can reach in his mental processes something existing in itself 'out there' and beyond himself, but rather in determining how the pure phenomena of cognition can reach something which as such is not immanent in them, that is to say, of how the absolute self-giveness of cognition itself can reach something which is not self-given in the same way.[46]

---

46. *Ibid.*, pp. 4-7 (2-4).

A First Introduction to Husserl's Phenomenology

Eidetic Abstraction

Let us now suppose for a moment that by means of the phenomenological reduction the realm of the pure phenomena is brought to the fore in the manner briefly indicated above. The next step to be taken consists then in trying to acquire *universally* valid insights concerning these phenomena, for we are not interested in these pure phenomena as such, but precisely in their necessary structure and, therefore, in their very essence. In addition to the phenomenological reduction we, therefore, need a second procedure, viz., eidetic abstraction which has to give us a new objectivity as absolutely given, namely, the objectivity of essences.

Once this procedure is applied to the pure phenomena in a legitimate way, it is no longer possible to posit the identity of the absolutely given and the genuinely immanent because what is universal is absolutely given but is not genuinely immanent. For the act in which man knows the universal is something singular and concrete, a concrete moment of man's stream of consciousness, while the universal itself which is supposedly given in self-evidence within the stream of consciousness, is not singular and concrete and, therefore, genuinely transcendent. If one then wants to formulate the real meaning of the phenomenological reduction in a clearer way, one has to say that the reduction intends to exclude what is transcendent in the sense of everything that is not absolutely given to pure intuition. If epistemology wants to be an inquiry within the realm of pure self-evidence and, nonetheless, also an inquiry into essences, its subject matter cannot consist in the genuinely immanent, but rather in the a *priori* within the realm of the absolute self-given data. However, it is clear that even when the domain of investigation is delineated in this way, one of the most important tasks of epistemology is still left untouched, namely, the explanation of the meaning of the absolutely given, the absolute clarity of the given and, thus, the absolutely intuitive self-evidence which gets hold of itself here.[47]

---

47. *Ibid.*, pp. 7-10 (5-7).

The Origin of Husserl's Phenomenology

Intentionality and Constitution

We have just seen that the sphere of absolute clarity, as the sphere of immanence in the strict sense, reaches no further than does self-giveness. Once we have entered this sphere by means of the phenomenological reduction, we have to reflect upon our own cogitations and try to appraise their genuine content and to lift that which is intuited into consciousness of universality. All this seems at first to be very simple but, upon closer investigation, it becomes clear that the realm of the self-givenness reaches further than the givenness of the cogitation as such and the ideation which grasps it in its universality. For in every cogitation, even after the reduction, we must make a distinction between the appearance and that which appears, and this within the realm of the purely given as such. This means that in phenomenological epistemology we have two different absolute data: the givenness of the appearing *(noesis)* and the givenness of that which appears *(noema)*. And here we must again make the remark that the noema is immanent, although it is not genuinely immanent inasfar as it is not a concrete part of the appearance as such. Every intentional cogitation manifests itself as a form of consciousness constituting something self-given which is not contained within what is real, and is not at all found *as* cogitation.

On the lowest level of the phenomenological consideration, it seemed at first very easy to understand what is meant by evidence. Evidence seemed to be only a question of intuition: my intuitive grasp 'sees' the things which are simply there before me in consciousness. My intuitive glance simply looks at them and takes them just as they are. Upon closer investigation, however, this intuiting glance appears to be completely different from such a simple 'seeing'. For it becomes clear here that it is meaningless to speak of things which simply are there for me and only have to be intuited. This 'simply being there' appears to be essentially connected with a complex of different experiences possessing their own specific structure, such as perception, memory, phantasy, etc. Things are not in consciousness as matches in a box, but in and through these experiences things are constituted in such a way that they, nonetheless, are in no way 'really' contained in these experiences. For every thing 'to be given' means in this or that way to come into being in and through our lived experiences and to be presented by them.

33

We find everywhere that marvelous intentional relationship between the knowing act and the object known. The task of phenomenology is not to intuit this relationship and to describe it, but to explain how an object of knowledge is constituted in our knowing acts. Within the sphere of pure self-givenness and evidence we must analyze and describe all the modes of presentation and the correlates which become manifest in them. Only in this way shall we see how the 'transcendent' real objects are found and known in our knowing activities, namely, as those which at the outset where 'meant' only, and how the sense of this meaning is continuously fulfilled in the progressing coherence of knowledge in an original act of synthesis.[48]

Prospectus

It will be evident that in this brief outline of the fundamental themes of a phenomenological epistemology many questions remained unsolved. For this reason we shall return to these topics in the following chapters. However, before explaining what exactly is meant by reduction, eidetic abstraction, intentionality, and constitution, we must first present an account of the main ideas contained in the famous article *Philosophy as Rigorous Science* which Husserl published in the periodical *Logos* in 1911.

---

48. *Ibid.,* pp. 10-14 (8-12).

CHAPTER TWO

'PHILOSOPHY AS RIGOROUS SCIENCE'

1. *Rigor and Radicalism in Philosophy*

Genesis of Husserl's Article

In 1911, between the publication of the first edition of the *Logical Investigations* (1900-1901) and the first volume of *Ideas* (1913), Husserl wrote an article entitled *Philosophy as Rigorous Science*. In this article, which appeared in the review *Logos*, Husserl tried to defend the position that philosophy should be a rigorous science. That philosophy must be a strict and rigorous science does not mean that philosophy has to imitate the empirical sciences. Philosophy is to be an 'ideal' science which is not concerned with factual facts, that is, with objects that somehow are measurable. The object of philosophy belongs to another world than that of the objects considered by the different empirical sciences. The object of philosophy is not factual but ideal. And as ideal this object originates from consciousness, which in this context cannot be described in empirical terms as this is done, for instance, in empirical psychology. The object of philosophy constitutes a world of its own. Philosophy as a strict science is possible, not because philosophy can be reduced to one of the empirical sciences, but because it is possible to arrive at a truly scientific knowledge of the ideal objects which also may be called the essences of things.

Although Husserl did not conceive this 'scientific' philosophy as something that is easily attained, he did regard it as attainable, precisely because he was convinced that it is possible to deliver consciousness from all factual and contingent elements which are contrary to the truly scientific character that philosophy should possess. In 1911, however, this complete purification of consciousness was still an ideal to be materialized in a far future. Husserl's whole life and his whole philosophy can be looked upon as a constant search to attain such a complete purification.[1]

---

1. Quentin Lauer, *The Triumph of Subjectivity*, pp. 27-29.

Be this as it may, around 1903 it had become clear to Husserl that his new ideas about pure logic, described in the *Logical Investigations,* must have significance far beyond this limited area. In the decade following the publication of the second volume of this work, Husserl began to apply his phenomenological method to several different philosophical topics. This application of the method gave him a better understanding of its meaning. It also led him to transform it considerably and to develop a completely new philosophy.

This development began with Husserl's repudiation of his earlier characterization of phenomenology as a descriptive psychology, as we have seen in Chapter One. Phenomenology now became the study of the essential structures of the acts and contents of consciousness, a study to be based not on merely empirical generalizations, but on the intuitive grasp of the essences of the things themselves.

Although the years 1901-1913 were very productive, Husserl did not publish very much. His major efforts went into the preparation of lectures in which he tried to test his ideas before his students. In these lectures Husserl was chiefly interested in concrete phenomenological analyses. In these analyses he first turned his attention toward various types of consciousness and, especially, toward different types of knowledge, paying special attention to their claim to validity. From this point of view Husserl wrote phenomenological analyses of perception, consciousness of images, memory, etc. Later he focused attention on our consciousness of internal time and the constitution of the 'thing'. The lectures on our consciousness of internal time, given in 1905 and in 1910, and later published by Heidegger in 1928, show most concretely the fruits of Husserl's studies of intentionality during these years.

It was not until 1907 that Husserl was ready to express his new conception of phenomenology in a purely theoretical way, rather than limit himself to its concrete applications. As we have seen in the preceding chapter, partly influenced by a rather profound study of Descartes's and Kant's philosophy, partly challenged by his professional disappointments during the year 1906, Husserl undertook to re-examine his entire program of philosophy. He wanted to reformulate it in terms of a new 'critique of reason,' for which his new phenomenology would have to provide the foundations. As we have mentioned, it was this program which he explained in his five lectures at Göttingen in 1907.[2]

Scope of the Logos Article

Husserl's article in *Logos* was a simple and clear explanation of this new philosophy for a broader public. It was intended as an introduction to phenomenology rather than as an explanation of its fundamental theses and method. The first part of the article describes the necessary conditions under which philosophy can claim to be a 'rigorous' science. It is in this part of the article that Husserl resumes the main topic of the first volume of the *Logical Investigations:* he again attacks 'naturalism' and 'psychologism' as being incapable of deciding epistemological and metaphysical problems.

In the second part of the article Husserl focusses attention on 'historicism'. According to him, historicism, which had doubted the possibility of a genuinely scientific philosophy because of the philosophers' failures in the past, had led to unacceptable forms of relativism and skepticism concerning all metaphysical knowledge. Against this historicism Husserl claims that the validity of any kind of knowledge can neither be proved nor disproved by merely historical facts.

The article concludes with a vigorous protest against any attempt to substitute a so-called *Weltanschauung* for scientific philosophy. It is Husserl's view that it is not right to replace philosophy with an ideological view of the world comprising an interpretation of reality together with certain norms and rules for man's life. In this part of the article Husserl gives a brief report of the controversy and correspondence with Wilhelm Dilthey on this topic. Although Husserl does not deny that Dilthey's empirical and classifying typology of 'world views' is legitimate and even willingly grants its usefulness, he maintains, on the other hand, that the goal of a 'world view' is too restricted, because it wants to provide the individual with a unifying perspective of life, while science and philosophy essentially aim at an indefinite future because their tasks are never finished. *Weltanschauungen*, therefore, must be kept strictly separated from science and philosophy, for *Weltanschau-*

---

2. Herbert Spiegelberg, *op. cit.*, vol. I, pp. 118-120.

ungen are always subject to all the modifications which flow of necessity from man's changing perspectives.[3]

The Crisis of Scientific Thought

As we have mentioned, Husserl at first specialized in mathematics and physics. It was only after several years of study that he decided to become a philosopher. When at last, under the influence of his interest in psychology and under Brentano's direction, he began to study philospohy, he soon arrived at the following conclusions:

1. There is a great difference between, on the one hand, the scientific character of mathematics and physics and the results which they have attained since Galileo, Descartes, and Newton, and on the other hand, the character and results of philosophy.

2. There has practically never been any clear theory of the sciences, and this absence has been one of the most important reasons why philosophy could not develop into a strict and rigorous science. Yet every philosopher since Plato's days has nursed this ideal in one way or another.

3. From Brentano's lectures in particular, Husserl gained the conviction that philosophy nevertheless, and at least in principle, offers a field of serious work; philosophy too can be treated in the spirit of a strict science.

4. Philosophy can not be founded on the sciences but precisely must give to the different sciences a radical foundation.

In order to show that the last statement is not in contradiction with the first one, Husserl points to the fact that despite the practical and technical triumphs of the different sciences, science as a whole has run into theoretical problems which defy all conventional solutions. There exist not only certain defects in the foundation of mathematics, which first caught Husserl's attention, but there are also important theoretical problems in physics, which ultimately would lead to the theory of rela-

---

3. *Ibid.*, p. 121.

tivity and to quantum mechanics; these two physical theories, while solving some important questions, would bring to light many new theoretical problems. Although in 1911 Husserl was not yet fully aware of the direction modern physics was going to take under the stimulating leadership of thinkers such as Einstein, Lorentz, Bohr, Rutherford and Planck, it became gradually clear to him that enlarged control over nature was bought at the price of diminished intelligibility in the foundations of the respective sciences. There was, therefore, no longer any reason for accepting the verdict of the exact sciences as the final answer to all conceivable questions. And in the psychological and social sciences the theoretical problems were even so great that one had to ask whether these sciences had managed to acquire a strictly scientific character.

According to Husserl, it is possible to solve all these problems, but only under the condition that we first try to found philosophy itself as a rigorous science, then to transcend 'naturalism' and, finally, to fill the gap between science and philosophy with the help of what Husserl calls 'regional ontologies'. Husserl, then, was hopeful that philosophy, at least after a phenomenological reorganization, would be able to assist the 'objective' sciences in the clarification and the critique of their unclarified fundamental concepts and assumptions.[4]

Philosophical Radicalism

Husserl's quest for scientific rigor thus leads logically to another demand: namely, philosophy must be a radical science. Radicalism here means the necessity to return to the roots and first beginnings of all knowledge, to its ultimate foundations. This spirit of radicalism, which at first had led Husserl from mathematics to philosophy, was destined to guide his search for a philosophy more rigorous and more radical than any of those known to him. The same spirit also made him attempt to make his own philosophy constantly more radical.

Where are these ultimate roots of knowledge to be found? Husserl's first answer was very simple: in the things themselves, in the original phenomena to which all our concepts and ideas ultimately refer. Gradually, however, in the process of going down to the last roots of these

---

4. *Ibid.*, pp. 76-82 (passim).

phenomena themselves by means of phenomenological analyses, Husserl reached the conviction that these roots must lie even deeper. They must be sought in the very consciousness of the knowing subject to whom these phenomena appear, and ultimately in what he would call later 'transcendental subjectivity'.

One of the most disputed expressions of Husserl's radicalism is his intention to make his phenomenology be a philosophy free from every presupposition. This 'freedom from every presupposition' is sometimes misunderstood as if Husserl wanted to start philosophizing from absolute zero, even unaided by language and logic. This, however, was never his intention. For him the expression simply means the attempt to eliminate only all presuppositions which have not been thoroughly examined. It should be understood, therefore, not as freedom from all presuppositions, but only as freedom from unverified and unverifiable presuppositions.[5]

Descartes and Husserl

It will be useful to emphasize here the relation which in this respect clearly exists between Husserl's and Descartes' ways of thinking. First of all, both were dissatisfied with the philosophy of their day. This dissatisfaction was due especially to the fact that philosophy was in no way truly scientific and radical; yet philosophy must be radical and, therefore, also strictly scientific if it is not to be altogether without meaning. Secondly, both rejected every historical form of philosophy and required a radical, new, and strictly personal starting point for the whole of philosophy; in this way they explicitly denied the essentially historical character of philosophy. Both, finally, were patently deficient in the knowledge of the history of philosophy itself.

Let us briefly illustrate the point with a few quotations. In his *Discourse on Method* Descartes relates that from his childhood he had been familiar with the study of literature and that he was ardently desirous of instruction since he was given to believe that by their help a clear and certain knowledge of all that is useful in life could be acquired. But as soon as he had finished the entire course of study, he completely changed his point of view. He had so many doubts and found so many

---

5. *Ibid.*, pp. 82-84.

errors that all his attempts at learning appeared to have taught him nothing else than that he was ignorant. On the other hand, he was especially delighted with mathematics, on account of the certitude and evidence of its deductions. But he did not yet have a precise knowledge of its true use, for he thought that it contributed only to the advancement of the mechanical arts.

Concerning philosophy he says that he prefers to mention only that it has been studied for many centuries by the most outstanding thinkers without having produced anything which is not disputed and consequently uncertain. He goes on to say that he himself had not enough presumption to hope to succeed better than others. When he noticed how many different opinions philosophers have held on the same subject, despite the fact that only one of them can ever be true, he decided to consider almost as false any opinion which was merely probable.[6]

And in his *Meditations Concerning First Philosophy* he writes that after several years he became again aware of the fact that, from his earliest years, he had accepted many false opinions as true, and that consequently what he afterwards had based on such principles, was highly doubtful and uncertain. And he continues that from that time he was deeply convinced of the necessity of undertaking, once and for all, the task to set aside all the opinions which he had previously accepted among his beliefs and start again from the very beginning, if he wished to have any firm and constant knowledge in the realm of the sciences.[7]

Husserl's Avoidance of Descartes' Scientism

Although Descartes and Husserl moved in the same sphere of thinking with respect to philosophy and its historical evolution, there were also important points in which they completely differed from each other. One of the most important points is that Husserl managed to avoid Descartes' fundamental mistake in the philosophy of science, a mistake which ultimately leads to scientism. According to Descartes, there is no essential distinction between science and philosophy.

---

6. Descartes, *Discourse on Method and Meditations*. Translated, with an Introduction, by Laurence J. Lafleur (New York: The Bobbs-Merrill Co., 1960), pp. 5-8.
7. *Ibid.*, p. 75.

A First Introduction to Husserl's Phenomenology

In a well-known passage from one of his letters Descartes says that the first part of philosophy is metaphysics, which contains the principles of knowledge, among which is the explanation of the principal attributes of God, of the immortality of the human soul, and of all the clear and simple notions which are in it. The second part of philosophy is, in his view, physics in which, after having found the true principles of material things, the philosopher examines generally how the whole universe is composed, and then in particular what is the nature of the earth and of all the bodies in it, plants, animals, and men, so that he afterwards will be able to discover the other sciences which are useful to man. Thus, Descartes concludes, philosophy as a whole is like a tree whose roots are metaphysics, whose trunk is physics, and whose branches are all the other sciences. These reduce themselves to three principal ones, viz., medicine, mechanics, and morals.[8]

According to Husserl, such a view of the relations between science and philosophy necesssarily implies that the infinite totality of all beings constitutes a rational unity which can be explained by a single universal science making use of only one method, namely, the deductive method of mathematics. This assumption, however, is in contradiction with the very nature of the sciences which *de facto* exist.[9] For this reason Husserl does not intend to construct a scientific philosophy on the pattern of mathematics, but, following Kant, he wants a philosophy that, albeit in a completely different way, will lead to the analogous but absolute indubitability of its basic insights. According to him, Descartes' ideal is out of the question, because we have to admit that there is an essential distinction between philosophy and science.

In *The Idea of Phenomenology* Husserl says, therefore, that there are people who believe in a harmonic unity of all the sciences, even in methodological aspect. This conception corresponds perfectly to the ideal of philosophy proposed in the seventeenth century, when everybody believed the welfare of philosophy to depend on the claim that methodologically philosophy had to follow the example of the exact

8. Descartes, *Principles of Philosophy*, in *A Discourse on Method. Together with the Meditations and Excerpts of the Principles.* Trans. by J. Veitch, with an introduction by A. D. Lindsay (London: Everyman's Library, 1935), p. 211.

9. Edmund Husserl, *Krisis*, pp. 18-20.

sciences, and evidently in the first place of mathematics and mathematical physics. However, Husserl says, such a positivism is entirely unacceptable. In his view there can be no doubt about the fact that philosophy lies in a completely new dimension; it needs wholly new starting points and a wholly new method, through which it is perfectly distinguished from the other sciences.

It was precisely Husserl's intention to develop a philosophy which is able to found itself in a radical way, and which then will be able to provide the natural sciences, and even mathematics and logic, with the absolutely indubitable foundations which they themselves cannot provide. The fact that the foundation of philosophy must possess an absolute indubitability that is essentially distinct from the indubitable character of logic, mathematics, and other sciences, is one of Husserl's fundamental intuitions. But as we will see, it was only later that this intuition could be brought to light in a more convincing way by phenomenology itself.[11]

2. Philospohy as a Rigorous Science

After these historical explanations, we must now look at Husserl's own text. In this chapter, however, we will confine ourselves to the first part of Husserl's *Logos* article, because we intend to deal with the question concerning the relation between phenomenology and psychology in one of the following chapters. We intend to report Husserl's ideas partly in the form of a free translation, partly in the form of a paraphasing survey, in order to make his text more readable and understandable.[12]

Philosophy Has Always Claimed to Be a Strict Science

From the very beginning philosophy has always claimed to be a strict science. It has pressed this claim forward with variable energy, but has never completely abandoned it. On the other hand, however, philosophy

---

10. Edmund Husserl, *Die Idee*, 23-24 (18-20).
11. Quentin Lauer, *Phénoménologie de Husserl. Essai sur la genèse de l'intentionalité* (Paris: Presses Universitaires de France, 1955), pp. 4-7.
12. Edmund Husserl, *Phil. str. W.*, pp. 289-293 (71-79).

has never been able to live up to its claim of being a strict science either. This assertion is true even of its most recent period, from the Renaissance to the present, in which, despite the multiplicity and contradictory character of its orientations, philosophy has gone forward in one clear direction. The dominant characteristic of modern philosophy consists in this that, rather than surrender naïvely to the philosophical impulse, it wants to become a strict science by means of critical reflection and by ever more profound methodological investigations.

The only mature fruit, however, of these efforts have been the foundation and the independence of the different positive sciences. Philosophy, even in the particular sense in which it is now beginning to become distinct from these sciences, lacks as much as ever the character of being a rigorous science. The very meaning of the distinction between philosophy and science remains scientifically uncertain and the relation of philosophy to the different sciences is still a matter of dispute. Especially the question of whether philosophy demands fundamentally new attitudes and, therefore, also new methods, is still unanswered. This situation convincingly shows that scientific clarity has not even reached the question of what kind of a problem a philosophical problem really is.

According to its historical goal, philosophy is the most rigorous of all sciences, for it represents man's imperishable demand for pure and absolute knowledge. Yet it is still incapable of materializing this demand and of assuming the form of a strict science. Kant loved to repeat that one could not learn philosophy but only to philosophize. In this statement Kant clearly confesses that philosophy is supposed to be unscientific, for science can be taught and learned always and everywhere in fundamentally the same way. If philosophy cannot be learned, this is because it still lacks objectively founded and comprehended insights and because its problems, methods and theories have not yet been defined in clear concepts.

The Imperfection of Philosophy

But it is not enough to say that philosophy is an imperfect science; it simply is not yet a science at all. As a science it has not yet even started. All sciences are imperfect, even the exact sciences. These sciences are still incomplete, first, because a limitless horizon of open possibilities still lies before them, and, furthermore, because there remain still many gaps even in the realms which have already been scientifically developed. Nevertheless, these sciences have a subject matter, and this matter is continuously expending in new directions. No reasonable person will doubt the objective truth of the theories proposed by mathematics and the natural sciences. Here there is, generally speaking, no room for private 'opinions' and personal 'points of view', and to the extent that there still are 'opinions' in particular points, everybody admits that the science in question is not yet really established as such.

The imperfection of philosophy, however, is of an entirely different kind. Philosophy does not possess a doctrinal system which is still incomplete and imperfectly elaborated, but it has none whatsoever. Every question of philosophy remains controverted, every position is a matter of individual conviction, and every thesis only the interpretation given by a 'school' or 'trend'.

It may be true that the positions presented by ancient and modern philosophers are based on serious intellectual activity. They may even have prepared the way for a scientifically rigorous philosophy. Nevertheless, at present they offer nothing that can be recognized as the basis for a philosophical science.

This avowal needs to be made candidly, precisely by those modern philosophers who want to give evidence that an important revolution is going to take place in philosophy and are willing to prepare the ground for a future philosophical 'system'. For, the outspoken admission that all previous philosophy lacked a really scientific character immediately gives rise to the question of whether philosophy should continue to aim at being a rigorous science. And furthermore, what is a revolution in philosophy supposed to mean? Does it imply a departure from the idea of a rigorous science? And what is supposed to be the meaning of the 'system' which allegedly seems to be the ideal in our philosophical research? Is it to be a philosophical 'system' in the traditional sense which like a Minerva springs forth completely from the head of some creative genius, but is destined to be relegated later, together with other 'Minervas,' to the silent museum of philosophy's history? Or is it to be a philosophical 'system' of doctrines which, after a long and thorough preparation, really begins afresh with a foundation free of doubt and rises up as a skillful construction, each stone set upon stone, each as solid as the other, and laid down according to a plan clearly drawn up in advance. But there is still no agreement on the answers to these question.

Philosophy Has Never Become a Rigorous Science

The revolutions which lead to real progress in philosophy are those which discredit the claims of former philosophies to be scientific by means of a critique of their allegedly scientific procedures. For such a revolution is inspired by the fully conscious will to establish philosophy in a radically new fashion as a rigorous science. First of all, it concentrates all its energy on systematically examining and clarifying the conditions of strict science which the former philosophers naïvely overlooked or misunderstood, in order to clear the way for a reconstruction of the philosophical 'system'. Such a fully conscious will for rigorous science dominated the Socratic-Platonic revolution of philosophy and also the scientific reaction against Scholasticism, especially the Cartesian revolution. Its impulse carried over to the great philosophers of the seventeenth and eighteenth centuries; it renewed itself with radical vigor in the critique of Kant and still dominated Fichte. Again and again these revolutionary thinkers directed their research toward true beginnings, decisive formulation of problems, and correct methods.

Only with romantic philosophy did a change occur. However much Hegel insisted on the absolute validity of his method and his doctrine, his system lacked precisely the rational critique which makes a 'scientific' philosophy possible. Hegelian philosophy, like romantic philosophy in general, in the years that followed, either weakened or falsified the impulse to arrive at a rigorous philosophical science.

As is well known the progress of the exact sciences caused reactions against Hegelianism and gave a very powerful impulse to the naturalism of the eighteenth century. Hegelianism itself, on the other hand, largely determined the ideological world-view-philosophy with its typical relativism, historicism, and, therefore, skepticism.

'Philosophy as Rigorous Science'

The view defended in this article, Husserl continues, is based on the conviction that the interests of human culture demand the development of a rigorously scientific philosophy. Consequently, if a new philosophical revolution is to be justified, it must be inspired by the desire to lay a new foundation for philosophy as a rigorous science. This purpose is by no means foreign to the present age, for it animates precisely the naturalism which dominates our time. Naturalism starts with a firm determination to realize the ideal of a rigorously scientific reform of philosophy. It even believes, both in its earlier and its modern forms, that it has already realized this ideal.

However, when we look at naturalism from the standpoint of principle, it becomes clear that it proceeds in a way which from the very start is rooted in an erroneous theory. Taken from a practical point of view, this constitutes a growing danger for our culture. It is, therefore, important to criticize naturalism in a radical way. In particular, there is need of a positive critique of principles and methods rather than a purely negative critique based on consequences only. For, only a positive critique can preserve our confidence in the real possibility of a scientific philosophy, a confidence which was threatened by the realization of the absurd consequences flowing from a naturalism built on strictly empirical sciences. It is because of these absurd consequences that contemporary philosophy is in fact anti-naturalistic in its orientation. Still influenced by historicism, it seems to turn away from the ideal of a scientific philosophy and to turn toward a philosophy of the ideological 'world-view-type'. But let us focus attention first on naturalism itself.[18]

Naturalistic Philosophy

After this general introduction Husserl goes on to say that naturalism arose from the discovery of nature considered as the totality of spatio-temporal beings subject to the laws of nature. The progressive realization of this idea in ever new natural sciences guaranteed strict knowledge in regard to many realms of investigation and made naturalism constantly expand. In a similar way historicism developed later from the 'discovery of history' and constantly guaranteed new 'human-

---

13. *Ibid.*, pp. 289-293 (71-79).

istic sciences'. In harmony with each one's dominant habit of interpretation, the naturalist tends to regard everything as nature, while the humanist sees everything as 'mind', as a historical creation. In this way both are inclined to distort the sense of everything that cannot be seen in their perspective. The naturalist sees only nature, and especially physical nature. Whatever is, he says, is either physical or psychical. If it is physical, it belongs to the totality of physical nature; if it is psychical, it is merely a variable which depends on the physical, or at best is a secondary 'parallel accompaniment'. Whatever is, therefore, belongs to psychophysical nature, that is to say, it is wholly determined by rigid laws.

Extreme and consistent naturalism in all its forms implies as characteristic traits, on the one hand, the naturalization of consciousness with all its intentionally immanent data, and, on the other, the naturalization of ideas and consequently of all ideals and norms.

Without realizing it, naturalism ultimately refutes itself. Let us take formal logic as an example to explain this. The principles of formal logic, the so-called laws of thought, are interpreted by naturalism as natural laws of thinking. Such an interpretation implies the absurdity which is typical of every form of skepticism, as is explained in detail in the *Logical Investigations*. One could submit also naturalistic axiology and ethics to a radical criticism of the same kind. For theoretical absurdities lead inevitably to absurdities in theories dealing with values and ethical norms. Be this as it may, it should be evident that the naturalist sets up and tries to justify theories which deny precisely what he presupposes, whether it be in constructing formal theories or in justifying values and norms as the best. The naturalist teaches, preaches and moralizes; but he denies what every sermon and every demand presuppose if they are to have meaning at all. Unlike the ancient skeptics, however, he does not say explicity that the only rational thing to do is to deny reason. The absurdity of his position remains hidden from him, precisely because of the fact that he constantly naturalizes reason.

The Ideal of a Rigorous Science with Respect to Philosophy

Naturalism which wanted to base philosophy on strict science and establish it as a strict science, is now completely discredited. Hence its theoretical goal seems to be discredited too, especially if we keep in mind that even among non-naturalists there is a widespread tendency to regard positive science as the only strict science and to recognize philosophy as scientific only if it is based on this kind of science. That tendency, however, is only a prejudice. And, therefore, it would be a fundamental error to give up the ideal itself solely because of the falsity of that prejudice.

The merits and chief strength of naturalism in our time lie precisely in the energy with which it seeks to realize the principle of scientific rigor in all the realms of nature and of mind, both in theory and practice, and in the energy with which it tries to solve the problems of Being and of value in the manner of 'exact natural science'. In all modern life there is perhaps no idea that progresses more powerfully and more irresistably than the idea of science. Nothing will be able to stop its victorious march. In fact, with respect to its legitimate aims, science encompasses everything. Conceived in its ideal perfection, it would be reason itself and could tolerate no other authority equal or superior to itself. The domain of strict science encompasses, therefore, also all the theoretical, axiological, and practical ideals, which naturalism—by giving them an empirical meaning—at the same time and even necessarily distorts.

General convictions, however, carry little weight if one cannot give them a foundation. Hope for establishing a science signifies little if one is incapable of tracing a path leading to its goals. If, then, the idea of philosophy as a rigorous science, concerned with the above-mentioned problems and all problems essentially related to them, is not to remain vain, we must see a clear possibility of realizing it. The clarification of the problems and a penetration into their true sense must reveal methods which are adequate for dealing with these problems because they are demanded by the very essence of these problems. That is what has to be accomplished. However useful and indispensable the negative critique and refutation of naturalism from its consequences may be, it contributes very little to this positive purpose.

The situation is altogether different when we engage in the necessary positive critique of the foundations, methods and accomplishments of naturalism. This kind of critique distinguishes and clarifies; it compels us to pursue the proper sense of the philosophical motives which, as a rule, are only vaguely and equivocally formulated as problems, and for this reason, it can serve to help us in a positive way. With this end in view we will comment more in detail now on that characteristic of naturalism which was above particularly emphasized, namely the naturalization of consciousness.

The Naïve Character of All Natural Science

All natural sciences are naïve with respect to their point of departure. The nature which they want to investigate is simply there for them. It is taken for granted that things are there such as things at rest, in motion, changing in unlimited space, and temporal things in unlimited time. We perceive them, we describe them by means of simple empirical judgments. Natural science wants to know these evident data in an objectively valid and strictly scientific manner.

The same is true also with respect to nature in the broader psychophysical sense. The psychical does not constitute a world for itself; it is given as an ego or as the experience of an ego, and reveals itself empirically as bound to certain physical things, called bodies. This, too, is a self-evident pre-given datum. The task of psychology, then, is to investigate scientifically this psychical element in the psycho-physical constitution of nature, to determine it in an objectively valid way. Every psychological determination is, therefore, of necessity psycho-physical, that is to say, it has a never-absent physical connotation.

Empirical psychology is sometimes concerned with pure events of consciousness and not with those which depend on the psycho-physical order in the ordinary and more restricted sense. Even then, however, these events are thought of as events of nature, that it, as belonging to human or animal consciousnesses, which for their part are obviously connected with human or animal bodies. To eliminate that connection with nature would strip the psychical of its character as an objectively, temporally determinable fact of nature; in short, it would no longer be a psychological fact. Accordingly, every psychological judgment involves the existential positing of physical nature, either explicitly or implicitly.

We may conclude, therefore, Husserl continues, that if there are decisive arguments to prove that the physical sciences of nature cannot be philosophy, that they can never serve as a foundation for philosophy, and that they can have a philosophical value for the purpose of metaphysics only on the basis of a prior philosophy, then all these arguments are equally applicable to psychology. Now, Husserl thinks, there is no lack of such arguments.[14]

Natural Science Cannot Serve as a Basis of a Theory of Knowledge

In dealing with the most important of these arguments, Husserl takes his starting point in the remark that all the methods of empirical science are reducible to experience. It is true, of course, that natural science in its own way is very critical with respect to experience. Nevertheless, no matter how good this critique may be, as long as we remain within the domain of natural science, there remains the possibility of a completely different and indispensable critique of experience. We mean, Husserl says, a critique which puts into question all experience as such as well as the kind of thinking that is proper to empirical science.

How can experience as consciousness give us an object? How can experiences confirm or rectify each other, and not merely invalidate or confirm each other subjectively? How can the play of a consciousness whose logic is empirical, make objectively valid statements, statements which are valid for things which are in and for themselves? Why are the 'playing rules' of consciousness not irrelevant to things? How can natural science be intelligible in absolutely every case, to the extent of claiming at every step to posit and to know a nature which is 'in itself', that is, in opposition to the subjective flow of consciousness? All these questions become enigmas as soon as one reflects seriously upon them. As everyone knows, the theory of knowledge is the discipline which wants to answer these questions. Up to the present, however, in spite of all the thoughts great scholars have devoted to them, it has not answered these questions in a way that is scientifically clear, unanimous, and definitive.

---

14. *Ibid.*, pp. 294-298 (79-87).

A First Introduction to Husserl's Phenomenology

One needs only to remain with rigorous consistency on the level of this problematic to see how absurd it is to base a theory of knowledge on natural science. If, generally speaking, certain enigmas are, in principle, inherent in natural science, then it is self-evident that their solution in principle transcends natural science.

It also becomes clear that in principle every prescientific supposition of nature must be excluded from a theory of knowledge which is to retain its univocal sense. It must exclude also expressions which imply the thetic existential positing of things in the framework of space, time, and causality. The same applies obviously also to all existential positings concerning the 'being there' of the investigator himself, his psychical faculties, etc.

Phenomenology of Consciousness

If the theory of knowledge wants to study the problems of the relationship between consciousness and Being, it can have before its eyes only Being as the correlate of consciousness: Being as perceived, remembered, expected, represented, imagined, identified, distinguished, believed, etc. It is clear, then, that its study must aim at scientific knowledge of the essence of consciousness itself, at that which consciousness itself 'is' according to its essence and in all its various form. At the same time, however, the study must aim at what consciousness 'means', as well as at the different ways in which it 'tends' to the objective order, and at the way it ultimately 'demonstrates' the objective order as that which 'really' is.

It is precisely consciousness itself that must make evident and wholly intelligible the statement that objectivity is and manifests itself cognitively as being so. This task requires a study of consciousness in its entirety, since in all its forms consciousness enters into possible cognitive functions. To the extent, however, that every act of consciousness is 'consciousness-of', the essential study of consciousness includes also that of consciousness' meaning and consciousness' objectivity as such. On the other hand, the clarification of all fundamental kinds of objectivity is indispensable for the essential analysis of consciousness, just as to study any kind of objectivity in its general essence means to concern oneself with the modes in which objects are given. All such studies, therefore, are included under the general title 'phenomenological'.

We meet here, Husserl concludes, a discipline which is a science of consciousness, but a science which is not psychology. It is a 'phenomenology' of consciousness, as opposed to a natural science about consciousness. It is to be expected, of course, that phenomenology and psychology are closely related, for both are concerned with consciousness, though not in the same way, but according to a different 'standpoint'. What we mean is that psychology is concerned with 'empirical consciousness', with consciousness from the empirical standpoint, as an empirical being in the order of nature, whereas phenomenology is concerned with 'pure' consciousness, that is, consciousness taken from the phenomenological point of view.[15]

Husserl develops this idea extensively and takes great pains to explain what is to be understood here by phenomenology and also to describe the precise relationship between phenomenology and empirical psychology. I shall return to this part of the article in one of the following chapters.

3. Husserl's Criticism of Naturalism

Although in the *Logos* article Husserl already touches upon many fundamental insights of his later transcendental phenomenology, one could, nevertheless, say that his criticism of naturalism and psychologism, his view on radicalism as the leading idea of modern and contemporary philosophy, and his critique of Dilthey's historicism constitute the kernel of this article. In the last sections of this chapter I shall restrict myself to a brief consideration of Husserl's criticism of naturalism and his view on radicalism in philosophy in order to focus attention on some basic insights which are of great importance to an understanding of Husserl's transcendental phenomenology in the different phases of its later development. I shall return to the other subjects mentioned in one of the following chapters.

---

15. *Ibid.*, pp. 298-302 (87-91) and 302-322 (91-122) passim.

Husserl's View on Experience

In order to make the basis of Husserl's criticism of naturalism more understandable, one must take his starting point in Husserl's own view of experience. Husserl is of the opinion that nature manifests itself in a series of changing appearances or 'phenomena'. A material thing presents itself to man in and through a multiplicity of aspects or perspectives. ". . . the thing is the intentional unity, that which we are conscious of as the one and self-identical object within the continuously ordered flow of perceptual multiplicities, as they pass from the one into the other . . ." "It can 'appear' only with a certain 'orientation', which necessarily carries with it predelineated in advance systematical possibilities of always new orientations . . .".[16]

Everyone will agree that the physical thing itself does not belong to the concrete content of the perception itself as cogitation, because it is obvious that this thing itself is transcendent in regard to the 'world of appearances'. But even those appearances, although we refer to them habitually as 'merely subjective', do not belong to the real content of perception, but are also opposed to it as transcendent. Let me give a concrete example. I see a table. Keeping the table steadily in view as I go around it, I have continuously the consciousness of the bodily presence of one and the same table. But my perception of it is one that changes continuously; it is a continuum of changing perceptions. When I close my eyes and keep my other senses inactive in relation to the table, then I have no perception of it any more. When I open my eyes again, the perception returns. It evidently does not return to me as individually the same. Only the table is the same. The perceived thing can be, without being perceived; but the perception itself is what it is only within the steady flow of consciousness. The perceived thing in general, *but also all its parts, aspects, and phases, whether the quality in question be primary or secondary, are necessarily transcendent to the perception.* The color of the thing seen is not a real phase of the consciousness of color; certainly, it appears, but even while it is appearing the appearance must be continuously changing. The *same* color

---

16. Edmund Husserl, Ideen I, p. 94 (119); p. 97 (122).

appears 'in' continuously varying *patterns of perspective color-variations*. The same holds true for every sensory quality, also for the primary qualities.[17]

However, the series of changing phenomena refers to an enduring, stable, and 'objective' thing which claims to possess an independent existence of its own, and to transcend the mobile stream of perception. In the perception of one side of an object, this object as a whole manifests itself as something which, irrespective of the relativism, multiplicity, and change of the 'subjective' appearances, posits itself as standing there as a temporal unity of enduring or changing properties.[18]

The duality, however, which in the experience of a corporeal thing we are pointing to here, must be understood in the right way. The phenomena do not manifest themselves as separated from the object they refer to. The relation between phenomena and object, therefore, is different from the relation between a sign or an image and the thing which they signify. The thought that the transcendence of the thing is that of an image or sign, Husserl says, has proved misleading. The image-theory is often zealously attacked and the sign-theory substituted for it. But both theories are not only incorrect but even nonsensical. The spatial thing which we see is, despite all its transcendence, perceived; we are consciously aware of it as given in its bodily presence. We are not given an image or a sign in its place.[19]

One must, however, realize here that a material thing can manifest itself in perception only in an inadequate way; material objects cannot be given with complete determinacy and with similarly complete intuitability in any limited finite consciousness. The complete giveness is prescribed only as an 'idea' in the Kantian sense, as a connection of endless processes of continuous appearing and, correlatively, as a continuum of appearances determined *a priori*.[20] In other words a spatial thing is nothing but an intentional unity, which, in principle, can be given only as the unity of such phenomena.[21] That is why one, furthermore, has to

17. *Ibid.*, pp. 92-93 (117-118).
18. Edmund Husserl, *Phil. str. W.*, p. 310 (104).
19. Edmund Husserl, *Ideen I*, pp. 98-99 (123).
20. *Ibid.*, pp. 350-351 (366).
21. *Ibid.*, p. 98 (122).

admit a certain identity between each phenomenon and the appearing thing itself, because each appearance of the thing somehow contains the whole thing.[22]

Thus, the appearance of the material thing in and through a multiplicity of perspectives (*Abschattungen*) is essentially charactistic of the thing as such. It is not an accidental caprice of the thing, nor an accident of our human constitution that 'our' perception can reach the things themselves only and merely through their perspectives. On the contrary, it is evident, and it follows from the essential nature of the spatial thing itself as such, that a being of such a structure can, in principle, be given in perception only by way of perspectives.[23]

Natural Sciences

However, the sense (*Sinn*) of the experience of the material world does not consist exclusively of the relation between the phenomena and the 'unity' which they constitute. The unities of which the phenomena are the one-sided perspectives only, that is to say, the corporeal things themselves to which they refer, manifest themselves as incorporated in the totality of our corporeal world that binds them all together with its one space and its one time. They are what they are only in their unity; only in the connection with each other do they retain their identity.[24] It is the physicist who, pressed by the relativism characteristic of our immediate experience, tries to transcend this relativism by constructing the transcendent world of physics from these pure appearances of our concrete life.

The manner in which the world of physics is constructed by scientific thought is motivated by the effective content of the concrete world. Realities are given as unities of immediate experience, as unities of diverse sensible appearances. Stabilities, changes, and relationships of change, all of which can be grasped sensibly, direct cognition everywhere, and function for it like a 'vague' medium in which true, objective,

---

22. Edmund Husserl, *L. U.*, vol. III, pp. 148-149.
23. Edmund Husserl, *Ideen I*, p. 97 (122).
24. Edmund Husserl, *Phil. str. W.*, p. 311 (104).

physically exact nature presents itself, a medium through which thought, as empirically scientific thought, determines and constructs what is true.[25]

The world of physics is a unity of spatio-temporal Being which is in harmony with the exact laws of nature.[26] Concepts such as 'atom' or 'electron' take the place of the sensible qualities. The real as a whole which is constituted this way is governed by the law of causality. And while in the concrete but subjective world of our immediate experience we are dealing with things, in the ideal but objective world of science we meet only series of causalities, the intertexture of which constitute the thing, that is, the 'substance' of its properties. The corporeal things are what they are only in this unity; only in the causal relation to or connection with each other do they retain their individual identity (= substance), and this they retain as that which carries 'real properties'. All physically real properties are causal. Every material being is subject to laws of possible changes, and these laws concern the identical thing, not by itself but in the unified, actual and possible totality of the one nature. Each physical thing has its nature, as the totality of what it, the identical, is, by virtue of being the intertexture of causalities within the one all-nature. Real properties are a title for the possibilities of transformation of something identical, possibilities pre-indicated according to the laws of causality. And thus this identical, with regard to what it is, is determinable only by recourse to these laws.[27]

The sciences of nature try to transcend the vague and approximate character of our naïve experience and to reach an ideal objectivity and an ideal being which in our concrete experience only announces itself. That is why Husserl says that natural science "simply follows consistently the sense of what the thing so to speak pretends to be as experienced, and calls this—vaguely enough—'elimination of secondary qualities', 'elimination of the merely subjective in the appearance', while 'retaining what is left, the primary qualities'. And that is more than an obscure expression; it is a bad theory regarding a good procedure."[28]

---

25. *Ibid.*, p. 311 (104-105).
26. *Ibid.*, p. 294 (79-80).
27. *Ibid.*, p. 310 (104-105).
28. *Ibid.*, p. 311 (105).

Naturalism

That which Husserl calls 'naturalism' is nothing but a wrong interpretation of the sense *(Sinn)* of the sciences of nature according to which the objectivity of the physical world is to be identified with objectivity as such, and physical reality and its conditions with reality and its conditions in general. In this way, however, naturalism forgets that the physical world necessarily and even in its very essence refers to the 'subjective' world. For, physical nature, although it pretends to transcend our naïve experience, exists only in relation to that experience. What is studied and investigated in physical science, was already somehow intended in our pre-scientific perception. The physical thing is nothing foreign to that which appears in a sensory body, but something that manifests itself in it and in it alone indeed in a primordial way, a way that is also *a priori* in that it rests on essential grounds which cannot be annulled. Moreover, even the sensory determining-content of the *x* which functions as bearer of the physical determinations does not clothe the latter in an alien dress that conceals them: rather it is only insofar as the *x* is the subject of the sensory determinations that it is also subject of the physical, which on its side announces itself in the sensory. In principle, the thing of which the physicist speaks can be given only sensorily, in sensory 'ways of appearance'. In the shifting continuity of these ways of appearance the thing manifests itself as one identical element. It is this element which the physicist in relation to all experienceable systems that can come under consideration as 'conditioning circumstances', subjects to a causal analysis, to an inquiry into real necessary connections.[29]

The consequence of this is that where the sciences of nature are still right, naturalism is already wrong. For, by interpreting the ideal world, which science discovers by taking its starting point in the fleeing and changing world of perception, as absolute Being of which the world of perception is supposed to be only a subjective experience,[30] naturalism denies the internal sense of this experience itself. Physical nature has meaning only in relation to an existence which manifests itself first in

---

29. Edmund Husserl, *Ideen I*, p. 126 (145-146).
30. *Ibid.*, pp. 122-123 (143-144).

the relativism of the perspectives, and that precisely is the mode of being characteristic of corporeal reality.

And in order to be consistent naturalism even reduces the totality of Being to the mode of being characteristic of physical reality: " . . . the natural scientist has the tendency to look upon everything as nature" and is, therefore, "inclined to falsify the sense of what cannot be seen in his way".[31] Spiritual as well as ideal being must form part of nature, if it really wants to be called 'being'. In regard to 'spiritual' being Husserl formulates his point of view as follows. Every psychological determination is by that very fact psychophysical, which is to say in the broadest sense that it has a never-failing physical connotation. Even where empirical psychology concerns itself with determinations of bare events of consciousness and not with dependences that are psychophysical in the usual and narrower sense, those events are thought of, nevertheless, as belonging to nature, that is, as belonging to human or animal consciousnesses that for their part have an unquestioned and co-apprehended connection with human and animal organisms. To eliminate the relation to nature would deprive the psychical of its character as an objectively and temporally determinable fact of nature, that is, of its character as a psychological fact. Thus let us hold fast to this: every psychological judgment involves the existential positing of physical nature, whether expressly or not.[32] In a general way we may say according to Husserl that the naturalist sees only nature, and primarily physical nature. Whatever is, is either itself physical, belonging to the unified totality of physical nature, or it is in fact psychical, but then merely as a variable dependent on the physical, at best as a secondary 'parallel accompaniment'. Whatever is belongs to psychophysical nature, which is to say that it is univocally determined by rigid laws.[33]

Naturalism and Materialism

The profound meaning of these quotations is not so much that they attribute to naturalism the fundamental theses of materialism, because

---

31. Edmund Husserl, *Phil. str. W.*, p. 294 (79).
32. *Ibid.*, pp. 298-299 (86).
33. *Ibid.*, p. 294 (79).

naturalism is not a metaphysical doctrine. These quotations only want to show that for naturalism the objectivity itself of a psychic phenomenon implies the physical world. That is to say, for naturalism being does not so much mean being corporeal and material, but only 'being at the same level as material reality'; the reality of psychic phenomena disappears as soon as one denies the fact that it essentially belongs to nature in the sense of physical reality. That is why Husserl sees the real source of naturalism in the fact that it conceives the existence of the totality of being 'in the image of' the material and corporeal things, and that, consequently, it understands the way each being manifests itself in the manner characteristic of corporeal things which announce themselves in and through subjective phenomena of man's experience. This is also why, according to Husserl, it does not matter whether one interprets the fundamental insights of naturalism in an idealistic or a realistic way.[34] This is finally why naturalism has to defend the materialization, reification and naturalization of consciousness. For, as long as naturalism does not broaden its concept of Being, it will never be able to conceive the essence of consciousness as essentially different from the essence of a material and corporeal thing. And here again we can say that it does not matter whether one conceives consciousness on the same level as the physical world, or whether one resolves the physical world into the contents of consciousness, because in either case consciousness and the physical world are 'in' nature and possess the same modes of being and of manifesting themselves. Finally, it will be clear that once consciousness is 'naturalized', the essences as well as the subjective phenomena are to be naturalized, too. Then it becomes apparent that naturalism and psychologism are two different realizations of one and the same, fundamentally unacceptable, empiricist point of view.

Phases of the Process of Naturalization

Let us now briefly indicate the most important phases of this naturalization. First of all, if Being means Being-'in'-nature, then consciousness, by means of which nature is known and understood, must be part of nature in order to be able to exist. This means that consciousness

---

34. *Ibid.*, p. 294 (79-80).

must be described with the help of the same categories that are employed in the description of physical nature, namely, the categories of time, space, and causality. The necessary consequence of this point of view is that, for instance, the relation between the phenomena and reality (which announces itself in those phenomena), must be interpreted in terms of a causal relation.[35]

Secondly, once consciousnes is naturalized, all that is ideal and universal (such as numbers, geometrical entities, values, etc.) is to be naturalized as well, at least inasfar as one wants to attribute to them one or another form of 'reality'. If this view is further developed in a consistent way, it necessarily leads to an inadmissible form of empiricism and nominalism. In this context Husserl often refers to Locke, Berkeley, Hume and Stuart Mill.[36]

Thirdly, mathematical, logical, and ethical laws also can no longer refer to ideal entities which have a certain 'reality' or 'validity' of their own, but must refer to natural, psychophysical facts and, therefor, are to be explained in *psychology,* understood as a natural science. If we ask for exact philosophy, Husserl remarks, a philosophy which could be the analogue of exact mechanics, we are shown psychophysical and, above all, experimental psychology, to which, of course, no one can deny the rank of strict science. This, they tell us, is the long sought scientific psychology, that has at last become a fact. Logic and epistemology, aesthetics, ethics, and pedagogy have finally obtained their scientific foundation through it. In addition, strict psychology is obviously the foundation of all humanistic sciences and not less even of metaphysics.[37]

Finally, philosophy cannot use other methods than those employed by the natural sciences. Because natural science only recognizes physical experience as a legitimate source of knowledge and refutes every 'intuition' as well as every immediate grasp of essences, it is understand-

---

35. Edmund Husserl, *Ideen I,* pp. 122-130 (143-149).

36. Edmund Husserl, *L. U.,* vol. II, pp. 106-224, and *Erste Philos.,* vol. I, pp. 78-182.

37. Edmund Husserl, *Phil. str. W.,* p. 297 (84) ; *L. U.,* vol. I, pp. 102-109, 180-182.

able that Husserl concentrates all his attention on this thesis of naturalism, as we shall see in the following chapter.[38]

4. *The Question of the Radical Departure in Husserl's Later Philosophy*

Introductory Remarks

In the foregoing we have seen that in his *Logos* article Husserl defends the thesis that philosophy has to be a strict and rigorous science. According to a rather generally accepted view Husserl's commitment to the ideal of philosophy as a rigorous science never wavered, but only assumed different forms in the midst of a rapidly changing intellectual climate.[39] In an essay entitled *The Decisive Phases in the Development of Husserl's Phenomenology,*[40] Biemel has shown that the long evolution through which Husserl passed between 1891 and 1911 led to this famous article. Biemel is of the opinion that this article is the "rock upon which Husserl's whole philosophy is based". Biemel also suggests that the ideal described in this article was one of the most important guiding principles in *all* Husserl's later investigations. In 1951 De Waelhens[41] for the first time called this opinion in question and a few years later Merleau-Ponty shared this point of view in his article on Husserl's philosophy in *Les Philosophes Célèbres.*[42] Spiegelberg believes that this view is due to a misunderstanding of some of Husserl's later manuscripts.[43] It is true, Spiegelberg says, that Husserl, in his manuscripts written after 1930, sometimes seems to be saying that philosophy as a rigorous science "is a dream now ended". But, Spiegelberg continues, the context shows then that Husserl speaks with bitter irony about the times, not about himself; these negative statements do not so much apply to the ideal as to the possibility of obtaining

---

38. *Ibid.,* pp. 194-199 (79-87).
39. Herbert Spiegelberg, *op, cit.,* vol. I, p. 77.
40. Walter Biemel, "Les phases décisives", p. 54
41. Alphonse De Waelhens, "Husserl et la phénoménologie", *Critique* 7 (1951), p. 1054.
42. Maurice Merleau-Ponty, *Les Philosophes Célèbres* (Paris: Mazenot, 1956), p. 17, p. 427.
43. Herbert Spiegelberg, *op. cit.,* vol. I, p. 77.

the necessary support from like-minded scholars to implement this ideal. Although I do not agree with Spiegelberg's motivation, no one would doubt, I think, that Husserl maintained the ideal throughout his whole life, as can easily be shown from his *Cartesian Meditations* and even from his last book *The Crisis of the European Sciences*. On the other hand, however, both De Waelhens and Merleau-Ponty were also correct in positing that Husserl perforce abandoned his original view the moment he became aware of the real meaning of the history of man's philosophy, as is clearly in evidence in the second volume of his *First Philosophy* (1925).

Be this as it may, even if we should adopt the point of view that Husserl, everything considered, maintained his original view, we still should have to explain how this ideal is to be understood. Therefore the balance of this chapter will be devoted to a discussion of the following problems: 1) the extent to which Husserl abandoned this ideal in his *First Philosophy* and some of his later manuscripts and nevertheless re-assumed it in his last publications; 2) Husserl's view on the question of the radical departure in his last publications and his critique of Cartesianism; 3) the manner in which Husserl's radicalism is really to be understood.

a. HUSSERL'S REJECTION OF CARTESIANISM

Husserl's 'First Philosophy'

In the winter of 1923-1924 Husserl presented a series of lectures in which he—in a historical and a systematical way—tried to defend the thesis that transcendental phenomenology is the first realization of the age-old idea of a 'First Philosophy'. It was Husserl's intention in this work to describe a new road leading to transcendental phenomenology and containing all the important insights which already had come to light in his philosophical investigations from 1913 on. This series of lectures was, therefore, supposed to describe not only the *idea* of transcendental phenomenology as already briefly indicated in *Ideas* (1913), but also to present all the meditations and 'pre-meditations' on the road leading to such a philosophy, and especially the meditations on the absolute starting point or origin of this road. 'First Philosophy' is a truly universal science which gives itself an absolute foundation, because it begins in and proceeds from a really absolute starting point. It is, therefore, that science which is *first* because of inner and even essential motives.[44] It is a science which intends to bring about the ideal which Descartes saw but never was able to realize and, therefore, aims at an absolute radicalism; it is a science of a completely new and absolute 'beginning'.[45]

When he started to prepare the course in 1923, Husserl was deeply convinced that in this new, historical and systematical approach he had found the way to show the true radicalization of transcendental phenomenology in a definitive manner. In the spring of 1924, however, it became clear to him that such a road is blocked and that a foundation of this view seems even to be completely impossible. Between 1924 and 1930 he rewrote several sections of the historical as well as of the systematical part of the lecture series, but the more he studied the problems involved in such an approach to phenomenology the more he became convinced of the problematic character of his original idea. Finally, in 1930, he decided to give up his plan to publish the lecture series and immediately started investigations in a completely new direction, investigations which finally led to the insights described in *Crisis*.[46]

Impossibility of the Cartesian Ideal

When Husserl started to write his lecture course, which even then was intended as an immediate preparation for the publication of the two volumes on 'First Philosophy', he thought he was able to show that transcendental phenomenology is the harmonious synthesis and the crown of all important ideas brought to the fore in modern and contemporary philosophy. However, what, as a matter of fact, the systematic part of *First Philosophy* shows us is that Husserl against his will had to dis-

---

44. Edmund Husserl, *Erste Philos.*, vol. II, p. 5; p. 4.
45. *Ibid.*, p. 154.
46. Ludwig Landgrebe, *Der Weg der Phänomenologie* (Gütersloh: Gerd Mohn, 1963), pp. 163-167.

sociate himself from a tradition whose fundamental ideas he precisely hoped to materialize. What is enacted in this book before the eyes of the attentive reader is exactly the breakdown of transcendental subjectivism as the ultimate completion and crowning of modern rationalism, because it becomes unmasked as an a-historical apriorism.[47]

The problems which Husserl experienced in his description of phenomenology from the viewpoint of the idea of an absolutely founded science, can perhaps be briefly described as follows. 1) Husserl wanted to discover a domain of apodictical evidences which imply the necessary insight that their contradiction is absolutely impossible, because only such a domain can constitute the ground and basis of an absolute justification of all knowledge and science. 2) The apodicticity Husserl was looking for must have the character of an essential insight, that is, an insight whose essential characteristics are universality and necessity. 3) At the same time, however, Husserl determined apodicticity, in the sense of apodictic evidence, as the immediate consciousness of the presence of what is meant 'in its bodily self-hood', the immediate presence of consciousness to 'the things themselves'. 4) However, such an immediate presence of consciousness to 'the things themselves' is only materialized in and by experience, and all experience ultimately originates in intuition (*Anschauung*). 5) But insights, the essential characteristics of which are an unconditional necessity and universality, that is to say, insights into 'eternal' and 'necessary' truths, cannot be drawn from experience which is necessarily tied to the factical and, therefore the contingent.[48]

In 1924 Husserl was fully aware of the fact that neither Plato's *thigein*, nor Descartes' closed *cogito*, nor Kant's regression from a factical *cogito* to the conditions of its possibility could bring a solution for this problematic. That is why phenomenology, in Husserl's view, has to tread a completely new road in order to show in what sense transcendental subjectivity could be truly considered to be a domain of absolute experience. Husserl thought that his transcendental reduction was able to justify a distinction between a mundane and a transcendental subjectivity, and to explain in a radical way that the abso-

---

47. *Ibid.*, pp. 164-165.
48. *Ibid.*, pp. 171-173.

lute domain of the essentially intentional consciousness can legitimately be considered as a domain of transcendental experience which, as closed in itself, is not dependent any more on the factical and the contingent. However, describing this domain of transcendental experience in a transcendental 'egology', Husserl gradually became aware of the fact that every experience is and remains world-experience. Analysis and description of this insight not only led Husserl to the problematic of the 'life-world', but also to intricate problems concerning intersubjectivity and historicity. Maintaining his original ideal Husserl now tried to solve the problems concerning intersubjectivity in his *Cartesian Meditations,* while—still maintaining his ideas—he attempted to solve the 'life-world' problem and the problematic concerning philosophy's historicity in *Crisis* and his last manuscripts, employing a completely new approach to transcendental phenomenology. Both these attempts were not completely successful. Although Husserl had sometimes felt this clearly, he must nevertheless have been of the opinion that—at least in principle—a really radical and scientifically rigorous philosophy is and remains realizable.[49] Be this as it may, we shall return to these problems in one of the chapters to come.

b. RADICALISM AS THE LEADING IDEA IN 'CARTESIAN MEDITATIONS' AND 'CRISIS'

Descartes' Influence According to the 'Cartesian Meditations'

In the first two sections of his *Cartesian Meditations* Husserl points out that the reading of Descartes' works gave him a new impulse when between 1901 and 1906 he conceived the first idea of his transcendental phenomenology. The study of Descartes' *Meditations Concerning First Philosophy* directly caused the transformation of his phenomenology from a descriptive psychology into a new kind of transcendental philosophy. That is why he called his transcendental phenomenology a neo-Cartesianism, even though he had to reject nearly the whole doc-

---

49. *Ibid.,* pp. 173-175.

trinal content of Descartes' philosophy. His intention was precisely to develop Descartes' methological ideas in an absolutely radical way.

According to Husserl, the aim of Descartes' *Meditations* was a complete reform of philosophy into a science based on an absolute foundation. In Descartes' view this implied a corresponding reform of all the sciences. For all sciences are non-autonomous members of the all-embracing science, philosophy. Moreover, the different sciences can develop into genuine sciences only within the systematic unity of philosophy. But as they have developed historically, the sciences do not correspond to this ideal. They have no ultimate grounding on the basis of absolute insights. Hence there is need for a radical rebuilding of the sciences that satisfies the idea of philosophy as the all-inclusive unity of the sciences. This reconstruction must be made by means of one and the same absolutely rational grounding.

Descartes wanted to realize this ideal through a philosophy turned toward the subject himself. This turning to the subject occurs on two different levels. I must first withdraw into myself; within myself I must overthrow all the sciences which I have hitherto accepted; within myself I must try to rebuild them again. For philosophy and wisdom are personal affairs of the philosopher. Philosophy must arise as my self-acquired knowledge, tending to universality, a knowledge which I can justify from the beginning and at each subsequent step by virtue of my own absolute insights. This choice implies that I want to begin in absolute 'poverty', that is, with an absolute lack of knowledge. The first thing I have to do is to reflect on how I can find a method which promises to lead to genuine knowledge. What I am doing here is not literature; it is my personal but not my private concern. It is the prototype that every real beginning philosopher has to follow.

Secondly, there is a return to my ego in a more profound sense, a return to my ego as the subject of my pure cogitations. This return is affected by means of a radical, methodic doubt. Aiming with radical consistency at absolute knowledge, I refuse to accept anything as existent, unless it is made secure against any conceivable doubt. In this way I hope to find something that is absolutely evident. The certainty of my sense experience, however, with which the world is given in natural life, cannot withstand every critique. Therefore, the existence of the world remains unacceptable, at least at this first stage of our consideration. I retain only myself, as the pure ego of my own pure cogitations, as possessing an absolutely indubitable existence. Next, my ego tries to philosophize in a kind of solipsistic fashion. I seek *apodictically* certain ways through which, within my own pure interiority, an objective exteriority can be deduced.

According to Husserl, Descartes tried to realize this ideal by deducing, first, God's existence and veracity and then, by means of them, objective nature, the duality of finite substances and finally the objective ground for metaphysics and the natural sciences. All these inferences are made according to guiding principles that are 'innate' in the pure ego.[50]

Renewal of Descartes' Radicalism

For Husserl, the most important question was whether Descartes' ideas were really able to solve all our problems about science and phillosophy. After three centuries of brilliant development, Husserl says, the sciences find themselves in a crisis with respect to their foundations, fundamental concepts and methods. But when they attempt to reform those foundations, they neglect to resume Descartes' *Meditations*.

In philosophy, on the other hand, these *Meditations* exercised great influence precisely because they went back to the pure *ego cogito*. Descartes inaugurated an entirely new kind of philosophy by radically turning away from naïve objectivism to transcendental subjectivism. This turning manifests itself also in the inadequate attempts made by Spinoza, Leibniz, and Kant, but seems to tend toward some radical final form. But even here the divisiveness of contemporary philosophy makes one think. There is no unity in aims, problems and methods. Instead of a serious scientific philosophy we have a philosophical literature, which grows beyond all bounds and almost without any coherence. A serious collaboration and a firm intention to produce objectively valid results, that is, results that have been refined by mutual critique, could perhaps

---

50. Edmund Husserl, *Cart. Med.,* pp. 43-45 (1-3).

help us. But how can such a collaboration be reached when there are almost as many philosophies as there are philosophers?

Our situation, Husserl says, is similar to the one which Descartes encountered in his youth. It is time, therefore, to renew radicalism. We must overthrow the immense philosophical literature and begin with new *Meditations Concerning First Philosophy*. Of course, we should not take over the content of Descartes' meditations, but renew the radicalism of their spirit with even greater vigor.[51]

Kant and Metaphysics

It is perhaps interesting to mention that the principle Husserl used in his critique of Descartes' philosophy is, in principle at least, identical with one of the most important ideas of Kant's philosophy of science. In the *Preface* to the second edition of his *Critique of Pure Reason*, Kant makes the following fundamental statement about the pursuit of metaphysics:

> If after elaborate preparations, frequently renewed, it is brought to a stop immediately it nears its goal; if often it is compelled to retrace its steps and strike into some new line of approach; or again, if the various participants are unable to agree on any common plan or procedure, then we may rest assured that it is very far from having entered upon the secure path of science, and is indeed a merely random groping. In these circumstances, we shall be rendering a service to reason should we succeed in discovering the path upon which it can securely travel, even if, as a result of so doing, much that is comprised in our original aims, adopted without reflection, may have to be abandoned as fruitless.[52]

According to Kant logic, mathematics and physics have already entered upon the secure course of science a long time ago; metaphysics, on the other hand, has not yet managed to attain to the secure scientific method. This will become evident, he said, if we apply the tests proposed

---

51. *Ibid.*, pp. 45-48 (4-6).
52. Immanuel Kant., *Critique of Pure Reason*. Translated by Norman Kemp Smith (London: Macmillan Comp., 1963), p. 17 and pp. 17-37 (passim).

at the beginning of the above-mentioned *Preface*. We find that reason perpetually comes to a standstill when it attempts to gain *a priori* the perception even of those laws which the most common experience confirms. It is constantly compelled to retrace its steps and to abandon as useless the path on which it has entered. Moreover, those who are engaged in metaphysical pursuits are far from being able to agree among themselves.

This leads us to the question of why metaphysics has not yet found the sure path of science. Kant thinks that the examples of mathematics and natural philosophy (physics), which reached their present condition by a sudden revolution, are sufficiently remarkable to fix our attention on the essential circumstances of the change which has proved so profitable to them, and to induce us to make the experiment of imitating them to the extent that their analogy with metaphysics permits this. Hitherto it has been assumed that our knowledge must conform to the objects; but the attempts to ascertain anything about these objects *a priori,* by means of concepts, and thus to extend the range of our knowledge, have been wrecked by this assumption. Kant, therefore, wants to try to be more successful in metaphysics by assuming that the objects must conform to our cognition. We must try to do just what Copernicus did in attempting to explain the celestial movements.

Descartes' Fundamental Mistake

When we compare these quotations, it becomes immediately evident that for both Husserl and Kant one of the most important reasons why modern philosophy in its different forms is inadmissible, lies in the fact that there is no agreement about its object, method and results. But let us go back to Husserl's view regarding Descartes' philosophy of science. According to Husserl, Descartes' principal mistake was that he presupposed an ideal of science, the ideal approximated by mathematics and mathematical science of nature. The fateful prejudice of this ideal dominated philosophy for centuries. For Descartes, it was *a priori* certain that the all-embracing science he intended should have the form of a deductive system, in which the whole structure, in a geometric fashion, rests on an axiomatic foundation as the absolute ground of the deductions.

'PHILOSOPHY AS RIGOROUS SCIENCE'

This presupposition, however, says Husserl, is nothing but a prejudice which we must try to avoid. It is in this point that Husserl transcends Descartes' point of view and fundamentally agrees with Kant. Husserl, however, rejects Kant's point of view too, because, according to him, Kant also was not yet able to see the fundamental necessity of a transcendental reduction, which is the absolutely necessary presupposition for a really 'transcendental' philosophy.[53] This is explained in a particularly convincing way in Husserl's last book: *The Crisis of the European Sciences.*[54]

Husserl's Radicalism in 'Crisis'

I think that no one will question whether in his last publication Husserl maintained the fundamental thesis explained in the *Cartesian Meditations.* True, the perspective is completely changed; Husserl is looking for an absolutely new road which could lead him to a new, transcendental form of philosophy, his transcendental phenomenology; the '*Lebenswelt*' idea occupies a central place. But all this does not change the fact that Husserl maintained his original claim that his transcendental phenomenology is to be considered—at least in principle —as a realization of the ideal which moved philosophy since Plato's days. This is particularly clear from the central sections of the book.[55] This idea is also reassumed in a manuscript which as paragraph 73 is added by the editor to Husserl's text as the conclusion of this work.[56] However, no one can deny either that this ideal itself underwent a very important change inasfar as Husserl explicitly became aware of the essential historicity of man's thinking, which implies that this idea can be materialized *in principle* only, because it means "an infinity of life and striving for reason" and apodicticity.[57]

I do not want to go into further details here, because it is my intention to deal with Husserl's *Crisis* in Chapter Nine. These brief remarks may suffice to substantiate my thesis that, although Husserl changed

53. Edmund Husserl, *Cart. Med.,* pp. 48-50 (7-9).
54. Edmund Husserl, *Krisis,* pp. 5-9, 91-123, and passim.
55. *Ibid.,* pp. 15-17, 101-104, 190-193.
56. *Ibid.,* pp. 269-276.
57. *Ibid.,* p. 275.

the meaning of his claim, he, nevertheless, even in his last publication maintained the very essence of his original view, namely, that philosophy can and must be a rigorous and, therefore, radical science. Let us, therefore, now turn to the question of what precisely in Husserl's view is to be understood by this claim of radicalism.

c. ON THE MEANING OF 'RADICALISM' IN PHILOSOPHY

Philosophy as a Radical and Apodictical Foundation of Science

As we have seen several times, Husserl explicitly claims that his phenomenology is to be understood, in principle at least, as the fulfillment of Cartesian radicalism. We have also seen that Husserl was very well aware of the fundamental difference between Descartes' radicalism and the radicalism characteristic of transcendental phenomenology. In his view, this difference was so great that in fact there are not two fundamental principles which Descartes' and his own philosophy have in common.[58]

On closer investigation of Descartes' and Husserl's points of view, however, the question seems to be legitimate whether Husserl really has understood the deepest intention of the Cartesian philosophy and whether the difference between the two forms of radicalism is not even greater than Husserl originally thought it was. That is what we have to investigate now.

There can be no doubt about the fact that both Husserl and Descartes were deeply convinced that philosophy's task consists in establishing a radical, and therefore apodictic, foundation of true science. In formulating this point of view Descartes opposed the late Renaissance philosophy which he incorrectly identified with 'Scholasticism' as such, while Husserl's claim of radicalism was born out of a thorough criticism of 'naturalism' and 'psychologism', which in Husserl's view were the two most important forms of twentieth century positivism, on the one hand, and neo-Kantianism on the other. It is clear that this difference in historical context constitutes a first point which explains why Des-

---

58. Edmund Husserl, *Cart. Med.,* p. 43 (1).

cartes' and Husserl's preoccupation in this respect are oriented in completely different directions.[59]

Descartes' and Husserl's Views on Philosophy's Radicalism

But there is more, inasfar as the meaning of philosophical radicalism itself is different in the two philosophies. This will become immediately clear if we realize that there is a great difference between the crisis of science which Descartes referred to in the sixteenth century, and the crisis of science's foundations which Husserl tried to cope with. Descartes formulated his claim of radicalism in reference to an uncertain science and a decayed philosophy. His return aimed at assuring the basis of an unshakable certitude, of a cornerstone for the edifice of future science. Husserl, on the other hand, found himself in the presence of a mature and secure science which 'only' suffered from a crisis in its foundations. Descartes wanted to establish the foundations of a science yet to come and, therefore, had to turn toward metaphysics. Husserl, on the other hand, wanted to discover the foundations of a science already built up and, therefore, had to reflect on a knowledge which was already there in order to try in this way to grasp more originally what is already present. In doing so, Husserl learned from Kant that such a reflection will end in relativism unless one performs that reflection on a deeper, that is, a transcendental level. Seen from this point of view, it will be clear why Husserl's attempt of radicalization is different from that intended by Descartes, not only in regard to its content but also with respect to its method. It even becomes problematic in this perspective whether the process of radicalization and the quest for a radical point of departure refer to one identical goal.

Both Descartes and Husserl were of the opinion that the process of radicalization presupposes a suspension of judgment. In Descartes this suspension of judgment has to take the form of a methodic doubt, because he found himself standing before a doubtful science. In Husserl's case the domain of investigation was already occupied by a science that

59. Pierre Thévenaz, *What is Phenomenology? and Other Essays*. Edited with an Introduction by James M. Edie and a Preface by John D. Wild (Chicago: Quadrangle Books, Inc., 1962), pp. 97-99.

is certain; there is nothing to be eliminated here, but the philosopher has only to free his view; that is why the suspension of judgment in Husserl's case consists in a phenomenological reduction, that is to say, in a change of perspective, which enables the philosopher to see how the phenomena of the sciences got their meaning in an original constitution.

But in both cases the process of radicalization takes the form of a struggle against the evident. Such a struggle is necessary because evidence is not identical with apodicticity. It is, therefore, necessary to detach oneself from every evidence which is not yet apodictical; this means, first, that we have to detach ourselves from our naïve evidences by means of the sciences; but it means, furthermore, that we clear away at the very heart of the evidence a more profound layer of naïveté characteristic of the sciences in order to bring to the fore the apodictic evidence which only can give us the radical point of departure the philosopher is looking for. In Descartes' and Husserl's philosophies these two reductions, however, are motivated by two completely different considerations. Descartes tries to render harmless the illusory evidences of dreams and hallucinations on the one hand, and the possible deception of an 'evil genius' on the other.

Husserl's *epoché* shows us a completely different preoccupation. It is not oriented toward an elimination of illusion and error, but a means of neutralizing our natural belief in the world. It intends to modify our relation to the world and to open up a new domain of experience by disclosing transcendental subjectivity. Husserl's reduction is a modification of the ego's attitude in relation to the world, and therefore, a change of intentionality. Transcendental intentionality is a special attention to the world, uncovering the relation of the world to its transcendental source which gives it its meaning. While Descartes' *epoché* makes the world disappear in order to open up consciousness' 'essential' structure as attention, Husserl's reduction, on the contrary, makes the world appear in regard to its meaning and, thus, discloses the essential structure of consciousness as intention. Instead of losing itself in the world which it experiences, consciousness, being intentional, discloses it by grasping itself as intention, that is, as consciousness of meaning. That is why the radical point of departure for Descartes lies at the very center of a centripetal consciousness, whereas for Husserl it is to be found at the final point of its centrifugal intention.

Finally, in both cases the process of radicalization is a reflexive procedure. But in Descartes' view reflection tends to guarantee to the philosopher an Archimedean point, whereas for Husserl who sees consciousness as essentially intentional, reflection is a way of giving sense on an always deeper level. That is why one could say that in Descartes one finds a virginal beginning and a linear method, going forward without returning, while in Husserl we find a circular movement which revolves around its point of departure radicalizing it without ever truly leaving it.[60]

Root of the Difference Between Descartes' and Husserl's Views

In order to be able to explain the difference between the two radical points of departure in detail we must take our starting point in the fact that in Descartes' philosophy the realization of the reflexive return consists in that *attention* materializes the coincidence of consciousness with itself, while in Husserl's phenomenology *intention* accomplishes the coincidence of consciousness with the world. For Descartes, a thought is not only consciousness of its object but always, at the same time, consciousness of itself as consciousness; it is this 'concomitant' reflection which materializes the coincidence of the ego with itself. This coincidence was already given in the very beginning, but attention passed over it in order to concentrate on the object. This coincidence can become distinct consciousness of self whenever the attention is directed to it. The method of the methodical doubt has the effect of transforming this natural evidence from psychological consciousness into apodictic evidence merely by intensifying attention.

For Husserl consciousness is intentional, and even completely intentional. That is why consciousness of self can exist only in a change of intentionality and even in this change consciousness remains essentially an opening onto the world. Caught up in its centrifugal movement it cannot avoid losing itself in the world except by re-grasping this world in the unity of its meaning. The true radical origin Husserl is aiming

---

60. *Ibid.*, pp. 99-104.

at consists in a recovery of the world, a recuperation of the world which, on the one hand, as total intention must manifest itself as a spectacle laid out before the disinterested spectator, and, on the other hand, as 'hidden teleology', as the 'product' of a constituting achievement which gives it its meaning. If in Husserl's philosophy one speaks of the coincidence of consciousness with itself, this means nothing but the coincidence of transcendental consciousness with the *totality* of its own intentions, that is, the world. This coincidence is according to Husserl the true radical point of departure. It will be clear that such a coincidence is inaccessible and can only be aimed at so that the search for the radical point of departure must consist in the process of a growing radicalization in philosophy. This seems to be the reasons why Husserl calls himself 'the perpetual beginner' who discovered that he was necessarily "on the way."[61]

Concluding, we must say with Thévenaz that in spite of the superficial similarities which Husserl liked to point out between Descartes and himself, and in spite of his care to develop the Cartesian ambition more faithfully than Descartes himself, we are dealing here with two irreducible attitudes. Descartes' philosophy does not lead to Husserl's phenomenology as to its most radical culmination. From Descartes there is no way to a genuinely transcendental philosophy.[62]

---

61. *Ibid.*, pp. 105-108.
62. *Ibid.*, p. 110-111.

CHAPTER THREE

FACT AND ESSENCE

1. *Phenomenology as the Study of the General Essence of Consciousness*

Phenomenology and the Foundation of Logic. The Study of Essences

In his *Logical Investigations* Husserl defined his new science of phenomenology as a descriptive psychology dealing with the general essence of consciousness and with the essences of it various structures.[1] Although it was evident to him since 1903, that this definition ambiguously and even incorrectly spoke of descriptive psychology, he never gave up the characterization of phenomenology as a science of the general essence of consciousness and its various structures. True, he gradually realized that his study of the relation between facts and essences in his *Logical Investigations* did not solve all the problems which could and should be asked in this context. However, he did not see in this limitation any reason to doubt the positive value of these inquiries or to minimize their fundamental importance for phenomenology. On the contrary, he repeatedly returned to the study of the relationship between facts and essences and tried in this way not only to solve the questions left open in his first investigations, but also to give a more radical basis to the original insights which they had disclosed.

Unlike the first volume of the *Logical Investigations,* which gives us a refutation of psychologism, the second volume presents detailed studies of logic and epistemology. In these studies Husserl admits that the linguistic analyses normally contained in books dealing with the foundation of logic, indeed, are indispensable for the philosophical account of logic, because only with the help of such analyses is it possible to define the true objects of logic. This admission does not imply, however, that those analyses will suffice to give logic a *radical* foundation. What is needed is something more fundamental, namely, a study of epistemology and, therefore, of the pure phenomenology of consciousness.

---

1. Edmund Husserl, *L. U.,* vol. II, p. 2.

The subject matter of such a discipline consists of experiences whose *essential* universality is to be analyzed *in intuition,* and not of experiences as events occurring in the natural world. The essences apprehended in essential intuition and the connection between them are to be described by means of concepts and laws. These concepts and laws, inasfar as they refer to essences, must have an *a priori* character. This realm of the *a priori* precisely is the sphere whose investigation critically prepares and philosophically clarifies the foundations of logic.

Phenomenology, then, wants to bring to light the sources from which the fundamental concepts and the ideal laws of pure logic arise, and to which they must be traced back, if we want to arrive at the clarity and distinctness that is required for a critical understanding of pure logic. The terms 'phenomenological' and 'epistemological' are still used here synonymously, and their interchangeability gives away the restricted character of Husserl's earlier investigations.

The objects investigated by pure logic are always given in a grammatical form. These objects are also couched in concrete physical experiences which either intend meaning or fulfill this intention, and which together with the linguistic expressions constitute a phenomenological unity. The logician now has first to study descriptively the characteristics of the acts involved in these unities inasfar as such a study is needed for his logical purposes. It will be evident that especially a study concerning our judgments will be of great importance here. However, the logician is not interested in a judgment as a concrete psychological phenomenon, but only in its very essence taken in its universality as apprehended in abstraction. But although the phenomenological analysis of concrete judgments does not belong to the proper domain of pure logic, it will nevertheless be clear that such an analysis will be very helpful in logical investigations. For, everything that is logical must be given in concrete and intuitive fullness and studied as such, if one is to bring to the fore the evidence of the *a priori* laws based upon it.

The goal of phenomenological analyses is therefore to give an epistemological foundation to the logical concepts and laws and to clarify their ultimate meaning. This is possible only if the logical concepts as unities of meaning are taken in the way they manifest themselves in original *intuition,* and such an intuition is, in turn, possible only by means of an *ideating abstraction* on the basis of concrete experiences. In the repeated performance of this abstraction and by means of a free variation of the content in this way brought to the fore, the logical concepts must be confirmed time and again before we, ultimately, will be able intuitively to grasp those concepts in their self-identity. It is for this reason that we cannot content ourselves with mere word-analyses, although it remains true that we have to begin our study with those analyses in our investigations concerning the meaning of the laws formulated in pure logic. Finally, however, we must return *to the things themselves.* Only by means of completely developed *intuitions* are we able to see *with evidence* that what is given in an actually performed abstraction is really that which the verbal meaning of the laws signifies.

A phenomenology of logical experience wants to give us as extensive a descriptive understanding of the psychical experiences and of the meanings inherent in them, as is necessary to give firm meaning to all fundamental logical concepts. In the past the fundamental logical concepts have been insufficiently clarified and numerous equivocations were the consequence of this situation. This was the main reason why pure logic and epistemology remained in a backward state. The phenomenology of the essences of the different forms of experience wants to give us the necessary clarifications. Because the clarification of logical ideas, such as 'concept', 'object', 'truth', 'proposition', 'matter of fact' and 'universal law', leads to the central questions of epistemology, epistemology is inseparable from the elucidation of the fundamental problems of pure logic.

Husserl carefully stresses the difference between the 'pure' description and essential intuition of phenomenology and the empirical description of natural science. Psychology is concerned with perceptions, judgments, feelings, etc., insofar as they refer to real 'conditions' of animal beings. Hence all propositions and statements of psychology apply to the natural world. Phenomenology, on the other hand, is not interested in the real 'conditions' of animal being or even in those which belong to an only *possible* natural world. Phenomenology is interested in perceptions. judgments, and feelings *as such,* in their *a priori* nature, in their very *essences.* At the same time, however, phenomenology provides the necessary foundation of empirical psychology, for essential insights in the very essences of perceptions and feelings are evidently applicable to the corresponding empirical 'conditions' of animal beings.[2]

For our purpose it is of some importance to dwell briefly on Husserl's theory of abstraction. First, however, we must mention some distinctions in the domain of 'meaning', which are of interest in this context. According to Husserl then *'meaning'* is that which an expression signifies. There is an essential distinction to be made between *'meaning'* and *'object meant'*, for sometimes different expressions having different 'meanings' refer to one and the same object. There is also a very important distinction to be made between *the multiple acts of meaning* and *the one identical meaning* to which they all refer and point. This ideal identical meaning is for Husserl an *ideal entity,* and not only a psychological datum. It was this concept of identical ideal meaning which led Husserl to the problem of generalities and universals.

At this point Husserl encountered the problems raised by British empiricism and especially the objections of the nominalist trend. With Berkeley, Husserl rejected Locke's doctrine of general ideas. The solution of the nominalistic group, following Berkeley and Hume, should also be rejected. After carefully examining the most important empiristic solutions of the problem, Husserl was able to show that all these solutions imply absurd consequences. At the same time, Husserl could show that there are special acts of *ideation,* which empiricism had overlooked and in which general essences are genuinely apprehended, although it remains true that general essences are given only on the basis of an intuitive apprehension of particular examples. Nevertheless, Husserl concludes, the act of ideation itself, which supposes abstraction but is not identical with it, is an original type of immediate experience.

Husserl's investigations do not solve all the question that can be raised about the nature of essences, but they do establish at least their 'existence' insofar as they show that the meaning of universal propositions can be satisfied only by the admission of general essences. These

---

2. Marvin Farber, *op. cit.,* pp. 196-221 (passim), esp. pp. 211-216.

essences are evidently entities *sui generis,* but they have a mode of being that makes it possible to formulate true propositions about them.[3]

Phenomenology as the Ultimate Foundation of All Knowledge. Inquiry into Essences Within the Context of Absolute Self-givenness

From the later perspective of transcendental phenomenology, Husserl's *Logical Investigations* were only a necessary first stage of phenomenological philosophy. The work dealt primarily with the philosophical foundations of logic and in no way completely surveyed the meaning of phenomenology as a whole. As we have seen, it was only in *The Idea of Phenomenology* that Husserl broadened his perspective and for the first time stated the program of a universal phenomenology conceived of as the ultimate foundation and critique of *all* knowledge. We must add here, however, that with respect to the question of the relationship between fact and essence, Husserl continued to maintain the view he had proposed in the *Logical Investigations.*

When in *The Idea of Phenomenology* Husserl for the first time mentions the question of the relationship between fact and essence, he simply notes that it is easy to understand that not only singularities but also generalities, general objects and general states of affairs, can be absolutely self-given. This insight is, according to him, of decisive importance for the very possibility of phenomenology. For it is proper to phenomenology to analyze and inquire into essences within the realm of absolute self-givenness. It is even necessary that this be its proper character, for phenomenology wants to be a science and a method for elucidating the possibilities of knowing and valuing them on the basis of their essential grounds. These are generally questionable possibilities, and their analysis and investigation, therefore, are general inquiries concerning essences. Analysis of essences necessarily tends to insights oriented to essences and universal objects.[4]

The inquiry concerning essences, therefore, is undoubtedly an inquiry into the general. The question, however, must be asked whether general essences and general states of affairs are self-given in exactly the

---

3. Herbert Spiegelberg, *op. cit.,* vol. I, pp. 105-106.
4. Edmund Husserl, *Die Idee,* p. 51 (40-41).

same way as, for instance, this concrete cogitation. Does not the general, as such, transcend our knowledge? True, general knowledge, as an absolute phenomenon, is immediately given; but the general itself is not immediately given in it, since the general, according to its very nature, is precisely that which remains identical in an unlimited number of possible acts of knowing dealing with the same content. The transcendence of the general over the concrete act of knowledge is evidently undeniable. Every singular act of knowledge and, therefore, every real element of this singular phenomenon also, is singular. Therefore, the general, which as such is precisely not a singularity, cannot be actually contained in this singular consciousness of a generality.

Yet it would be unreasonable to object to the transcendence of the general. For, the absolute phenomenon, the reduced cogitation, has the validity of an absolute self-givenness, not because it is a singularity, but because it *manifests itself* as an absolute self-givenness in the *pure intuition* performed after the phenomenological reduction. In pure intuition we immediately see such a self-givenness, and in the same way we see immediately the general as such in pure intuition. And this means that also the givenness of the general as such is a *purely immanent* givenness which, as immanent and therefore as immediately given, is absolutely evident.[5]

Consequently we must admit the possibility of the general's evident self-givenness in every evident cogitation. When I perceive a color and perform a reduction on this act, I obtain the pure phenomenon 'color'. If I then effect a pure abstraction I acquire the 'essence': phenomenological color as such, by means of ideation. The same holds good for every act of consciousness which immediately or mediately presupposes perception. But it is not correct to draw from this the conclusion that fully evident knowledge of essences necessarily presupposes a singular perception which gives us the paradigmatic singularity as something that is actually present now. On the other hand, however, it is true that such knowledge points to a singular experience, on the basis of which it necessarily must constitute itself.

---

5. *Ibid.*, pp. 55-57 (43-45).

FACT AND ESSENCE

The ideating abstraction by means of which the essence as such is constituted, can also take its starting point in a presentation made by our imagination. For the difference between the mode in which the being is posited by perception, and the mode in which it is posited in an act of imagination is irrelevant to the constitution of the *eidos* in question. The 'red', for example, of mere phantasy is specifically the same as the 'red' of perception. The consciousness of generality can, therefore, be based just as well on the basis of perception as on that of a corresponding imagination; if such a consciousness is had at all, then that which is general, the idea 'red', itself is grasped. It is intuited in the same way, and this admits of no difference between a picture and the original.[6]

"Ideas Concerning a Pure Phenomenology and Phenomenological Philosophy"

Between 1901 and 1913 Husserl began to exert influence outside Göttingen, not only by his writings but also through visits and exchanges of students and teachers. Especially in Munich there was a group of devoted adherents. Alexander Pfänder, Adolf Reinach, Moritz Geiger and, for some time, Max Scheler were the leading members of this group. From the contacts of this group with Husserl came the plan of publishing the review *Jahrbuch für Philosophie und phänomenologische Forschung*. The first issue, which appeared in 1913, opened with the first volume of Husserl's important book *Ideas Concerning a Pure Phenomenology and Phenomenological Philosophy*.

In this work Husserl tried to explain the basic principles and the main ideas of his new phenomenology as an all-embracing philosophical discipline. Of this project only the first volume, entitled *General Introduction to Pure Phenomenology*, was published in 1913. Preparing the second volume, *Phenomenological Studies Concerning Constitution*, Husserl met with so many problems that he had to lay it aside for a time. It appeared only posthumously in 1952. The lecture course on *First Philosophy*, given in 1923-1924 and published in 1956 and 1959, may be considered as a partial realization of the original plan

---

6. *Ibid.*, pp. 57-60 (45-49).

for the third volume. What posthumously has been published as the third volume of the Ideas, namely *Phenomenology and the Foundation of the Sciences,* is a part of the original second volume and was later substituted by Husserl himself for Volume Three.

Because of what Husserl says here regarding theory, method and basic insights, the first volume of the *Ideas* surpasses the others in importance. The first of its four major sections contains a brief survey and partly a reformulation of his view on essences and our knowledge of essences, as explained in his *Logical Investigations.* According to Husserl himself, this doctrine is basic for the understanding of phenomenology in relation to other descriptive sciences. He regarded this part as a necessary presupposition for every kind of phenomenological investigation.[7]

It is often said that the relation between this first section and the three other sections of the first volume of the *Ideas* is not very clear. It is true that at first sight this section seems to be superfluous. Moreover, it is not altogether improbable that Husserl wrote this section only after he had finished the others. However, this section may also be considered in connection with his investigations concerning the relation between fact and essence, as we find them in his *Logical Investigations* and *The Idea of Phenomenology,* investigations whose results could be only very briefly and concisely indicated above. When the doctrine contained in the first section of the *Ideas* is viewed in this connection, it becomes clear that they elucidate one of the most important features of Husserl's phenomenological philosophy as a whole. For this reason we will present here some of the most striking ideas of this section as an introduction to Husserl's final idea of phenomenology.

2. *Fact and Essence*

Natural Knowledge and Experience. Fact and Essence

Natural knowledge begins with experience and remains within experience. And since experience is experience of the world, the total field of possible research governed by our theoretical knowledge of the 'natural

---

7. Herbert Spiegelberg, *op. cit.,* vol. I, pp. 124-128.

standpoint' can be expressed in one word: 'the world'. Accordingly, the sciences proper to this 'natural standpoint' are sciences of the world. And, therefore, from this standpoint the meaning of the expressions 'true being', 'real being' and 'being in the world' coincide.

Every science has its own domain as the region of its research. To all its correct assertions there correspond certain intuitions as the original sources of its scientific justification. In these intuitions objects of the region in question appear as self-given and, in part at least, as given in a primordial sense. The object-giving intuition, now, of the first and natural sphere of knowledge and of all its sciences is 'natural experience', and the primordial object-giving experience here is 'perception'. In 'external perception' we have primordial experiences of physical things, but memory and anticipating expectation cannot be called primordial experiences. We have a primordial experience of ourselves and of our own states of consciousness in 'internal perception', but we do not have such an experience of others and their lived experiences, for those experiences occur in and through 'empathy'. We 'behold' the lived experiences of others by perceiving their bodily behavior. Although this 'beholding' in and through empathy is an intuitional object-giving act, it is no longer a primordial object-giving act. The fellow man with his psychical life is apprehended as 'there in person', and as one with his own body, but, unlike the body, his psychical life is not given to our consciousness in a primordial way.

The world is the totality of objects that can be known through experience and through theoretical knowledge based upon direct and present experiences. The sciences of the world, i.e., the sciences of our natural standpoint, include not only the 'natural sciences', but also sciences such as biology, physiology and psychology, and the so-called 'Geisteswissenschaften', namely history, the social sciences and the different 'cultural sciences'.[8]

Sciences of experience are *sciences of fact*. The cognitive acts which are ultimately based upon primordial experiences, posit reality in *individual* form; they posit it as having a spatio-temporal existence, as something existing here, and at this point of time, and as having this particu-

---

8. Edmund Husserl, *Ideen I*, pp. 10-12 (45-46).

lar duration, as having a real content whose essence could just as well be present in any other point of time. They posit it, moreover, as something which is present now at this place and in this particular physical shape, although the same real being, so far as its essence is concerned, could just as well be present in any other place and in any other form or shape. Every individual being as such is, generally speaking, accidental or contingent, inasfar as it is such and such but essentially could be other than it is.

Even if there are definite laws of nature, according to which *these* particular consequences must in fact follow whenever *those* conditions exist, such laws express only an order that in fact does obtain but might be quite different. Presupposing that the objects thus ordered are, when considered in themselves, accidental and contingent, these laws refer already from the very beginning to the *essences* of the objects of possible experience. For when we state that every fact can be 'essentially' other than it is, we express that it belongs to the meaning of every contingent thing and event to have an essential being and therefore an *eidos* that can be apprehended in all its purity. An individual object is not simply an individual, a 'this-here', but being constiuted thus and thus in itself it has its own mode of being, its own essential predicables which qualify it *qua* being as it is in itself. Whatever belongs to the essence of an individual can also belong to another individual.[9]

Essential Insight and Individual Intuition. Ideation

The term 'essence' indicates that which in the intimate self-being of an individual tells us 'what' it is. Every such 'what' can be expressed in an idea. Empirical or individual intuition can be transformed into essential insight by *ideation*. The object of such an insight is the corresponding *pure* essence or *eidos,* regardless of whether this essence be the highest, or a more specialized category, or even the fully 'concrete'.

This insight, which *gives* the essence and, in the last resort, in primordial form, can be *adequate,* but it can also be more or less imperfect or *inadequate*. In case of an inadequate insight, the inadequacy is not limited only to greater or lesser clearness and distinctness. For in

9. *Ibid.,* pp. 12-13 (46-47).

certain categories of being essences can be given only one-sidedly, although evidently several, but never all sides can be given successively. Hence, correlatively, the concrete and individual particularities corresponding to these categories can be experienced and represented only in inadequate, 'one-sided', empirical intuitions. This assertion applies to every essence belonging to the realm of the thing-like, physical and material being.[10]

No matter of what kind an individual intuition may be, whether adequate or inadequate, it can always change into essential intuition, and the latter, whether adequate or not, has the character of an object-giving act. This means that the essence (*eidos*) is a new type of object. *Just as the datum of individual and empirical intuition is an individual and concrete object, so the datum of essential intuition is a pure essence.*

It is very important to realize that there is no question here of a mere superficial analogy, but of a radical correspondence in nature. Essential insight is still intuition, and the eidetic object is still an object. The generalization of the correlative concepts 'intuition' and 'object' is therefore not accidental, but is demanded by the very nature of things. Empirical intuition, and more specifically sense experience, is conciousness of an individual object and, as intuition, it brings this object to givenness; as perception, it brings the object to primordial givenness, to the consciousness of grasping the object in a primordial way in its authentic reality. In a similar way, essential intuition is the consciousness of something, of an 'object', a something toward which one's glance is directed, a something that is self-given within this glance.

Thus, every possible object, or logically expressed, every subject of possibly true predications, has its own way of coming under a glance that presents, intuits and meets it eventually in its authentic reality, its 'bodily selfhood'. Accordingly, essential insight *is* intuition, and if there is question of an insight in the pregnant sense of the term, it is a primordial object-giving act, which grasps the essence in its authentic reality. On the other hand, it is a fundamentally unique and novel kind of intuition.

---

10. See Chapter II of this book.

It is undoubtedly intrinsically proper to essential intuition that it should be based on a primary factor of individual intuition, namely, the striving for the 'visible' presence of the individual fact. However, as is mentioned above, essential intuition does not presuppose any apprehension of the individual or any assumption as regards its reality. Consequently, no essential intuition is possible without the free possibility of directing one's glance to an individual counterpart, either given in perception or in imagination. Reversely, no individual intuition is possible without the free possibility of performing an act of ideation and directing one's glance to the corresponding essence which exemplifies itself in every individual, visible thing. Nevertheless, the two kinds of intuition remain fundamentally different, although, as we have seen, they are essentially related too. Thus, to the essential differences between the two kinds of intuitions correspond the essential relations between individual and concrete being and essence, between fact and *eidos*.[11]

The *eidos* or pure essence can be exemplified intuitively in the data of either experience or phantasy. Hence, if we want to grasp an essence itself in its primordial form, we can start either from the corresponding empirical intuitions, or from intuitions of a purely imaginative order. If in the play of phantasy we create spatial forms of one kind or another, or melodies, social events, fictitious events of everyday life, or acts of satisfaction or dissatisfaction, or whatever we want to imagine, we can through ideation secure from this source a primordial and even, on occasion, an adequate insight into pure essences: e.g., essences of spatial form as such, of melody as such, of social event as such, or essences of a relevant special type of them.

From all this it follows that the positing of the essence, with the intuitive apprehension that immediately accompanies it, does not at all imply the positing of any individual existence. Pure essential truths do not assert anything about facts. Consequently, from them alone we are not able to infer even the smallest truth about the real world.[12]

---

11. Edmund Husserl, *Ideen I*, pp. 13-16 (48-50).
12. *Ibid.*, pp. 16-17 (50-51).

FACT AND ESSENCE

Judgments About Essences and Judgments of Eidetic Generality

Another point still remains to be considered here. Judgments about essences and essential relationships on the one hand, and eidetic judgments in general, on the other, are not one and the same thing. For eidetic knowledge does not have essences as its objects in all its propositions and statements. Another point is closely connected with this. Although the intuition of essences is a form of consciousness analogous to natural experience and to the apprehension of concrete existence, and although in this intuition an essence is objectively grasped, as is an individual in natural experience, this intuiton is not the only consciousness which brings the essences to the fore while excluding the positing of any concrete existence. For we can be intuitively aware of essences and can even apprehend them in a certain manner, without their becoming objects *about* which we have consciousness.

To explain this point more in detail, let us focus attention on the difference between *judgments about essences* and judgments which in an indeterminately universal way and without positing anything individual, still *judge about the individual as an instance of essential being*. For instance, in geometry we judge as a rule not about the *eidos* 'straight', 'angle', or 'triangle', but about the straight line and the angle in general, about *individual* triangles in general. Such judgments have the character of 'pure' and absolutely unconditioned generality.

In order to give a noetic foundation to these judgments, taken inasfar as they deal with individual instances in the way just described, one needs a certain intuition of essences, a certain 'apprehension' of them. This immediate apprehension as well as the objectifying intuition are based on the conscious awareness of individual instances of the essence, but not on their being experienced as being real. Moreover, mere presentations of phantasy are able to give us the instances; of that which is intuited there, we are conscious: it appears, but it is not apprehended *as* existing. This becomes immediately clear when, for instance, we judge in an essential and purely general way that a color in general is different from a sound in general. For in that case, an instance of the essence 'color' and an instance of the essence 'sound' are intuitively present to us as instances of their own essences; and phantasy-intuition, which does not involve the positing of concrete existence, and essential intuition are present at the same time; but the latter does not function as an intuition which *objectifies* the essence in question. However, it belongs to the essence of the situation that at any time we are free to assume the corresponding standpoint in which the essence is objectified. But if we do so, the judgment itself must also undergo a change, and reads then, for instance, as follows: the generic essence 'color' is different from the generic essence 'sound'.

Conversely, every *judgment about an essence* can be transformed equivalently into an unconditionally universal *judgment concerning instances* of this essence as such. In this respect pure judgments relating to essences, i.e., pure eidetic judgments, have a common feature, regardless of their logical form. This common characteristic is that they posit no individual being, even[13] when, in pure essential generality, they judge about what is individual.

Essential Generality and Essential Necessity

Every eidetic particularization or individuation of an eidetically general state of affairs, inasfar as it is such a general state of affairs, is said to be an essential necessity. Essential generality and essential necessity are therefore correlates. Furthermore, the corresponding judgments are usually also called 'necessary'. However, it is important *not* to say, as is also usually done, that essential generality itself *is* necessity. Be this as it may, the consciousness of a necessity, or more specifically, the consciousness of a judgment in which we become aware of a certain matter as the specification of an eidetic generality, is called 'apodictic' and the judgment itself is said to be an apodictic consequent of the general proposition or judgment to which it is related.

The connection which the eidetic judging concerning the individual in general has with the positing of the individual as concretely existing, is also very important. The essential generality can be transferred to an individual or to an indeterminate realm of individuals which are posited

---

13. *Ibid.*, pp. 17-19 (51-53).

as concretely existing. Every 'application' of geometrical truths to concrete cases in nature, posited as real, is an example of this transference. The state of affairs set down as real is then a *fact* insofar as it is an individual state of *real* affairs, and an *eidetic necessity* insofar as it is an instance of an essential generality.

Care should be taken not to confuse the *unrestricted generality* of natural laws with *essential generality*. The proposition 'all bodies are heavy' does not intend to claim that any concrete thing in particular within the universe really exists. Nevertheless, this proposition does not have the unconditioned generality of eidetically general propositions, for it implies a reference to concrete existence, namely, the spatio-temporal reality, since only all *real* bodies are heavy. On the other hand, the proposition 'all material things are extended' possesses eidetic validity and can be taken as *purely* eidetic, if in regard to the subject of this statement every reference to concrete existence is excluded as irrelevant. It states something which has its pure ground in the essence of material things and in the essence of extension as such, i.e., something into which we can have an insight in unconditional generality.[14]

Sciences of Facts and Sciences of Essences

We have seen above that each individual object has its own essence, just as conversely to each essence there corresponds a series of possible individuals as its factual individuations. This connection gives rise to a corresponding relationship between sciences of facts and sciences of essences.

There are pure sciences of essences such as pure logic, pure mathematics, pure theory of time, pure theory of space, pure theory of movement, etc. In all their considerations these sciences are wholly free from positing any actual facts. Differently expressed, in these sciences no experience *as* experience, that is as consciousness which apprehends *reality,* can take over the function of offering a logical ground. If experience plays a role in these sciences, it is not *as* experience. For example, the geometrician who draws figures on the blackboard and experiences them, provides as little ground for his seeing and think-

---

14. *Ibid.,* pp. 19-21 (53-55).

ing the geometric essences as does the 'physical' act of producing those figures. Whether he draws his lines in an imaginary world or on the blackboard does not make any difference here. The physicist, however, acts quite differently. He observes and experiments, he determines what is concretely there just as he experiences it. For him experience is an act which gives a foundation which mere imagining could never replace. It is for this reason that 'science of fact' and 'science of experience' are equivalent expressions.

Accordingly, the essential characteristic of pure eidetic science is that its procedure is exclusively eidetic. From start to finish it discloses no factual meaning that is not eidetically valid. The expression 'a factual meaning that is eidetically valid' refers to a factual meaning which either is immediately open to primordial insight because it is directly based on essences in which we have a primordial insight, or can be 'inferred' through pure reasoning from axiomatic factual meanings of this type.[15]

It is evident, then, that eidetic science is in principle unable to take over any of the theoretical results attained by empirical sciences. For the reference to reality which appears in the immediately valid premises of the empirical sciences reappears in all their derivative propositions. From facts nothing ever follows but facts.

Although eidetic science is intrinsically independent of any science of facts, the opposite holds for the sciences of facts themselves. No fully developed science of facts can exist without an admixture of eidetic knowledge; every science of facts depends on formal and material eidetic sciences. For, in the first place, it is obvious that an empirical science, no matter where it finds the ground on which it bases its judgments through mediate reasoning, must proceed according to the formal principles of logic. Generally speaking, since, just as any other science, empirical science is directed toward objects, it is necessarily bound by the laws which pertain to the essence of objectivity-in-general. Hence it cannot be indifferent to the group of formal-ontological disciplines which, apart from formal logic in the narrow sense of the term, include the disciplines which used to be classified under the term 'formal *mathesis universalis*'. Secondly, every fact includes an essential structure of a

---

15. *Ibid.*, pp. 21-22 (55-56).

material order, and every eidetic truth pertaining to the pure essence therein included must lead to a law that governs the given concrete instance and, in general, every possible instance.[16]

Regions and Regional Categories

Every concrete empirical objectivity, together with its material essence, has its proper place in a highest material genus, a 'region' of empirical objects. To the pure regional essence there corresponds, therefore, a 'regional eidetic science', a 'regional ontology'. Accordingly, every empirical science which deals with the entities belonging to a given region, will be essentially related to the regional and formal ontologies in question. In other words, every factual and empirical science has its essential theoretical basis in eidetic ontologies. For instance, an 'eidetic science of physical nature in general' (namely, the ontology of nature) corresponds to all the natural sciences, insofar as to actual nature there corresponds an *eidos* that can be apprehended in its purity, viz., the essence 'nature in general' with the limitless horizon of essential structures included in it. If we are to construct the idea of a completely rationalized empirical science of nature, obviously the realization of this idea will be essentially dependent on the cultivation of the corresponding eidetic sciences. It will depend, not only on the cultivation of the formal *mathesis universalis* which is related similarly to all the sciences, but, in particular, on the constitution of material-ontological disciplines which analyze in rational purity the essence of nature and also all essential articulations of nature's objectivities as such. The same holds good, of course, for all other regions.

To support this view we may appeal again to the development of the natural sciences. Their era of greatness in the modern age arose precisely from this that geometry, which in the ancient world had already been highly developed along pure eidetic lines, was in one sweep made fruitful for the physical method. It was clearly realized that it is of the essence of a material thing to be a *res extensa* and that consequently geometry is an ontological discipline concerning an essential feature of such a thing, namely, its spatial form. But it was also realized that the

---

16. *Ibid.*, p. 23 (56-57).

universal, regional essence of the things goes much farther. The evidence for this assertion is that, at the very beginning of the modern era, there was development because a series of other sciences was created, and their purpose was to play a role analogous to the one played by geometry in the rationalization of the empirical. The rich variety of the mathematical sciences orginated from this impulse.[17]

Region and Category

If we place ourselves within the realm of any eidetic science, for instance, within the ontology of nature, we find ourselves normally directed not toward essences as objects, but toward the objects of the essences which, in the case selected, are subordinate to the region called 'nature'. Let us note here, that the term 'object' is a name given to different but connected entities, such as 'thing', 'property', 'relation', 'substance', 'group', and 'order'. These different entities clearly are not equivalent, but may refer to a type of objectivity which has, so to speak, the privilege of being the primordial objectivity, and with respect to which all others are in a certain sense mere differentiations. In the example chosen, the 'thing' has evidently this privilege in reference to its properties and relations. If we try to clarify this formal order, the important concept 'category', as related to the concept 'region', will spontaneously emerge.

'Category' is a term which, on the one hand, refers to a determinate region, but, on the other, serves to specify such a material region in relation to the form of region in general, that is to say, in relation to the purely formal essence 'object-in-general' and its typical 'formal categories'. What is meant by *formal categories* can easily be explained by starting with *pure* logic, which is the eidetic science of 'object-in-general'. According to this science, object is everything that is, and its meaning can be fixed in an endless variety of truths. But, as a whole, these truths lead back to a small number of immediate truths, the so-called 'axioms' of the pure logical sciences. Now we define the pure basic concepts of logic which figure in these axioms as *logical categories,* or categories of the logical region, that is the categories of 'object-in-general'. These con-

17. *Ibid.,* pp. 23-26 (57-59).

cepts, as they figure in the total system of axioms, determine the logical essence of 'object-in-general', and express the unconditonally necessary and constitutive determinations of 'object-as-such'. As examples of logical categories, we may cite such concepts as 'property,' 'state of affairs,' 'relation,' 'identity,' 'class,' 'genus,' and 'species'.

However the fundamental concepts of the various kinds of propositions which belong to the very essence of proposition-as-such, have their proper place here also. They belong here in reference to the essential truths which not merely link together objects-in-general, but, moreover, connect them in such a way that pure truths concerning signification (*Bedeutung*) can be transformed into pure truths concerning objects. Nevertheless, the categories of signification must be distinguished from the formal categories in the strict sense of the term, for they constitute a group possessing a distinctive character.

By 'categories', therefore, we understand, on the one hand, concepts in the sense of meanings, and, on the other also, and even primarily, the formal essences themselves which find their expression in these significations.[18]

Other Important Distinctions. Again Region and Category

Another important distinction in the realm of formal objectivities is is that between syntactic forms and syntactic substrates. This distinction is connected with a division of the formal ontological categories into 'syntactic categories' and 'substrative categories'.

We understand by *syntactic objectivities* those which are derived from other objectivities with the help of 'syntactic forms'. The categories now which correspond to these 'syntactic forms' are called *syntactic categories*. Examples of these categories are, for instance, 'substantive meaning', 'relation', 'unity', 'numerical quantity', 'order', etc. In order to explain this further, we must point to the fact that every object, insofar as it can be made more explicit and related to other objects, in brief, insofar as it is logically determinable, takes on different syntactic forms. In this way, as correlates of thinking (taken in its determining function) objectivities of a higher order are constituted such as 'qual-

---

18. *Ibid.*, pp. 26-29 (59-62).

ities', 'qualitatively determined objects', and 'relations between such objects'. If the thinking is predicative, there gradually arise expressions and apophantic structures of meaning which reflect the syntactic object-ivities according to all their forms and divisions in 'meaning syntaxes' that correspond exactly to them. All these categorial objectivities can—just as objectivities in general as well—again function as sub-strata of higher categorial constructions.

Conversely, every such categorial construction refers to *ultimate substrata,* to objects of the lowest grade, to objects which are no longer constructions of a syntactico-categorial kind and which contain in them-selves no further trace of those ontological forms which are mere cor-relates of man's thinking. Accordingly, the formal region of objectivity-in-general is divided into ultimate substrata and syntactic objectivities. Syntactic objectivities, then, are derived from other objectivities by means of syntactic forms. The categories which correspond to these forms are called 'syntactic categories'.[19]

Moreover, within the realm of essences as a whole, a new set of categorial distinctions are to be made. Every essence, whether it has a determinate content or is purely logical and formal, has its proper place in a hierarchy of essences, in a hierarchy of generality and speci-ficity. The series necessarily has two limits that do not coalesce, namely downward the 'lowest specific difference' or the 'eidetic singularity', and upward a 'highest genus'. *Eidetic singularities* are essences which of necessity refer to other essences as their genera, but have no further specifications with respect to which they themselves might be genera. Likewise, that genus is highest which has no other genus above it.

In this sense, in the realm of pure, logical entities, the genus 'mean-ing-in-general' is the highest genus; in the same realm a categorical proposition is an eidetic singularity, while 'proposition-in-general' is a mediating genus. To give another example: 'numerical-quantity-in-general' is a highest genus, while 'two', 'three', etc. are its eidetic singu-larities.[20]

From what is said, it will be clear that it is very important to make a clear distinction between generalization and formalization. In the pro-

---

19. *Ibid.,* pp. 29-30 (62-63).
20. *Ibid.,* pp. 31-32 (63-64).

cess of *generalization* one remains in one and the same realm of entities, while *formalization* is the reduction of what has material content to a formal generality of a purely logical kind. In the same way, one must clearly distinguish between specialization and 'deformalization', the latter being understood as the process of filling out with content that which first was an 'empty' logico-mathematical form only.[21]

We must consider here also the distinction between 'full substrata with positive content', together with the corresponding full 'content-laden syntactic objectivities', and the 'empty substrata' together with the 'syntactic objectivities' formed from them and consisting in the modifications of the empty 'object-in-general'. However, the empty substratum is not empty in itself; it has a fixed content consisting of the totality of the positive contents belonging to the structure of pure logic, with all the categorial objectivities out of which these contents are constituted.

In the class of objectivities with positive content we find 'ultimate content-laden substrata' as the nuclei of all syntactic constructions. To the class of these nuclei belong the 'substrative categories', which are divided into ultimate substantive essences, and the "this-there's" as the pure syntactically formless individual units (the *tode ti's*). Between the formless ultimate essence and the pure syntactically formless individual units there exists an essential connection which consists in this that every 'this-there' has *its* essential substantive quality, possessing the character of a formless substrative essence, in the sense mentioned above.[22]

We call a categorial form 'dependent' insofar as it refers of necessity to a substratum of which it is the form. Substratum and form, then, are essences which refer to each other. In this broadest sense, the category 'essence', for example, is dependent upon all determinate essences. In the same way the categorial form 'object' is dependent upon all 'material' objects. In a narrower sense, the concept 'dependence' is identical with 'being contained in', 'being one with', 'being connected with' in the stricter sense of the term.

---

21. *Ibid.*, pp. 32-34 (64-66).
22. *Ibid.*, pp. 34-35 (66-67).

When we now use the term 'dependence' in this stricter sense, we are able to describe the difference between the categorial concepts 'abstractum', 'concretum', and 'individual' in the following way. A dependent essence is an *abstractum;* an absolutely independent and self-sustaining e s s e n c e is a *concretum,* while a 'this-there' whose s u b-s t a n t i v e e s s e n c e is a concretum, is called an *individual.* The individual is the primordial object demanded on purely logical grounds, the logical absolute to which all the logical modifications refer. A concretum is always an *eidetic* singularity, since genera are in principle dependent. Thus, eidetic singularities are divided into abstract and concrete singularities.[23]

By means of the concepts 'individual' and 'concretum' it is possible also to define the concept 'region' in a stricter way. The region is precisely the highest and most inclusive generic unity belonging to a concretum, that is, the essentially unitary connection of the *summa genera* which belong to the lowest differences within the concretum. The eidetic range of the region includes the ideal totality of the concretely unified systems of differences of these genera while the individual range includes the ideal totality of possible individuals corresponding to such concrete essences.

Every regional essence determines essential truths. These truths are grounded in it as this generic essence, but are not mere specifications of formal-ontological truths. The system of truths having their ground in the regional essence constitutes the content of the 'regional ontology'. The totality of the fundamental truths, i.e., the totality of the regional axioms, limits and defines the system of the 'regional categories'. These are not merely specifications of purely logical categories, but are distinguished by the fact that, through regional axioms, they express the features characteristic of the regional essence and, therefore, express in eidetic generality that which must *a priori* pertain to an individual object of the region. The application of such, not purely logical, concepts to given individuals is apodictic and unconditionally necessary. It is governed by the regional axioms.[24]

---

23. *Ibid.,* pp. 35-37 (67-69).
24. *Ibid.,* pp. 37-38 (69-71).

Conclusion

So far we have been concerned entirely with purely logical considerations and did not mention any material sphere and any concrete region. We limited our task to drawing up a scheme concerning the foundations of pure logic and presented this scheme as an example of the logically originated fundamental constitution of all possible knowledge or of the objects proper to such knowledge. According to this scheme individuals must be determinable in terms of concepts and laws, which may be called *a priori* principles. All empirical sciences must be based on their own regional ontologies, and not merely on pure logic which is common to all sciences.

These statements also give rise to the idea of a task to be performed, namely, to determine, within the horizon of our individual intuitions, the highest genera of *concreta,* and in this way to distribute all intuitable individual entities according to regions of being, each region in principle pointing to an eidetic science and one or more empirical sciences. However, the radical distinction of these regions in 'material things' and 'souls', for instance, in no way eliminates partial overlapping, because, in the given example, the latter has its ground in the former, and by this reason the theory of the soul is based on that of the body.

The problem of a radical classification of the sciences is mainly a question of separating the regions from one another, and for this again we need, as a prerequisite, pure logical studies of the kind we have briefly outlined here. However, we need also a phenomenology whose nature and goal must be described in the following in a more accurate way.[25]

3. *Regional Ontologies and Phenomenology*

The preceding pages briefly describe Husserl's view on the relation between fact and essence and its logical consequences. For the greater part these considerations are borrowed by Husserl from the second and third volumes of the second edition of his *Logical Investigations* (1913). The ideas mentioned contain many difficult problems which

25. *Ibid.,* p. 39 (70-71).

cannot be considered here in detail, as their study would exceed a mere introduction to Husserl's philosophy.[26] There are, however, other problems with which we have to cope here, because they appear to be very important for the proper understanding of Husserl's phenomenological philosophy as a whole; such as, for instance, the question concerning the status of being of essences, the problem of how we are able to know them truthfully, and the problem regarding the relation between regional ontologies and phenomenological philosophy. For the balance of this chapter I shall briefly dwell on the last problem only; it is my intention to deal with the other two problems in the next chapter.[27]

Regional Ontologies and Empirical Sciences

There is no doubt about the fact that in dealing with the so-called 'regional ontologies' Husserl in 1913 took his starting point in the idea that in its many directions the world of our immediate experience has already become the object of scientific determination in which everything that our pre-scientific and daily experience finds merely in a vague and naïve way is grasped in exact concepts and explanatory theories. Each science has its own domain of investigation, but it is not able to furnish this domain for itself; this domain is pre-given to it in advance inasfar as in our pre-scientific experience beings immediately manifest themselves as being comparable with and distinguishable from one other.

Our pre-scientific experience *a priori* precedes all sciences of experience and equally *a priori* predelineates their different domains of investigation. Husserl calls the totality of objects that each science investigates in its own and typical way, a 'region'. In this way he speaks, for instance, of the 'region of physical nature', the 'region of psychical beings', etc. What all the objects of a certain region have in common

---

26. See, for instance, Suzanne Bachelard, *La logique de Husserl. Etude sur logique formelle et logique transcendentale* (Paris: Presses Universitaires de France, 1957).

27. See for the following, C. Lannoy, "Phenomenologie, ontologie en psychologie in het werk van Edmund Husserl", *Tijdschrift voor Philosophie*, 11 (1949) 391-416; L. Landgrebe, "Seinsregionen und regionale Ontologien in Husserl's Phänomenologie", *Studium Generale*, 9 (1956), 313-324 (also in *Der Weg der Phänomenologie*, pp. 143-162.)

and, therefore, what characterizes them, is, according to Husserl, fixed in the categories which are germane to each region. Together they co-constitute the 'regional categories' or the fundamental and basic concepts of that region. In these basic concepts are all the *a priori* presuppositions contained under which each multiplicity of beings which are immediately given in our pre-scientific experience can be conceived and understood as belonging together in such a way that they can become the object and theme of one or the other science. Because these basic concepts constitute the typical mode of intelligibility and, therefore, also the object-character of the objects of the sciences in question, the sciences in which the categories of a determinate region are discovered, are called 'regional ontologies'. That is why every empirical science which is engaged in the scientific investigation of a determinate domain of beings, is to be founded in a regional ontology in which the basic concepts of this science are to be explained in a radical way.[28]

According to Landgrebe, Husserl in 1913 considered these sciences to be philosophical sciences.[29] It is my opinion, however, that this cannot be so. For, already in *The Idea of Phenomenology* (1907) Husserl characterized the difference between philosophical and non-philosophical disciplines by pointing to the fundamental difference between the philosophical and the natural attitude, whereas in the same book the formal ontologies are explicitly classed under the sciences of the natural attitude.[30] In a note of 1916[31] referring to the first lecture, Husserl adds the material ontologies and makes again the explicit remark that all these ontologies belong to the realm of the 'natural' sciences, that is to say, to the sciences of the natural attitude. That Husserl in 1913 was of the same opinion is not only clear from the remark with which he concludes his 'logical investigations',[32] but especially from the passage in which he explicitly says that the formal ontologies as well as the material ontologies must be 'disconnected' through the phenomenological

28. Ludwig Landgrebe, *loc. cit.,* pp. 313-314.
29. *Ibid.,* pp. 314-315.
30. Edmund Husserl, *Die Idee,* p. 19 (14-15).
31. *Ibid.,* p. 79.
32. Edmund Husserl, *Ideen I,* p. 39 (71).

reduction.[33] Here Husserl even claims "the absolute independence of phenomenology from all sciences, including the eidetic sciences", that is, from the formal and material ontologies; this claim is motivated there by 'the philosophical functions' which phenomenology has to perform.[34] In the third volume of the *Ideas*, which according to Marley Biemel was written in its first draft in 1912,[35] Husserl says that it is one of the most important tasks of phenomenological philosophy to give the eidetic, regional ontologies their ultimate foundation.[36]

Be this as it may, when Husserl claims that every empirical science is to be founded in a regional ontology, this evidently does not mean that the regional ontologies should have to precede the empirical sciences. On the contrary, it is Husserl's view that regional ontologies can be built up only by starting from a subsequent reflection on the conditions under which such a domain of beings could be delineated. Regional ontologies explicitate what in unconditioned generality and necessity must belong to a certain object if it really is to be the object of investigation of the correlative empirical science; that is to say, regional ontologies must determine and describe the essential structures of every possible object of the different empirical sciences which deal with the entities belonging to the region in question. That is why Husserl also speaks of 'eidetic sciences' in contradistinction to 'sciences of facts' On the other hand, however, it also follows from the foregoing that, although it is true that the regional ontologies follow after the corresponding empirical sciences in the order of time, they, nevertheless, as eidetic sciences precede those sciences *de jure*.[37]

Formal and Material Ontologies

In *Ideas* (1913) a formal ontology which makes abstraction from all the regional distinctions of the different objects, is put ahead of the

33. *Ibid.*, pp. 140-144 (158-163); see also E. Levinas, *Théorie de l'intuition dans la phénoménologie de Husserl* (Paris: J. Vrin, 1963), p. 21-22.
34. Edmund Husserl, *Ideen I*, p. 144 (162).
35. *Ibid.*, vol. II: Einleitung des Herausgebers, p. *xvi*.
36. *Ibid.*, vol. II, pp. 79-85
37. *Ibid.*, vol. I, p. 23 (56-57), pp. 164-168 (185-188). Ludwig Landgrebe, *loc. cit.*, p. 315 C. Lannoy, *loc. cit.*, pp. 408-409.

regional ontologies.[38] It is the science which deals with the formal idea 'object-in-general'. Its subject matter consists in the conditions under which anything whatsoever can be a legitimate object of man's thought and science, and under which, therefore, this object can be explained and described by every science. The fundamental concept or the basic category of formal ontology thus consists in the empty 'object-in-general'. Although, on the one hand, one could say that this formal ontology is a branch of logic as universal analytic, it is, on the other hand, also true that it comprises the whole *mathesis universalis* (formal logic, arithmetic, pure analysis, set theory, etc.)[39]

The regional or material ontologies try to investigate all the conditions which from the point of view of their subject matters are necessarily presupposed in the different empirical sciences. They have to focus attention on the *eidos*, that is, the universally operative and necessary essence of the objects of the empirical sciences. It is these essences of the different objects of the empirical sciences which in formal ontology are investigated in the reduced form of 'object-in-general'. The subject matter of formal ontology, therefore, does not consist in the class of essences, but "in a mere essence-form, which is indeed an essence, but a completely 'empty' one",[40] that is to say, "an essence which in the manner of an empty form fits all possible essences, and which in its formal universality has the highest material generalities subordinated to it".[41] However, the formal region is not on a par with the material regions; "it is properly speaking no region at all, but the pure form of region in general only".[42] Formal ontology, therefore, investigates a completely new dimension of being, namely, the necessary conditions of being-object.[43]

Let us try to explain this important distinction from a different point of view. It is Husserl's idea that the structure of being on which the material ontologies focus all their attention is not everywhere the

38. Edmund Husserl, *Ideen I*, p. 23 (56-57).
39. *Ibid.*, p. 27 (60).
40. *Ibid.*
41. *Ibid.*
42. *Ibid.*
43. C. Lannoy, *loc. cit.*, pp. 406-408.

same: different regions of being have a different constitution and therefore, can not be described with the help of the same categories.[44]
Certainly, one can universally apply the categories 'object', 'relation',
etc. But the structure which is expressed in these concepts common to
all regions of being is merely formal. Therefore, the concept 'object in
general' is *not* the supreme genus of which the basic concepts of the
different material regions are to be the various species. The categories
that express the material structure of being which, for instance, defines
nature as nature and consciouness as consciousness, are not mere
specifications of formal categories; that is to say, they are not the results of the addition of a *differentia specifica* to a *genus proximum*. This
is why Husserl stresses the difference between genus and form, between generalization and formalization, and between specialization and
deformalization.[45]

The General Ontology of the World of Immediate Experience

At any rate, in 1913, Husserl had not yet mentioned the possibility and even necessity of a "general material ontology of the world
of immediate experience," which in the lecture series *Phenomenological
Psychology* (1925) constitutes the core of his investigations. Once
Husserl saw the necessity, not only of a material ontology of nature as
nature, of consciousness as consciousness, of society as society, etc., but
first and foremost a general material ontology of the world of immediate experience as such, it became clear to him that the subject
matter of the different regional ontologies cannot be determined by
taking one's starting point in the empirical sciences, but must be drawn
from the general material ontology of the world of immediate experience.
However, all that was said in 1913 about formal ontology as well as
about the description of the meaning and function of the material
ontologies is maintained in 1925. Husserl then only adds a new science,
namely the general ontology of the world of immediate experience as
such, which in regard to the material ontologies has a foundational

---

44. *Ibid.*, pp. 26-27 (59-60).

45. E. Levinas, *op. cit.*, p. 21. See also: Edmund Husserl, *Ideen I*, pp. 32-34
(64-66).

function. The consequence of this evidently is that the relation between regional ontologies and the corresponding empirical sciences is to be determined in a different way. But even then Husserl explicitly maintains that every material ontology whatsoever must ultimately be founded on transcendental phenomenology.[46]

We shall return to these questions in the last chapters of this book, because the development of Husserl's thought in this respect is closely connected with his later view on phenomenological phychology and with the 'life-world' problematic which forms the kernel of Husserl's last publication.

---

46. Edmund Husserl, *Phän. Psych.*, pp. 52-72; *Ideen III*, pp. 23-24; *Erste Phil.*, pp. 212-218.

CHAPTER FOUR

EVIDENCE

Introduction

In Chapter Three we have seen that according to Husserl every individual fact has its own essence,[1] just as conversely to each essence there corresponds a series of possible individuals.[2] An individual object is not simply a mere 'this-there', but being constituted thus-and-thus 'in itself' it has its own proper mode of Being, its own *eidos* which can be apprehended in all its purity.[3] The term *'eidos'* or 'essence' is here taken to mean that which in the intimate self-being of an individual discloses to us 'what' it is.[4]

Asking himself how we are able to know such an *'eidos'*, Husserl posits that every essence can be "set out as an Idea". And trying to explain this enigmatic statement Husserl continues that every empirical intuition can be transformed into an intuition of an essence by means of the process of *ideation*. Of whatever kind the empirical intuition may be, "it can always pass off into the intuition of an essence". Just as the datum of empirical intuition is an individual object, so the datum of 'essential intuition' is a pure essence. And just as empirical intuition is consciousness of an individual object and intuitively brings it to givenness, so 'essential intuition' is the consciousness of an 'object' toward which conciousness directs its glance as toward something 'self-given'. And, finally, just as in perception consciousness grasps the individual object in its 'bodily' selfhood, so is genuine essential intuition a primordial dator intuition grasping the essence in its 'bodily' selfhood.[5]

In developing this point of view Husserl touches only in passing upon two problems which are very important for a proper understanding of his theory concerning the relation between fact and essence. These questions are: what mode of Being is characteristic of essences

---

1. Edmund Husserl, *Ideen I*, p. 12 (46-47).—In this and the following chapters the term 'Being' always indicates the German term 'Sein', whereas 'being' is used as a translation for the term 'Seindes'.
2. *Ibid.*, p. 21 (55).
3. *Ibid.*, pp. 12-13 (47).
4. *Ibid.*, p. 13 (48).
5. *Ibid.*, pp. 13-14 (48-49).

and how do we know them? In formulating his own view on these questions, which as we shall see are closely connected, Husserl first tries to define his position against empiricism and positivism, on the one hand, and classical idealism, on the other.

Empiricism and positivism deny that general essences can be considered to be given in the genuine sense of the term. Husserl tries to explain that in this matter the empiricist and the positivist suffer from a prejudice which prevents them from seeing that more is given than individual and singular data and more than singular facts. What phenomenology objects to, with respect to empiricism and positivism, is not their battle against unverified and unverifiable metaphysical 'nonsense', but the fact that they dogmatically restrict givenness to particular experiences and thereby implicitly reject any intuition of general essences and general relations. If positivism means nothing but basing all sciences without any prejudice whatsoever upon the 'positive', that is, upon what can be primordially apprehended, then it is 'we who are genuine positivists,' Husserl claims.[6] Classical idealism, on the other hand, falls short inasfar as it never was able to develop a consistent theory of self-evidence, which is essential in every theory of intuition.

In any case, it is against the background of this critical excursion that Husserl tries to define his own point of view concerning the questions mentioned. There it becomes clear that Husserl presupposes that self-evidence based upon intuition is the ultimate criterion of all truth and that the principle that intuition is the ultimate source which justifies all our knowledge is even the leading idea of his phenomenology as a whole. That is why finally explicitly formulates this basic principle and tries to elucidate its meaning and purpose. Let us try to explain this in more detail, taking up again the considerations of our foregoing chapter concerning fact and essence.

1. *Naturalistic Misconceptions*

Necessity of an Epoché with Respect to All Previous Philosophy

According to Husserl the general discussion of essences and sciences of essences as contrasted with facts and the sciences of facts, con-

---

6. *Ibid.*, p. 46 (78).

cerned the essential foundations of pure phenomenology, as a science of the essential Being of things and for understanding the position of phenomenology with respect to all empirical sciences. In presenting these determinations, Husserl claims, we did not argue from a pre-established philosophical standpoint and did not even make use of gen-erally accepted philosophical theories. Instead we have given expres-sion to certain distinctions that are directly given to us in intuition. We took these distinctions exactly as they presented themselves immediately, without adding any hypotheses or interpretations, and without reading into them anything derived from traditional or modern theories. State-ments brought to the fore in this way are genuine principles and 'real beginnings'. If, as is the case here, they are so general that they cover all regions of Being, they are certainly fundamental in a philosophical sense.

In the fundamental statements we have formulated in this way we have presupposed nothing, not even a determinate conception of phil-osophy itself. We must try to maintain this standpoint during the whole of our phenomenological investigations and abstain from making any judgment concerning the theoretical content of any previous philosophy. Thus our whole further discussion must remain within the limits im-posed by this 'philosophical *epoché*'. On the other hand, however, this *epoché* does not force us to abstain from speaking of philosophy as a historical fact, of philosophical movements that have once existed and somehow determined the general scientific convictions of man.[7]

Empiricism Identifies Experience with the Primordial Act

It is within the limits of such an *epoché* that we now must become involved in a debate with empiricism. For, if philosophy has any 'fun-damental' principles in the genuine sense of the term, that is, principles which radically can be grounded only through what is given immediately in intuition, the issue of the contest concerning such intuition does not depend on the possession of a certain idea of philosophy. What com-pels us to oppose empiricism is merely the fact that 'ideas', 'essences'

---

7. *Ibid.*, pp. 40-42 (72-73).

and 'knowledge of essences' are denied by empiricism, whereas such a denial contradicts the immediately given phenomena.

Let us frankly admit that empiricist naturalism has its origin in founded motives. Radically opposed to all 'idols', it seeks to indicate and establish the right of autonomous reason to be the only authority in matters of truth. To pass rational judgment upon facts and things means to be guided by the things themselves, to get away from mere talk, to go back to the facts, to question them in their self-givenness, and to lay aside all prejudices foreign to their very nature. In the view of the empiricist, another way of expressing the same idea is to say that all science must arise from experience and that all mediated knowledge must be based upon immediate experience. Therefore, for empiricism genuine science means exactly the same as science of experience. 'Ideas' and 'essences' as opposed to facts are only scholastic entities, meta-physical 'ghosts' which are to be swept away by means of Ockham's razor. We must be grateful to modern natural science, to have delivered us from these philosophical 'spooks'. Science is concerned only with the real world of facts pertaining to experience. Whatever does not belong to this world of facts is purely imaginary, and a science based on imagination is simply an imaginary science. Essences belong to the realm of speculative *a priori* constructions, through which, in the first half of the nineteenth century, idealism in its ignorance of scientific knowledge of nature used to impede the progress of true science.

However, all those empiricist remarks are based on misunderstandings and prejudices, no matter how noble the motives may have been which originally inspired them. The basic mistake of empiricism here is that it identifies the fundamental requirement of a return to the 'things themselves' with the requirement that all knowledge must be founded upon experience. Accepting the naturalistic limitation of the realm of knowable 'facts', it simply takes for granted that only experience can give facts themselves. But facts are not necessarily facts-of-nature. For the fact-world in the ordinary sense of the term is not necessarily identical with reality as such, and it is only with the fact-world of nature that the primordial dator act 'experience' is concerned. Immediate intuition, not only the sensory 'seeing' of natural experience, but 'seeing' in general as primordial dator consciousness of any kind whatsoever is the ultimate source and justification of all rational statements. That is why for 'experience' one must substitute the more general term 'intuition.' That is also why one must refuse to identify science in general with science of experience or empirical science.[8]

Idealistic Obscurities

There are obscurities also on the opposite side. Idealism accepts only a pure thinking *a priori* and thus rejects the fundamental thesis of empiricism. However, Husserl says, it fails to explain in a convincing way what it genuinely means when it posits that there is such a thing as pure intuition in which essences are primordially given, just as individual realities are given in empirical intuition. It fails, likewise, to realize that the concept 'dator intuition' encompasses *every* process of insight involving judgment, and in particular the insight into unconditionally universal truths. Idealism does not know that the concept 'dator intuition' can be differentiated in various ways and, in particular, that it has differentiations which are parallel to the logical categories. It is true that in classical idealism there is question of self-evidence, but instead of considering it as a process of insight somehow connected with ordinary seeing, it speaks about a 'feeling of self-evidence' which like a mystical *'index veri'* colors the judgment with a feeling. Such interpretations are possible only so long as one does not know how to analyze types of consciousness by viewing them purely in their essence, instead of making ethereal theories about them. These so-called feelings of self-evidence or of intellectual necessity are simply fictions.[9]

2. The Existence and Our Knowledge of Essences

The Reproach of Platonic Idealism

It is often said that Husserl's view on essences must be considered a new form of Platonic realism. Since the appearance of the second volume of the *Logical Investigations* this remark has been made time and

---

8. *Ibid.*, pp. 42-47 (74-78).
9. *Ibid.*, pp. 47-48 (78-79).

again, and the polemics directed against his *Logos* article have been going in the same direction. The criticism claims that Husserl conceives of essences as objects to which one has to ascribe 'genuine Being' as to all other objects, and also the capacity to be intuited as in the case of empirical realities.

Husserl refutes this criticism by positing that it was never his intention to defend the thesis that the term object is identical with empirical objects and that reality and empirical reality are one and the same thing.[10] If 'object' is to be defined as 'anything whatsoever', then no one can deny that essences are objects, although they do not have the same status of Being as this tree here before my window. Furthermore, all the critics who deny that essences are 'genuine' objects, seem to forget that they continually make use of essences in their thinking and speaking and that they explain them away only because of their epistemological *a priori* standpoints. The critics take their starting point in the epistemological presupposition that it is *a priori* impossible that there could be any such thing as essences and intuition of essences. When language suggests to us that there are such 'things', then these must be the consequences of certain 'grammatical hypostatizations' which, therefore, do not give cause for abstruse 'metaphysical' considerations. What we call 'essences,' the critics say, are only the real mental products of our own 'abstraction' which are somehow to be connected with our 'real' experiences. Because of this abstraction essences must be certain 'concepts' and these concepts are 'mental constructions' only. Therefore, the terms 'essence', 'eidos', 'Idea', refer only to psychological facts.

In Husserl's view essences are certainly concepts, but concepts are not mental products, not psychological facts. Although it is true that my number-presentation here and now is a psychological fact, this does not mean and imply that the number itself which is presented here, has *also* to be a psychological fact. On the contrary, its non-temporal Being is evident; to refer to it as a psychological fact or as a mental construct, therefore, is an absurdity. And if the term 'concept' were to mean a 'mental construct', then such things as pure numbers could not be concepts.[11]

---

10. Edmund Husserl, *L. U.*, vol. II, pp. 106-224, especially pp. 106-107, 124-125, 147, 155, 187, 223-224. See also E. Levinas, *Théorie de l'intuition*, pp. 151-153.
11. Edmund Husserl. *Ideen I*, pp. 48-50 (80-82).

Essence and Fiction

However, one could say that no one can deny either that essences must have their origin in individual intuitions and that, therefore, a certain form of abstraction must play a role in the 'construction' of essences. Furthermore, in many cases we just construct ideas at pleasure; especially in the latter cases it is clear that concepts must be psychological products.

In dealing with this objection Husserl agrees with his opponents that those 'conceptual constructions', just as in the case of free fancy, certainly take place spontaneously, and also that what is spontaneously produced must indeed be a product of mind. However, Husserl says, one has to make a clear distinction here between the act of presentation and that which is presented in this very act, between the living experience of thinking or of imagining and the object *qua* thought or imagined. Whereas the thinking of a mathematical entity and the imagining of a centaur are spontaneous and, therefore, products of the mind, the objects meant in and by these acts are not mental products at all, but 'ideal' entities. In other words, Husserl says, it is impossible to identify consciousness of essences with those essences themselves.

But are those essences not mere fictions just as the centaur mentioned above? And is speaking of the 'existence' of essences, therefore, not very suspect? Husserl answers this objection by saying that here, too, there is an analogy between individual facts and essences. For things can be perceived and therewith recognized as 'real', or as doubtful, or even as illusory. The same holds true of essences. Thus it follows that they, just like other objectivities, have meanings given to them which can be right and wrong. Husserl concludes therefore that notwithstanding all these objections one must maintain the thesis that intuition of essences is a primordial dator act which as such is analogous to sensory perception and not to imagination.[12]

Ideation

The proceding pages contain many difficult problems which cannot be considered here, since their study would exceed a mere introduction to

---

12. *Ibid.,* pp. 50-52 (82-83).

Husserl's philosophy. Only on one point must we dwell here briefly, because it appears to be very important for a proper understanding of Husserl's phenomenological methods, namely the process of ideation.

As we have mentioned, Husserl uses the term 'essence' to indicate what a thing is.[13] Every essence can be expressed by an idea. Every empirical and individual intuition can be transformed into an essential insight by means of a so-called 'ideation'. The object of such an insight, called 'pure essence' or 'eidos', is a new kind of object. Consequently, essential insight is a new kind of intuition.[14] However, Husserl claims, essential intuition, according to its very nature, is based on an individual intuition, although it does not presuppose any apprehension of an individual's reality. Hence it is certain that no essential intuition is possible when the ego cannot freely direct its regard to an individual counterpart. Conversely, no individual intuition is possible unless there is a free possibility of carrying out an act of ideation. All this, however, does not alter the fact that the two kinds of intuition are fundamentally different.[15]

Husserl does not go into detail here as far as the methodological aspects of this viewpoint are concerned. He focusses attention only on the following points: 1) phenomenology is either a science of essences or no science at all; 2) phenomenology is a science whose objects do not at all depend on mental constructs; 3) phenomenology is a science in which the essences known are in no way dependent on their concrete factual realizations; 4) nevertheless, it is true that our knowledge of essences must take its starting point in our knowledge of facts.[16]

From this it follows of necessity that an essential insight into the very nature of things requires, among other things, that the essences of things, in one way or another, be disengaged from everything that is simply contingent and accidental to them. This is to be done by the above-mentioned ideation. But neither in his *Logical Investigations*, nor in *The Idea of Phenomenology*, nor in his *Ideas* does Husserl give a clear description of the procedure of ideation. Husserl later returned

---

13. *Ibid.*, p. 13 (48).
14. *Ibid.*, pp. 13-14 (48-49).
15. *Ibid.*, pp. 14-16 (49-50).
16. *Ibid.*, pp. 13-16 (48-50), 50-52 (82-83).

to the subject, not only in his *Phenomenological Psychology* (1925),[17] but also in the *Cartesian Meditations* (1931).[18] The most important description of ideation, however, is found in Husserl's *Experience and Judgment*,[19] edited by Ludwig Landgrebe and published in 1939. The last part of this book deals with the nature of pure essences as obtained by the 'eidetic reduction', which instead of ideation is called now 'the method of free variation'. Husserl describes this method here in a way that is similar to the brief idications given in the *Ideas* which were later developed in *Phenomenological Psychology*.

The Method of Free Variation

In *Experience and Judgment*[20] Husserl argues that an experienced or fancied object can be interpreted as an example of a certain *eidos* and, at the same time, as a prototype for modifications by a series of free variations in phantasy. All these variations have concrete similarities with some given prototype, and the complex of new instances, produced in phantasy, is permeated with an invariant identical content, in terms of which all these arbitrary variations remain congruent while their differences remain irrelevant. This invariant element imposes limits on all possible variations of the same prototype; it is that element without which an object of this kind can neither be thought of nor intuitively imagined. The intuition characteristic of the *eidos* is founded on the manifold of the variants produced in the process of arbitrary variations, but the *eidos* can be grasped purely as such. This intuition of the *eidos* consists in the active apprehension of that which was passively pre-constituted. The examplar chosen as point of departure acts as the proto-type of ever new images, which are created by association in passive phantasy or by fictitious transformation in active phantasy. The es-sence of the method, therefore, consists in this that in our phantasy we

---

17. Edmund Husserl, *Phän. Psychol.,* pp. 72-87.
18. Edmund Husserl, *Cart. Med.,* pp. 103-107 (69-72).
19. Edmund Husserl, *Erf. u. Urt.,* pp. 410-428.
20. See for the following also Alfred Schuetz, "Type and Eidos in Husserl's Later Philosophy", *Philosophy and Phenomenological Research,* 20 (1959). 147-165,) pp. 158-161.

try to change a perceived object in as many different ways as possible.

Let us take an example of the noematic order. I see this table here. Next, I merely imagine things which could be called a table but are quite different from this table: large and small, high and low tables, tables with one, three, four an more legs, tables of different shapes, etc. In all those variations of the originally given table, I find the essence 'table' without which nothing can be a table. We eliminate in this way every accidental and contingent aspect of this table, in order to find what is essential for table as such. When the essence 'table' is passively pre-constituted in this way, it is possible by active intuition to grasp this essence itself.

As we have mentioned, there are important differences between empirical and eidetic generalities. The former are contingent not only in the sense that their formation begins with a particular that is given contingently in factual experience, but also in the sense that the conceptualization proceeds on the basis of comparison with likewise contingently given similarities. In the natural attitude the experienced world is given to us as the universal persistent ground of Being and as the universal field of all our activities, no matter what we are interested in. The formation of a pure *eidos,* however, may not depend on these contingencies of what is factually given, but must be capable of laying down rules for the experience of all empirical particularities. By the process of ideation we eliminate the relationship of our experience with the world and we liberate the environmental horizon of the variants from attachment to any experiential activity. By doing so, we place ourselves in a world of pure phantasy and of pure possibilities. Each of these possibilities can become the center of a set of possible pure variations arbitrarily made; from each of them we may arrive at an absolute pure *eidos,* provided the sets of variations can be connected to a single type of thing.

Still aiming at pure possibilities we may impose limitations on the activity of pure phantasy. Such a limitation, however, should not be confused with concrete specifications of concepts like 'table' or 'house'. Empirical concepts are not genuine specifications of pure essences, but typical generalizations, ranges of anticipation of experiences, outlined by

115

actual experiences. On the other hand, eidetic generalities can always be related to appearing realities. For instance, any actually emergent color is at the same time possible in the pure sense; any one of them can be taken as an example and changed into a variant. Thus, we can transpose all actualities to the level of pure possibilities. But if we do so, even this free arbitrariness appears to have its own limitations. That which can be varied arbitrarily, has necessarily laws determining the characteristics which an object must have in order to be of this or that particular type.

These brief remarks, evidently, do not solve all problems; but they seem to suffice for a first understanding of Husserl's eidetic reduction.[21]

3. *The Principle of All Principles*

Formulation of the Principle of Evidence

After clearing the ground by critical, explanatory and methodological remarks, Husserl now proceeds to formulate the basic principle of his phenomenological philosophy.

No conceivable theory, he says, can mislead us in regard to the 'principle of all principles', that every primordial intuition is a legitimate source of knowledge, and that whatever presents itself in 'intuition' in primordial form, in its authentic reality, is to be accepted simply as that which it presents itself to be, but only within the limits in which it thus presents itself. Let us not forget, Husserl remarks, that any theory can derive its truth solely from primordial data. Thus, any statement which limits itself strictly to expressing this meaning accurately, is really an 'absolute beginning' and a true principle. This assertion applies especially to essential judgments that are general in form, and it is to these that the term 'principle' is usually limited.

It is in this sense, Husserl continues, that every scientist is perfectly justified in following the 'principle' that all assertions about facts of nature must be based upon experience. For, Husserl says, that assertion *is* a principle; it is drawn immediately from sources of general insight. At any time one can readily convince oneself of this point by explaining

---

21. Edmund Husserl, *Erf. u. Urt.*, pp. 410-428 (passim).

the meaning of the expressions used in formulating the principle, and by bringing to the fore in their pure givenness the essences to which these expressions refer. In a similar fashion one who investigates the realm of essences, just as anyone who uses and expresses himself in universal propositions, must follow a parallel principle. Such a principle *must* exist, for the very principle admitted above, namely, that all knowledge of facts is grounded on experience, is not itself open to empirical insight. The same is true of every other principle and, in general, of all knowledge concerning essences.[22]

The scientist who works in the realm of the positive sciences rejects knowledge of essences only when he 'philosophizes' and lets himself be deceived by empiricist sophisms. In Husserl's opinion he does not reject it when, as a scientist, he places himself upon the normal standpoint of empirical science and gives reasons for his convictions; for then, he largely lets himself be guided by essential insights, viz., the insights of pure mathematics. And as anyone can observe, these mathematical disciplines do not proceed empirically and are not founded upon observation and experiment.

Empiricism, however, refuses to admit this and claims that numberless experiences have served to give a foundation to our mathematical insights. The collective experience of all races of mankind and, perhaps, even of the races of animals before man has accumulated immense stores of arithmetical and geometrical impressions and these stores have been integrated in man's habits of apprehension. It is from this source, empiricism claims, that our geometrical insight draws its inspiration. In reply, Husserl says, one may ask on the basis of what experience do we know of these alleged accumulated stores which no one has ever observed? Since when are long-forgotten and entirely hypothetical experiences to be preferred to actual and carefully tested experiences, when we want to give a foundation to a science, and especially to the most exact of all sciences? The physicist observes and experiments, and he rightly refuses to be satisfied with prescientific experiences, let alone with instinctive apprehensions and hypotheses concerning experiences which are merely alleged to have been intuited.

---

22. Edmund Husserl, *Ideen I*, pp. 52-53 (83-84).

Or should we say, Husserl continues, that we owe the insights of geometry to the 'experiences of our imagination', that they are inductively derived from experiences in the functioning of our imagination? But, Husserl says, why then does the physicist make no use of such marvellous 'experiences of our imagination'? For no other reason, of course, than that experiments conducted in imagination would not be real but imagined experiments.

In Husserl's view the correct standpoint with respect to all such interpretations is to point to the intrinsic meaning of mathematical assertions. In order to know, and to know beyond doubt, what a mathematical axiom states, we should not turn to philohophical empiricists, but to consciousness. For it is in consciousness that as mathematicians we grasp axiomatic matters with perfect insight into its axiomatic character. All we have to do is hold on to this intuition and we will see with certainty that the axioms express pure relations between essences without any aid from facts of experience. Instead of philosophizing and psychologizing about geometrical thought and intuition from without, Husserl concludes, we should determine their intrinsic meaning through direct analyses.[23]

Science and Philosophy

For Husserl it is thus evident that scientists only *speak* skeptically about mathematics and everything eidetic, but through their eidetic method they *act* dogmatically. Physical science has grown to greatness by disregarding ancient skepticism and abandoning even the attempt to overcome it. It refused to worry over such 'crucial' problems as the possibility to know the 'external' world, or to ask how the age-old difficulties implied in this possibility were to be solved. Instead it occupied itself with the method that natural science should follow if it wants to be as perfectly as possible an *exact* science of nature. In the prephilosophical and, in a good sense, *dogmatic* sphere of inquiry, to which all the empirical sciences belong, the right attitude is deliberately to discard all skepticism, all 'natural philosophy' and theories of knowledge, in order to find the data of knowledge there, where they

---

23. *Ibid.*, pp. 53-54 (84-86).

actually face us, no matter what epistemological difficulties may subsequently arise concerning the possibility of such data being there.

It is for these reasons, Husserl continues, that an important division must be made in the field of scientific inquiry. On the one hand, we have the sciences of the dogmatic standpoint. They face the facts and are not conecrned about any epistemological or skeptical problems. They start from the primordial givenness of the facts they deal with and, in verifying their ideas, always return to these facts. They investigate the nature of the immediately given facts and ask what conclusions can be drawn from that natural foundation concerning those facts. On the other hand, we have the rigorous investigations of the epistemological, that is, the *specifically philosophical standpoint.* They are concerned with the skeptical problems about the possibility of man's knowledge. Their object is, first, to solve these problems in principle and in a general way and, then, to study the bearing which their solutions have on the critical task of determining what meaning and value for knowledge can be attributed to the results of the 'dogmatic' sciences. At any rate, so long as a highly developed critique of knowledge constituted with complete rigor and clearness is lacking, it is right to separate the field of dogmatic research from all critical forms of inquiry.[24]

4. *The Theory of Evidence*

Problems and Tasks of a Phenomenology of Evidence[25]

As any other form of intuitionism Husserl's phenomenology accepts as its final criterion of truth the direct evidence or self-givenness of intuitively grasped data. Consequently, phenomenology also must answer the criticisms directed against self-evidence as a reliable criterion of truth, and must try to solve the real problems raised by these critiques. Is phenomenology better equiped to solve the real problems raised by this criticism than other intuitionist systems have been able to do?

---

24. *Ibid.*, pp. 54-57 (86-88).

25. See for the following section in general Herbert Spiegelberg, "Phenomenology of Direct Evidence", *Philosophy and Phenomenological Research*, 2 (1942), 427-456, pp. 427-429.

As we have seen, one of the principal characteristics of the phenomenological method consists in the careful observation, analysis and description of immedately given phenomena in their irreducible nature and in their full variety. An accurate and consistent use of this method, therefore, should safeguard us against pseudo-evidences and help us attain true intuitions. Moreover, if this method is applied to the phenomenon of self-evidence itself, it offers considerable assistance in clarifying this concept and its foundations.

Another very important point is that phenomenology makes a clear distinction between predicative and pre-predicative evidence and is able to show that every predicative evidence is ultimately founded upon a pre-predicative experience, which as such is given immediately in intuitional experience.

Lastly, phenomenology makes also distinctions between different kinds of self-evidence. Such distinctions may serve to reduce and sometimes even to remove the seeming contraditions between the different conflicting phenomena which at times all seem to claim genuine self-evidence. More specifically, these distinctions may make it possible for us to separate genuine self-evidence from pseudo-self-evidence.

With respect to this last point, in Husserl's writings we often find the distinction between *adequate* and *inadequate* self-evidence. A thing in the real world, for instance, a three dimensional object like a house or a tree, can appear only with inadequate self-evidence, because the perception in which it is given is, as we will see, 'adumbrative' and therefore one-sided. Such inadequate self-evidence, as distinguished e.g., from the adequate self-evidence of a simple arithmetical insight, is capable of increase and decrease.

Secondly, Husserl stresses the difference between *assertoric* self-evidence and *apodictic* self-evidence. The former refers to empirical individual objects or conditions, while the latter is an insight into general essences and essential relationships which apodictically excludes any alternatives. As a rule, only apodictic self-evidence is considered to be really adequate.

Thirdly, Husserl distinguishes between *pure* and *impure* self-evidence, according as such self-evidence includes or does not include an element of fact; between *purely formal* or analytic and *material* or synthetic *a priori* self-evidence; between *theoretical, axiological,* and *practical* self-evidence; and between *immediate* and *mediate* self-evidence.

Finally, in his *Formal and Transcendental Logic* Husserl distinguishes between *self-evidence of distinctness* and *self-evidence of clearness.* The former is supposed to be present in a judgment that is explicitly made and not merely contained vaguely and confusedly in a causal idea or in a sentence which is 'merely' read and repeated. Self-evidence of clearness, in addition to being distinct, presents also the object to which the judgment refers.

Especially important is also Husserl's hierarchy of self-evidences in which the pre-predicative self-evidence of individual objects appears as primary and basic.

A complete phenomenology of self-evidence would have to explain all these distinctions in detail and to face all the problems which they imply. It would have to indicate to what extent these distinctions refer to *intrinsically* different types of self-evidence, and not merely to extrinsic differences flowing from the different kinds of objects involved.

It is evidently impossible for us to perform all these tasks in an introductory study.[26] We will restrict ourselves to an attempt to clarify Husserl's conception of self-evidence and to describe the most important of the distinctions mentioned. Husserl never wrote a complete phenomenology of self-evidence, but in his various works incidentally mentioned only those insights which in the particular context seemed indispensable. Hence we will have to compare and combine different passages. A necessary consequence of this procedure is that we must sometimes quote his words without their original context.

What Is Self-evidence?

In the first volume of the *Logical Investigations* Husserl mentions that one of the prejudices of psychologism is concerned with the *locus*

---

26. See, for instance, Gaston Berger, *Le cogito dans la philosophie de Husserl* (Paris: Aubier, 1941), pp. 78-88. Quintin Lauer, *Phénoménologie de Husserl,* pp. 129, 133-138, 143-145, 245-251, 256-259, 261, 265-267, 271, 293-303, 312-314, 348-351. Stephan Strasser, "Beschouwingen over het vraagstuk van de apodicticiteit en de critische verantwoording der Phaenomenologie", *Tijdschrift voor Philosophie,* 8 (1946), 226-270.

of truth and the nature of evidence. Truth, he mentions, is believed to reside in the judgment, and evidence is taken to mean a 'peculiar feeling' which somehow guarantees the truth of the corresponding judgment. Hence it follows that, if logic deals with truth, the laws of logic are principles of psychology. For they are principles which explain the conditions upon which the presence or absence of that 'feeling' depends.[27]

Husserl, however, does not admit that truth resides in judgment, and he also denies that pure logical propositions say anything at all about evidence and its conditions. They can be related to experiences of evidence only by way of application. The evidential propositions arising from such an application retain their *a priori* character; consequently, the conditions of evidence which they express are not psychological or real conditions. Evidence is not a 'feeling' which guarantees the truth of a judgment, but the experience in which we become aware that it is in conformity to the truth. It is possible, of course, to study the natural conditions in which evidence arises and disappears according to the testimony of our experience. The examination of such conditions is a task of psychology. However, the evidence of judgment is subject not only to such psychological conditions but also to ideal ones. These ideal conditions refer to the relationship between evidence and truth. If the classical definition of truth (*adaequatio rei et intellectus*) is interpreted to mean the complete agreement between that which is meant and that which is immediately given as such, we may say that this agreement is *experienced* in the evidence, insofar as the evidence is the actual adequate identification of these two. In and through evidence the truth is 'present' in fact.[28]

For a deeper insight into the essence of evidence we need more accurate distinctions, which can perhaps best be introduced through the following consideration. Phenomenology wants to be a strict and rigorous science. Like any other science, phenomenology must consist of scientific statements; that is, its propositions must accurately express our

27. Edmund Husserl, *L. U.*, vol. I, pp. 128-129. See also *Quentin Lauer, Phénoménologie de Husserl,* pp. 129-151 (passim); Marvin Farber, *op. cit.*, pp. 131-132.

28. Edmund Husserl, *Die Idee,* pp. 58-63 (46-51); Marvin Farber, *op. cit.,* p. 444.

scientifically formed and interconnected philosophical judgments. For this reason a study concerning the foundation of philosophy should begin by clarifying our 'judicative activity' and the judgments constituted in it. First of all, we must consider here the distinction between immediate and mediate judgments. The meaning of mediate judgments is so much related to other judgments that judicatively believing them presupposes belief in these other judgments. Moreover, the distinction between immediate and mediate judgments demands that we clarify man's tendency toward *grounded* judgments and therefore also the grounding activity itself in order to show the correctness, the truth of those judgments. The grounding of mediate judgments presupposes the grounding of the immediate judgments implied in the meaning of these mediate judgments. Once this grounding has been made in an explicit way, we can later freely return to it and to the truth shown in it. By virtue of man's freedom to reactualize such a truth while realizing that it is one and the same truth, this truth becomes his permanent possession and, as such, is called a 'cognition'.

Going further in this direction and explicitating more accurately what is meant by 'cognition' and its grounding, we arrive at the idea of evidence. In a genuine grounding, judgments reveal themselves as correct, as agreeing; in other words, the grounding is an agreement of the judgment with the judged state of affairs itself. More precisely expressed, judging is 'meaning' (and as a rule, merely supposing) that this or that exists and has this or that determination. That which is judged then is merely a supposed state of affairs. However, there is sometimes a privileged judicative 'meaning', a judicative possessing of the state of affairs itself. This 'possessing' is called *evidence*. In it, the state of affairs instead of being merely 'meant' from a distance is present as 'itself'; the judger possesses it itself. A merely supposing judging can be adjusted to the affairs themselves by being consciously converted into the corresponding evidence. This conversion is internally characterized as the fulfilment of what was merely 'meant'; it is a synthesis in which what was 'meant' agrees with what is itself given; it is an evident possessing of the correctness of what was previously 'meant' from a distance.[29]

---

29. Edmund Husserl, *Cart. Med.*, pp. 50-52 (9-11).

Predicative and Pre-predicative Self-evidence

Another point must be stressed here to supplement the preceding remarks. The judgment in the broadest sense, i.e., something meant as being, and evidence in the broadest sense must be distinguished from pre-predicative judging and pre-predicative evidence. For, all our judging functions in our pursuit of knowledge, which generally speaking is always knowledge of 'being'. Thus, being is pre-given to every act of knowledge as a possible object of our judging. If this is true, all knowledge presupposes pre-given objects; objects must be pre-given if our judgments are to lead to real and true knowledge. Moreover, if these judgments are to be evident judgments, the objects themselves have to be given with evidence.[30]

We must therefore make a distinction between *predicative* and *pre-predicative* evidence. Pre-predicative evidence simply is self-givenness in the way in which an object can consciously be characterized in its givenness as being there itself in its authentic reality, in contrast with a mere supposing representation. An object of external perception, for instance, is evidently given as 'it itself' in contrast with its mere representation in memory or imagination. For this reason we will call 'evident' any consciousness which, in reference to its object, must be characterized as immediately giving this object itself, whether or not this self-giving is adequate. In this way our terminology differs from the common usage which restricts evidence to adequate self-givenness. This is why we have to emphasize that every type of object has its own way of giving itself (= evidence), and also that, as we will see, adequate evidence is not possible for every object.

The evident givenness of an object does not always have to take the form of a predication. An object, as a possible substratum of a judgment, can be evidently given, even though it is not necessarily judged in a predicative judgment. But an evident predicative judgment concerning an object is impossible unless this object itself is given with evidence. In the problems concerning evidence, therefore, we must distinguish questions concerning the evidence of the pre-given objects themselves

---

30. Edmund Husserl, *Erf. u. Urt.*, p. 11.

from questions dealing with the evident predicative judgments based on the evidence of those objects. The latter are studied in formal logic; the former are not considered by classical formal logic but constitute a very important theme in our phenomenological investigations.[31]

At any rate, evidence is, in a very wide sense, an 'experiencing' of something that is; it is a 'mental seeing' of something itself. Evidence, however, which includes all experiencing in the usual and more restricted sense, can be more or less perfect. All our prescientific experiences and evidences are only more or less perfect. Their imperfection, as a rule, consists in this that they are incomplete, one-sided and at the same time relatively obscure and indistinct, accordingly as the givenness of the affairs themselves is qualified. Differently expressed, the 'experiences' are infected with 'empty' components, with expectant and attendant meanings. This imperfection is removed by a synthesizing series of further experiences in which the attendant meanings are 'filled' and realized in actual experience. The question of whether adequate evidence does not necessarily lie 'at infinity' need not concern us here.[32]

The Primordial Dator 'Vision'

Let us now consider the question of evidence more accurately by introducing a few more distinctions. First of all, we must mention the distinction between 'positional experience' in which what is posited acquires primordial givenness and positional experiences in which it does not acquire this givenness; in other words between 'perceiving' acts, understood in the broad sense of this expression, and non-perceiving acts. A recollective consciousness, e.g., of a landscape, is not given in a primordial sense, for the landscape is not perceived in the very act of perception. In saying this, we do not want to claim that recollective consciousness is not an independent legitimate source but merely that its legitimacy is not the one proper to 'seeing'. Phenomenology extends this kind of opposition to *all* types of positional experiences. We can, for instance, predicate 'blindly' that $2 + 1 = 1 + 2$, but we can also

---

31. *Ibid.,* pp. 11-14.
32. Edmund Husserl, *Cart. Med.,* pp. 52-55 (11-14).

make the same judgment with insight. In the latter case the state of affairs, the synthetic objectivity which corresponds to the synthesis made in this judgment, is primordially given, it is grasped in a primordial way. This is no longer so after the living fulfilment of the insight, for it changes at once into the obscurity of a retention. As such, it may still be rationally more perfect than any other confused consciousness of the same noematic meaning, e.g., an 'unthinking' reproduction of something that was previously learnt and perhaps even with insight; yet it is no longer a primordially given consciousness.

These distinction are not concerned with the pure meaning or/and its position; for these are the same for both members of every pair of examples and the meaning in question may be consciously and intuitively grasped as being identical every time. The distinction is concerned with the way in which the mere meaning is or is not 'filled', for, as a mere *abstractum* this meaning requires additions in the form of supplementary phases, in order to give the content of consciousness (its *noema*) full development.[33]

But fullness of meaning is not the only requisite; we are also concerned with the 'how' of its 'filling'. One mode of experiencing the meaning is the 'intuitive' way. It makes us aware of the 'meant object as such' through direct mental vision. A particularly striking example is the case in which the mode of direct vision is the primordial object-giving mode. In that case the meaning in the perception of a landscape is perceptively 'filled', and we become aware of the perceived object with its colors, forms, etc., in the mode of the 'embodied'. Similar distinctions exist in all act-spheres. The situation again has two parallel aspects, one noetic, the other noematic.

Here, as in every kind of rational consciousness, the expression 'to belong to' has a very special meaning. We say, for instance, that to the bodily appearing of a thing positionality 'belongs' in all cases inasfar as every such appearing necessarily implies the positing of the thing's existence. Positionality is not only one with this appearing in a general

---

33. Husserl understands by *'noema'* the object meant as such, whereas the *'noesis'* is the act of consciousness which is correlative to such a *noema*. The adjectives *'noematic'* and *'noetic'* respectively refer to *noema* and *noesis*. For a fuller explanation of these terms see Chapter VI.

way, but even in a unique sense: it is motivated by it, not merely in a general way, but even 'rationally motivated'. This assertion means that the positing has its original basis of legitimacy in the primordial givenness of the appearing thing. When there is a question of other forms of givenness, there may also be a ground of legitimacy; but in these forms we do not find the privileged original ground, which plays such a prominent part in the relative evaluation of the grounds of legitimacy.

The positing of the essence or essential relationship that is primordially given in our vision of essential being likewise 'belongs' to the meaning in its mode of givenness. This positing again is a rational positing and, as a believing certitude, it is an originally motivated positing; it has the specific character of 'understanding'. If the positing is 'blind', if the meaning of the words is determined on the basis of a vague act-background of which we are only confusedly aware, the insight lacks of necessity a rational character; the rational character is essentially incompatible with such a mode of givenness of the state of affairs or, alternatively, with such a noematic accompaniment of the nucleus of meaning. On the other hand, this incompatibility does not exclude a secondary rational character as is exemplified by the imperfect reproduction of essential cognition.

Insight or self-evidence in general, therefore is an entirely distinctive occurrence; its heart is the unity of a rational positing with that which essentially motivates it. The reference to *motivation* in an excellent way fits the relation between noetic positing and the posited noematic meaning in its mode of intentional fullness.

The twofold meaning of the term 'self-evidence', as applied both to noetic characters or full acts (self-evident acts of judging) and to noematic positions (self-evident posited meanings) is a case of the general and necessary ambiguity proper to expressions that are concerned with the phases of correlation between noesis and noema. The phenomenological indication of the source from which these ambiguities arise renders them harmless, and even allows us to recognize that they are indispensable.

The expression 'fulfilment' contains another ambiguity of an entirely different type. Sometimes the expression refers to 'fulfilment of intention', as a characteristic which an actual thesis assumes through a special mode of meaning; sometimes it refers to the peculiar property which the meaning in question has of hiding the wealth of motives on which the thesis can be based in accordance with reason.[34]

Assertoric and Apodictic Self-evidence

The pairs of examples used above also illustrate two other essential differences. What we ordinarily call 'self-evidence' and 'insight' is a positional doxic and adequate dator consciousness which excludes that the state of affairs could be different; the thesis is motivated in a very exceptional fashion through the adequacy of the given material, and is in the highest sense an act of reason. The above mentioned arithmetical example of $1 + 2 = 2 + 1$ may serve to illustrate this point through comparison with the example of a landscape. In the case of the landscape there is a seeing, but no experience of self-evidence, in the ordinary meaningful sense of the term, as a 'seeing into'. When the two examples are studied more closely, we are struck by a twofold difference. In the arithmetical example we are dealing with the *essence,* but in the other with this *individual;* secondly, in the eidetic example the primordial giveness is *adequate,* but in the example from the sphere of experience it is *inadequate.* Both differences are of importance with respect to the type of evidential vision involved.

Regarding the first difference, on phenomenological grounds we may say that the *'assertoric seeing'* of an individual, e.g., the awareness of this concrete thing or this individual state of affairs, is in its rational character essentially distinct from 'apodictic seeing', from 'seeing into' an essence or essential relationship. 'Assertoric seeing' is distinct also from the modification of the 'apodictic seeing into' which may occur through the mixing of the essential and the individual. Such a mixing happens when an insight is applied to something assertorically seen, or more generally, when we know that a posited particular being must of necessity be such and such.

Evidential vision and insight, understood in the ordinary meaningful sense, are, as mentioned, taken here to mean the same, namely

34. Edmund Husserl, *Ideen I,* pp. 333-336 (350-353).

'apodictic seeing into'. We propose now to separate the two terms, because we need a more general term, which should include both 'assertoric seeing' and 'apodictic seeing into'. It is an important phenomenological discovery that these two belong to the same genus and that, understood in a still more general way, rational consciousness in general indicates a supreme genus of thetic modalites. Within this supreme genus the acts of 'seeing,' taken in its widest sense and in reference to primordial givenness, constitute a well-defined class.

In giving a name to the supreme genus, one has the choice of extending either the meaning of the term 'seeing', or the meaning of the terms 'seeing into' and 'evidential vision.' It would be most suitable to select the term 'evidential vision' in reference to the most general concept. In that case the expression 'primordial evidential vision' could be used to indicate every rational thesis whose motivation is based on the primordial character of what is primordially given. We should then have to make a further decision between the assertoric and apodictic forms of evidential vision, and reserve the term 'insight' to designate this apodictic character. Proceeding still farther, we could oppose pure insight and impure insight, including in the latter the cognition of the neccessity affecting an element of fact, whose existence does not need to be self evident. Likewise, in a very general way, we could oppose pure and impure evidential vision.[35]

It is interesting to see how Husserl later defined assertoric and apodictic evidence. In the *Cartesian Meditations*[36] he determines this difference as follows.

Although the idea of 'perfect evidence' through harmonizing experiences constantly guides the scientist in his work, he attributes a higher dignity to a different kind of evidence as regards its perfection. The most perfect kind of evidence is 'apodictic' evidence, which can occur even in the realm of inadequate evidences. Apodicticity is absolute indubitability in a very special sense, it is the absolute indubitability that the scientist must demand of all his 'principles'. Its superior value manifests itself when, with respect to groundings that are already evident in and by themselves, he attempts to find further grounds for them at a higher

---

35. *Ibid.*, pp. 336-338 (353-354).
36 Edmund Husserl, *Cart. Med.*, pp. 55-57 (14-16).

level by going back to principles in order to give them the highest possible value. Analyzing this procedure, it becomes clear that apodicticity must be characterized in the following way.

Any evidence is the grasping of something in the mode of 'it itself' with complete certainty of its being such and such, a certainty therefore that excludes every reasonable doubt. However, it does not follow that complete certainty eliminates that what now is evident could conceivably later become doubtful or that its being such and such could conceivably prove to be an illusion. As a matter of fact sense experience furnishes us with actual examples in which this happens. Moreover, this possibility of becoming doubtful, or of not being such and such, which remains despite evidence, can always be recognized beforehand by critically reflecting on what the evidence in question shows us.

An *apodictic evidence,* however, is not merely certainty of the state of affairs, but in critical reflection manifests itself endowed with the remarkable characteristic that the non-being of the state of affairs in question is absolutely unimaginable and inconceivable. It eliminates every doubt in advance. Moreover, the evidence of that critical reflection likewise has the character of apodicticity. And the inconceivable character of the opposite of what presents itself as apodictically evident is apodictically evident also. The same applies to every critical reflection on a higher level. Be this as it may, in case of an *assertoric evidence* the non-being of the state of affairs in question is, at least in principle, always imaginable and conceivable.[37]

Adequate and Inadequate Self-evidence

The second of the two differences, as we have noted, is that between adequate and inadequate self-evidence. This distinction is closely connected with that between adequate and inadequate givenness. Its discussion will give us also an opportunity to describe a remarkable type of 'impure' evidential vision. In inadequate self-evidence the positing act grounded on the bodily appearance of the 'thing itself' is indeed rational, but the appearance is never more than a one-sided 'imperfect' appearance. We are conscious not only of the object as appearing in bodily form, but also of the *thing itself* unqualifiedly, of the whole in its col-

---

37. *Ibid.,* p. 56 (15-16).

lective meaning, even though this meaning is only one-sidedly intuited and still undetermined in various respects. Of course, that which appears must not be divorced from the 'thing' as though it were something separately existing. The correlate of meaning of that which appears constitutes a dependent part within the full meaning of the 'thing', and this part has unity of meaning and independence only within a whole in which there are necessarily empty and indeterminate component parts.

In principle, a thing in the real world can appear only 'inadequately' within the finite limits of appearance. Essentially connected with this inadequacy is the fact that no rational positing which is based on an appearance presenting itself so inadequately, can be 'definitive'. Such a particular positing is not equivalent to the plain statement 'The thing is real', but only to the assertion 'It is real unless further experience adduces stronger rational motives and shows that the original positing is hereafter to be cancelled'. Moreover, the positing is rationally motivated only by the appearance, i.e., the imperfectly fulfilled perceptual meaning, in and for itself, considered in its particular detail.

The sphere of beings which can in principle be only inadequately given is the sphere of 'transcendents' in the sense of realities 'outside' consciousness. Phenomenology of reason has to study the various occurrences within this sphere that have been predelineated in advance. It has to show how the inadequate consciousness of being-given, the partial appearing is related to one and the same determinable X throughout the endless stream of new appearances which are constantly merging into one another. It has also to indicate the essential possibilities which present themselves here.

The first of these possibilities is a series of experiences which are constantly motivated along rational lines through the rational positings that are continuously at our disposal. Experience in this case runs a course in which the empty 'places' of preceding appearances are filled again and the interdeterminacies become more closely determined. It thus constantly advances toward a thoroughly harmonious 'filling' of the original meanings, and this fulfillment is accompanied by an increasing intelligibility. Secondly, there are also opposite possibilities: cases of fusions or polythetic syntheses in which there is disagreement or a different determination of that X which we are constantly aware of as one and the same—different in the sense of being out of harmony with the original bestowal of meaning.

Every region and category of objects has phenomenologically not only a corresponding basic kind of meaning or position, but also a fundamental type of primordial dator consciousness of this meaning. There is also a corresponding fundamental kind of primordial self-evidence, which is essentially motivated by a primordial givenness in conformity with the above-mentioned basic divisions.

But at any rate, every such self-evidence in the broad sense we have given to it is either *adequate* or *inadequate*. If it is adequate, it is in principle incapable of being made either stronger or weaker; in other words it is without graded differences of weight. If it is *inadequate,* it is capable of increase or decrease. Whether in any given context either adequate or inadequate self-evidence is possible depends on the generic type of this context and therefore is fixed *a priori.* Hence it would be simply absurd to demand that the perfection which self-evidence has in one context, e.g., that of essential relationships, be present also in other contexts which essentially exclude it.

We must add another remark here. The original meaning of the concepts 'adequate' and 'inadequate' refers to the modes of presentation. We were forced to transfer this meaning to the essential features of the rational positings themselves that are grounded on these modes. And we were able to do so because the two are essentially connected. This transference results of course in a slight but inevitable equivocation. Fortunately such an equivocation is without danger as soon as one recognizes the equivocation as such, and thus can make a clear distinction between the derived and the original meaning.[38]

Husserl makes still other distinctions and analyzes also other examples. However, the preceding pages should suffice for a general understanding of this aspect of his phenomonological philosophy itself as such, which is all that is intended here. Moreover, we will have to return to his theory of evidence in the following chapters. There we hope to find an opportunity to delve deeper into some of the problems mentioned in the foregoing.

---

38. Edmund Husserl, *Ideen I,* pp. 338-341 (354-357).

CHAPTER FIVE

PHENOMENOLOGICAL REDUCTION

1. *Necessity of a Phenomenological Reduction*

The Term 'Reduction' in Husserl's Philosophy

In the preceding chapters we have repeatedly met the terms 'reduction' and *'epoche'*. In Husserl's writings these terms can have a variety of meanings and for this reason he adds to the term 'reduction' different qualifiers such as 'philosophical', 'psychological', 'eidetic', 'phenomenological', and 'transcendental'. Although it is our intention to limit ourselves in this chapter to the phenomenological reduction in the strict sense, which Husserl in his later works usually calls 'transcendental' or 'transcendental-phenomenological' reduction, we will first briefly indicate the meaning of the other reductive procedures.

In general, reduction or *epoche* means that philosophical procedure through which we return to the origins of our knowledge of which our everyday thinking has mostly lost sight. The reduction which Husserl calls 'philosophical *epoche*' has to lead us to a philosophical attitude which in one way or another is perhaps, at least implicitly, admitted by every philosopher. This *epoche* demands that the philosopher place himself at a distance with respect to the solutions which in the course of history have been proposed for the different philosophical problems. Undoubtedly, in every philosophy there is a historical element; nevertheless, philosophy requires primarily my personal insight. That is why I must at first adopt a neutral position with respect to the solutions of the problems in question. In developing my philosophical insights, I may not argue academically from a philosophical standpoint that is fixed in advance. I cannot base my personal insights on traditional, or even generally recognized, philosophical theories, but I must try to base them on an immediate intuition. I must take the original phenomena exactly as they present themselves, without adding any hypotheses or interpretations and without reading into them anything suggested by ancient or modern theories. Only positions taken up in such a way can be real principles and real 'beginnings'. When they are so general that they cover the all-embracing regions of Being, they are certainly fundamental in a philosophical sense and belong themselves to philosophy. I must try not to presuppose anything, whether a science or a philosophy. The philosophic *epochē*, which Husserl wants us to perform, should consist, when explicitly formulated, in this, that regarding the theoretical content of all previous philosophies, we shall abstain from making any judgment at all, and that our whole discussion shall respect the limits imposed by this abstention up to its very end.[1]

The *eidetic reduction* drops all references to the particular and individual in the immediately given phenomena because, unlike the natural sciences, philosophy necessarily is a science of essences. In his earlier works Husserl calls this method 'ideating abstraction' and in his later works he often speaks of 'the method of free variation', as we have already seen in Chapter Four.

What is meant by the *psychological reduction* may be clarified in the following way. As we have seen, about 1903 Husserl came to the conclusion that there is an essential difference between his phenomenological philosophy and descriptive psychology. At first, it was not easy for him to determine the function of psychology within the framework of his changing conception of phenomenology. Gradually, however, he realized that descriptive psychology is distinct not only from pure phenomenology but also from traditional empirical psychology. For Husserl, empirical psychology is the study of physical entities in all their aspects as parts of the psycho-physical organism. Phenomenological or descriptive psychology, on the other hand, studies the fundamental types of psychological phenomena. It deals only with psychical entities and events as 'unities of meaning', as they appear to us in our intentional acts. It is interested only in the essences of these physical activities and realities, and describes them in intentional analyses. A necessary presupposition of such a study is, first, the eidetic reduction from facts to essences, and then a reduction from 'objective' things to 'unities of meaning', given in my own subjectivity as a real psychological entity in the world. It is this last reduction which Husserl sometimes calls 'psychological reduction'.[2]

---

1. Edmund Husserl, *Ideen I*, pp. 40-41 (72-73).
2. Edmund Husserl, *Phänom. Psychol.*, pp. 187-192, 217-222, 281-284, 292-295, 312-315, 335-344. *Cart. Med.*, p. 107 (72-73).

PHENOMENOLOGICAL REDUCTION

Preliminary Description of the Phenomenological Reduction

As we have mentioned several times, according to Husserl, we must make a radical distinction between philosophical and non-philosophical sciences. One of the most characteristic features of the non-philosophical sciences is the fact that they deliberately put aside all skepticism and every kind of critique of knowledge, in order to describe and explain only the facts themselves as accurately and objectively as possible exactly as they immediately manifest themselves to us. Philosophy, however, neither wants to nor may presuppose anything whatsoever, and therefore is obliged to pursue critical inquiries into the very possibility of human knowledge and science.[3]

Thus, on one side, we have the sciences of the dogmatic attitude, which are oriented to the things themselves and are not concerned with skeptical and epistemological problems. These sciences simply take their starting point from things and ultimately return also to the things as they are given in primordial experience. They examine things precisely inasfar as they immediately manifest themselves to man in order to draw from them every possible immediate or mediate conclusion. On the other side, we have the sciences of the epistemological and specifically philosophical attitude. They explicitly want to consider all the skeptical problems concerning the possibility of our knowledge and of science. They begin by trying to solve these problems in principle and in general in order to be able to draw from these general insights conclusions which authorize us to attach a definite sense and value to the dogmatic sciences and their results.[4]

We have mentioned also that, according to Husserl, a fully convincing epistemology does not yet exist. If we really want to realize the fundamental intention of philosophy, an intention, moreover, that defines its very essence, we must try to find a radically founded answer to the critical and epistemological problems. In order to find such an answer, we must necessarily disregard the results of the dogmatic sciences and even abandon the natural attitude in general. According to the 'principle of all principles' we can adhere only to what manifests itself to us

---

3. Edmund Husserl, *Die Idee*, pp. 17-26 (13-21).
4. Edmund Husserl, *Ideen I*, pp. 54-57 (86-88).

in apodictic evidence; only apodictically evident insights can constitute the starting point and the real beginnings of our philosophical investigations. Thus philosophy is impossible without applying the reduction to every datum and insight that is not yet apodictically evident.[5] The question, however, is: How are we to make such a reduction?

Before we can answer that question we must first try to describe as briefly and as accurately as possible what precisely are the basic convictions of the natural attitude and the dogmatic sciences. Only then will we be able to explain the real meaning and nature of the 'phenomenological reduction'.

The Dogmatic Natural Attitude. Possibility of the Epochē

According to Husserl, man generally and ordinarily lives in the natural attitude. Since we have already explained in detail what is meant by this attitude we need only to summarize here its essential elements. With Husserl, we came to the conclusion that, in the natural attitude, I find continually present and 'standing over against me' the one spatio-temporal fact-world to which I myself belong, as well as all other men who are in this world and related to it in the same way as I. This fact-world I find to be 'out there', and I take it exactly as it gives itself to me as something existing out there. To doubt or to reject the data of the natural world does not destroy the general thesis of the natural standpoint itself. 'The' world is a fact-world that is always there. At most this world is here or there 'other' than I supposed it to be; this or that particular point may be an illusion or a hallucination and, therefore, must be deleted from it. But the 'it' itself always remains, in the sense of the general thesis, a world that has its Being 'out there'. The goal pursued by the sciences of the natural standpoint is to know this world more comprehensively, more perfectly than is possible through naïve explanations; they want to solve all the problems of scientific knowledge which offer themselves from the standpoint of the natural attitude.[6]

---

5. Edmund Husserl, *Cart. Med.,* pp. 48-61 (passim), (7-21). See for the following as a whole also Chapter I of this book.

6. Edmund Husserl, *Ideen I,* pp. 57-63 (91-96).

Instead of persevering in this natural attitude, Husserl says, we want to alter it now radically. First, however, we must convince ourselves that such an alteration is possible in principle. According to the general thesis of the natural standpoint the real world around us is at all times known, not merely in general as something apprehended, but as a fact-world that has its Being 'out there.' This thesis, however, does not consist in an explicit existential judgment. It is and remains implicit during the entire time this standpoint is adopted; that is to say, it perdures so long as our life runs its course of natural endeavor. What has been perceived at any time has in its totality and in all its distinct aspects the character of 'being present out there'. This character can function essentially as the basis of an explicit or predicative existential judgment that is in agreement with the character upon which it is founded. If we express the judgment in question, we know very well that we simply put into the form of a statement and express via a predication something that was already contained somehow in the original experience.

The unexpressed thesis can be treated in exactly the same way as the thesis of the explicit judgment. A procedure of this kind that can be followed at any time is, for instance, Descartes' attempt to doubt everything. However, Husserl remarks, let us add at once that Descartes had an entirely different aim in mind and that the reduction is something completely different from the Cartesian doubt. Nevertheless, methodologically it has its advantages to compare the reduction with Descartes' doubt. The attempt to doubt everything is part of man's freedom at any moment. We can attempt to doubt everything, no matter how convinced we are of that which we doubt, even if the evidence which gives us certainty is wholly adequate.

Husserl invites us now to consider the essential implications of such an act. One who attempts to doubt, he points out, tries to doubt some form or other of Being. This attempt does not affect the form of Being itself. One who doubts whether an object, whose Being he does not doubt, is constituted in this or that way, doubts only about the way it is constituted. It is clear, however, that we cannot both doubt the Being of anything and, at the same time and in the same act of consciousness, bring what is contained in this Being under the terms of the natural thesis, thereby conferring upon it the character of 'being actually there'. In other words, Husserl claims, we cannot at the same time both doubt and hold for certain one and the same quality of Being.

It is likewise evident that the attempt to doubt any object of consciousness with respect to its actually being there necessarily implies a certain suspension of the natural thesis. This is precisely what interests us here. In phenomenology the suspension is not a transformation of the thesis into its antithesis, and neither is it a transformation of the thesis into a presumption, indecision, or doubt. Rather is it something wholly unique, Husserl claims. For we do not relinquish the thesis we have adopted; we do not modify our conviction, but it remains unchanged in itself so long as we do not introduce new motives of judgment; and this is precisely what we abstain from doing here. Nevertheless, the thesis undergoes a modification; while remaining unchanged in itself, we put it, as it were, out of action, we disconnect it, we 'bracket' it. It still remains there 'between brackets', as Husserl puts it. Differently expressed, the thesis is a 'lived' experience, but we make no use of it; and by that, of course, we do not mean that kind of non-use resulting from ignorance of the thesis. As in all similar expressions, we are dealing here with signs pointing to a definite but unique form of consciousness, which joins the original simple thesis, whether or not this thesis actually or even predicatively posits existence and changes its value in a very special way. This changing of value is an affair of our full freedom; it is the opposite of any cognitive attitude that would have a bearing on the thesis but would be incompatible with it.

If the attempt to *doubt* is applied to a thesis which, as we assume now, is certain and expressly adhered to, the 'disconnection' takes place in and through a modification of its antithesis; we suppose the non-being of the thesis, so that this antithesis becomes the partial basis of the attempt to doubt. In Descartes' case this is so evident that his universal attempt to doubt is precisely an attempted universal denial. However, Husserl points out, we may disregard this possibility here, for we are interested only in the phenomenon of 'bracketing' or 'disconnecting'. Although this phenomenon can very easily be detached from the attempt to doubt, it obviously can appear in other contexts also, and even independently. The peculiar *epochē* can be used in relation to every thesis. As Husserl sees it, it is a certain refraining from judgment which is compatible with the *undoubted* and *indubitable* conviction based on self-evidence. The thesis is merely 'put out of action', 'bracketed'; it receives the modified status of being a 'bracketed thesis', and the judgment in which it is founded simply becomes a 'bracketed judgment'.

Let us add here, Husserl concludes, that nothing prevents us from speaking of 'bracketing' with respect to an object which is to be posited, regardless of the region or category of Being to which it belongs. 'Bracketing', then, means that every thesis related to this object must be disconnected, changed into a 'bracketed' thesis. Finally, the term 'bracketing' is more suitable for the sphere of objects, and the expression 'to put out of action' better fits the sphere of acts of consciousness.[7]

The Phenomenological Epochē

Husserl goes on to say now that the universal *epochē*, taken in the sharply defined new sense he has given to it, could replace the Cartesian attempt to doubt everything. However, there are good reasons for limiting the universality of the *epochē*, Husserl says. For if we leave it as inclusive as it is, there would be no room left for unmodified judgments. For *every* thesis and *every* judgment can be freely modified to any extent, and every object that we can judge can be placed between brackets. But our design was precisely to discover a new scientific domain through the method of bracketing, and it is for this reason that its universality is to be limited.

Husserl is of the opinion that the following limitation is to be made. We 'put out of action' the general thesis which is characteristic of the natural standpoint; we 'bracket' whatever it contains concerning the nature of Being. The entire natural world, therefore, which is continually 'there for me' and will ever remain there, is a fact-world of which I remain conscious, even though I decide to put it 'between brackets'.

By doing so in absolute freedom, Husserl continues, I do *not deny* this world, as though I were a sophist; I do *not doubt* that it is there,

---

7. *Ibid.*, pp. 63-66 (96-99).

as though I were a skeptic; but I use the 'phenomenological *epochē*', which completely bars me from making use of any judgment that concerns spatio-temporal being as 'being out there'.

Accordingly I disconnect all sciences concerning this natural world, even though they stand before me on as firm a foundation as ever; I even continue to greatly admire them. I merely make no use whatsoever of their principles and laws and do not make my own any of their propositions. None of their evident propositions serves me as a foundation—so long as any of them is understood as these sciences themselves understand it, as a truth concerning the realities of the world. I accept it only after I have 'bracketed' it; I accept it only in the modified consciousness I have of the judgment as disconnected and not in the role it plays within the science in question as a proposition which claims to be valid and whose validity I recognize and utilize.

This *epochē* or reduction should not be confused with the one demanded by positivism but which positivism itself does not always respect. We are not concerned here with removing the prejudices which endanger the positive character of our research. Our aim is not to constitute a science free from theory and from metaphysics by reducing all its foundations to immediate data, or to find the means to reach this aim. While we do not question the value of such undertakings, our demand goes in a different direction. The whole world as placed within the framework of nature and presented as real in experience, taken absolutely free from all theory, exactly as it is experienced in reality, and as it is made manifest in and through our chains of experiences, is no longer valid for us; it must be 'bracketed' as untested but also as uncontested. Likewise, all theories and sciences, positivistic or non-positivistic, which are concerned with this world, no matter how good they may be, are subjected to the same reduction.[8]

The Phenomenological Residuum

Although the preceding considerations show us the meaning of the phenomenological reduction, we still do not know how serviceable this

---

8. *Ibid.*, pp. 67-69 (99-100).

reduction may be. For what can possibly remain when the whole world is 'bracketed', including ourselves and our own thinking? Knowing that Husserl is interested in a new eidetic science, one would be inclined to reply that the world as fact is disconnected, but not the world as 'eidos', nor any other sphere of essential being. As a matter of fact, such a disconnection of the world does not mean that, e.g., the number series and the arithmetic relative to it are disconnected.

Husserl, however, does not aim in this direction. His goal is to penetrate into a new region of Being, whose distinctive character has not yet been defined, a region of *individual* Being, as is every genuine region. What exactly this region is will have to be determined more accurately at a later time. Now we want only to briefly indicate this region.

We proceed, in the first instance, by disclosing simply and directly what we see. And because the being to be disclosed in this way is none other than that which we refer to on essential grounds as 'pure experience', 'pure consciousness' with its pure correlates of consciousness, on the one hand, and its pure ego, on the other, it follows that we must start with the ego, consciousness and experience as given to us from the natural standpoint.

I, a real human being, am a real object like others in the natural world. I perform cogitations, acts of consciousness, and these acts, as belonging to this human subject, are events of the same natural world. The same holds true of the entire changing stream of my other experiences. The specific acts of the ego shine forth distinctly in this stream; they merge into one another, enter into combinations, and constantly undergo modifications.

Two points are to be noted here. First, in its widest sense, the term 'consciousness' includes *all* experiences. Secondly, even in our scientific thinking we are locked up in the natural attitude; we are grounded in habits that are firmly established since they have never seemed to mislead us. For these reasons we consider all these data of psychological reflection to be real world events, experiences of 'animal' beings. It is so natural to see them only in this light that although we are familiar with the possibility of changing our standpoint and are in search of a new domain of objects, we failed to notice that the new domain emerges from these very centers of experience through the adoption of the new standpoint. Moreover, instead of keeping our eyes turned toward these centers of experience, we turned them away and sought the new objects in the ontological realms of arithmetic, geometry, and the like. But in these realms nothing truly new could be gained.

Thus, we must keep our eyes on the sphere of consciousness and study what we find immanent in it. At first, before we have carried out the phenomenological reduction in the strict sense, we must subject the very essence of this sphere of consciousness to a systematic analysis which, however, need not be exhaustive. What we lack most of all is a kind of general insight into the essence of consciousness in general, and more especially into the essence of consciousness insofar as in and through its essential being, the natural fact-world becomes known. In these studies we must try to arrive at the full insight which we want—namely, that consciousness in itself has a being of its own which is absolutely unique because it remains unaffected by the phenomenological reduction. Consciousness, therefore, remains as a 'phenomenological residuum', as a region of Being which is, in principle, unique and can become the domain of a new science: phenomenology.

Only through this insight will the phenomenological *epochē* deserve its name; it is the operation required to make accessible to us pure consciousness and subsequently the whole penomenological region. In this way we will be able to understand why this region and the corresponding new science were destined to remain unnoticed for such a long time. From the natural viewpoint nothing can be seen save the natural world. So long as the possibility of the phenomenological attitude was not understood, and the method of referring the objectivities emerging in that sphere to a primordial form of apprehension had not been seen, the phenomenological world had to remain unknown.

Important epistemological reasons justify us in calling pure consciousness a 'transcendental consciousness', and the operation through which it is acquired 'transcendental reduction'. As we will see, this reduction involves several successive steps in the process of disconnecting and 'bracketing'; hence the method will assume the character of a gradual reduction whose different phases however constitute a unity.

Be this as it may, in this way it should become clear what is still left when our phenomenological *epochē* has bracketed the universe, which normally is understood as the totality of Being. The reduction opens to us the absolute region of Being, the region of absolute and transcendental subjectivity in which the totality of Being, the whole universe, is 'contained' in a special way, as we will see. First, however, we must make a brief systematic analysis of the essence of the sphere of consciousness.[9]

2. *Consciousness and Reality*

The Essence of Consciousness. Intentionality

Husserl begins his investigation concerning the relation between consciousness and reality by saying that he wants to make a series of remarks in which we do not have to trouble ourselves about the phenomenological reduction. We are directed to an external world, he says, and without abandoning the natural standpoint, we can reflect psychologically upon our ego and its experiences. Exactly as if we had never heard of the phenomenological reduction, we can devote our attention to the essential nature of 'this consciousness-of-something.' We retain only the general principle that every individual event has an essence which can be grasped in its eidetic purity and, in this purity, must belong to a field that is open to eidetic inquiry. In accordance with this principle, the universal fact of nature, conveyed by expressions such as 'I am,' 'I think', 'I am conscious of', 'I have a world standing over against me,' has an essential content, and it is to this content alone that we now want to pay attention. We want to grasp and to fix in adequate ideation the pure essences of the situations in question.

Restricting the topic of our inquiry even further, Husserl continues, we limit it to consciousness, to our conscious experiences in general. As

9. *Ibid.*, pp. 69-74 (101-103).

our starting point we take consciousness in a pregnant sense that suggests itself spontaneously and is most simply expressed in the Cartesian *cogito*. This *cogito* includes every case of 'I perceive,' 'I remember,' 'I fancy,' 'I judge,' 'I feel,' 'I desire,' 'I will,' and all other similar experiences of the ego. This ego itself, however, we leave out of consideration here, for we will be concerned with it later.

We want to consider conscious experiences in the entire fullness of concretion with which they figure for every ego in the totality of the concrete context (the stream of experiences) and to which they are closely attached by their own essences. Considered in this fashion, every experience in the stream, which our reflection can grasp, evidently has an essence of its own which is open to intuition, it has a content that can be considered in its singularity in and for itself. We will attempt to grasp this individual content of the cogitation in its pure singularity, and describe its general features, while excluding everything which cannot be found in the cogitation as it is in itself. We must describe also the unity of consciousness which is required by the intrinsic nature of the cogitations, and in such a way that they could not be without this unity.

Let us begin with an example. Before me lies this piece of white paper. I see it, touch it. The perceptual seeing and touching of the paper, as the full concrete experience of the paper that lies here and now as truly given precisely with these particular qualities, is a cogitation, a conscious experience. The paper itself, however, with its objective qualities, its spatial extension, its objective location in reference to that spatial thing which I call 'my body', is not a cogitation, but a *cogitatum;* it is not a perceptual experience, but something perceived.

Before pursuing this point farther, let us broaden the illustration. In perception, taken in the strict sense as an explicit awareness, I am turned toward the object, the paper, and I apprehend it as being this here and now. This apprehension is a singling out, for every perceived object has a background in experience. Around the paper lie books, pencils, and other things. In a certain sense these are also 'perceived'; they are perceptually there in the field of intuition. But while I was turned toward the paper, I did not focus attention on them; I did not apprehend

144

them, not even in a secondary sense. They appeared but were not singled out.

Every perception of a thing has such a zone of background awarenesses (referring to the *outer horizon*), and taken together these also are a conscious experience, or more briefly a 'consciousness of'. What we are saying here applies to that zone of consciousness solely which belongs to the essence of a perception as being-turned-toward an object and further to whatever belongs to the proper essence of this zone. It is, however, implied here that certain modifications of the original experience are possible. We refer to these possibilities as a free turning of our gaze from the paper that was first perceived to objects which had already appeared before, of which we had been implicitly aware and of which, now that we have directed our gaze to them, we are explicitly aware, perceiving them 'attentively'.

What we have stated here concerning perceptual experiences obviously applies also to all other experiences, essentially different though they be, such as recollection, representation, etc. It is obviously true also of all such experiences that their focal point is surrounded by a marginal zone, because the stream of experiences can never wholly consist of focal actualities. All such experiences essentially reveal also that remarkable modification which transfers consciousness from the mode of actual orientation to the mode of non-actuality, and vice versa.

A general feature belonging to the essence of every actual *cogito* is that it is a consciousness *of* something. But according to the preceding remarks, the modified cogitation is likewise and in its own way consciousness and consciousness of the same something as the corresponding unmodified consciousness. The essential property of consciousness in its general form, therefore, is preserved in its modifications. All experiences which have this essential property in common may be called '*intentional experiences*', or acts in a very wide sense of this term. Insofar as these experiences are consciousness of something, they are 'intentionally related' to this something.

Let us emphasize, however, that there is no question here of a relationship between the psychological event called 'experience' and some other real being called 'object'. There is likewise no question here of a psychological connection between these two in 'objective reality.' On the contrary, we are concerned with experiences in their essential purity, with pure essences, and with that which is implied in the essences *a priori* with absolute necessity.

The statement that an experience is the consciousness of something does not refer to the experiential fact as 'lived' within the world or within a given psychological context, but to the pure essence of experience grasped ideationally as pure idea. The very essence of an experience includes not only *that* it is a consciousness of, but also that of which it is a consciousness, and in what determinate or indeterminate sense it is this consciousness.[10]

Immanent and Transcendant Perceptions

Husserl points out next that, although at this point he will not continue the descriptive analysis of intentional experiences in their essential nature, attention must be drawn to certain aspects that have a bearing on further developments. He states that if an intentional experience is carried out in the manner of an actual *cogito*, the subject directs itself within this experience toward the intentional object. To the cogitation itself belongs an immanent 'glancing-toward' the object, a directedness which originates from the ego and can never be absent. This glancing of the ego toward something harmonizes with the particular act involved; it is perceptive in perception, fanciful in fancy, and volitional in the act of willing. Consequently, this 'having in one's glance,' which belongs to the essence of the cogitation, to the act as such, is not in itself again a proper act. In particular it should not be confused with perceiving, fancying, or other types of acts related to perceptions. It is to be noted here also that the intentional object of a consciousness should not at all be identified with the apprehended object and the act of apprehending should not be identified with the mode of the *cogito* in general, but with a special mode of act, capable of being assumed by every consciousness or every act that does not yet possess it. If consciousness assumes this mode, its intentional object is

---

10. *Ibid.*, pp. 74-81 (103-109), passim.

not known merely in a general way and brought within the directed glance of the mind, but it is an apprehended or perceived object.[11]

To these considerations we must now add the following. Living in the *cogito,* we do not have the cogitation itself consciously before us as an intentional object; but it can at any time become such an object. To the essence of the *cogito* belongs, in principle, the possibility of reflexively directing the mental glance toward itself, in the form, of course, of a new cogitation and by way of a simple apprehension. In other words, every cogitation can become the object of a so-called 'inner perception,' and eventually the object of a reflexive valuation. The same applies in correspondingly modified ways, not only to real acts, in the sense of acts of perception, but also to acts of which we are aware in fancy, in memory, or in empathy. We can reflect 'in' memory, empathy, etc., and in these various possible modifications make the acts of which we are aware into objects of acts of apprehending and of the acts which are founded upon this apprehension.

With these remarks, Husserl says, we may connect the distinction between *transcendent* and *immanent* perceptions and acts in general. By 'immanently directed acts' we mean those acts which are essentially constituted in such a way that their intentional objects, if they exist at all, belong to the same stream of experience as these acts themselves. An example of immanent perception is found wherever one act is related to another act of the same ego. Intentional experiences which do not have this relationship, are 'transcendently directed'; for instance, all acts directed toward essences or toward intentional experiences of other ego's.

In the case of an immanently directed, or more briefly, an immanent perception, the perception and the perceived essentially constitute an immediate unity, viz., the unity of a single concrete cogitation. The perceiving act conceals its object here in itself in such a way that it can be separated from it only by means of abstraction, and only as something that is essentially incapable of subsisting alone. If the perceived is an intentional experience, e.g., when we reflect upon a conviction that is still alive in us, two intentional experiences are connected; at

---

11. *Ibid.,* pp. 81-82 (109-110).

least the second of these is dependent and, moreover, not merely founded upon the first experience but, at the same time, intentionally directed toward it.

This type of 'real' self-containedness is a distinctive characteristic of immanent perception and of the mental attitudes based upon it; it is absent from most of the other cases of immanent relationship between intentional experiences, such as, for instance, the remembering of remembering.

Transcendent perceptions and the other transcendently related intentional experiences are clearly related in a very different way. The perception of a thing not only does not contain in itself the thing itself, but is also without any essential unity with the thing, assuming of course that this thing does exist. A unity that is determined solely by the proper essence of the experiences themselves can be none other than the unity of the stream of experiences. Differently expressed, it is only with experiences that an experience can be united into a single whole whose essence in its totality encompasses the essences of those experiences and is based upon them.[12]

Consciousness and Natural Reality

The essential characteristics of experience and consciousness which we have been able to lay bare are stepping stones toward the goal we want to attain, viz., the discovery of the essence of that pure consciousness which is to determine the limits of the phenomenological field. Our inquiry into these characteristics was eidetic; but the individual examples of the essences we have referred to as experience, stream of experiences, or consciousness in its various senses, belong as real events to the natural world. To the extent that we used these examples, we have not abandoned the basis of the natural standpoint. Individual consciousness is interwoven with the natural world in a twofold way: 1) it is some *man's* consciousness, and 2) at least in many of its particularizations it is a consciousness of this world, says Husserl.

We must now ask the question: How can consciousness have an essence of its own, if it is so intimately connected with the real world?

---

12. *Ibid.,* pp. 84-86 (111-113).

To what extent must the material world be something fundamentally different and excluded from the experience's own essential nature? And, if consciousness really is 'alien' and 'other' with respect to the real world, how can it be interwoven with the whole world which is alien to it? For it is easy to convince oneself that the material world is the fundamental stratum to which all other real being is essentially related. The material world, however, clearly manifests that in it consciousness and thingness form a connected whole, for they are connected within the particular psychological unities which we call 'animals' and 'men', and ultimately within the real unity of the world as a whole. Can the unity of a whole be other than the unity effected through the essential natures proper to its parts, so that these parts must have some community of essence instead of being fundamentally heterogeneous?

Let us look for the ultimate sources giving rise to the general thesis of the world which I adopt when I assume the natural attitude and which enables me as a conscious being to discover 'over against me' a world of things, to ascribe to myself a body in this world, and to find a proper place for myself in it. This ultimate source is obviously sense experience; but for our purpose it is sufficient here to consider sense perception, for in a certain sense the latter plays among the acts of experience the role of an original experience. Every perceiving consciousness has the characteristic of being the consciousness of the 'bodily' self-presence of an individual object; hence, it is sufficient for us to consider the perception of an individual thing as representative of all other perceptions and experiences.

The natural wakeful life of the ego is a continuous perceiving, whether actual or potential. The world of things and our body within this world are continuously present to our perception. How then can consciousness itself separate the perceiving being as a concrete thing in itself from that within consciousness of which we are conscious, viz., the perceived being as standing 'over against consciousness' in and for itself? Yet it is this precisely that the phenomenological reduction tries to materialize.

Husserl says that in every naïve perception I see and grasp the thing itself in its authentic reality; the perceived thing is real and itself really given, given 'bodily' in perception. Here perceiving, considered simply as consciousness and apart from the body and the bodily organs, appears as something that in itself is essenceless, an empty look of an empty ego toward the object itself, which nevertheless immediately grasps it in an astonishing way.[13]

However, one who is not naïve but a man of science, who as such continues to remain in the natural attitude, may point to the familiar distinction between secondary and primary qualities, according to which secondary qualities are merely subjective, and only the geometrico-physical qualities objective. This distinction, however, disregards the fact that the primary qualities cannot be perceived apart from the secondary qualities. Thus, he would have to say that the whole essential content of the perceived thing, all that is present in the body, with all its qualities and everything that can ever be perceived, is 'mere appearance,' and that the 'true thing' is what physical science says of it. The 'true being,' therefore, would be entirely and fundamentally something that is defined differently from that which is given in perception as bodily reality. As strictly experienced, the thing gives merely an empty X, which becomes the bearer of mathematical determinations and of the corresponding mathematical formulae. It does not exist in perceptual space but in an 'objective space' of which perceptual space is a mere 'symbol,' a Euclidean manifold of three dimensions that can be represented only symbolically.

Let us accept this and let that which is given 'bodily' in any perception be a mere 'appearance,' merely subjective. The sensible content of that which is given in perception, thus, continues to be considered as other than the true thing as it is in itself, but the empty X, the substratum, of the perceived determinations continues to be viewed as that which is determined through an exact method in the form of physical predicates. All physical knowledge serves accordingly, and in the reverse sense, to indicate the course which experience can take with respect to the sensible things it meets and the events in which they figure. It helps us therefore to find our way in the world of actual experience in which we all live and act.[14]

---

13. *Ibid.*, pp. 87-89 (113-115).
14. *Ibid.*, pp. 89-91 (115-117).

PHENOMENOLOGICAL REDUCTION

Perception and Its Transcendent Object

All this being presupposed, we must ask the question: What pertains to the concrete real nature of the perception itself precisely as cogitation? Obviously it is not the physical thing; being radically transcendent it transcends also the whole world of appearances. But even the world of appearances, though we refer to it habitually as 'merely subjective,' does not belong in all the details of its things and events to the real content of perception, but is opposed to it as transcendent. Let us consider this more closely, for hitherto we have spoken only in a passing way of the transcendence of the thing. It is our task now to gain a more profound insight into the relation of the transcendent to the consciousness that knows it, and to see how this mutual relationship is to be understood, Husserl continues.

Let us leave aside the whole of physics and the entire domain of theoretical thought, and remain within the framework of simple intuition and the syntheses belonging to it, including perception. It is then evident, that intuition and the intuited, perception and the perceived thing, although they are essentially related to each other, are in principle and of necessity not really and essentially one.

Let us again start with an example. Keeping this table steadily in view while I circle it and change my position in space, I have continually the consciousness of the bodily presence 'out there' of this one and same table, which in itself remains unchanged throughout. But the perception of the table changes continually; it is a continuum of changing perceptions. Now I close my eyes. Since my other senses are inactive in reference to the table, I have now no perception of it. I open my eyes, and the perception returns. Can I say that the *perception* returns? Let us be more careful. Under no circumstances does it return to me as individually the same perception. Only the table is the same, and I know it as identical through my synthetic consciousness which connects my new perception with my recollection. The perceived thing can be without being perceived, without my being aware of it and perhaps without itself changing at all. But the perception itself is what it is only within the steady flow of consciousness; it is itself constantly in flux; the perceptual 'now' is constantly passing over into the following consciousness of the just-past and at the same time a new 'now' comes forth. The perceived thing in general, and all its parts, aspects, and phases, whether the qualities in question be primarily or secondary, are necessarily transcedent to the perception.

An experiencing consciousness of one and the same thing which looks all around its object, and thereby continually confirms the unity of its own nature, possesses essentially and necessarily a manifold system of continuous patterns of appearances and perspective variations. In and through these patterns and variations all objective phases of the 'bodily' self-given which appear in perception, manifest themselves perspectively in definite continua.

We now see also what really and indubitably belongs to the real content and nature of the concrete intentional experiences, referred to here as 'perceptions of things.' The thing is an intentional unity, i.e., that which we are conscious of as one and identical with iself in the continuously ordered flow of perceptual patterns as they merge into one another; and these patterns themselves always have their definite descriptive nature, which is essentially related with that intentional unity. To every phase of perception, for instance, there necessarily belongs a definite content in the way of perspective variations of color, shape, etc. These variations are counted among the sense data. These sense data are 'besouled' within the concrete unity of perception through 'apprehending' acts. But we must keep clearly in mind here that the sense data which exercise the function of presenting color and shape in perspectives differ wholly and in principle from color and shape *simpliciter;* they differ, in short, from all the generic aspects which a thing can show. The perspective variation, though expressed in the same terms as the 'perspected' thing, differs from it generically and in principle. The perspective variation is an experience, the 'perspected' thing is spatial.[15]

Being as Consciousness and Being as Reality

In Husserl's opinion the preceding considerations have shown that the thing transcends its perception. We can claim with an absolutely

---

15. *Ibid.,* pp. 91-95 (117-120).

unconditioned generality, he says, that a thing cannot be given as really immanent in any possible consciousness. Thus, a fundamental and essential difference arises between Being as experience and Being as thing. The regional essence 'experience' and more specifically the regional subclass 'cogitation' has in principle the property of being perceivable through immanent perception, but it is of the essence of a spatial thing that immanent perception is not possible. This inability to be perceived immanently and, therefore, generally, to find a place in the system of experiences belongs essentially and in principle to the thing as such; it belongs to every reality, in the genuine sense of this term. (This sense we still have to determine later.) Thus we say that the thing itself is transcendant, thereby expressing the most fundamental difference between two ways of Being, called 'consciousness' and 'reality'.

A fundamental difference in the mode of being-given accompanies this opposition between immanence and transcendence. Immanent and transcendent perceptions differ, of course, first of all because the intentional object contained in the character of the bodily self, is, in the one case, really immanent to the perceiving, but not so in the other. Secondly, and that is more important, they differ because of the mode of being-given; for we perceive the thing through the perspective manifestations of its determinate qualities which in any given case are real, whereas an experience itself does not have any perspectives.[16]

It would, however, be a fundamental error to suppose that perception does not reach the thing itself. The claim is sometimes made that the thing in itself and in its 'ipseity' is not given to us as such. This claim is absurd. It implies that there is no essential difference between transcendent and immanent. The idea that the transcendence of the thing is that of an image or sign has proved deceptive here. The image-theory is often vigorously attacked and replaced by a sign-theory. But both theories are not only incorrect but even absurd. In spite of its transcendence, the spatial thing which we see is perceived; we are consciously aware of it as given in its bodily form. We are not given an image or a sign in place of the spatial thing and therefore must not substitute consciousness of a sign or of an image for a perception.

---

16. *Ibid.*, pp. 95-98 (120-122).

In acts of immediate intuition we intuit an 'itself', says Husserl. In this case no apprehensions at a higher level are built upon the basis of these apprehending acts of intuition; nothing, then, is known for which the intuited could serve as a sign or an image. For this reason the intuited must be said to be immediately intuited as an 'itself'. What is intuited in perception is still uniquely characterized as 'bodily' in contrast to the modified character proper to Being 'presented to the mind' in memory or in the play of free fancy. The perception of a thing does not present something that is not present as if it were a recollection or a fancy; it presents and apprehends an 'itself' in its 'bodily' presence. It does this in accordance with the apprehended object's own meaning, and to suppose that it acts differently is precisely to go against its own sense. Moreover, when it is a question of the perception of *things,* then it is its essential nature to be a perception operating through perspectives.[17]

Husserl goes on to say that the perception of things is inadequate to a certain extent, and this inadequacy too is an essential necessity. In principle a thing can be given 'in one of its aspects' only, i.e., in this or that particular perspective only. A thing can be given merely in modes of appearing; the factors that are of necessity involved in its mode of appearing are: 1) a nucleus consisting of what is really and effectively presented; 2) a surrounding zone of apprehension consisting of marginal co-data of a non-proper kind; 3) a more or less vague indeterminacy. This indeterminacy necessarily refers to the determinability of a rigorously prescribed style. It points to possible patterns of perception, which, by continually merging into one another, fuse in the unity of a single perception. In this single perception the continuously perduring thing in constantly new series of perspectives continually reveals new aspects. Meanwhile, the marginal co-apprehended phases of the thing gradually come into the focus of real presentations as real data; the indeterminacies define themselves more clearly and finally become clear data themselves; and reversely, what is clear subsides into the unclear, and the presented into the non-presented. To remain forever incomplete in this fashion is an essential feature of the

---

17. *Ibid.,* pp. 98-100 (122-124).

correlation between the thing and its perception. If the meaning of a thing becomes determined through what is given in a new thing-perception (and what else could determine its meaning?), it must necessarily remain incomplete and refer us to unified and continuous series of possible perceptions. However, any one of these possible series unfolds into an endless number of directions in systematically ordered ways and unfolds endlessly in each direction. In principle there remains always a margin of determinable indeterminacy, no matter how far we proceed in the empirical way, and no matter how far the continua of actual perceptions of the same thing extend.

We may even say that Being in general, understood as Being for an ego, can be given only through appearances. For, otherwise, the transcendent would really be a being which could also become immanent, whereas what is immanently perceivable is merely immanently perceivable and nothing more. Let us explain this point more accurately.

Experience, we have said, does not present itself. This implies that the perception of an experience is plain insight into something which in perception is given *as absolute*, and not as an identity uniting modes of apperance through perspective continua. Everything we have stated concerning the givenness of things loses its meaning here. The experience of a feeling has no perspectives. If I look at it, I have an absolute before me; it has no aspects which might present themselves now in this way and then in that. For this reason, we must maintain the assertion: it is an essential characteristic of what is given through appearances that none of its appearances gives the matter in question in an absolute form but presents merely one side of it; on the other hand, it is an essential mark of what is immanently given to be given precisely as an absolute which simply cannot present aspects in varying perspectives.

But the following distinction is to be noted also. Even an experience is never perceived in its completeness; it cannot be grasped adequately in its full unity. It is essentially something that flows, and starting from the present moment in the stream of experience we can 'swim after it' by turning our gaze reflectively toward it, while the stretches we leave behind in our wake are lost to our perception. Only

155

in the form of retention or in that of retrospective remembering do we have any consciousness of what has immediately flowed past us. Ultimately, the whole stream of my experiences is a unity of experience with respect to which it is in principle impossible to obtain a complete perceptual grasp by 'swimming' with it. But this incompleteness which belongs to the essence of our perception of experience, differs fundamentally from the imperfection which is of the essence of 'transcendent' perception, i.e., perception by means of a presentation which varies perspectively through such a thing as appearance.[18]

The Indubitability of Immanent Perception.
The Dubitability of Transcendent Perception

As Husserl emphasizes, the consequences of these considerations are important. Any immanent perception immediately and necessarily guarantees the existence of its object. If reflective apprehension is directed to my experience, I apprehend an absolute 'self' whose existence is, in principle, undeniable. It would be absurd to maintain the possibility that an experience given in such a way does not truly exist. For every stream of experiences, and every ego as such, it is, in principle possible to secure this self-evidence: each one of us bears in himself the guarantee of his absolute existence as a fundamental possibility. It is conceivable that an ego might have only fancies in its stream of experiences; what floats before the mind may be mere fiction; yet the floating itself, the consciousness producing the fiction is not itself imagined, and the possibility of a perceiving reflection which apprehends absolute existence belongs to the essence of this consciousness as it does to every experience.

On the other hand, the thing-world, as we know, Husserl continues, has as its essential characteristic that no perception, no matter how perfect, gives us anything absolute within its domain. With this feature another is essentially connected, namely, that every experience, no matter how far it extends, leaves open the possibility that that which is given does not exist, in spite of the persistent consciousness of its 'bodily' self-presence. It is an essentially valid law that the existence

---

18. *Ibid., pp.* 100-103 (124-127).

of a thing is never imposed of necessity by virtue of its givenness, but in a way always remains contingent. It can always happen that further experience will compel us to abandon something that has already been affirmed and justified in the light of empirical rules.

In Husserl's opinion, it is accordingly clear that everything which is there for me in the world of things is, in principle, only a presumptive reality. I myself, on the contrary, for whom it is there, I myself (my experience in its actuality) am 'absolute reality', given through a positing that is unconditioned and simply indissoluble. In this way the thesis of my pure ego and its personal life, which is necessary and patently induitable, stands opposed to the thesis of the world which is contingent and subject to doubt.

Husserl continues by reminding us that these reflections also show that no proofs drawn from empirical considerations of the world can give absolute certainty concerning the world's existence. The world is not doubtful in the sense that there are rational grounds which could offset the enormous power of unanimous experiences; yet such a doubt is *conceivable*. The reason is that the possibility of its non-being is in principle never excluded. Therefore, the existence of the world is not *apodictically* evident.[19]

3. *Absolute Consciousness as Theme of Phenomenology*

The World as Correlate of Consciousness

Husserl is of the opinion that with this conclusion our study has reached its climax. However, he says, before drawing a final conclusion from it, we must first focus attention on the following consideration. When we mentally destroy the objectivity of things as a correlate of empirical consciousness, there is no limit beyond which we cannot go. We must always keep in mind that it is as things of experience that things are what they are. Experience alone determines their meaning, and when we are dealing with things based on facts, it is actual experience in its orderly empirical connections which determines their meaning. This assertion applies to every conceivable kind of transcendence

---

19. *Ibid.*, pp. 106-110 (130-132).

which might be treated as real or possible. An object that is in itself is never out of relation with consciousness and its ego. The same holds also for the whole world.

Let us now recall the *possibility* of non-being which, as we have seen, belongs essentially to every thing-like transcendence. It is then evident that the Being of consciousness, and in general of every stream of experiences would not be affected in its own existence by the nullification of the thing-world. For the nullification of the world means, correlatively, precisely that in every stream of the ego's experience certain ordered empirical connections would be excluded. But this exclusion does not imply that other experiences and the corresponding experiential systems are excluded. Thus, no real thing, nothing that consciously presents itself through appearances, is necessary for the Being of consciousness itself. Immanent Being is, therefore, indubitably absolute in the sense that in principle it does not need anything to exist. On the other hand, the world of transcendent things is related unqualifiedly to consciousness, consciousness evidently taken here as actual consciousness.

Thus consciousness, understood in its purity, must be considered to be a self-contained system of Being, a system of absolute Being. Nothing can penetrate into this system and nothing can escape from it; it has no spatio-temporal exterior and cannot be inside any spatio-temporal system; it can neither be affected causally by anything nor exert causality upon anything (causality being understood here in the normal sense of natural causality, as a relation of dependence between realities).

On the other hand, according to its own meaning, the whole spatio-temporal world to which man and the human ego claim to belong as individual realities, is merely an intentional being, i.e., a being which has the purely secondary or relative sense of a Being-for-a-consciousness. It is a Being which consciousness posits in its own experiences; and it is, in principle, intuitable and determinable only as the element common to the motivated manifolds of appearances, but beyond this it is nothing at all.[20]

---

20. *Ibid.*, pp. 110-117 (133-139), passim.

PHENOMENOLOGICAL REDUCTION

Pure Consciousness as the Field of Phenomenology

According to Husserl, the meaning which Being has in ordinary speech is inverted here. The Being which for us is first, is in itself second, i.e., it is what it is only relative to the first. Reality is not in itself something absolute, which becomes connected with something else only in a secondary way. Absolutely speaking it is nothing at all and it has no absolute essence whatsoever. It is essentially something which, in principle, is only intentional, only known, only consciously present as an appearance.

It should be evident that in contrast to the natural standpoint whose correlate is the natural world, a new standpoint must be available which despite the 'disconnecting' of the psycho-physical totality of nature, leaves a residue—the whole field of absolute consciousness. Instead of living naïvely in experience and subjecting the transcendental nature which we experience to theoretical inquires, we make a phenomenological reduction. Instead of naïvely performing the acts proper to consciousness (which constitutes nature) with its transcendent theses, we put all these theses 'out of action.' We direct our gaze of apprehension and theoretical inquiry to pure consciousness in its own absolute Being. It is pure consciousness which remains as the phenomenological residue we tried to find. We have 'suspended' in this way the whole world with all its things, living creatures, men, ourselves included. By doing this, we have literally lost nothing but we have gained the whole of absolute Being which, properly understood, conceals all transcendencies in itself and constitutes them within itself.

In the natural attitude we simply perform the acts through which the world is there for us. We live in a naïve and unreflective way in our acts of perceiving and experiencing. When we pursue natural science, we make reflections as required by the logic of experience, and in these reflections the realities given in experience are determined in terms of thought. When we place ourselves in the phenomenological standpoint, however, we cease to perform these cogitative theses; we place between brackets those that have been made; instead of performing them, we reflect upon them, and these acts we apprehend as absolute Being.

We now live entirely in such acts of the second level, whose datum is the basic field of phenomenology.[21]

Transcendental Subjectivity

In Husserl's view the result of these radical meditations is that we now have neither a science that we accept nor a world that exists for us. Instead of simply existing for us and of being naturally accepted in our experiential belief in its existence, the world is now for us merely something that claims to be. Moreover, the same reduction applies to the intramundane existence of all other egos; hence we may no longer speak communicatively or in the plural. For other human beings and animals are data of experience for me only because I sensitively experience their organisms; and, since the validity of this experience is called in question, I may not use it. At the same time, I lose, of course, everything that pertains to social life and culture. Briefly put, not only corporeal nature but the entire concrete surrounding world in which I live is for me, from now on, merely a *phenomenon of being*, instead of something that really is.

In this way I disregard the reality that might pertain to this phenomenon and also the possibility that at a future time I may critically decide that the world exists. Nevertheless, this phenomenon itself, as mine, is not nothing but is precisely that which makes such a critical decision possible. Accordingly, it makes possible everything that has for me sense and validity as true Being. Moreover, the fact that I have abstained and still abstain from every belief involved in or based upon sense experience, so that the existence of the experienced world remains unaccepted by me, still leaves this abstaining itself be what it is: it exists, together with the whole stream of my experiencing life. Moreover, this life is continually *there for me*. With respect to the field of the present, it is continually given to me perceptually with the most primordial originality as 'it itself'; and with respect to the past, now these and now those phases are again given to consciousness in memory, i.e., they are given as the 'past phases themselves.' By reflecting, I can grasp what is present as present, what is past as past, each as 'it itself'.

---

21. *Ibid.*, pp. 118-119 (139-141).

Meanwhile the world which is experienced in this reflectively grasped life continues, in a certain manner at least, to be for me experienced as before, and with precisely the same content it has at any particular time. It continues to appear as it appeared before. The only difference is that reflecting philosophically I no longer accept the natural belief in existence that is involved in experiencing the world, even though it is true that this belief too is still there and grasped by me consciously.

The same applies to all the processes of meaning that, in addition to the processes of world-experiencing, belong to my stream of life: the non-intuitive processes of 'meaning' certain objects, of judging, valuing and deciding, etc. The same applies in particular to the taking of positions that is necessarily involved in those processes when I am in the natural and non-reflective attitude. For, precisely this taking of positions always presupposes the world, it always involves belief in its existence. Here too the fact that the philosophically reflecting ego abstains from taking a position does not mean that they disappear from its field of experience. The concrete lived experiences remain that to which the ego's attentive regard is directed, but the attentive ego, as a philosophizing ego, practices abstention with respect to what it intuits. Likewise, everything 'meant' in these accepting or positing processes of consciousness, such as the 'meant' judgment, theory, value, or end, continues to be completely retained, but as a mere 'phenomenon' only.

Accordingly, the suspension of all positions taken toward the 'already-given' objective world does not leave us with nothing. On the contrary, it gives us possession of something. What I, the one who is meditating, acquire by it is my pure living, with all the pure lived experiences that make up this living, and everything 'meant' in them purely as 'meant' in them, viz., the universe of mere phenomena. The *epoché* is the radical and universal method by which I apprehend myself purely as ego, with my own pure conscious life, in and through which the whole objective world exists for me and is exactly as it is for me. The world is for me nothing but the world existing for and accepted by me in my conscious cogitations. It obtains its entire meaning and acceptance as existing solely from those cogitations. In these conscious and intentional activities my whole worldly life goes on, including my life of scientific inquiry and search for grounds. Through my living, my experiencing, thinking, valuing, and acting, I can enter no other world than the one that obtains its meaning and acceptance in and from me. By putting myself above this whole life and refraining from any belief that takes the world simply as existing, i.e., by directing by glance solely to this life itself as consciousness of the world, I gain myself as the pure ego, with the pure stream of my cogitations.

Thus, the Being of the pure ego and its cogitations is prior to the natural existence of the world. Natural being is a realm whose existential status is secondary, for it always presupposes the realm of transcendental Being. The fundamental phenomenological method of the transcendental *epoché* which leads back to this realm of transcendal Being, is called the transcendental-phenomenological reduction.[22]

The Apodictic Evidence of Transcendental Subjectivity

In his *Cartesian Meditations* Husserl further elaborates the meaning of the transcendental reduction in a few brief sections which because of their clarity seem to be exceptionally appropriate for concluding this long chapter. Husserl says there that in order to be able to serve as the basis for apodictic judgments, the experience of my transcendental ego must be apodictically evident. For according to our interpretation of the 'principle of all principles' only then can there be question of arriving at a true and apodictic philosophy. The question then is: Does the transcendental reduction make possible an apodictic evidence of the Being of transcendental subjectivity; and, secondly: What is the range covered by this apodictic evidence? As we have seen, undoubtedly there is apodicticity in the proposition 'I am'. However, the problem of the range covered by our apodictic evidence remains urgent. For undeniable self-experience offers only a nucleus that is *immediately* experienced with strict adequacy, namely, the ego's living present, while beyond this living present there extends an indeterminately general presumptive horizon, which comprises what, strictly speaking, is not experienced but is necessarily 'also-meant'. The presumption which is *implicit* in the apodictic evidence of the *cogito* is subject, therefore,

22. Edmund Husserl, *Cart. Med.*, pp. 58-61 (18-21).

to critique with respect to the possibilities of its fulfilment and their range.

One could say that adequacy and apodicticity of evidence do not have to go together. But even then the following questions remain: To what extent can the transcendental ego be deceived about itself and its own life? And to what extent does it have components that are absolutely indubitable?[23]

In the wake of Descartes, it seems easy to grasp the pure ego and its cogitations. Nevertheless, his ideas contain several prejudices and much 'scholasticism.' Influenced by his admiration for mathematical and natural sciences, he could easily fall for the prejudice that in the 'ego cogito' one is dealing with an apodictic 'axiom,' which together with other axioms can serve as the basis for a deductively explanatory science patterned on geometry. Descartes, moreover, thought that in our apodictic pure ego we have saved a little tag of the world, leaving us only with the problem of inferring and deducing the rest of the world from it through rightly conducted arguments based on our innate principles. In this way, the ego became a 'thinking substance' and the starting point for inferences based on the principle of causality. In this manner Descartes became the father of an absurd transcendental realism.

We can escape all these prejudices if we remain true to the principle of pure intuition and accept nothing but that which we find actually given in the field of pure consciousness.[24]

The Psychological and the Transcendental Ego

Continuing in this vein, it is true, Husserl says, that the reduction leaves me and my life untouched in their existential status, regardless of whether or not the world exists. But we must emphasize here again, he tells us, that this ego with its life, which necessarily remains for me after the reduction, is not itself a part of the world. True, as apperceived in natural experience, I am a theme of positive and objective science; the psychic life, for instance, considered by psychology, is

---

23. *Ibid.,* pp. 61-63 (22-23).
24. *Ibid.,* pp. 63-64 (23-25).

taken there as psychical life in the world. But for me, the meditating ego, who in the attitude of the reduction posits himself exclusively as the basis upon which all objective acceptances and their objective bases are accepted, there is no longer any psychological ego and there are no longer psychical phenomena.

Thus by the phenomenological reduction I reduce my natural human ego and my psychical life to my transcendental-phenomenological ego, the realm of transcendental-phenomenological self-experience. The objective world, the only world that can ever exist for me, this world with all its objects derives the entire meaning and existential status which it has for me, from me as the transcendental ego. And this ego discloses itself only through the transcendental-phenomenological reduction.

The concepts 'transcendental' and its correlate 'transcendent', then, must be derived solely from our phenomenological attitude. Just as the transcendental ego is not a part of the world, so neither is the transcendent world a part of my ego. This 'transcendence' is essential to the intrinsic meaning of anything worldly, despite the fact that it is solely from my experiencing that anything worldly can acquire any meanings determining it. If this 'transcendence', which consists in being not really included in the ego, is essential to the intrinsic meaning of the world, then the ego itself which contains within itself the world as an accepted meaning and which is necessarily presupposed by this meaning, is legitimately called 'transcendental,' in the phenomenological sense of the term. And any philosophical problem arising from this correlation is said to be a 'transcendental-philosophical' problem.[25]

4. *The Doctrinal Content of the Transcendental-Phenomenological Reduction*

Husserl first mentioned the necessity of a reduction as a necessary condition for an absolutely radical and 'transcendental' foundation of philosophy in the summer of 1905 in the *Seefelder Blätter*. However, he did not yet accurately describe there his vaguely seen idea or deter-

---

25. *Ibid.,* pp. 64-65 (25-26).

mine the nature, function and meaning of the phenomenological reduction. In *The Idea of Phenomenology* the fundamental ideas concerning the phenomenological reduction were for the first time clearly expressed in their full meaning, and the essential relationship between reduction and constitution was likewise explicitly indicated. In this same period also Husserl turned to Descartes as the model of such a radical return to that which is given beyond every possible doubt. However, he immediately emphasized that his reduction should not be interpreted as a Cartesian doubt. The latter denied, at least temporarily, the existence of the things reduced, while Husserl did not deny that existence but only placed it between brackets.[26]

In this point also Husserl's thinking underwent an evolution. This becomes particularly clear when we study the manuscripts he wrote between 1907 and 1913 and the innumerable writings of the last fifteen years of his life which explicitly deal with this problem. However, there is no doubt that this evolution reached, with respect to the very essence of the phenomenological reduction as such, its final stage before he published his *Ideas* in 1913. It is true that after 1915 Husserl constantly restudied the problems connected with the reduction, without, however, ever changing his mind about the cardinal aspects of this central idea of his phenomenological philosophy. In these new studies he merely tried to make the procedure more radical and to determine the positive meaning and doctrinal content of the reduction more accurately than he had done in his earlier writings.[27]

As Husserl proceeded in his phenomenological investigations, it became increasingly clear to him that more was involved than a mere suspension of existential belief. Yet it was not easy for him to determine the additional aspects of the reduction. Even in the last decade of his life Husserl believed that no adequate account of the phenomenological reduction had appeared as yet; in fact his correspondence referred to it as the most difficult thing ever attempted in philosophy. Boehm's edition of the second part of Husserl's *First Philosophy* (1923-1924), which

---

26. See Biemel's *Introduction* to Edmund Husserl, *Die Idee*, p. *viii*.

27. Walter Biemel, "Les phases décisives dans le développement de la philosophie de Husserl", p. 55. See also Herbert Spiegelberg, *op. cit.*, Vol. I, pp. 133-134.

appeared under the title *Theory of the Phenomenological Reduction,* provides us with some information about the intermediate stages of the evolution. It shows Husserl's struggling with the problems of the correct starting point of the reduction, but it hardly clarifies the reduction itself and certainly contains no significant change of its essence.[28]

The problems which drew Husserl's attention in the last fifteen years of his life were the exact way in which the necessity of the reduction is to be justified, the relation between reduction and analysis, between reduction and constitution, between the reduction and the 'life-world', and finally the accurate description of the difference between the psychological and the transcendental reduction. Especially these issues explain why the phenomenological reduction remains one of the most enigmatic concepts of Husserl's philosophy, as is evident from the many different interpretations given to it by Husserl himself, his disciples, and his later interpreters.[29] Since it is our intention to deal with Husserl's view of intentional analysis, constitution, the 'life-world' and psychology in the following chapters, we shall here touch only briefly upon the first problem. First, however, we must make another remark.

It is sometimes claimed that we must distinguish several different steps in Husserl's transcendental reduction. This claim is sometimes explained in the following way. The reduction has, first of all, its positive and its negative aspects. In its negative aspect the reduction guarantees that no foreign elements will be admitted into the later analyses. This negative aspect has its counterpart in the various levels of reduction. The constant application of the reduction presents, therefore, a gradual penetration into the pure subjectivity as the sole ground and source of all objectivity. According to Lauer, Husserl nowhere explicitly describes the different stages of the process as a whole. However, Lauer claims, transcendental subjectivity can be understood only if we realize that there are at least six levels of reduction, each of which results in a subject of greater purity. Only when the subject is at its greatest purity,

---

28. See Boehm's *Introduction* to Edmund Husserl, *Erste Phil.,* vol. II, pp. *xii-xlii* (passim). See also Herbert Spiegelberg, *op. cit.,* vol. I, pp. 135-136.

29. Eugen Fink, "Operative Begriffe in Husserls Phänomenologie", pp. 321-322. See also Herman L. Van Breda, "La réduction phénoménologique", in *Husserl,* pp. 307-318, p. 307.

do we have the strict science of phenomenology as Husserl understood it. Only when the subject has been purified to the extent of being absolutely pure subjectivity, can it be the universal *a priori* source and ground of objectivity. According to Lauer one has to wade through all of Husserl's works, published and unpublished, in order to discover just what the six levels of reduction are.[30]

Although there is some truth in this view, it seems to me that there is only one transcendental-phenomenological reduction which is to be clearly distinguished from the so-called 'psychological reduction,' the eidetic reduction and the reduction of the world of culture to the original 'life-world.' We hope to deal with the first and the last form of reduction in one of the following chapters. It is true that in the transcendental reduction we must make a distinction between a negative and a positive aspect. We may also admit several aspects and even stages in this transcendental reduction, but these stages are so closely connected and interrelated that it seemed to be of more importance to put the stress on the unity of the procedure than on its different phases.

Be this as it may, we must now return to the important question mentioned above: What is the exact meaning of the inhibition of our existential belief concerning the world? In a remarkable study of this question Van Breda points out that perhaps we can summarize Husserl's final answer to this question in the three following theses: 1) The phenomenological reduction is for Husserl that procedure which enables him to attain a truly philosophical level. 2) This procedure forbids Husserl to opt either for an objectivistic or for a subjectivistic attitude in philosophy; its aim is to establish him within the transcendental relation between *cogito* and *cogitatum*. 3) For Husserl the problem concerning the reduction, at least in its profoundest sense, is solely the discovery of the authentically metaphysical dimension.[31]

---

30. Quentin Lauer, *Phénoménologie de Husserl*, p. 340 (note 4), 361 (note 1). See also Walter Biemel, "Husserls Encyclopaedia-Britannica Artikel und Heideggers Anmerkungen dazu", *Tijdschrift voor Philosophie*, 12(1950), 246-280, pp. 257-268. Gaston Berger, *Le cogito dans la philosophie de Husserl*, pp. 55-60. H. Boelaars, "Husserls reducties en haar betekenis voor het Thomisme", *Tijdschrift voor Philosophie*, 6(1944), 333-376, pp. 345-362.

31. Herman L. Van Breda, "La réduction phénoménologique", pp. 307-308.

In principle I agree with Van Breda that in this way the doctrinal content of the phenomenological reduction is indicated in a clear but still preliminary way. The question is how the second and the third theses are to be interpreted. Since this interpretation touches the very intricate problem of Husserl's transcendental idealism, I shall revert to this question in the last chapter of this book, for Husserl's answer of the question is essentially connected with his view on constitution.

CHAPTER SIX

INTENTIONALITY

Although Husserl's doctrine of intentionality is already implicitly contained in his *Philosophy of Arithmetic,* he did not present a detailed and accurate description of it until he wrote the second volume of the *Logical Investigations.* The doctrine is presented there within the context of logical questions which are not essential to phenomenology as such. For this reason Husserl reverted to the explanation of intentionality in his work *Ideas,* dealing there only with those elements and topics which are characteristic of phenomenology in the proper sense.

All of Husserl's later works presuppose the description of intentionality given in the *Ideas,* and his conception of it never underwent any change, although the dynamic structure of intentionality was emphasized more in the later works. The same applies to the link between intentionality, on the one hand, and synthesis and constitution, on the other.[1]

In this chapter I shall limit myself to a brief paraphrase of Husserl's view on intentionality as the basic idea of phenomenology. Nevertheless, a few remarks with respect to the ideas of intentionality found in Husserl's *Logical Investigations* seem to be indispensable. These remarks will be limited to points which seem to be necessary for an understanding of the evolution of Husserl's thought between 1901 and 1913.

1. *Intentionality in the 'Logical Investigations'*[2]

Between 1896 and 1900 Husserl developed the essential insights pertaining to his new philosophy of intentionality. Our consciousness is

---

1. A. Diemer, *Edmund Husserl. Versuch einer systematischen Darstellung seiner Phänomenologie* (Meisenheim a.Gl: Hain, 1956), pp. 45-72 (passim).
2. See for the following in general Edmund Husserl, *L.U.,* vol. II, 5. *Untersuchung* (per totum). See also Herbert Spiegelberg, *op. cit.* vol. I, pp. 107-111 and pp. 39-42. Marvin Farber, *op. cit.,* pp. 11-14, 339-341. Ludwig Landgrebe, *Phänomenologie und Metaphysik* (Hamburg: Schröder, 1949), pp. 59-69. E. Levinas, *Théorie de l'intuition,* pp. 65-76. Gaston Berger, *Le cogito dans la philosophie de Husserl,* pp. 47-50. Quentin Lauer, *Phénoménologie de Husserl,* pp. 56-59, 89-95. A. Diemer, *op. cit.,* pp. 45-56. Pierre Thévenaz, *What is Phenomenology?,* pp. 48-50.

intentional; it is 'openness to,' 'relation to.' This relation is, strictly speaking, identical with the fundamental and constitutive structure of consciousness; it is a relation between a 'meaning' act and that which is 'meant,' its object, the latter being defined as meaning (*Sinn*).

It was during the preparation of the *Logical Investigations* that Husserl discovered the concept of intentionality. At the time he was seeking a radically philosophical explanation of mathematical and logical beings. In this process and while also trying to arrive at their essential structures and indicate a foundation for their proper value, Husserl formulated the thesis that the nature of these beings is exclusively to be objects of consciousness. To say this is tantamount to saying that these logical and mathematical beings are, in the most fundamental sense, meanings-for-me. In this specific instance intentional analysis, he claims, demonstrates that consciousness is to be thought of as a relation *sui generis* to an apprehended object.

Husserl explicitly mentioned several times that he owed his conception of intentionality to Brentano. According to Brentano, now, every psychical phenomenon is characterized by what the medieval Scholastics called the intentional 'inexistence' of an object. Brentano called this characteristic of every psychical phenomenon the 'reference to a content', or 'the directedness to an immanent object'. This concept enabled Brentano to distinguish between psychical and physical phenomena. He held that everything psychical is characterized by such an intentional relation to an object. Any psychical phenomenon, he claimed, contains something as an object, but not always in the same way. Thus, in a presentation something is presented, in a judgment something is acknowledged or rejected, and in desire something is desired. Brentano regarded this 'intentional inexistence' as exclusively proper to psychical phenomena; for this reason he defined them as phenomena which intentionally contain an object in themselves.[3]

There can be no doubt about Husserl's dependence on Brentano for the concept of intentionality and the field it opened to descriptive analysis. Nonetheless Husserl thought that Brentano had failed to grasp what intentionality *really* is and make it philosophically useful. For

---

3. Franz Brentano, *Psychologie vom empirischen Standpunkt*, Oskar Krauss ed., (Leipzig: Felix Meiner, 1924), 3 vol., vol. I, pp. 125-126.

Brentano every intentional experience was a phenomenon and the term 'phenomenon' denoted an appearing object as such. In this sense Brentano spoke of objects which 'enter into consciousness,' and he added that consciousness enters into relationship with objects in this or that particular way, or that intentional experiences contain something in themselves as an object. According to Husserl, such expressions are questionable, for they may lead to the following two misinterpretations: 1) There should be a real relation between consciousness and the things known; 2) There should be a relationship between two things found immanent in consciousness, namely, between act and intentional object; hence one psychical content is included in another.

Let us first consider the second misinterpretation. The expression 'immanent objectivity' is used to denote the essential characteristic of intentional experiences. An object is 'meant' in an intentional experience; it is 'aimed at' in an experience of presentation, of judgment, or any other cognitive act. It is essential to such experiences that there be a reference to an object, that an object be 'intentionally present.' Such an intentional experience may occur even if the object does not exist. In that case, 'meaning' the object is and remains an experience; but the object is merely 'meant', and is really nothing. If I present the god Jupiter, then this god is a presented object; it is 'immanently present' in my act. Of course, the descriptive analysis of this intentional experience will not disclose the god Jupiter as being in it; hence, the 'immanent' object does not belong to the descriptive immanent nature of the experience; therefore, it is not at all immanent. But it is also not 'outside the mind'; that is, it really is not at all. That, however, does not prevent my presenting-the-god Jupiter from being real. On the other hand, if the intended object does not exist, nothing needs to be changed phenomenologically. With respect to consciousness the given is essentially the same, whether the presented object exists, is imaginary or even absurd. For this reason, it is better to avoid the term 'immanent objects' and to use the expression 'intentional object' which is not open to similar objections.

As for the first-mentioned misinterpretaion, there is no question of a real relation, but only of an intentional relation between consciousness and the things known. Husserl, therefore, chose his own terminology in such a way that such disputable presuppositions and ambiguities were excluded as much as possible. He avoided the expression 'psychical phenomenon' and spoke of 'experience' or, more exactly, of 'intentional experience.' The term 'intentional' designates the characteristic of intention, the reference to something objective. As a briefer expression he uses the term 'act.' 'Intention' is understood here in the sense of 'aiming at,' and is applicable to acts of theoretical and practical aiming. The image of 'aiming at,' however, does not apply equally well to all acts; hence Husserl was forced to distinguish a narrower and a wider concept of intention.[4]

Immediately after the publication of the *Logical Investigations* Husserl realized the fragmentary character of his first philosophical inquiries concerning intentionality. Intentionality is not only a characteristic feature of the acts of consciousness, but it is the very essence of consciousness itself. In his *Idea of Phenomenolgy* in which he expressed this conviction for the first time, Husserl's main interest still appeared to be mostly epistemological.[5] For this reason he reverted to the topic in the *Ideas* in order to explain the fundamental and full meaning of intentionality as completely and clearly as possible.

2. *Intentionality as the Main Theme of Phenomenology*

In the preceding chapter we have explained that the Cartesian *cogito* possesses apodictic evidence and that, according to Husserl, there seems to exist a possibility of grounding all actual and possible knowledge in this apodictic evidence. The question, however, is: How can this be done? What can we do philosophically with a 'transcendental ego'? True, in the order of knowledge, the existence of this ego is prior to all objective being because, in a certain sense, this ego is the basis on which all objective cognition rests. And although, with Descartes, we endeavor to find in transcendental subjectivity the ultimate ground of all knowledge and all science, and even of the existence of

---

4. Edmund Husserl, *L.U.*, vol. II, pp. 378-379. Marvin Farber, *op. cit.*, pp. 11-14, 339-341.
5. Edmund Husserl, *Die Idee*, pp. 55-56 (43-44).

an objective world, Husserl claims, we must ask whether this priority truthfully means that the transcendental ego is, in the usual sense, the epistemological basis on which all objective knowledge is founded.[6]

The Idea of a Transcendental Ground of Knowledge

Dealing with this problem, Husserl in his *Cartesian Meditations* explicitly posits that in his opinion the Cartesian discovery of the transcendental ego has really disclosed a new idea concerning the foundation of knowledge, namely, the idea of grounding it transcendentally. But rather than trying to use the *ego cogito* as an apodictically evident premise in deductive processes, one has to direct his attention to the fact that the phenomenological *epoché* opens up an infinite realm of being of a new kind, namely, the sphere of transcendental experience. And wherever there is a new kind of experience, a new science is bound to arise.

Here, however, a difficulty manifests itself. For no matter how absolute the apodictic evidence of the ego's existence may be for this ego itself, this evidence does not necessarily hold good also for the existence of the many data of transcendental experience. On the other hand, the bare self-identity of the 'I am' is not the only thing that is given as indubitable in transcendental self-experience. Detailed analyses are needed, therefore, to discover and to describe everything that is absolutely indubitable within the field of our transcendental experience.[7]

In those analyses the weight of transcendental evidence of the *ego cogito* has to be shifted from the identical ego to its manifold cogitations, the stream of conscious life in which this ego lives. The ego can at any time direct its reflective attention to its conscious life, its perceiving and imagining, its asserting, valuing or willing life. It can contemplate this life, explicitate and describe its content.

To follow this procedure does not mean that one has to limit oneself to psychological descriptions based on purely internal experience, for a purely descriptive psychology of consciousness is not a transcendental phenomenology determined in terms of the transcendental-phenomenological reduction. The pure psychology of consciousness merely runs

---

6. Edmund Husserl, *Cart. Med.,* p. 66 (27)
7. *Ibid.,* pp. 66-70 (27-31).

parallel to the transcendental phenomenology of consciousness. These two must at first be kept strictly separated, for as we have seen, the failure to distinguish them is typical of psychologism and makes a genuine philosophy impossible. One must constantly bear in mind here that transcendental-phenomenological research may on no condition neglect to make use of the transcendental reduction. Accordingly, the difference between a psychological and a transcendental-phenomenological investigation of consciousness is very profound, although the two may have parallel contents. The psychological investigation makes use of data belonging to a world whose existence is presupposed, but the transcendental-phenomenological investigation does not take the parallel data and their contents as existing, since the phenomenological attitude accepts the world only as a reality phenomenon.

But there is still another point of crucial importance. One should not forget that the *epoché* of all worldly being does not remove the fact that the manifold cogitations concerning these intramundane beings contain a relation to these beings *as mere phenomena;* in other words, every consciousness and every conscious process is, in itself, consciousness of something no matter what ontic status this objective 'something' may have. The transcendental *ego cogito* must, therefore, be broadened by an addition. Each cogitation 'means' something and contains in itself as 'meant' its characteristic *cogitatum.* Moreover, each *cogito* does so in its own fashion. For instance, the table-perception 'means' a table, this individual table here, and 'means' it in the way proper to perception, but a table-memory 'means' a table in the way proper to memory.

Conscious processes are also called 'intentional,' but in this context the term 'intentionality' simply indicates the universal fundamental property of consciousness to be consciousness *of* something. Every *cogito* contains its *cogitatum*.[8]

This fundamental relation has to be explained here in a more detailed and accurate way. First, however, we must focus attention upon other important characteristics of consciousness.[9]

---

8. *Ibid.,* pp. 70-72 (31-33).
9. Edmund Husserl, *Ideen I,* pp. 174-177 (194-197).

Natural and Transcendental Reflection

Among the most general features pertaining to the essential structure of the pure sphere of experience, Husserl says, one has to consider, first of all, reflection. The reason is that reflection has a universal methodological function, since the phenomenological method proceeds entirely through acts of reflection. Let us begin by recapitulating what we already know and then seek to penetrate more profoundly into the matter by investigating that type of phenomenological study which is made both possible and necessary by reflection.

Every ego lives its own experiences, which include much that is real and intentional. The expression 'it lives them' does not mean that it apprehends them explicitly after the manner of immanent experience. But it is ideally possible for every experience that is not explicitly included in the ego's glance, to be apprehended by this glance. When this happens, a reflective act of the ego is directed toward this experience so that it becomes an object for the ego. Again, the reflections themselves are experiences, and therefore can serve as the basis of new reflections, and so on to infinity.

The experience as really lived 'now,' as it first becomes the focal point of reflection, presents itself as really lived, as being 'now.' It presents itself also as 'having just been,' and insofar as it was unnoticed as 'not reflected upon.' In our natural attitude we unthinkingly take it for granted that experiences do not exist only when we turn to grasp them in immanent experience and that, if in immanent reflection they are still objects of awareness as 'having just been,' then they were really existent and were really lived by us.

In continuing to clarify this idea, Husserl says, we are further convinced that it is also reflection, which in an on the basis of recall, tells us about our former experiences which were 'then' present, 'then' immanently perceptible, although they were not immanently perceived. The same must be said, according to the naïve natural view, for anticipation and foreseeing expectation. We have here, first, the immediate 'protention' which is the exact counterpart of immediate retention. Next we have here the anticipation which *re*produces in the more proper sense of the term, but re-presents quite differently from recall whose counterpart it is. Here the intuitively expected of which, through the reflection possible 'in' anticipation, we are foreseeingly aware as 'presently coming,' has at the same time the meaning of 'what will be perceived,' just as the recalled has the meaning of 'what has been perceived.' Thus, we can reflect in anticipation also and bring to consciousness experiences as belonging to the anticipated as such, even though the anticipation itself does not offer the proper standpoint for having these experiences. We do so each time we say that we will see what is coming and, in saying this, our reflecting glance has turned toward the coming perceptual experience.

Let us now, Husserl says, make use of the phenomenological reduction. In the natural attitude we look upon the world as already given as existent, even in our reflections, but in the transcendental-phenomenological reflection we give up this standpoint. The transcendental-phenomenological experience consists in this that we look at and describe the particular transcendentally 'reduced' *cogito,* but abstain from participating, as reflecting subjects, in the natural positing of existence by the original act and our natural ego. Moreover, we can transform every particular *cogito* into a case illustrating an essential generality and make it our own within the framework of pure intuition.

In this way, Husserl emphasizes, we can examine all this from a transcendental-phenomenological standpoint and even eidetically, whether at a higher level of generality or at the level corresponding to the essential conditions proper to special types of experience. The whole stream of experiences 'lived' in the fashion of unreflecting consciousness can be made the subject of a scientific study concerning the nature of the stream. This study should aim at systematic completeness and extend to all the possible intentional aspects included in the experiences, and also to the experiences of modified consciousness which may be in them and their intentional aspects.

The study of the stream of consciousness takes place through various acts of reflection of a special type. These acts themselves, in their turn, belong to the stream of experiences, and in corresponding reflections on a higher level can become objects of phenomenological analysis. Analyses of this kind lay the foundation of a general phenomenology and of the methodological insights that are indispensable to its development.[10]

The term 'reflection', as the foregoing analysis shows, is an expression indicating the acts in which the stream of experiences, with its manifold events and intentionalities, can be grasped and analyzed in the light of its own evidence. Generally speaking, reflection modifies the previous experience in an essential fashion. The previous experience loses its original mode, and reflecting makes an object out of what previously was an experience, but does not make it objective. Thus, reflection does not repeat the original process, but considers it and explains what can be found in it. Reflection is a new intentional experience which, with its characteristic of 'referring back' to the earlier process, is awareness precisely of that earlier experience itself. It is an experiential knowing to which we owe all conceivable knowledge and cognition of our intentional life. This description holds also for our phenomenological reflection.

To put it differently, in phenomenological reflection there is a doubling of the ego: the phenomenological ego establishes itself, as a 'disinterested onlooker,' above the naïvely interested ego. This doubling itself can be experienced in a new reflection. As transcendental, this new reflection likewise demands the same attitude of looking-on-disinterestedly, for the ego's sole remaining interest is to see and to describe adequately what it sees, purely as it is seen, as that which is seen and seen in this or that fashion.

As Husserl sees it, it is in this way that all events of our life-turned-toward-the-world are made capable of description, without any accompanying or expectant meanings and prejudices. Only in this purified condition can they become themes of a universal critique of consciousness, as is demanded by our aim to arrive at a radical grounding of philosophy. Evidently, however, everything depends here on keeping the description absolutely free of any prejudices, so that we can satisfy the principle of pure evidence. This requirement means that we must restrict ourselves to the pure data of transcendental reflection; hence

---

10. *Ibid.*, pp. 177-181 (197-200). *Cart. Med.*, pp. 72-73 (33-35).

these data must be taken precisely as wholly free of any interpretation that reads into them more than is genuinely seen.

If we follow this methodological principle and remember that every *cogito* is a *cogito cogitatum*, it becomes evident that every description must have two sides: on the one hand, description of the intentional object as such (noematic description), and on the other description of the modes of the *cogito* itself (noetic description). Thus it should be clear that through the universal reduction the world is not simply lost for phenomenology. We retain it as *cogitatum*, not only with respect to particular realities, but also with respect to the world itself as the necessary background of our whole natural life.[11]

We must now devote our attention to other important characteristics of consciousness.

The Relation of Every Experience to the Ego

Husserl was especially convinced that among the general essential characteristics proper to the transcendentally purified field of experience, special mention was to be made of the relation which every experience has to the pure ego.

Every *cogito*, he tells us, is characteristically an act of the ego, an act proceeding from the ego and actually living in the ego. But when I perform the phenomenological reduction, the whole natural world is suspended, including 'I myself.' Only pure experience, as an act with its own essence, remains as residue. I also see, however, that although the apprehension of the same act taken as human experience could be different in many aspects, yet no reduction can remove the form of the *cogito* and the 'pure' subject of the act. Being-directed-toward-an-object, being-occupied-with-it, adopting-an-attitude, undergoing-something, all these contain of necessity in their very essence that they are 'something from the ego.' This ego is the pure ego, which no reduction can ever remove.

The experiencing ego, however, is not something that could be taken 'by itself' and made into an object of inquiry in its own right. Apart

_____

11. *Ideen*, p. 181 (200). *Cart. Med.*, pp. 73-75 (35-36).

from its way-of-being-related, it is completely devoid of essential components; it has no content that could be unfolded; it is pure ego and nothing else. Despite their necessary relationships, however, we continue to distinguish the experience itself from the pure ego which experiences, and again, the pure subjective phase of the way-of-experiencing from the ego-diverted content of the experience.

Thus, the essential nature of the sphere of experience contains a two-sided fact of great importance: 1) Every *cogito,* as a *cogito,* is directed to an object or *cogitatum;* 2) It is also and of necessity a *cogito* of this ego.

This fundamental fact can also be expressed by saying that in every experience we must distingnuish between a subjectively and an objectively oriented aspect. To this two-sideness there corresponds a diversion of our investigation into two parts. One is concerned with pure subjectivity, the other with whatever belongs to the constitution of objectivity as referred to its subjective source. The inquiry which we propose to pursue here will be concerned mainly with the objectively oriented aspect, for this aspect presents itself first when we give up the natural attitude.[12]

Time and Consciousness of Time

As Husserl states it, another characteristic which needs to be discussed here is phenomenological time. Let us begin by noting the difference between objective or cosmic time and phenomenological time, the unitary form of all experiences within a *single* stream of experiences of a single pure ego. Through the phenomenological reduction consciousness has forsaken not only its apperceptive connection with material reality and its relations in space, but also its setting in cosmic time. The phenomenological time, which belongs essentially to experience as such, is not to be measured by any position of the sun, by any clock, or other physical means; it cannot be measured at all. The same holds true for the modes in which its intrinsic content is presented and the derivatives of these modes, the modally determined 'now,' 'before' and 'after,' simultaneity, succession, etc.

---

12. *Ideen,* pp. 194-196 (213-215).

Cosmic time is related to phenomenological time in a way which is somewhat analogous to that in which the extension pertaining to the immanent essence of a concrete meaning content stands to objective spatial extension, that is, to the extension of the appearing physical object, which manifests itself in visual perspectives through the sense data by means of which it appears.

Moreover, the term 'time' indicates a completely self-contained sphere of problems. It will become clear later that the transcendental absolute which we have laid bare by the reduction, is not yet really ultimate, because it is something which in a unique sense constitutes itself in something else that is truly absolute. However, in these preliminary investigations we can leave the problems concerning time-consciousness out of consideration, without making our investigations less rigorous.

In any case, the essential property of experiences that is expressed by the term 'temporality' indicates not only something that belongs in a general way to every experience, but also a necessary form which binds one experience to another. Every real experience is necessarily one that has duration, and through this duration it takes its place in an endless continuum of durations, in a concretely filled continuum. It necessarily has a temporal sphere that is concretely filled and extends endlessly on all sides. This tells us at once that this experience belongs to a single endlessly extended stream of experiences.

Again, it belongs to the essence of the situation that the ego is able to direct its regard to the way in which the temporal factor is given, and to know with self-evidence that there cannot be any enduring experience outside a continuous flow of modes of being-given as the unitary factor in the process. Moreover, the ego can know with self-evidence that this mode of being-given pertaining to the temporal experience is itself also an experience, although of a new kind and dimension. For instance, I am able to pay attention to the experience of joy in all its purity, and follow its temporal phases while the experience endures from the beginning until its end. But I can also look at the way in which this experience manifests itself: its mode of actual 'now,' this 'now's' link with continuously new 'nows' or the continuous passing of the actual 'now' into a 'just-gone now.'

Husserl maintains that the actual 'now' necessarily has the nature of a point; its punctual character points to a form that persists through the continuous change of content. The same applies to the continuity of the 'just-gone'; it too is a continuity of forms with ever new contents. The form receives continually a fresh content; a new impression, corresponding to an ever-new point of the duration, continually attaches itself to each impression united with the experience of 'now'; the impression continually transforms itself into a retention, and this retention continually into a modified retention, etc. To all this we must add continuous changes in an opposite direction: there is also a continuous 'after' corresponding to the continuous 'before'; and there is a 'protentional' continuum corresponding to the retentional continuum.[13]

Every present moment of experience, even that of the initial phase of a newly developing experience, has necessarily a 'before' as its limit. In principle, this 'before' cannot be an empty 'before,' since a mere form without content is pure nonsense. Every newly beginning experience has necessarily been preceded in time by other experiences; the past experience is continually filled with content. In a similar way every present moment of experience has necessarily an 'after' as a limit, and that limit likewise is not empty.

To the now-consciousness the consciousness of the 'just past' is necessarily attached, and this consciousness again is itself a 'now'. No experience can cease without a consciousness of its ceasing and its having ceased, and that consciousness is a 'now' filled with a new content. The stream of experience is an infinite unity, and the form of this stream is one that necessarily encompasses all the experiences of the pure ego.

The general characteristic of consciousness which we have just indicated, considered as a possible datum for our reflection, is part of a still broader characteristic. The latter can be expressed in this basic and essential law: every experience implies not only temporal succession in

---

13. *Ibid.*, pp. 196-199 (215-218). See also *Cart. Med.*, pp. 109-111 (75-79), and especially Edmund Husserl, *The Phenomenology of Internal Time-Consciousness.* Edited by Martin Heidegger, translated by James S. Churchill, with an Introduction by Calvin O. Schrag (Bloomington: Indiana University Press, 1964), pp. 98-126.

an essentially self-contained system of experiences, but also comes under the rubric of simultaneity. In other words, every present moment of experience has about it a horizon of experiences which also share in the primordial 'now'-form, and which, as such, constitute the one primordial horizon of the pure ego, its total primordial 'now'-consciousness.

This horizon enters as a unity into the structure of the past modes of experience also. Every 'before' as a modified 'now,' is the center of endless stretches of what has simultaneously been. Thus, the previously-given descriptions should be completed with a new dimension; and not until we bring in this dimension do we have the *whole* phenomenological temporal field of the pure ego. From any one of its experiences as a center, this ego can measure the whole field according to the three dimensions of 'before,' 'after,' and 'simultaneous.'

Accordingly, these two are necessary correlates: *one* pure ego and *one* stream of experiences which is filled with content in all these three dimensions, which is essentially coherent in all its fillings, and which progresses through the continuity of its content.[14]

Something else still is essentially related to this fundamental form of consciousness. If in its reflection the regard of the pure ego rests on a particular experience, it is *a priori* possible for the ego to redirect its regard to other experiences insofar as this experience is connected with them. But it is in principle impossible that this connected whole of experiences can be given in its entirety through a single pure regard. Nevertheless, this connected whole can in a certain way be grasped intuitively. To grasp it, the regard must follow the line of 'unlimited progressive development' of immanent intuitions, it must go from the experience on which the regard has been fixed to new experiences within its horizon, and from the fixing of the regard on these to that of their horizons, etc. Advancing continuously in this fashion from one apprehension to another, we apprehend in a certain way the stream of experience as a unity. But we do not apprehend it like a single experience, but in the manner of *an idea in the Kantian sense.*

From these reflections we can draw the eidetically valid and self-evident conclusion that no concrete experience can be independent in the

---

14. *Ideen I*, pp. 199-201 (218-219).

full sense of the term. Each experience needs to be completed in reference to some connected whole, and the form and kind of this whole is not left to our free choice but has simply to be accepted.[15]

Intentionality

Husserl feels that one is now able to return to intentionality, which in his opinion is to be considered as the general theme of 'objectively' oriented phenomenology. As we have seen, intentionality is an essential characteristic of the sphere of experiences in general. For, in one way or another, all experiences in exactly the same sense participate in intentionality, although we cannot say that every experience has intentionality as it has a temporal character. Intentionality characterizes consciousness, in the pregnant sense of the term, and permits us to describe the whole stream of experiences both as a stream of consciousness and as the unity of one single consciousness.

In the preceding considerations intentionality was understood as the unique characteristic of experience to be consciousness *of* something. It was in the explicit *cogito* that we first encountered this marvelous property to which all metaphysical enigmas of theoretical reason ultimately lead us back: to perceive is to perceive something; to judge is to judge something; to value is to value a certain value; to act concerns action, to do aims at a deed, to love at the beloved, to rejoice at the object of joy. In every wakeful *cogito* a regard of the pure ego is directed to the object of the correlate of consciousness then considered, and the ego has consciousness of this object in one of its typical variations.

However, as we have learned from phenomenological reflection, this orientation of the ego in presenting, thinking, valuing, etc., this directedness toward the correlate object, cannot be found in every experience, whereas intentionality may always be concealed in it. For instance, it is clear that the objective background, from which the perceived object of the cogitation emerges when it is singled out by the glance of the ego, is an objective background in a sense that can really be experienced. For, even while we are turned toward the pure object in the mode of the

---

15. *Ibid.,* pp. 201-203 (220-222).

cogito, various objects appear; we are intuitively aware of them; they blend into the unity of a single intuition, the unity of a consciously grasped field of objects. We face here a potential field of perception in the sense that a special perception can be directed toward everything that in this way appears.

But we cannot call it a potential field of perception in the sense that the object in the field cannot be objectively grasped at all until the ego's glance turns toward other objects in the field. For, the variations of the sensory perspective (e.g., variations of the visual perspective) are experienced as present in a single visual field as soon as for the first time they shape themselves into intuitive appearances of objects.

Intentionality includes also experiences which proceed either from the background of actual consciousness, such as the awakening of emotions, the first beginning of judgments, and nascent wishes, or from different depths of background, i.e., they are farther from or nearer to the pure ego, which, as it lives wakefully, is the center of reference in the passing thoughts. A desire, a wish or a judgment can be 'fulfilled' in a specific sense—namely, by the ego which plays an active role in this fulfillment. However, such modes of consciousness may already be present and emerge in the background without being 'fulfilled' in this way. Yet in their own essential nature these emerging actualities are already a consciousness of something. Accordingly, we do not include in the essence of intentionality that which pertains specifically to the *cogito,* viz., the 'glance-toward', the ego's 'turning-to'; on the contrary, we take this cogitation to be a special modality of the general function called 'intentionality'.[16]

In the following pages we must more accurately try to determine this original insight into the very essence of intentionality in both its static and dynamic aspects. As we will see, the static consideration endeavors to determine everything that is concretely found in every lived experinece; in other words, it is interested in its real components. The dynamic consideration, on the other hand, wants to describe the genesis and evolution of intentionality.[17]

---

16. *Ibid.,* pp. 203-205 (222-224).
17. A. Diemer, *op. cit.,* pp. 77-79. Edmund Husserl, *Car. Med.,* pp. 10-11 (76-77).

3. Static Description of Intentionality

Sensible Hylē and Intentional Morphē

Elaborating the first aspect of this subject, Husserl goes on to explain that in the static consideration of intentionality we begin by making an essential distinction between experiences which we could call 'primary contents' and experiences or phases of experiences which are bearers of the specific quality of intentionality.

To the primary contents belong unitary sense experiences, sense contents, such as the data of color, touch, and sound. They should not be confused with the appearing phases of things, such as their color qualities and their roughness, for these reveal themselves experientially only through the primary contents. The same applies to sense impressions of pleasure, pain, tickling, etc. Such concrete data of experience are found as components in concrete experiences of a more comprehensive type which as whole are intentional. With respect to these sensible phases, the latter are, as it were, an animating or meaning-giving layer which makes the concrete intentional experience take form and shape out of the sensible elements that in themselves contain nothing intentional.

In the whole phenomenological domain, as Husserl explains it, this remarkable duality and unity of sensible *hylē* and intentional *morphē*, play a dominant role. As a matter of fact, these 'matter' and 'form' concepts impose themselves, when we consider clear intuitions, or clearly-formed valuations, volitions, etc. Intentional experiences are there as unities which come about through the giving of meaning. Sense data offer themselves as material suitable for intentional 'informing', or giving of meaning, at different levels.

The sensible *hylē* and the intentional *morphē* might also be called 'formless materials' and 'matterless forms'. We may add in passing that the expression 'primary content', which was used in the *Logical Investigations,* no longer covers the situation. The expression 'sense experience' likewise should not be used any longer, since it indicates not only hyletic but also intentional experiences; for, even a sense experience consists of hyletic data and intentional *morphē*. This is the reason why we prefer to speak of 'hyletic data', 'material data', 'materials', 'sensible materials', or 'sensory materials'.

That which forms the materials into intentional experiences and thereby introduces the specific element of intentionality, is identical with that which gives its specific meaning to our use of the term 'consciousness'. We will call it 'noesis' or 'noetic phase'.

To avoid every ambiguity we will therefore say that the stream of phenomenological Being has a double bed: one material and the other noetic. Phenomenological analyses which are specifically concerned with the material aspect may be called 'hyletic-phenomenological analyses', and those that study the noetic phases may be referred to as 'noetic-phenomenological analyses'. Noetic analyses are the most important and fruitful analyses of Phenomenology.[18]

Noesis and Noema

It is easy to indicate the characteristic of intentional experience in its general form, for everyone understands the expression 'consciousness is consciousness of something'. It is more difficult, however, to obtain a pure and correct grasp of the phenomenological characteristics of the corresponding essence, since this 'consciousness of something' appears to be at the same time both very obvious and very obscure.[19]

Concerning this aspect of intentionality Husserl tells us that we must make a clear distinction between the real components of our intentional experiences and the intentional correlates or the components of these correlates. Thus, on the one hand, we have to distinguish the parts and phases disclosed by a real analysis of the experience which treats this experience as an object like any other. On the other hand, every intentional experience is the consciousness of something. Every intentional experience, by virtue of its noetic phase, is noetic; it is essential to it to contain in itself some kind of meaning or perhaps many meanings, and on the basis of this essential characteristic of giving meaning, and in harmony with it, to develop further phases which, through it, become themselves 'meaningful'.

Examples of such noetic phases are: directing the pure ego's glance to the object intended by virtue of the regard's gift of meaning, i.e.,

---

18. *Ideen I*, pp. 207-212 (226-230).
19. *Ibid.*, pp. 216-218 (235-236).

to that which the ego has in mind as something 'meant'; apprehending this object, holding it in a steady grasp while the glance shifts to other objects which have come within its reach; likewise the effects of bringing out, relating, com-prehending and assuming the various attitudes of belief, presumption, valuation, etc. All this may be discovered in the relevant experiences, no matter how different they may be in themselves. Just as this series of examples indicates that there are real components in the experiences, so also does it point, under the heading 'meaning', to components that are not real. In this way we come to the distinction, briefly indicated above, between *noesis* and *noema*. For, to the manifold data of the real noetic content, there corresponds at all points a variety of data that can be displayed in truly pure intuition, and in a correlative 'noematic content', or 'noema'.

Perception, for instance, has its noema, and at the basis of this noema its perceptual meaning, i.e., the 'perceived as such'. Likewise, recollection has as its own noema, the 'remembered as such'. Everywhere we must take the noematic correlate, which, in a very broad sense, is here referred to as 'meaning', precisely as it is immanent in the experience of perception, judgment, etc.

As phenomenologists, we now have to ask the essential question: What is the 'perceived as such'? What are its essential phases as noema? We will get the answer to these questions by yielding fully to what is essentially *given*. It will allow us faithfully to describe 'that which appears as such' in the light of perfect self-evidence.[20]

Continuing in this vein Husserl claims that in phenomenologically pure experience we find indissolubly belonging to the essence of perception the 'perceived as such', for instance, under the headings 'material thing', 'plant', 'tree'. The quotation marks are important here, for they express the radical modification made in the sense of the words. The tree, for example, as it exists in nature is quite different from this perceived tree as such. The former can be destroyed or burned, but the meaning of this perception is indestructible and cannot be separated from its essence.

---

20. *Ibid.*, pp. 218-221 (237-240).

It is to be noted that for the phenomenologist as well as for the psychologist the perceived, as meaning, should not include anything that does not really appear in the perceptual manifestation of the appearing reality. Moreover, what appears must be included in the perceived precisely as it is presented to us in the actual perception. A special kind of reflection may lead to the discovery of this meaning, as it is immanent in perception. The phenomenological judgment has to adjust itself and give faithful expression only to that which is apprehended in this perception.[21]

It is the fundamental characteristic of all intentionality that not only perception but every intentional experience has its intentional object, i.e., its objective meaning. To have a meaning is the cardinal characteristic of all consciousness, it is that on account of which consciousness is not only just experience, but meaningful and noetic experience.

Husserl reminds us, however, that we must not forget that the meaning of an act does not exhaust the full noema. Likewise, the noetic side of an intentional experience does not consist exclusively in the strict meaning-giving phase to which meaning specifically belongs as a correlate. As we will show presently, the full noema consists in a chain of noematic phases, and the phase of specific meaning supplies only a kind of necessary nucleus. Further phases are essentially grounded in this nucleus, and for that reason they too should be called phases of meaning.

To state again the only clear conclusion we have reached, intentional experience is undoubtedly such that, from a suitable viewpoint, a meaning can be extracted from it. The situation which defines this meaning for us cannot remain concealed. This situation is such that the non-existence of the presented or ideally constructed object in its plain and simple sense cannot deprive the presented object, as such, from the relevant presentation. In other words, a distinction must be made between the presented object and its presentation. As a matter of fact, the scholastic distinction between 'mental', 'intentional' or 'immanent' object and 'real' object, points to the same correlation. However, from a first apprehension of a distinction affecting the nature of consciousness

---

21. *Ibid.*, pp. 221-222 (240-241).

to its correct, phenomenologically pure determination and valuation, is a giant step and this step scholasticism failed to take.

Someone would perhaps suggest that the real object can be separated from the intentional object by saying: in experience the intention is given with its intentional object; this object, as such, belongs inseparably to it and therefore really lives in it. What the experience intends or presents is and remains with it, whether or not the corresponding 'real object' exists in reality. However, when we try to separate the real object from the intentional object in this way, by making the latter a real factor immanent in experience, we have to face the difficulty that now two realities must confront each other, whereas only one of them is present and possible. I perceive the tree there in the garden; that tree and nothing else is the real object of the perceiving intention. Obviously, a second, immanent tree, or even an 'inner image' of the real tree, is not *given,* and to assume that there is such a tree leads only to absurdity.

Husserl makes it clear that we must therefore restrict ourselves to what is given in pure experience. Through the phenomenological reduction every 'real' object is 'bracketed'. Hence, abiding by this suspension, we must try to describe only that which is self-evidently contained in the 'reduced' phenomenon. If we do this, it appears that every perception contains this: it has its noematic meaning, its 'perceived as such', which, as correlate, belongs to the phenomenologically reduced perception. In other words, any perception is a consciousness of a real world —the reality of which is placed between brackets—and this perceptually appearing world can be described as such.[22]

The Noema in Non-perceptual Experiences

According to Husserl what has been said here concerning perception applies to all types of intentional experience. Memory, after reduction, yields the 'remembered as such'; expectation, the 'expected as such'; phantasy the 'fancied as such'. In each of these experiences the object considered may be, for example, a tree in bloom, and in each of them

---

22. *Ibid.,* pp. 223-226 (241-245).

this tree may appear in such a way that the faithful description of what appears as such has to make use of the same expressions. Yet the noematic correlates are essentially different. In one case the character of that which appears is described as bodily reality, in another as fiction, and in a third as recollection. The characters in question are not added to, but found as inseparable features of the perceived, fancied, or remembered as such. They are features of the meaning of perception, that of fancy and that of memory, and they are found to belong of necessity to these in correlation with the respective types of noetic experience.

All this leads us to the remark that within the complete noema we must distinguish essentially different strata, grouped around a *central nucleus*. This nucleus is the pure 'objective meaning', i.e., that which in the above-mentioned examples could be described in identical objective terms regardless of the type of intentional experience.[23]

We must now describe the meaning of noesis and noema in the case of a derivative act. Let us take as an example the predicative judgment. The noema of a judgment is the judged content of the judgment as such. But this content, at least insofar as its central nucleus is concerned, is nothing other than that which we ordinarily refer to as the judgment.

To grasp the full noema, we must grasp it as we find it in reality, in the full noematic concreteness in which we are conscious of it when we concretely judge. Note that the judged content of the judgment is not to be confused with the matter judged about. When the judging process takes place on the basis of a perceiving act that plainly posits something, the noema of this presenting act becomes part of the judging act taken in its full concreteness. The presenting noesis likewise becomes a constitutive part of the essence of the concrete noesis of the judgment. The 'presented as such' receives the form of the apophantic subject or object. The object 'concerning which', and in particular the object we use as subject of our judgment, is the matter judged about. The whole that is formed out of this matter, the content

---

23. *Ibid.*, pp. 226-228 (245-246).

of the judgment as content, constitutes the full noematic correlate, the meaning of the judgment as experienced.

However, the phenomenological reduction must not be neglected here. If we wish to obtain the pure noema of our judgment as experienced, this reduction demands that we suspend the delivery of the judgment. If we do this, we find facing us in their phenomenological purity: 1) the full concrete essence of the judgment as experienced, i.e., the noesis of the judgment, apprehended concretely as essence; and 2) the noema of the judgment which belongs to the noesis and is necessarily one with it, i.e., the delivered judgment as *eidos*.[24]

These remarks briefly indicate some very important features of the relationship between noesis and noema. It is our intention to return to this fundamental phenomenological topic in the following chapter. The preceding descriptions suffice, we hope, as a preliminary idea of these two cardinal poles of the intentionality of consciousness: noesis and noema.

4. Dynamic Description of Intentionality

Functional Problems

Husserl leaves no room for doubt that as far as he is concerned the greatest of all phenomenological issues are the functional problems, i.e., the problems involved in the constitution of the objective field of consciousness. They concern the way in which, e.g., the noeses which animate the hyletic material and merge into unitary manifolds and continuous syntheses, bring forth the consciousness of something in such a way that in and through it the objective unity of the objectivities can be consistently and rationally determined.

The viewpoint of function is the central viewpoint of phenomenology. The inquiries to which it gives rise cover nearly the entire phenomenological sphere. All phenomenological analyses ultimately serve in one form or another as integral parts or lower grades of functions. Instead of analyzing, describing and classifying single experiences, the study of details is governed by the teleological view of their function in making *synthetic unity* possible.

---

24. *Ibid.*, pp. 232-237 (250-255).

For instance, in the sphere of experience, the functional method pays attention to the many forms of conscious continua and of discontinua of conscious experiences that are internally united through a common bond of meaning, through the unifying consciousness of one and the same objective datum which appears now in this perspective, and then in that, and presents itself either intuitively or as determined by thought. It seeks to discover how objective unities of every kind, immanent but not real, are 'known' or 'supposed'; how the identity of these suppositions is constituted by conscious formations that are of different types but whose structure is essentially fixed; and how these formations should be described along strictly methodical lines. The functional method, moreover, investigates how the unity of the objective content of every objective region and category can and must, in accordance with conscious insight, be disclosed or exposed as corresponding to 'reason' and 'unreason' respectively.

We must therefore study in the most general and comprehensive fashion how objective unities of every region and category are consciously constituted. We must systematically show how all the connections of our real and possible consciousness of these unities as essential possibilities are fixed by the essential nature of these types of consciousness: the simple or secondary intuitions intentionally related to them, the thought-formations of lower and higher levels, the confused and the clear, the expressed and the non-expressed, the pre-scientific and the scientific, up to the highest formations of strictly theoretical science. All fundamental types of possible consciousness, and the modifications, fusions, syntheses which essentially belong to them, must be made evident and systematically studied in their eidetic generality and phenomenological purity. We must study also how through their own essence they pre-figure all possibilities of being; and how the existing objects by virtue of absolutely fixed and essential laws are the correlates of conscious connections having a definite essential content, just as, conversely, the Being of systems thus articulated is equivalent to the existing objects. And in all these investigations we have to keep in mind that they refer to all regions of Being and all levels of generality.

From its pure eidetic and phenomenological standpoint which suspends the transcendent in every shape and form, phenomenology arrives inevitably at its own ground of pure consciousness, at this whole system of problems which are transcendental in the specific sense. For this reason it is rightly called 'transcendental phenomenology'. On its own ground it must come to the point where instead of treating experiences as dead material, as systems of content which simply are but 'mean' nothing, it masters its own group of problems which present experiences as intentional, solely by virtue of their eidetic essence as 'consciousness of'.[25]

Actuality and Potentiality of Intentional Life

As Husserl sees it, the most important problems of a genetic and dynamic study of intentionality are concerned with the different forms of synthesis: the synthesis uniting a multiplicity of aspects given in a multiplicity of acts into the experience of a single object, the synthesis uniting the different phases of a particular experience into the unity of a single total experience, the synthesis uniting the whole of conscious life into an all-embracing *cogito* which synthetically comprises all particular conscious processes and intends the world as horizon of every particular *cogitatum*. The fundamental form of this universal synthesis, which makes all other syntheses of consciousness possible, is the all-embracing consciousness of internal time. The correlate of this consciousness is immanent temporality itself as constant infinite horizon.[26]

The multiplicity, however, of the intentionality which belongs to any *cogito* relating to the world is not exhausted by considering cogitations as *actual* lived experiences. On the contrary, every actuality implies potentialities which, rather than being empty possibilities, are intentionally prefigured with respect to content. In addition, they have the character of possibilities that can be actualized by the ego. This feature indicates another fundamental characteristic of intentionality. Every lived experience has a horizon, which changes with the alteration of the links of consciousness to which the experience belongs and with the modification of the experience itself in the different phases of its flow.

---

25. *Ibid.,* pp. 212-215 (230-233).
26. Edmund Husserl, *Cart. Med.,* pp. 77-81 (39-43).

This horizon is an intentional horizon of reference to potentialities of consciousness which belong to the experience itself. For example, to every external perception there belongs its reference from the genuinely perceived sides of the object of perception to the sides that are also 'meant', though not yet explicitly perceived but only anticipated at first, with a non-intuitional emptiness as sides coming into view. There is a continuous 'protention' which in each phase of the perception has a new sense. Moreover, the perception has inner horizons made up of other possibilities of perception, which we could have if we actually took a different course of perception. Finally, every perception always has a horizon of the past, as a possibility of recollections that can be awakened and have their horizons of possible recollections.

All this was already mentioned in the foregoing. Here we want to focus attention on the fact only that these horizons are *predelineated potentialities* in the sense that we can ask any horizon what lies in it; we can explicitate, unfold, and uncover its potentialities. By doing this we uncover the objective meaning that is implicitly meant in every actual *cogito,* though never with more than a certain degree of determination. This meaning, this *cogitatum* as *cogitatum,* is never present to our consciousness as a finished datum; it is clarified only through the explicitation of the given horizons.

The predelineation itself is always imperfect. But despite its indeterminateness it has a determinate structure, that is, a determination and an openness which are both immediately given in any experience. This openness prior to further determinations is precisely what constitutes the horizon. As contrasted with the case of pure anticipating acts of imagining there occurs here, by means of an actual continuation of perception, a 'fulfilling' further determination, but it too always refers to new horizons.

Husserl explains thus that every consciousness is characterized essentially not only by being *somehow* able to change into continually new modes of consciousness of the same object, but also by being able to do so according to these horizon-intentionalities. The object is like an identity-pole, always meant as having a meaning that is still to be actualized. In every moment of consciousness it points to a noetic intentionality that pertains to it according to its meaning and that can and must be explained through intentional analyses.[27]

Husserl tells us further that, as we have seen, every perceived object is perceived in an outer horizon. The horizon of all possible horizons is the world. This horizon, however, is a horizon *sui generis;* it is not the synthesis of all possible horizons, but this total horizon is pre-given to every concrete horizon. The world is indeed that to which every being refers but, at the same time, it is also that from which every being ultimately must be understood and has its sense and meaning. The same applies to every particular horizon. The world is the root and goal of the particular horizons; it is transcendent in the strict sense of this term.

This transcendent total horizon manifests itself in every being and shows how this being must be explicitated. This world appears in a world-experience, in which everything is experienced but which itself is never experienced. Therefore, a very deep sense of transcendence manifests itself in every experience in which the ego experiences the world as transcendent horizon from which and in which it understands every being and itself. The world is that to which the ego transcends itself in every concrete experience. The world as world-experience and the ego as experience of the world are nothing but the final intentionality of consciousness. From the viewpoint of the ego, this intentionality is not a static consciousness of the world, but a dynamic, continuous self-transcendence to the world; this intentionality *is* not, but it functions. That is why it is called 'functioning intentionality'.[28] We have to return to this theme in a subsequent chapter.

5, *Intentional Analysis*

Function of Intentional Analysis Within Phenomenology

In the foregoing we gained an understanding of the fundamental principle that phenomenology, as understood by Husserl, wants to found all knowledge on an apodictic evidence that is immediately rooted in intuition. We have also seen that the transcendental reduction dis-

---

27. *Ibid.,* pp. 81-83 (44-46).
28. Gerd Brandt, *Welt, Zeit und Ich* (The Hague: Martinus Nijhoff, 1955), pp. 13-25.

closes a field of transcendental experience which is given with such an evidence. According to Husserl it must be possible now to found every actual and possible knowledge on this apodictic evidence by uncovering this field of transcendental experience in its universal structure.[29]

What this realm is becomes more manifest, Husserl tells us, as soon as we realize that every *cogito* necessarily implies its *cogitatum*. If, however, consciousness essentially is consciousness of something, then not only the *cogito* itself is apodictically evident, but also its *cogitatum*, provided at least that we maintain the transcendental reduction and, furthermore, consider the *cogitatum* in question solely insofar as it is immediately given in this *cogito*.[30]

The transcendental-phenomenological reflection enables us therefore to analyze and describe the *cogitata* exactly as they were 'meant' (*noemata*) and to describe the *noeses* correlated to these *noemata*. Our universal *epoché* thus does not simply take away the world from phenomenology, but lets us retain it, after the reduction, as *cogitatum*.[31]

We must, however, as Husserl warns us, be very careful here. For at first sight in this way 'pure Being itself' may seem to be found in the evidence of every *cogito,* so that all we have to do simply is to intuit and grasp it. On closer investigation, however, it appears that in the transcendental sphere the different objectivities are not found in the cogitations as matches in a box, but are constituted in different types of synthesis, since what is meant (the object) is practically never identical with what immediately appears (*noema*).[32] Let us try to explain this.

Every inquiry into consciousness implies two sides, a noematic and a noetic side, which, however, descriptively are inseparable. One of the most important points in our analysis and description will be to describe and explain the syntheses which occur in every act of con-

---

29. Edmund Husserl, *Die Idee,* pp. 59-60 (46-48).
30. Edmund Husserl, *Cart. Med.,* pp. 66-70 (27-31).
31. *Ibid.,* pp. 70-75 (31-37).
32. Edmund Husserl, *Die Idee,* pp. 70-72 (55-57).

sciousness and which have their noematic and noetic sides. A die, for instance, is given continuously in perception as an objective unity in a multiplicity of modes of appearing and these modes are correlates of a multiplicity of individual noeses. How can we explain and describe that we experience a multiplicity of aspects, given in a multiplicity of individually different acts, as one and the same perception of one single object? Thus, once we have started the phenomenological task of describing consciousness concretely an endless horizon of facts discloses itself, and all these facts can be characterized as facts of synthetic structures which give noetic-noematic unity to the individual cogitations and their *cogitata*. Only the elucidation of the peculiar operation called 'synthesis' can make the disclosure of the *cogito* as 'consciousness-of' fruitful for philosophy. This elucidation is the task of the *intentional analysis*.[33]

The Proper Nature of Intentional Analysis

It should be evident that the intentional analysis of consciousness is wholly different from analyses in the usual, natural sense. Consciousness is not simply a whole made up of data of consciousness and, therefore, capable of being analyzed or divided into self-sufficient and nonself-sufficient elements or parts. True, in certain themes intentional analysis leads also to such distinctions and divisions, yet everywhere its peculiar attainment, as intentional, is to disclose the potentialities implicit in the actualities of consciousness. This disclosure results, on the noematic side, in an explicitation of what is consciously meant and, on the noetic side, in the explicitation of the possible intentional experiences themselves. Intentional analysis is guided by the fundamental principle that every consciousness is an intending of 'what is meant', but that at any time, this something 'meant' is more than what is given explicitly at that time. The intending-beyond-itself, which is implicit in any consciousness, must be considered to be an essential aspect of consciousness.

The phenomenologist's inquiry, however, does not arise from a naïve devotedness to the intentional object, purely as such. He wants also to describe the noetic manifolds of consciousness and their synthetic unity,

---

33. *Ibid.*, pp. 72-76 (57-60).

through which alone we have one intentional object. When the phenomenologist explores everything objective with its content solely as a correlate of consciousness, he does not consider and describe it simply only as *somehow* referring back to the corresponding cogito. Rather with his reflective glance he penetrates an anonymous cogitative life and uncovers there the definite synthetic courses taken by the manifold modes of consciousness. Beyond them, he uncovers the mode of ego-comportment, which leads to an understanding of how my consciousness makes it possible and necessary that this or that exisiting object with these determinations is intended in it, occurs in it as this or that meaning. It is to be noted here that the phenomenological explicitation of the perceived as such, is not restricted to its perceptual explicitation. On the contrary, the phenomenological explicitation shows what is included and non-intuitively co-intended in the very meaning of the *cogitatum*, by making present in imagination the potential perceptions which will make the invisible visible.

By explicitating their correlative horizons in this fashion intentional analysis brings the highly diverse anonymous lived experiences to the fore, including those which have a constitutive function in relation to the objective meaning of the *cogitatum* in question. Only in this way can the phenomenologist explain how, within the immanence of conscious life and in the variously determined modes of consciousness, it is possible to intend anything like fixed and permanent objective unities, and how this marvelous operation of constituting identical objects is performed for each category of objects. The horizon structure which belongs to every intentionality makes phenomenological analysis and description follow a completely new kind of method.[34]

The most universal type, within which everything particular is included as special form, is indicated by our first universal scheme: *ego-cogito-cogitatum*. The most universal descriptions which we have attempted concerning intentionality, its peculiar synthesis, etc., refer to this type. In the particularizations of this type and their descriptions the intentional object plays the role of a transcendental 'clue' to the typical infinite manifolds of possible cogitations.

---

34. Edmund Husserl, *Cart. Med.*, pp. 83-87 (46-49).

The point of departure is the object given directly at this particular time. From it reflection goes back to the mode of consciousness as it is at that moment and to the potential modes of consciousness included 'horizontally' in that mode; next, it goes to those modes in which the object might be differently intended as the same, such as perception, retention, recollection, and expectation. And each of those types is further particularized in its whole noetico-noematic structure, according as the intentional object is more particularized; e.g., as *cogitatum* as such, as anything whatsoever, as 'a single object', a 'concrete spatial thing', or 'an animate being.'

Each type disclosed by these clues is to be investigated in its noetic-noematic structure. It is to be systematically explicitated with respect to the modes of intentional flow pertaining to it, and with respect to their horizons and the intentional processes implicit in them. No matter how fluid the modes of consciousness may be, they are always restricted to a set of structural types, which remain invariably the same, as long as the objectivity intended remains this one type of this determinate kind.

To explicitate systematically this set of structural types is precisely the task of the transcendental theory. If this theory is restricted to an objective universality as its clue, it is called the theory of the transcendental constitution of any object whatsoever, as an object of the category or the region in question. It is this subject which will occupy us in the following chapter.[35]

In concluding Husserl makes clear that the peculiar attainment of intentional analysis is to disclose the potentialities implied in the actualities of consciousness. He sees intentional analysis as the general method of elucidation and explicitation of meanings, and that as such it consists in disclosing and disengaging those constituents which are necessarily implied in a certain meaning experienced in a given situation.[36] Concerning the perceptual apprehension of a material thing, for instance, the method requires that the examination of a given perception be not

---

35. *Ibid.,* pp. 87-89 (50-53).
36. Gaston Berger, *Recherches sur les conditions de la connaissance* (Paris: Aubier, 1942), p. 101.

confined to what presents itself in direct sense-experience. For, in fact, the meaning of a perception, the *cogitatum qua cogitatum*, the perceptual noema, the perceived thing as it presents itself before the experiencing subject's mind in and through the act under consideration, is only indicated in a merely implicit way by what is given in direct sense-experience. For a complete analysis and clarification of the perceptual meaning, a progressive explicitation of the inner horizon is required.[37] Thus, we have resorted to intentional analysis when, going beyond what is given in direct sense experience, we have pointed out the 'inner horizon' in its role as co-determinant of the perceptual meaning. From the noetic point of view, the explicitation of the inner horizon appears as a disclosure of anticipations with which the given perception is interwoven. These anticipations of potential perceptions, when actualized, will render visible what is unseen at the moment.[38] To submit a perception to intentional analysis amounts to considering it with regard to other perceptions, namely, the group of those related to the same thing. The material thing, as an objective unity, is constituted by perceptions concatenating themselves into one coherent systematic group. The thing is that which it progressively reveals itself to be through those perceptions. Since the thing derives the sense of its existence from the systematic concatenation and intertexture of these perceptions, the investigation of a single act of perception by the method of intentional analysis is founded on the contribution of that perception toward the constitution of the appearing thing. Such an investigation is concerned with the role the chosen single perception plays in the group to which it belongs and with which it is concatenated. Examining a single perception by the method of intentional analysis, we must concentrate upon the function which this single perception assumes in the synthesis of identification, which is the fundamental characteristic of the perceptual process.[39]

---

37. Edmund Husserl, *Cart. Med.*, pp. 77-78 (39-40).
38. *Ibid.*, pp. 78-79 (40-41).
39. *Ibid.*, pp. 79-81 (41-43). *Ideen I*, pp. 213-214 (231-232). See for *section 5* as a whole also Aron Gurwitsch, *The Field of Consciousness* (Pittsburgh: Duquesne University Press, 1964), pp. 199-305 (passim).

CHAPTER SEVEN

CONSTITUTION

1. Historical Introduction

Constitution: an 'Operational' Concept in Husserl's Phenomenology .

According to Fink, constitution is one of those concepts which Husserl never has explained accurately and completely. It is an 'operational' concept with which he continually 'works' without thematizing it explicitly. Although for Husserl himself this concept must have had a precise meaning, for us it remains ambiguous, as are many other basic concepts of his phenomenology such as 'phenomenon', 'production', 'achievement' and 'reduction'. Despite the fact that sometimes, or in the case of 'reduction' even often, Husserl explicitly thematized them, in fact these concepts remained 'operational' only.[1] Moreover, it is historically certain that Husserl's ideas underwent a long evolution also with respect to this point. In his older phenomenological studies he only spoke of the constitution of objects and objectivities in consciousness;[2] later he mentioned the synthetical constitution of acts or also of *synthesis*,[3] and finally he referred to the universal constitution of the whole of conscious life and even the transcendental constitution of the transcendental ego itself.[4]

Nevertheless, we should be prudent here. Without any doubt, Husserl's idea of constitution underwent a long and profound evolution with respect to the extent and the 'how' of the constitution; on the other hand, it is also historically certain that he never changed his mind regarding the essence and meaning of the constitution.[5] In his lecture series of 1907, *The Idea of Phenomenology*, Husserl presented

---

1. Eugen Fink, "Operative Begriffe in Husserls Phänomenologie", pp. 321-322 and pp. 335-337.
2. Edmund Husserl, *Die Idee*, pp. 67-76 (52-60). See also Biemel's *Introduction, ibid.*, p. *viii* and p. *ix*.
3. Edmund Husserl, *Ideen I*, pp. 212-215 (230-233), 291-293 (307-309), 338-341 (354-357).
4. Edmund Husserl, *Cart. Med.*, pp. 32-34.
5. Walter Biemel, "Les phases décisives dans le développement de la philosophie de Husserl", pp. 32-34.

the first outline of his transcendental phenomenology and tried to describe what constitution and constitutional problems really are and mean. When we compare this description with that offered in his *Cartesian Meditations* which were written when Husserl was about seventy years old, we find that they are essentially the same. In 1906 Husserl describes the meaning of constitution in general as the 'dissolution of Being in consciousness'.[6] In other manuscripts of this period he explicitly pointed out that his transcendental phenomenology is identical with a phenomenology of 'constituting' consciousness.[7]

The Meaning of Constitution in 'The Idea of Phenomenology' (1907)

It is very illustrative to see, how in *The Idea* this important concept for the first time is introduced within the context of a theoretical treatise concerning the meaning of phenomenology as a whole. Since Husserl apparently was not completely satisfied with the first draft of the fifth lecture in which this concept was explained in some details, we shall follow here his summary written immediately after the last lecture on May 2, 1907.[8]

In this summary Husserl says that on the first and lowest level of the phenomenological considerations, it seems at first very easy to understand what is meant by evidence. Evidence seems to be only a question of seeing and intuiting; my intuiting grasp intuits the things which are simply there before me; they are there in consciousness in a really evident intuiting, and my intuiting glance simply looks at them, grasps them, and takes them just as they are in themselves. Any difference between the things and their givenness is founded, then, in the things themselves which in themselves have all their distinctions.

On closer investigation and analysis, however, this intuiting glance appears to be completely different from such a simple 'seeing'. Although the indescribable and indistinct intuiting glance is to be maintained under the title 'attention', it will be evident that it is meaningless to speak here of things which simply are there for me and only have

---

6. See Walter Biemel's *Introduction* to Husserl's *Die Idee*, p. *viii*.
7. *Ibid.*, p. *ix*.
8. *Ibid.*, pp. 87-88.

to be intuited. This 'simply being there' appears to imply a complex of different experiences possessing their own specific structures, such as perception, phantasy, memory, retention, and expectation. Things are not in consciousness as matches in a box, but in and through these experiences things are *constituted* in such a way that they are in no way really contained in these experiences. For every thing 'to be given' means in this or that way to come into being in and through our lived experiences and to be presented by them. Moreover, things are not there first and subsequently impress 'pictures' of themselves on our consciousness. In our phenomenological reduction the things are 'in' the appearances, and only because they appear to us are they given in themselves. It is true that they appear as being independent of this individual appearance, but essentially they are inseparable from the appearing itself.

Everywhere we find that marvelous intentional relationship between the knowing act and the known object. The task of phenomenology is not to intuit this relation and to describe it, but to explain how an object of knowledge is constituted in our knowing acts. Within the sphere of pure self-givenness and evidence we must analyze and describe all the modes of presentation and the correlates which become manifest in them. Only in this way will we see *how* the transcendent real object is found and known in the acts of knowledge itself, namely, as that which at the outset was 'meant' only, and *how* the sense of this meaning is continuously fulfilled in the progressing coherence of knowledge in an original act of synthesis. Then we will experience how the objects of knowledge are continuously constituted, and how this constitution is predetermined by the fact that these objects essentially require such a gradual constitution. Phenomenology studies in a scientific and radical way the constitution of objectivities of every kind of consciousness, the acts of consciousness and their correlates, phenomena in an active and a passive sense.[9]

Constitution in Husserl's Later Works

In his *Ideas* and especially in the *Cartesian Meditations* Husserl's description of the essence and meaning of constitution is much clearer

---

9. *Ibid.*, pp. 11-14 (8-12).

and more radical. It is also true that the domain of constitution is considerably enlarged there. But with respect to the essence these descriptions seem to be identical to that of *The Idea of Phenomenology*.

In these later works, Husserl clearly explains again that the main intention of his constitutional phenomenology is to identify Being and intelligibility, to reduce Being to reason.[10] According to this view, not only is knowledge constituted in consciousness, but the very Being of that which is known is also so constituted. For only 'absolute Being' is Being in the full sense, and only consciousness and Being-in-consciousness are forms of 'absolute Being' which, thus, necessarily belong together. Now, since Being is in consciousness only as constituted by consciousness, Being is absolute only just as constituted. Thus, intentional constitution becomes a universal explanation or clarification of Being. Nothing is, except by a proper achievement of consciousness, whether actual or potential.[11] If, then, the task of philosophy is to understand Being, its method must be to penetrate the subjectivity wherein Being has its source and to clarify the original constitution of Being in and by that transcendental subjectivity.[12]

Compared with the analyses given in Husserl's later works, those presented in *Ideas* appear relatively static. They give only the order in which the different constitutive layers rest upon one another and in which they constitute themselves in consciousness. Husserl first tried to describe the constitution of the world of material things, then presented a description of the constitution of our body and, finally, that of the world of our personal life. A special feature of these constitutions is their final dependence on a pre-given *hylē*, the hyletic sense-data. The experience of such *hylē* involves at first sight the dependence of the transcendental constitution on factors that are not dependent upon the transcendental subjectivity. It is often said that this fact points to a 'realistic' element in the very core of constitutive phenomenology. However, it is merely a sign that these analyses are not yet completely radical

---

10. Edmund Husserl, *Ideen I*, pp. 329-333 (345-349) ; *Cart. Med.*, pp. 91-92 (56-57).

11. Edmund Husserl, *F. tr. L.*, p. 207.

12. Quentin Lauer, *The Triumph of Subjectivity*, pp. 79-80.

and that they have to be supplemented with more fundamental analyses. That is one of the reasons why Husserl's later works tried to trace the hyletic data back to a deeper kind of constitution of a completely active nature.[13]

That there is no abrupt shift in Husserl's thinking but rather an evolution and a radicalization can readily be seen in his various constitutional analyses of time-consciousness. We know already that this topic forms the major field in which Husserl tried to clarify the ultimate meaning of constitution. As we have seen, Husserl originally had inherited this topic from Brentano. Studying the problems connected with our consciousness of internal time again and again, he gradually came to the conclusion that it contained the clue to the universal phenomenological problem of constitution. In the investigations made between 1905 and 1910 the stress is put on the passive synthetic genesis of time and these descriptions do not yet supply any evidence for an active constitution of time.[14] However, from these analyses it became gradually clear to Husserl, that the constitution of internal time could throw more light on the constitution of the different types of objectivities.

His studies in this direction, performed between 1929 and 1938, are not yet published. But, as is clear from the investigations of Brand and Diemer, these studies do not offer more than the first indications of what Husserl hoped to demonstrate: the primal constitution of the stream of time by active hidden achievements of transcendental subjectivity which is presupposed in all other constitutions, such as the constitution of the hyletic data themselves and the intentional objectivities based on those data. It was in this way that Husserl tried to establish a new form of 'transcendental idealism'. The brief indications of the *Cartesian Meditations* and the analyses of the later manuscripts are suggestive, but they do not really show how all objectivities owe together with their being known their very Being itself to active achievements of transcendental subjectivities.[15]

---

13. Herbert Spiegelberg, *op. cit.* vol. I, p. 147.
14. See, for instance, Husserl's *The Phenomenology of Internal Time Consciousness,* pp. 98-126.
15. Gerd Brand, *op. cit.,* pp. 54-141 (passim). A. Diemer, *op. cit.,* pp. 143-175. See also: Herbert Spiegelberg, *op. cit.,* pp. 146-149.

Be this as it may, in his *Cartesian Meditations* Husserl introduces the constitutional problems in the following way. As we have seen, every inquiry into consciousness implies two sides, a noematic and a noetic side which, however, descriptively are inseparable. One of the most important things in our noetic-noematic analyses is to describe and explain the synthesis which takes place in every consciousness. For example, if I take the perceiving of a die as a theme of analysis and description, I see in pure reflection that this die is given continuously as an objective unity in a multiform and changeable multiplicity of manners of appearing. In their temporal flow these acts of perception are not an incoherent sequence of lived experiences, but rather merge in the unity of a synthesis, in such a way that in them one and the same die is intended as appearing. The one identical die appears now in close appearances now in distant appearances, in the changing modes of 'here' and 'there', over against an always co-intended 'absolute here'. Moreover, each manner of appearance in such a mode shows itself to be the synthetic unity pertaining to a multiplicity of manners of appearance belonging to that mode. Thus, the die here near by, appears as the same now from this side, now from that, and in every case shows me a determinate perspective. The same holds good for every aspect and property of the die: we always find the aspect in question as a unity belonging to a passing flow of multiplicities of acts. Thus, each passing *cogito* intends its *cogitatum* as a *cogito* possessing a describable structure of multiplicities that has a definite noetic-noematic composition which, by virtue of its essential nature, belongs to only this identical *cogitatum*. Now the question must be asked: How can we explain and describe that we experience a multiplicity of appearances given in a multiplicity of noeses, as the perception of one single thing? It is only by clarifying the so-called 'synthesis' that the discovery of the intentional character of the *cogito* can become fruitful.[16]

Now, the fundamental form of synthesis is identification. We first encounter it as an all-encompassing, passively flowing synthesis in the form of a continuous consciousness of internal time. Every experience has its internal temporality. In the experience of a die, for instance, we

---

16. Edmund Husserl, *Cart. Med.*, pp. 77-79 (39-41).

can make a distinction between the objective temporality of this die and the internal temporality of our die-perceiving. The noetic appearing flows away with the temporal phases which are the continually changing appearances of this identical die. The unity of these phases is a unity of synthesis. It does not consist in a being-stuck to one another externally, but in a connectedness that makes the unity of a single consciousness, in which the unity of one intentional objectivity as the same objectivity belonging to multiple modes of appearance becomes *constituted*. The one identical die as appearing is continuously immanent in the flowing stream of consciousness, it is descriptively *in* it, not as a real intrinsic component, but as something intentional, as its immanent objective meaning. This object of consciousness, as identical with itself during the flowing experience, does not come into the experience from without, but is an intentional effect produced by the synthesis of consciousness itself. Thus, also the immanent objective sense as a whole is constituted in and by consciousness.

One and the same die can also be intended in completely different types of acts, simultaneously or successively in separate perceptions, recollections, expectations, etc. Here again it is a synthesis which gives rise to consciousness of identity of one and the same immanent objective meaning.

Moreover, also in every consciousness of a plurality and a relational complex there is a synthesis. And finally the whole of conscious life is unified synthetically: it is an all-embracing *cogito,* synthetically comprising all particular conscious experiences and intending the world as horizon of every particular horizon.[17]

It is the task of the constitutional analyses of phenomenology to analyse, describe and explain the constitution which takes place in all these syntheses.[18]

2. *Constitutional Problems*

A More Accurate Description of Constitution

In the foregoing chapters we spoke repeatedly of 'synthesis', 'constitution', and 'genesis', without describing these terms accurately, and

---

17. *Ibid.,* pp. 79-81 (41-43).
18. Edmund Husserl, *F. tr. L.,* pp. 276-280.

without precisely indicating their meaning in the whole of transcendental phenomenology. Because these expressions point at the very heart of transcendental phenomenology we must try to explain them now by describing the problems to which they refer, the methods to be used in order to solve these problems, and the solutions themselves.

It is Husserl's claim that hitherto it was irrelevant to our intentional analyses whether their objects were Being or not really Being. Now however, we must try to deal with this distinction explicitly under the title Reason and Unreason as a correlative expression for Being and Non-Being.

By our *epoché* we have effected a reduction to our pure meaning act (*cogito*) and the 'meant' (its *cogitatum*), purely as 'meant'. The predicates 'Being' and 'Non-Being' now refer to the 'meant', not as an object but as an objective sense; truth and falsity refer to the 'meaning' act.

Husserl is of the opinion that, as is evident from the study of intentional analysis, these predicates are not *ipso facto* given as phenomenological themes, when 'meaning' act and objective sense are given and described. On the other hand, these predicates have their phenomenological origin in these correlative entities. As we have seen, the multiple modes of consciousness that belong together synthetically and pertain to every object meant, appear to be founded on an initial intending act which has the typical nature of a verifying and, in particular, an evidently verifying synthesis. When such a synthesis occurs, the object meant has, correlatively the characteristic of 'Being' or 'existing'; or else there are nullifying syntheses and then the object meant has, correlatively, the characteristic of 'Non-Being' or 'non-existing'. These synthetic occurrences are intentionalities of a higher level, which essentially and, in exclusive disjunction, pertain to every objective sense from the side of the acts and their correlates which in principle can be produced by the transcendental ego. Reason, thus, refers to the possibility of verification which transcendental subjectivity in principle always has, and verification refers to making evident. That is why we must return here to one of the preceding chapters in which the concept of evidence was explained.[19]

---

19. Edmund Husserl, *Cart. Med.*, pp. 91-92 (56-57).

Reality as the Correlate of Evident Verification

Husserl points out that in the broadest sense evidence indicates a universal primal phenomenon of our intentional life, viz., the mode of consciousness that consists in the self-appearance, the self-giving of a thing or state of affairs, in the final mode of 'it itself here', 'immediately intuited' and 'given originally'. For the ego this signifies not aiming confusedly at something with an empty expectant intention, but being with it itself, seeing and intuiting it itself. Every experience in the ordinary sense of the term is evident in this broadest sense.

In the case of most objects evidence is only an occasional occurrence in conscious life; nevertheless, it is also a possibility that could be the aim of an actualizing intention in any particular case. Thus, it is an essential fundamental characteristic of all intentional life. Any consciousness, without exception, either is itself already to be characterized as evidence, giving its intended object originally or it essentially tends toward conversion into original presentation of its object and therefore toward syntheses of verification which belong essentially to the domain of the 'I can'.

Within the realm of the transcendental reduction we can ask any vague consciousness, whether and to what extent—as long as the identity of the object meant is preserved—the meant object in the mode of 'it itself' corresponds to that consciousness. During the process of verification, however, verification can turn into its negative. Then it appears that Non-Being must be conceived of as a modality of Being in the sense of certain Being. Evidence thus appears to be correlated with Being and with all the modal variants of Being possible, Being probably, Being doubtful, etc.[20]

All these differences, moreover, are split into two by a difference that extends throughout the whole sphere of consciousness, namely, between reality and 'as-if-reality' of phantasy. So a new universal concept of possibility arises, which repeats in modified form all the modes of Being and repeats them as modes belonging to purely imagined non-

---

20. *Ibid.*, pp. 92-93 (57-58).

realties, in contrast to the modes belonging to reality itself in all its modalities.

Correlatively, all modes of consciousness are likewise divided into those of *positionality* and those of *quasi-positionality*. And to each of these modes there corresponds both a particular mode of evidence of its object meant, and of potentialities of making these objects evident. All this must be explained in phenomenology in an original process of *clarification* which ultimately is founded on a prefigurative intuition. This prefigurative intuition of a verifying fulfillment as such, however, furnishes a realizing evidence not that the content in question *is*, but only that it could be. For such an intuition only contains the meaning in an implicit way; if it would be a direct self-giving act, it would fulfil and verify its meaning with respect to its existential sense.[21]

These brief observations refer first of all to formally universal problems of intentional analysis and to investigations concerning the phenomenological origin of the principles and fundamental concepts of formal logic. At the same time, however, they make it evident too that these concepts in their formal-ontological universality point to a universal conformity of the structural laws of our conscious life, a harmony by virtue of which alone truth and reality are able to have meaning for us. True, the fact that objects in the broadest sense, such as real things, lived experiences, or numbers, exist for me, says nothing immediately about evidence itself; it says only that objects are accepted by me: they are for me as *cogitata* intended in the positional mode of 'certain believing'. However, we know also that we should have to abandon that acceptance, if a course of evident identifying syntheses were to lead to conflict with an evident datum, for we can be sure that something is real only as long as a synthesis of evident verification takes place. It is clear that truth and the true reality of objects are to be obtained only from evidence, and that it is through evidence alone that a really existing, true and rightly accepted object has meaning for us. Every claim of being right comes from evidence and therefore from transcendental subjectivity itself.[22]

---

21. *Ibid.,* p. 93 (58-59).
22. *Ibid.,* pp. 94-95 (59-60).

Constitutional Problems Concerning the World

Neither the identity of any object meant nor that of a truly existing object, nor the identity constituted in the adequation of the object meant as such with the object that truly is, is really an intrinsic moment of the transient lived experience of evidence and verification. However, we have here an *ideal immanence* referring to further complexes of possible syntheses as complexes that play an essential role here. For, every evidence founds for me an abiding possession. I can always return to this reality beheld in itself in a series of new evidences securing the first evidence. For instance, in the case of evidence of immanent data, I can return to them in a series of intuitive recollections which, as a potential horizon, creates the 'I can always do so again'. Without such possibilities there would be for me no fixed and abiding Being, no real nor ideal world. For both of these exist for us only thanks to the evidence, or the presumption, that we will always be able to 'make evident' in the future or to repeat acquired evidences of the past.

Thus, the particular evidence itself does not as yet produce for us any abiding Being. We must distinguish here between everything that exists 'in itself' and the accidental 'Being for me' of this particular act with its particular noema. On the other hand, however, the 'in itself' refers us also to a certain evidence, not to a particular evidence as a factual experience and its correlate, but to determinate potentialities which are grounded in the transcendental ego and its transcendental life, namely: 1) the infinity of intending acts which all relate to something as identical, and 2) the potential evidences which, as particular and factual experiences, are repeatable *in infinitum.*[23]

In another and even more complicated manner evidences refer to infinities of evidences relating to the same object. For they make their object itself given with an essential onesidedness because of the perspectivism and the inner and outer horizon we have spoken of. This one-sidedness is found not only in the totality of evidences of the real and objective world but also in every particular object in it.

The evidence pertaining to particular objects in a real objective world is rooted in 'external experience'; in this case there is no other

---

23. *Ibid.,* pp. 95-96 (60-61).

mode of self-presentation. As we have seen, this kind of evidence has an essential onesidedness which entails a multiform horizon of unfulfilled anticipations, which are in need of fulfillment. This imperfect evidence can be made more and more perfect by means of the actualizing synthetic transitions from evidence to evidence, but there is no imaginable synthesis here which is ever completed as an adequate evidence, because any such synthesis must always involve unfulfilled meanings. At the same time, there always remains the open possibility that the belief in Being will not be fulfilled and that what seemed to be does not exist. The external experience verifies objects of external experience only as long as the passively or actively continuing experiences together constitute a harmonious synthesis. That the Being of the world is, and necessarily remains, transcendent to consciousness does not at all alter the fact that it is only by our conscious life that everything transcendent becomes constituted, as something inseparable from consciousness; only conscious life, as world-consciousness, bears within itself inseparably the meaning 'world', 'this really existing world'. Only an uncovering of the horizon of experience ultimately clarifies the reality and transcendency of the world and, at the same time, shows the world to be inseparable from the transcendental subjectivity which ultimately constitutes the reality of meaning and Being.

The reference to harmonious infinities of further possible experiences manifestly signifies that every real object belonging to the world, as well as the world itself, is an infinite idea, related to infinities of harmoniously combinable experiences—an idea that is the correlate of the idea of a perfect experiential evidence and a complete synthesis of possible experiences.[24]

We must therefore conclude that 'true Being' and 'truth' indicate, in the case of any object meant or even able to be meant by me as transcendental ego, a structural differentiation among the infinite multiplicities of actual and possible cogitations, which relate to the object in question and thus can somehow go together to make up the unity of an identifying synthesis.

---

24. *Ibid.*, pp. 96-97 (61-62).

A really existing object indicates a particular synthesis within this multiplicity, namely, the system of evidences relating to this object and belonging together in such a way that they combine to make up one, perhaps infinite, total evidence. This *would* be an absolutely perfect evidence which *would* finally present the object itself just as it is. It is completely impossible to produce such an evidence: it is an idea in the Kantian sense only.[25]

The task of the transcendental constitution of really existing objectivity is to clarify with respect to all essential structures, the intrinsic structure of the dimensions of infinity that systematically make up the ideal infinite synthesis of this evidence. Besides those formally universal investigations which confine themselves to the formal-ontological concept of any object whatsoever as such, we have to explain the immense problems of that constitution which occurs with respect to each region of objects such as 'physical nature', 'living being', 'man', 'human community', 'culture', etc. Yet in every case we meet principally the same problem and have to use the same method.[26]

3. Development of the Constitutional Problems Regarding the Transcendental Ego Itself. Transcendental Idealism

The Problem of the Self-Constitution of the Ego

As Husserl sees it, we must at this point have come to the conclusion that objects exist for me, and that they are for me what they are only as objects of actual or possible consciousness. If this statement is to have any meaning, Husserl claims, we must be able to explain what is concretely involved in this 'existence as Being-for-me', to what kind of consciousness the statement refers, what the structure of consciousness is precisely, what exactly is meant here by 'possibility', and other similar questions. They can be answered only through constitutional investigations.

25. Edmund Husserl, *Ideen I*, pp. 348-351 (364-367).
26. Edmund Husserl, *Cart. Med.*, pp. 97-99 (62-64).
27. *Ibid.*, pp. 99-100 (65).

Moreover, only one method is possible here, the one required by the essence of intentionality and of its horizons. For, the transcendental ego is what it is solely in relation to its intentional objectivities. Among these, there are not only objects within its adequately verifiable sphere of immanent time, but also world objects which are shown to be existent only in its inadequate and merely presumptive external experience.

Thus, it is an essential property of the ego constantly to have systems of intentionality as actualities or potentialities. Each object that this ego ever 'means', thinks of, or values, indicates this object's correlative system and exists only as the correlate of that system.

An important element, however, is still missing in our explanations. The ego itself is existent for itself by continuously constituting itself as existing: it transcendentally constitutes itself. The ego grasps itself not only as a flow of life, but also as an I, who lives through the cogitations of this flow as the same 'I myself'.

Hitherto we paid attention only to the intentional relation between the *cogito* and its *cogitatum*. Our attention was focused only on that synthesis which polarizes the manifolds of actual and possible consciousnesses toward identical objects as synthetic unities. Here, however, we meet a second polarization, a second type of synthesis. It encompasses all the particular manifolds of cogitations as belonging to the identical ego, which, as the active subject of consciousness, lives in all experiences as related through them to all object-poles.[28]

Note, however, that this 'centering' ego is not an empty pole of identity. Rather, according to a law of transcendental genesis it acquires a new abiding property every time an act emanates from it and has a new objective meaning. When in an act of judgment I decide for the first time that something exists or is this or that, the flowing act passes, but from now on I am abidingly the ego who is thus decided: I am of this or that conviction. This does not mean merely that I remember that act now, or can remember it later, but so long as the act and its correlate are accepted by me, I can also return to them again and again, find them as mine and, correlatively, find myself as the ego which is convinced in this or that way.

---

28. *Ibid.*, p. 100 (66).

The temporal ordering of such determining properties of the ego manifestly is not a continuous filling of immanent time with lived experiences—just as the abiding ego itself, as the pole of the abiding ego-properties, is not an experience or a continuity of lived experiences, even though the ego is so related to the stream of the lived experiences. Since by its own active genesis, the ego constitutes itself as an identical substratum of ego-properties, it constitutes itself also as a fixed and abiding personal ego.[29]

From the ego as the identical pole and substratum of the habitual properties we must now distinguish the ego in full concreteness, which will be called the concrete 'monad'. The ego can be concrete only in the flowing manifold of its intentional life, along with the objects meant in its concrete acts.

This is to be understood in the following way. As ego, I have a surrounding world which is continually existing for me, and in which objects exist for me as already distinguished into objects with which I am acquainted and those which I only anticipate as objects with which I may become acquainted. The former, which are in the first sense existing for me, are such by an original acquisition of what I had never beheld previously, and by my explicitation of it through particular intuitions of its features. Thereby, in my syntheitc activity, the object becomes constituted originally, perceptively, in the explicit form of something identical having its manifold properties. Thus, my activity of positing and explicitating Being sets up a habituality of my ego by virtue of which the object, as having its manifold determinations, is mine abidingly. Such abiding acquisitions constitute my surrounding world, insofar as I am acquainted with it at this time, with its horizons of objects with which I am unacquainted, that is, objects yet to be acquired but already anticipated with this formal object-structure.

I exist for myself and am continuously given to myself in experiential evidence as 'I myself'. This is true of the transcendental ego and, correspondingly, of the psychologically pure ego; it is true, moreover, with respect to any sense of the word 'ego'. Since the monadic concrete ego includes the whole of actual and potential conscious life,

---

29. *Ibid.*, pp. 100-101 (66-67).

it is clear that the problem of explaining this monadic ego phenomenologically must include all constitutional problems without any exception. Consequently, the phenomenology of the self-constitution coincides
with phenomenology as a whole.[30]

Transcendental Analysis as Eidetic

With the doctrine of the ego as pole of its acts and as substratum
of its habitual properties we have reached the level of genetic phenomenology which deals with the problems of phenomenological genesis.
However, before we can clarify more precisely what genetic phenomenology is, we must once more reflect upon the phenomenological method.
We must try to apply a fundamental methodological procedure which
was already explained in the foregoing, namely the eidetic reduction.
In order to facilitate the approach to the constitutional problems, in our
considerations concerning analysis and constitution we have made use
of a merely empirical description, although this description remained
in the sphere of transcendental experience. The use of the method of
eidetic description transfers all empirical descriptions into a new and
fundamental dimension. This dimension is relatively easy to grasp now
that we have given a number of empirical descriptions.

The method of transcendental reduction, Husserl continues, reduced
each of us, as a Cartesian meditator, to his transcendental ego with its
concrete monadic contents as this *de facto* and exclusively absolute ego.
When I continue meditating, I find types that can be descriptively
formulated and intentionally explicated, and thus I am able to progress
step by step in the intentional uncovering of my 'monad' along the
fundamental lines that offer themselves to me. In the course of our
descriptions such expressions as 'essential necessity' and 'essentially
determined' forced themselves upon us. These phrases express a definite
concept of the *a priori,* first clarified and founded by phenomenology.

To clarify the matter let us look at some particular examples. Any
type of intentional, lived experience will do; therefore, take this perception. Let us think of it as explicitated and described by intentional

---

30. *Ibid.,* pp. 102-103 (67-68).

analysis with respect to noesis and noema. This can signify, and so we did understand it up to now, that only a type of the *de facto* occurrence in the *de facto* transcendental ego is in question and that these descriptions have an 'empirical' significance. But involuntarily our description was of such a universality that its results remain unaffected by the empirical facticity of the transcendental ego. Let us, says Husserl, make this clear first, and then fruitful for our method.

Starting from this particular table perception, we are able to practice the eidetic reduction. Our analyses of perception are then essential or eidetic analyses. All that we have said concerning syntheses belonging to the type 'perception', concerning horizons of potentiality, and so on, holds good, as can easily be seen, essentially for everything that can be formed by this free variation, and, accordingly, for every perception whatsoever. In other words, with absolute essential universality and with essential necessity this holds for every particular case and therefore for every *de facto* perception, since every fact can be thought of merely as an example of a pure possibility.

Though each single chosen type is thus raised from its environment within the empirically factual transcendental ego into the pure eidetic sphere, the intentional outer horizons pointing to its uncoverable nexus within the ego do not vanish, but these horizons themselves become eidetic only. In other words, with each eidetically pure type we find ourselves, not inside the *de facto* ego, but inside an *eidos* 'ego'; and constitution of one actually pure possibility among others implies, as its horizon, a purely possible ego, a purely possible variant of my *de facto* ego. Therefore, if we think of a phenomenology developed as an intuitively *a priori* science purely according to the eidetic method, all its eidetic researches are nothing else but uncoverings of the all-encompassing *eidos* 'transcendental ego as such', which comprises all pure possible variants of my *de facto* ego and this ego itself as possibility. Eidetic phenomenology, accordingly, explores the universal *a priori* without which neither I nor any transcendental ego whatsoever is imaginable. And since every eidetic universality has the value of an unbreakable law, eidetic phenomenology explores the all-embracing laws that prescribe for every factual statement about something transcendental the possible meaning of that statement.

Thus, to me as the meditating ego, guided by the idea of philosophy as the all-embracing science, grounded with absolute strictness, it becomes evident now that, first of all, I must develop a pure eidetic phenomenology, and that in the latter alone the first actualization of a philosophical science as a first philosophy can take place.

After a transcendental reduction, my interest is directed to my pure ego. But its uncovering becomes genuinely scientific only if I go back to the apodictic principles which pertain to this ego as exemplifying the *eidos* 'ego', that is, if I go back to the essential universalities and necessities by means of which the fact is to be related to its original fundaments. In this way we arrive at the methodological insight that, along with the phenomenological reduction, eidetic intuition is the fundamental form of all particular transcendental methods. Both of them together determine the legitimate meaning of transcendental phenomenology.[31]

Genetic Phenomenology

After this digression dealing with the meaning of the eidetic reduction within the realm of the constitutional problems of transcendental phenomenology, Husserl continues, we must return now to our original task of discovering the most important problems of phenomenology. In the following we are going to confine ourselves to problems arising within the limits of a purely eidetic phenomenology, so that the *de facto* transcendental ego and the particular data given in transcendental experience serve henceforth merely as examples of pure possibilities.

A brief description of a systematic sequence of problems and investigations concerning the transcendental ego as such, Husserl goes on to say, involves extraordinarily difficult problems, all the more difficult since we must try to find new approaches to the specific universal problems of the constitution characteristic of the transcendental ego itself. For, the universal *a priori* belonging to a transcendental ego as such is a definite *eidos,* which contains an infinity of *a priori* types of life's actualities and potentialities, along with the objects that can be constituted in this life as really existing objects. But in a unitarily possible

31. *Ibid.,* pp. 103-106 (69-72).

ego not all possible single types, which I find in my concrete ego, are compossible and not all compossible ones are compossible in just any order. For example, being scientific is only possible in man; and even then it is not really possible in a child. Restrictions of this type have their origin in an *a priori* universal structure and in a conformity to universal eidetic laws of coexistence and succession in an egological time. For whatever occurs in my ego, and eidetically in an ego as such, has its temporality and so participates in the system of forms that belong to the all-encompassing temporality.[32]

The eidetic laws of compossibility are rules that govern both actual and possible existence occurring simultaneously or in succession. They are laws of 'causality' in a very broad sense. However, to avoid an expression which easily evokes the prejudices of naturalism, we prefer to speak of 'laws of motivation'.

The universe of lived experiences which are the Being-content of the transcendental ego is a compossible totality only in the universal and unitary form of the flux, in which all particular experiences are concatenated as processes that flow within the flux.

Accordingly the most universal form, which belongs to all particular types of concrete lived experiences, together with the products that are flowingly constituted in its flux is a form of motivation, connecting all and governing within each single experience in particular. We may call it also a formal regularity characteristic of a universal genesis, according to which past, present, and future become unitarily constituted time and again, in a certain noetic-noematic form-structure of flowing modes of givenness. But within this form, life goes on as a motivated course of particular constitutive achievements with manifold particular motivations and motivational systems, which, according to universal regularities governing the genesis, make the universal genesis of the ego into a unity. The ego constitutes itself for itself in the unity of a history. And if it is true that the constitution of the ego conains all the constitutions of all its objectivities, then we must add here that the constitutive systems by virtue of which such and such objects exist for it, are themselves also possible only within the domain

---

32. *Ibid.*, pp. 107-108 (73-75).

of a genesis that remains in conformity with certain laws. At the same time, however, they are governed by the universal genetic form that makes the concrete monadic ego possible as a unity. That nature, a cultural world, a society, etc., exist for me as concrete monadic ego signifies: 1) that possibilities of corresponding experiences exist for me, and 2) that other modes of consciousness corresponding to them exist as possibilities for me which can be fulfilled or not fulfilled by certain experiences. We shall return to this topic in the following chapter.

As Husserl claims, problems concerning the psychological origin of the 'idea of space', the 'idea of time', the 'idea of physical thing', etc., present themselves in phenomenology as transcendental problems of intentionality, which have their particular places among the problems of a universal genesis.

Husserl holds that a systematic approach to the ultimate universalities pertaining to the problems characteristic of eidetic phenomenology is very difficult. The beginning phenomenologist has to take himself as his initial example. Transcendentally he finds himself as *the* ego, then as generally *an* ego, who already has a world, a world with nature, sciences, culture, etc., and with personalities of a higher order such as state and church. Although phenomenology developed at first on the static level, both these levels, the static and the genetic, are essential, and the latter is even the most fundamental.[33]

Active and Passive Genesis

If we consider first the principles of constitutive genesis which have universal significance for us as possible subjects related to a world, states Husserl, we find that there are principles of two fundamentally different types, namely, principles of *active* and principles of *passive* genesis.

In *active genesis* the ego functions as productively constitutive by means of lived experiences which are ego-acts of a special sort; for instance, the achievements of practical reason. The characteristic feature of these ego-acts is that they, through socialization concatenated

---

33. *Ibid.*, pp. 109-111 (75-77).

in a certain community and combined in a manifold, specifically active synthesis, originally constitute new objects on the basis of objects already given in modes of consciousness that give such objects beforehand. In this way, for instance, in collecting the collection is constituted, in counting the number, and in dividing the part. All these objects present themselves to consciousness as 'products'. Original consciousness of universality is also such an activity, namely, that in which the universal becomes constituted objectively. Many other examples could have been given here, such as the transcendental constitution of all cultural objects. Most of them presuppose the antecedent constitution of a transcendental intersubjectivity, as we shall see later on.

But although the higher forms of activities and 'products' of reason, all of which have the character of ideal objects, cannot be regarded as belonging to every concrete ego as such, it will be clear that, in regard to the lowest levels, such as experiential grasping, the situation will be different. But in *any* case, anything built up by active genesis necessarily presupposes, as the lowest level, a passivity that gives something beforehand; and analyzing this passivity we necessarily come upon the constitution by *passive genesis*. The ready-made objects that we meet in life as existent mere physical things, such as a star or a mountain, are given with the originality of the 'it itself' in the synthesis of a passive experience. As such it is given before every mental activity, which begins with the active grasping, characteristic of active genesis.

We must, furthermore, remark here that while the mental activities are forming their synthetic products, the passive synthesis that supplies them their material, still goes on. The physical thing given beforehand in passive intentions continues to appear in unitary intuitions. And no matter how much the thing may be modified therein by our active explanation, it continues to be given beforehand, the manifold modes of appearance continuously flow, and in their manifold passive synthesis, the one physical thing, with its typical shape and other characteristic features, appears. But even a synthesis of this form has its history which becomes manifest in the synthesis itself. It is owing to an essentially necessary genesis that I, the meditating ego, can experience a physical thing and can do so even at first sight.

That is why we in infancy had to learn to see physical things, and that such modes of consciousness had to precede all others genetically. In early childhood, the pre-given field of perception does not as yet contain anything that, at first sight, might be explicitated as a physical thing. But the meditating ego can penetrate into the intentional content of experiential phenomena themselves, and thus find intentional references leading back to a history, and accordingly bringing these phenomena to light as formations which presuppose other, essentially antecedent formations.

Husserl tells us that here, however, we soon come upon eidetic laws governing the passive forming of ever new syntheses. We encounter a *passive genesis* of the manifold apperceptions as formations that persist in a typical habituality, which is characteristic of them. These appear as data formed beforehand, as soon as they become actual, affect the central ego, and motivate its activities. Thanks to this passive synthesis, into which achievements of active synthesis also enter, the ego always has an environment of objects.[34]

Association

According to Husserl the universal principle of passive genesis governing the constitution of all objectivities which are given completely prior to every constitution of active genesis, is to be indicated by the term 'association'. Association, however, is here a matter of intentionality; and as such it can be brought to the fore descriptively in its primal constituting activity which then manifests itself as being governed by eidetic laws. Owing to the principle of association each passive constitution of lived experiences, of objects in immanent time, of all real natural objects belonging to the objective spatio-temporal world, can be made understandable. Taken in this way, association is a fundamental concept of transcendental phenomenology.

The traditional conception of association and of the laws of association which were, for instance, proposed by Hume and other thinkers, is only a naturalistic misinterpretation of the corresponding genuine, intentional concept. In phenomenology this concept receives an essen-

---

34. *Ibid.*, pp. 111-113 (77-80).

tially new definition. For association is not defined here in terms of a conformity to empirical laws governing complexes of data comprised in a human soul, but in terms of a conformity to eidetic laws which in a most comprehensive way rules the constitution of the pure ego. Association, therefore, refers here to a realm of the innate *a priori* without which an ego as such is inconceivable.

Only in the phenomenology of genesis comes the ego to light as an endless connection of synthetically concatenated achievements joined together in the unity of an all-encompassing genesis, at various levels, all of which conform to the universal abiding form, temporality. This form itself is built up in a continuous, passive, and completely universal genesis, which as a matter of essential necessity embraces everything new. In the mature ego, this many-leveled structure persists as an abiding system of forms characteristic of apperception and, consequently, also of the constituted objectivities; among these objectivities we also find those which belong to the objective universe with its fixed ontological structure. And this persisting itself is merely a form of synthesis, too.

Transcendental Idealism

From the foregoing it will be clear that phenomenology can be rightly characterized as a transcendental theory of knowledge. Such an 'epistemology' however, is to be clearly distinguished from the traditional theories of knowledge, Husserl claims.

The main problem of traditional epistemology is the problem of transcendence. This problem can be formulated in the following way: How can my knowledge abiding wholly within the immanence of my own conscious life, acquire objective significance for a world out there? According to traditional epistemology this problem is to be solved within the realm of the natural attitude. According to phenomenology, however, the whole problem becomes inconsistent in this way. For, how can I, as a natural man in the world, ask seriously and transcendentally how I get outside of my island of consciousness and how what presents itself in my consciousness can acquire objective significance for the world out there? It will be clear that, in formulating the question in this way, I apperceive myself as a natural man in the world and, in doing so, I have already presupposed the world outside of me which precisely is in question.

In Husserl's opinion there is only one way to avoid this inconsistency and that is the execution of the phenomenological reduction. For only then, says Husserl, comes to light that conscious life by which transcendental questions about the possibility of transcendental knowledge can be asked. But as soon as one tries to perform such a reduction, it becomes clear that all that exists for the pure ego is constituted in and by consciousness itself and that transcendency is nothing but an immanent existential characteristic, constituted within the ego itself. Every conceivable thing, whether immanent or transcendent, falls within the realm of transcendental subjectivity, as the subjectivity which constitutes all meaning and Being. The world and consciousness belong together essentially, and as belonging together they are concretely one, in the absolute concretion of transcendental subjectivity.

It will be clear, Husserl claims, that phenomenology is *eo ipso* transcendental idealism, though in a fundamentally new sense. It is neither a psychological idealism which tried to derive a meaningful world from senseless sensuous data; nor is it a Kantion idealism which believes in the possibility of a world of things in themselves, but a transcendental idealism as a consistently executed self-explicitation in the form of a sytematic egological science. The nature of this science is to be determined in a more accurate way in the following.[35]

---

35. *Ibid.*, pp. 113-114 (80-81).
36. *Ibid.*, pp. 114-121 (81-88) passim.

CHAPTER EIGHT

INTERSUBJECTIVITY

1. *The Problem of Intersubjectivity. First Attempt at a Solution Solipsism*

At the stage of the analysis briefly described in Chapter Seven, Husserl realizes that up to that time he had limited himself to a description of the original relation between reality and reason and, consequently, to the universal *a priori* laws of knowledge and Being. We have remained there, he says, on the level of a reflection in which the meditating ego needs only its own subjectivity, taken as an example of the *eidos* 'ego'. Before proceeding further with our inquiry, we must deal now with an apparently grave objection, he says. Is phenomenology not a purely solipsistic explanation of intentional constitution? For, when the phenomenological reduction 'brackets' the entire world as transcending our consciousness, the belief in the existence of other subjects is also suspended. The subsequent discovery that the world is ultimately the achievement of transcendental subjectivity constituted by its intentional acts, seems to make the conclusion inevitable that other egos are only 'projections of this solitary ego. If this conclusion is right, the world constituted by transcendental subjectivity could not possibly have an objective sense, that is, it could not be 'a world for everybody'.

Thus, the objection aims at the very claim of transcendental phenomenology to be a transcendental philosophy and, therefore, also at its claim that, in the form of a constitutional theory remaining within the limits of the transcendentally reduced ego, it can solve the transcendental problems pertaining to the objective world.[1]

Studying the problems implied in this objection, Husserl explicitly rejects solipsism as self-contradictory. On the other hand, however, he maintains that there can be no explanation of Being in any form outside intentional constitution, for Being must be explained in

---

1. Edmund Husserl, *Cart. Med.*, pp. 121-122 (89-90).

terms of reason. The preceding chapters have briefly explained the constitution of the different types of objectivity as well as the concomitant constitution of one's own subjectivity, but they did not explain the presence of other subjects. Yet only by means of other subjects can a solipsistic phenomenology be transcended. On the other hand, if other subjects are to be meaningful, also they must be constituted.

Such a constitution, however, seems to be without any reason and even completely impossible. In the first place, it is difficult to understand how *constituted* other egos could help us to solve the transcendental problems pertaining to the *objective* world *for everybody.* Secondly, we face here a dilemma: the constitution cannot be objective in itself, since the term of the constitution precisely is a subject, nor can it be subjective, since subjective constitution necessarily means to be a self-constitution. Is there, then, perhaps a third kind of constitution, one that is neither subjective nor objective, or is there a kind of synthesis of objective and subjective constitution in which is constituted an object that is, at the same time, a subject?[2]

Husserl's battle with this difficult problem began as early as his lectures of 1910-1911. Only in the last of the *Cartesian Meditations,* however, did he present a complete discussion of the matter. He tried to show there how the transcendental ego constitutes other egos as equal partners in an intersubjective community, which in turn forms the foundation for the objective, that is, the intersubjective world. Thus, the intersubjective community of egos, or, transcendental intersubjectivity, is introduced here as the very presupposition of the objective world for everybody. In 1910 Husserl was already aware of the problems involved in a theory of transcendental intersubjectivity. For a long time he studies those problems, but the solution which he proposed in the second volume of the *Ideas* was unconvincing and, as we shall see, soon rejected by Husserl himself.[3]

For this reason Husserl spent much time during the last fifteen years of his life trying to develop a more consistent theory of intersubjectivity

---

2. Quentin Lauer, *The Triumph of Subjectivity,* pp. 148-149.
3. Edmund Husserl, *Ideen II,* pp. 162-172, 172-200, 346-347, etc.

and intersubjective constitution. Whether his later theory, as explained in *Formal and Transcendental Logic* and especially in his *Cartesian Meditations,* offers an adequate solution of the solipsistic problem, is a point about which Husserl himself appears to have remained in doubt. Anyhow, he thought that his attempted descriptions at least deserved attention, even if they did not present a valid refutation of solipsism. On the other hand, he did not regard the problems concerning intersubjectivity as a reason for abandoning the constitutive explanation of all Being, since a solution of these problems was at least possible in principle, as easily can be shown.[4]

According to Lauer, the problems concerning intersubjectivity arise as soon as in the perspective of a phenomenological theory of constitution, we try to explain the universally valid objectivity of the world. We then need a 'universal' subject; but, according to the requirements of transcendental phenomenology, this 'universal' subject must also be a concrete subject. But a concrete universal subject can refer only to a concrete multiplicity of subjects. Since above we have only met our own transcendental subjectivity as an example of the *eidos* 'ego', we must now try to show by means of constitutional analyses that: 1) each subject must be self-constituted, for otherwise it can have no significance in a phenomenological context; 2) each subject must be constituted as such in each other subject, for otherwise a completely monadological universe will be the necessary result in which universe communication is impossible; 3) the constitution of the other must correspond to the other's self-constitution, for otherwise it will be invalid; 4) each subject must constitute a world of objectivity which is in some way identical with the world constituted by other subjects, for otherwise there will be no common ground for communication; 5) the world which each one constitutes must be a world comprising oneself and others, for otherwise the unity of the world will be destroyed.[5] Finally, it will be clear that all these statements will be without any real foundation, if they cannot be proved from the viewpoint of my transcendental ego. It is precisely this point which creates the greatest difficulties, as we will see.

---

4. Herbert Spiegelberg, *op. cit.,* vol. I, p. 158. Quentin Lauer, *op cit.,* p. 150.
5. Quentin Lauer, *op cit.,* p. 151.

A First Introduction to Husserl's Phenomenology

Empathy the Way to a Solution

From the very beginning it was evident to Husserl that we know the other as a subject. Although the supposition that each alien consciousness which I posit in my experience of the other (empathy) does not really exist, is not nonsensical, nevertheless *my* empathy itself is given in a primordial and absolute sense, not only essentially but existentially.[6] Thus, we must recognize in our field of objects some objects which are like none of the others. They present themselves not only as known by the knower, but also as knowing the knower, and this also is an immediate phenomenon. To be a subject means to have experiences; to be experienced as a subject means to be experienced as having experiences. Somehow, therefore, the experiences of others must form part of my intentional life, without at the same time being my experiences. Hence we are obliged to find an intentional category comprising a kind of experience of the other's experience. Like Theodor Lipps, Husserl referred to this kind of experience as 'empathy', although he did not follow Lipps in all his considerations.

From the very beginning Husserl likewise maintained that he had found in empathy the key to a constituted world which would be objectively valid for everybody. In his *Ideas* he describes this thought clearly for both the natural and the phenomenological attitude. Describing our natural attitude, he says that whatever holds good for me personally, also holds good for every other man whom I find present in my world-about-me. Experiencing them as men, I understand and accept them by means of empathy as ego-subjects, units like myself and related to their natural surroundings.[7] And I do this in such a way that I apprehend the world-about-them and the world-about-me *objectively* as one and the same world, which differs in each case only through affecting each consciousness differently. Despite these differences, we come to an understanding with our neighbors, and establish in common an *objective* spatio-temporal fact-world as the world about us

---

6. Edmund Husserl, *Ideen I*, pp. 106-107.
7. *Ibid.*, pp. 10-11 (45-46), 106-110 (130-132) L. (372-388).

that is there for all of us, and to which we ourselves nevertheless belong.[8]

Speaking about the constitutional problems, Husserl points out that within the sphere of the transcendental reduction the formation of the intersubjectively identical thing is a constitutive process of a higher order than, for instance, the constitution of my own objectivities given in my lived experiences. Its constitution is related to an indefinite plurality of subjects, who stand in a relation of 'mutual understanding'. The intersubjective world is the correlate of the intersubjective experience, mediated through empathy. Here we are therefore referred to the various wholes of sensory things already constituted individually by the many subjects, and further, to the corresponding perceptual manifolds belonging to the different personal subjects and streams of consciousness. This new factor of empathy and the question of how it plays a constitutive part in objective experience and gives unity to those separate manifolds must be explained in more detail.[9]

Finally, from the very beginning it was evident to Husserl that all our knowledge of the others is to some extent indirect. We have primordial experience of ourselves and our states of consciousness in so-called inner or self-perception, but we do not have direct experience of others and their vital experiences in and through empathy. We behold the living experiences of others through our perception of their bodily behavior. Although this beholding in the case of empathy is an intuitional dator act, it is no longer a primordial dator act.[10] The other is given to us not in a direct presentation, but only by way of appresentation. Appresentation is a process which acquaints us with aspects of an object that are not directly presented in themselves; we are familiar with such a process in our acquaintance with the rear of a building when we approach it from the front. In the latter case, however, direct presentations may follow later on, but not in the case of our knowledge of the other. What happens here is that when we perceive a body other than our own as 'there' rather than as 'here', we

---

8. *Ibid.*, pp. 61-62 (94-95).
9. *Ibid.*, p. 372-374 (387-388).
10. *Ibid.*, p. 11 (46).

apperceive it at once as the body of another ego by way of an assimilative analogy, a process which is not without problems.

On the basis of these principles Husserl tried to develop a theory of transcendental intersubjectivity in the second volume of his *Ideas*. In his third volume, however, he explained that the description of the problem of transcendental solipsism, that is more precisely, the relation between transcendental intersubjectivity and the objective world valid for me and for everybody, as indicated in the first volume and explained in the second, is incomplete. The reason of this is that the central thesis of transcendental idealism posits that only the transcendental subjectivity originally has meaning with respect to its Being and, thus, is an absolute Being, whereas the 'real' world is essentially relative to this absolute Being; this central thesis now is apodictically justified only if and when phenomenological explicitation of the transcendental ego succeeds in manifesting the other subjects which appear to me as transcendental in my transcendental life, within a transcendental we-community. Only in such a transcendental intersubjectivity a real and objective world is constituted as a world for everybody.[11]

It was for this reason that Husserl studied the problem again in *Formal and Transcendental Logic* and *Cartesian Meditations*. Since the ideas presented in the *Cartesian Meditations* essentially agree with those given in *Formal and Transcendental Logic,* and are more detailed and accurate, we will confine ourselves here to a brief description of the main ideas found in the *Cartesian Meditations*.[12]

2. *The Sphere of Transcendental Being as Monadological Intersubjectivity*

The Problem of Experiencing Someone Else

In the foregoing we have already seen that the doctrine concerning the constitution of the transcendental ego seems to lead to transcendental solipsism. With respect to such a conclusion, one could say that indeed

---

11. Edmund Husserl, *Ideen II*, pp. 172-200. *Ideen III*, pp. 10-21.
12. See for the foregoing also Alfred Schuetz, "Das Problem der transzendentalen Intersubjektivität", *Husserl*, pp. 334-365. Herbert Spiegelberg, *op. cit.*, pp. 158-159.

the world constituted in the ego is only a world for me and, therefore, only my idea; behind this idea there is somehow the world that exists in itself; the problem is only to find a way from the first to the second world. Or one could also claim that those questions about an eventual transcendency of the world and, therefore, the transcendency of the other egos cannot be asked by phenomenology.

According to Husserl it is much more fruitful to devote oneself to the task of a phenomenological explicitation of the explicit and implicit intentionalities in which the other egos are verified in the realm of our own transcendental ego, instead of trying to follow up those suggestions and to present dialectical arguments and metaphysical considerations in their favor. For only by means of such a phenomenological explicitation can the transcendental problem of the objective world valid for everybody be solved by phenomenology.[13]

First of all, Husserl claims, in my intentional analyses concerning the other ego, my transcendental guiding clue must be the experienced other himself, precisely as he is given to me in immediate and direct consciousness and manifests himself there with the noematic content belonging to him, and is taken now purely as a correlate of my own *cogito*. In other words, in many-sided analyses I must try to describe the other just as I experience him, namely, as being, as world-object, as physical thing, as governing psychically his natural organism, as psycho-physical object in the world, as subject for this world, as experiencing the world, and as experiencing me myself.

Then, within the limits of my transcendentally reduced pure conscious life, I experience the world, including the others, not as a formation of my own private synthesis, but as an intersubjective world that is actually there for everyone. Yet everyone has his own experiences, his own world phenomenon, while the experienced world exists in itself, over against all experiencing subjects and their world-phenomena.

Then I have to ask myself the question: What is the explanation of this? I hold fast, as I must do, to the insight that every meaning which any being whatever can have for me with respect to its 'what it is' and its 'that it is', is a meaning in, and arising from, my intentional

---

13. Edmund Husserl, *Cart. Med,* pp. 121-122 (89-90).

life and my constitutive syntheses. Therefore, I must begin with a systematic explicitation of the intentionality in which the Being of the others for me becomes established.

According to Husserl the first problem will be that of the 'thereness for me' of others. And this asks for a transcendental theory of experiencing someone else, a transcendental theory of 'empathy'. Such a theory contributes to laying the foundation for a transcendental theory of the objective world valid for everybody, as we hope to explain later.[14]

The Reduction to the Sphere of 'My Ownness'

Husserl claims that with respect to method we must first perform, within the universal transcendental sphere, a new kind of reduction. We must exclude from our thematic field everything that is here in question, namely, all constitutional achievements of intentionality relating to other subjectivities. This reduction to the transcendental sphere of my ownness (*Eigenheitssphäre*), that is, to the actual and potential intentionalities in which the ego constitutes itself in its ownness, thus, to my transcendental concrete I myself, has an unusual sense, as we will see.

In the natural attitude I find myself distinguished from and contrasted with others. If I abstract from others, I alone remain. But such an abstraction is not yet radical. For, such an aloneness does not modify the natural meaning of the world: to be experienceable by everyone. What we need here is a reduction by means of which come to the fore I myself and all that refers solely and exclusively to me myself as this transcendental ego. What is specifically proper to me as ego, my concrete being as a monad, purely in myself and for myself with an exclusive ownness, includes every intentionality and therefore also the intentionalities directed to the other; but also these intentionalities and their correlates shall at first remain excluded from our theme. If the ego in its ownness has been delimited, the question can be asked: How can my ego, within its ownness, constitute under the title 'experience of something other' precisely something *other,* that is to say, the other as other and all that presupposes the other as other? This question concerns, firstly, every possible other ego and, secondly, everything that

---

14. *Ibid.,* pp. 123-124 (90-92).

acquires determinations of meaning from the other egos, in short, an objective world in the proper and full sense of the term.

Let us try to characterize the ego's sphere of ownness and thus, correlatively, to perform explicitly the abstractive *epoché* yielding this new sphere. One remark, however, must be made in advance. The thematic exclusion of the constitutional achievements produced by the experience of something other, that is to say, the achievements referring to the other as other and all that presupposes the other as other, does not mean merely that we make a phenomonological *epoché* with respect to the naïve acceptance of the other's being. For the transcendental attitude is and remains presupposed here; everything that was previously for us in immediate consciousness is also here taken exclusively as a phenomenon, as a sense 'meant'. The above-mentioned abstractive *epoché*, then, is something completely new but one which presupposes the transcendental reduction.

As ego in the *transcendental* attitude, I attempt first of all to delimit, within my horizon of transcendental experience, that which is particularly my own. I begin by freeing that horizon abstractively from every thing that is alien (*Fremdes*). Thus we abstract from what gives men and animals their specific meaning as ego-like living beings and consequently also from all determinations of the phenomenal world whose meaning necessarily refers to and presupposes others as ego-subjects. In this way we retain a unitary coherent stratum of the phenomenon 'world' that is the correlate of my continuously and harmoniously proceeding world experience. Despite our abstraction, we can carry on continuously our experiencing intuition, while remaining exclusively in the retained stratum. This unitary stratum is distinguished by being essentially the *founding* stratum: I obviously cannot have the 'other' as an experiential meaning without having this stratum in actual experience; the reverse is evidently *not* the case.

In this way from the phenomenon 'world', appearing with an *objective* sense, a substratum becomes separated as the 'nature' included in my ownness, a nature that must always be carefully distinguished from nature as the theme of the natural sciences. True, nature as theme of the natural sciences is also the result of an abstraction, for it abstracts from everything psychical and from those predicates of the objective world that arise from persons. However, what is acquired by this scientific abstraction is still a stratum that belongs to the objective world itself and is therefore itself objective. But in the case of our abstraction the meaning 'objective', that is to say the meaning of being constituted intersubjectively, of being experienceable by everyone and being valid for everybody, disappears completely. Thus there is included in my ownness, as purified from every sense pertaining to other subjectivities, a sense, 'mere nature', that has lost precisely that 'validity for everybody'.

Accordingly, this peculiar abstractive sense-exclusion of what is alien, leaves us still a kind of 'world', a 'nature' reduced to what is included in my ownness. As having its place in this nature because of my bodily organism there remains also the psychological ego, with body, soul, and personal ego; and finally there are those predicates that get significance only and exclusively from this ego.

Something paradoxical manifests itself in this case. The psychical life of my psycho-physical ego, including my whole world-experiencing life and therefore including my actual and possible experiences of what is other, is wholly unaffected by this reduction. Consequently there belongs within my psychical Being the whole constitution of the world existing for me and, by the same token, the differentiation of that constitution into 1) the systems that constitute what is included in my ownness, and 2) the systems that constitute what is other. I, the reduced human ego, am constituted, accordingly, as a member of the world with a multiplicity of objects outside me. But I myself constitute all this in my consciousness and bear it intentionally in me.[15]

Results of This New Reduction Within the Sphere of the Transcendental Reduction

We must now try to describe the results of this new reduction in terms of our transcendental reduction. By means of the transcendental reduction I have become aware of myself as the transcendental ego which constitutes in its constitutive life everything that is ever objective for

---

15. *Ibid.*, p. 124-130 (92-99).

me. I am aware of myself as the ego of all constitutions which exists in its own actual and potential lived experiences and which constitutes in them not only everything objective, but also itself as identical ego. Now we must say: while I, as this transcendental ego, have constituted and am continually further constituting as a correlate the world that exists for me, I have now, by means of the new reduction, performed a mundanizing self-apperception, under the title 'ego in the usual sense', in corresponding constitutive syntheses.

By virtue of this mundanization everything included in my ownness, belonging to my transcendental and ultimate ego, enters now as something psychical into my psyche. Thus I find the mundanizing apperception. And now, from the psyche as phenomenon and part of the phenomenon 'man', I can go back to the all-inclusive absolute or transcendental ego. In this ultimate transcendental ego and the universe of what is constituted in it, a division of this ego's whole transcendental field of experience takes place, namely, the division into 1) the sphere of its ownness and the coherent stratum consisting in its experience of a world reduced to what is included in its ownness, and 2) the sphere of what is other. Yet every consciousness *of* what is other belongs in the *former* sphere. Whatever the transcendental ego constitutes in that first stratum, whatever it constitutes as non-other, as its own, that indeed belongs to this ego as a component of its own concrete essence. Within and by means of this ownness the transcendental ego constitutes, however, the 'objective' world as a universe of Being that is other than itself, and constitutes at the *first* level the other in the mode 'other ego'.[16]

Positive Characteristics of the Sphere of My Ownness

Husserl remarks that up to now we have only indirectly characterized the fundamental concept of that which is 'my own', namely, as nonalien (*Nichtfremdes*), a characterization that presupposes the concept of the 'other' (*des Anderen*). We must try now to characterize it positively as the ego in its ownness.

When in transcendental reduction I am reflecting on myself as transcendental ego, I am given to myself perceptually as this ego in this

16. *Ibid.,* pp. 130-131 (99-100).

grasping perception. I become aware that before this perception I was already given, already there for myself as a possible object of original intuition, although I was not explicitly grasped as such. I am given with an open infinite horizon of still undiscovered internal features of my own. As in a normal perception of a concrete material thing, my own being too is discovered by explication and gets its original sense by virtue of it. It becomes uncovered originally when my experiencing and explicitating glance is directed to myself, to my perceptually and even apodictically given 'I am', and to its abiding identity with itself in the continuously unitary synthesis of original self-experience. Whatever is included in this identical being's own essence, is characterized as its actual or possible *explicatum,* that is, as that in which I merely unfold my own identical being as what it, as identical, is in particular, namely, 'it in itself'.

According to Husserl there is, however, a difference between this self-perception and the explication of a perceptually given visual thing. Self-explication does not always go on in particular new perceptions in the proper sense. For when explicitating the horizon of Being that is included in my own essence, one of the first things I run into is my immanent temporality: my existence has the form of a stream of lived experiences. Since this self-explication goes on in the living present, it can find in a strictly perceptive way only what is given in the living present. In the most original manner conceivable it must uncover my own past by means of recollections. Therefore, although I am continually given to myself originally and can explicitate progressively what is included in my own essence, this explication is carried out largely in acts of consciousness that are not perceptions of aspects of my ownness with all its actualities and potentialities.

This transcendental self-experience possesses an apodictic evidence, but only in a restricted sense. In unqualifiedly apodictic evidence this self-explication brings to the fore only the all-encompassing structural forms in which I exist as ego. The explication of the single egological data, however, participates in this apodicticity only in an imperfect way; for example, as an evidence contained in my recollection of the past. Yet, even here, perfect apodicticity is given at least as an 'idea'.[17]

---

17. *Ibid.,* pp. 131-133 (100-103).

The ownness belonging to me as ego obviously extends not only to the actualities and potentialities of the stream of lived experiences. Just as it comprises the constitutive systems, so it comprises the constituted objects insofar as these are inseparable from the original constitution. This is true not only for hyletic data which become constituted as my own, as immanent temporalities within the limits of my ego, but also for all my habitualities, transcendent objects, and finally the entire reduced world. Since, however, we excluded from our consideration the intentional achievements produced by empathy, we have a nature that is constituted as a unity of spatial objects transcending the stream of lived experiences, but constituted as merely a multiplicity of objects of possible experience. This experience is purely my own life, and what is experienced in this experience is nothing more than a synthetic unity inseparable from this life and its potentialities.

In this way it becomes clear that the concrete ego has a universe of what is peculiarly its own, which can be uncovered by an original explicitation of its apodictic self-consciousness. This explicitation is itself, at least in principle, also apodictic. Within this original sphere of original self-explicitation we furthermore find a transcendent world which by reduction accrues to the ego's peculiar ownness on the basis of the intentional phenomenon 'objective world'.[18]

Immanent and Objective Transcendency. Course to be Followed by Our Intentional Explicitation

The undeniable fact that my own essence can be contrasted with something else, and that I can become aware of something other than I, presupposes that not all my own modes of consciousness are modes of my self-consciousness. Since actual Being is constituted originally by the fact that my experiences harmoniously grow together, my own self must contain, in contrast to my self-experience, yet other experiences united in harmonius systems. Now, the problem is *how* it is to be understood that the ego can always have in itself intentionalities in and through which it wholly transcends its own Being.

---

18. *Ibid.*, pp. 134-135 (103-105).

My experience of something that is not I, manifests itself as experience of an *objective* world, and therein of other egos. An important result of our new reduction now was that it brought to light an intentional substratum in which a reduced *world* shows itself as an *immanent* transcendency. In the order characteristic of the constitution of a world alien to my ego, this reduced world is the primordial transcendency, the primordial 'world', and, notwithstanding its ideality, it is still a determining part of my own concrete Being.

We must now try to explain *how* at the higher and founded level the sense-bestowal of the constitutionally secondary objective transcendency, namely, the 'objective world', takes place precisely as experience. And because the objective world is constantly there for me as already finished, this will be a matter of a static analysis of this experience itself in which we must try intentionally to uncover the manner in which it precisely gives sense.[19]

Constitution of the meaning of the objective world involves a number of levels. The first of these is the constitutional level of the other egos. Once the constitution of the other egos is explained, we must focus attention on the universal superaddition of sense to my primordial world whereby the latter can manifest itself as an 'objective world', as the identical world for everyone myself included. Thus, it is the other ego which makes it constitutionally possible that a new infinite domain of what is 'other', begins to appear as an objective world, to which all the other egos and I myself belong. But in this constitution of the objective world the others do not remain isolated; on the contrary, an ego-community as a community of monads becomes constituted in the sphere of my ownness, which in its communalized intentionality constitutes the one identical world. In this world all egos manifest themselves in an objectifying apperception as having the sense 'men', 'psycho-physical men as wordly objects'.

As Husserl explains it, by means of the aforementioned communalization of intentionality the transcendental intersubjectivity has an intersubjective sphere of its peculiar ownness, in which it constitutes the objective world. This objective world, however, does not transcend that

---

19. *Ibid.*, pp. 135-136 (105-106).

intersubjective sphere, but inheres in it as an immanent transcendency. The objective world as the ideal correlate of an intersubjective experience is essentially related to intersubjectivity. Consequently the constitution of the objective world necessarily implies a harmony of the named monads.[20]

Appresentation

Husserl holds that after the definition and the articulation of the primordial sphere, it is especially the first of the above indicated steps toward the constitution of an objective world which presents the greatest difficulties. These difficulties consist in the transcendental explicitation of experiencing someone else, in the sense in which the other did not yet attain the sense 'man'.

In the case of experiencing someone else, we generally say that the other ego itself as man is there before us 'in person'. Properly speaking, however, neither the other ego itself, nor its lived experiences or its appearances themselves, nor anything else belonging to its own essence, is given in my experience *originally*. For, if that which belongs to the other's own essence were directly accessible, it would be merely a moment of my own essence, and therefore, he himself and I myself would be *the same*. And the same holds true for his body, if the latter were nothing but the body that is merely a unity constituted in my actual and possible experiences. A certain mediating intentionality manifests itself here which, originating from the primordial world, makes present to consciousness a 'there-with-me' (*Mit-da*), which nevertheless is not itself there and never can become an 'itself-there'. We have here, accordingly, a kind of *appresentation*.

An appresentation occurs in external experience when, to give a concrete example, the front of a house which is actually seen, necessarily appresents its back. However, experiencing someone else cannot be a matter of just this kind of appresentation, since in external experience the verification by a corresponding fulfilling presentation is always possible, while such a possibility in the experience of someone else is

---

20. *Ibid.*, pp. 137-138 (106-108).

excluded in principle. The question, therefore, is how can the appresentation of another sphere in my original sphere be *motivated* as experience. It will be clear that a non-original presentation can do so only in combination with an original one; and only as demanded by the original presentation can a non-original presentation have the character of appresentation.

The perception that could function as the foundation here, is our perception of the primordially reduced world. The problems, however, are: What in particular must be taken into account in the perception of the reduced world? How is the motivation to be built up? And how does the very complicated intentional achievement of the appresentation in question become uncovered?

The term 'the other' means *'alter ego'*, and the 'ego' referred to in this expression is I myself, constituted within my primordial ownness as the psycho-physical unity, as primordial man, as personal ego, governing immediately in my body and immediately producing effects in the primordial surrounding world; the subject, moreover, of a concrete intentional life, a subject of a psychic sphere relating to itself and the world. All of that is already at our disposal; but as far as the intentionality by which it has become constituted is concerned, we have not yet investigated it here; that belongs to a different level and is the theme of investigations into which we have not yet entered.

Now, says Husserl, let us suppose that another man enters my primordial sphere. Within the realm of the primordial reduction this entrance must be described by saying that in the perceptual sphere belonging to my primordial world a body is presented, which, as primordial, is of course only an immanent transcendency. Since in *this* world my body is the only one that can be constituted originally as an animate organism, the body over there, which is nonetheless apprehended as an animate organism, must have derived its meaning from an apperceptive transfer of my animate organism. It will be clear then, that only a certain *similarity* within my primordial sphere connecting that body over there with my body, can serve as the motivation for the analogizing apprehension of that body as another animate organism. There is thus a certain assimilative apperception, but by no means an inference from analogy. For apperception is not an act of thinking and, therefore, not an act of inference. Every apperception in which we apprehend objects given beforehand, necessarily refers to a primordial instituting act, in which an everyday experience of the world involves in its anticipating apprehension of the object as having a similar sense, such an analogizing transfer of an originally instituted objective meaning to a new case.[21]

The Concept of 'Pairing'

If we attempt to describe the peculiar nature of that analogizing apprehension whereby a body similar to my own animate body within my primordial sphere becomes apprehended as likewise an animate body, we find 1) that the primordially instituting original is always livingly present and, therefore, that the primal institution itself is always going on in a living manner; 2) that what is appresented by virtue of the analogizing act can never attain actual presence and never become an object of proper perception; finally, 3) that ego and *alter ego* are always and necessarily given in an original 'pairing'.

Pairing, that is, the co-figuring occurrence as a pair and eventually later also as a group, is a universal phenomenon of the transcendental sphere. It is a primal form of that passive synthesis which we call association, in contrast to passive synthesis of identification. The characteristic trait of a pairing association is that, in its most primitive form, two data are given intentionally in the unity of one conscious act, which, on this basis and essentially already in pure passivity, as data appearing with mutual distinctness, phenomenologically found a unity of similarity, and thus are always constituted precisely as a pair—or in case there are more than two data involved, a group. We find here an intentional overlapping, coming about necessarily as soon as the data that undergo pairing become simultaneously intended; we find, more particularly, a mutual awakening and an overlapping of each other in regard to their objective sense. This overlapping has its degrees, the limiting case being that of complete identity. Be this as it may, the

---

21. *Ibid.,* pp. 138-141 (108-111).

important point here is that, as the result of this overlapping, there takes place in the paired data a mutual transfer of meaning.

In the apperception of the *alter ego* by the ego, pairing first occurs when the other enters my field of perception. I, as the primordial psycho-physical ego, occupy always the central place in my primordial field of perception; my living body is always there and likewise with primordial originality is equipped with the specific sense of an animate organism. Now in case there presents itself, as appearing in my primordial sphere, a body similar to mine and having determinations such that it must enter into a phenomenal pairing with mine, this body must appropriate its sense 'animate organism' from my body.

Husserl next asks whether or not this apperception is actually so transparent. What makes this organism another's rather than a second organism of myself? Obviously the *second* fundamental characteristic of the apperception in question plays an important part here, namely the fact that of the appropriated sense which is characteristic of bodily-hood as such, nothing can become actualized originally in my primordial sphere.[22]

But now, as Husserl explains, there arises for us the problem of making such an apperception understandable in its possibility. How is it possible that the transferred sense as far as its status of Being is concerned is appropriated as a set of psychic determinations existing in combination with that body over there, even though those determinations can never show themselves as themselves in the original domain belonging to the primordial sphere which alone is accessible?[23]

My Experience of Somebody Else

As Husserl views it, the appresentation, giving the other's psychic determinations which are not accessible originally, is combined with an original *presentation* of 'his' body as a part of nature given in my own-ness. In this combination the other's body and his ego are given in the manner characteristic of every transcending experience. Every experience, now, points to further experiences which probably will fulfill and verify the appresented horizons. It will be clear then, that, in case of

---

22. *Ibid.*, pp. 141-143 (112-113).
23. *Ibid.*, p. 143 (113-114).

an experience of someone else, the process of fulfillment can be effected only by *new appresentations* which proceed in a synthetical and harmonious way, and which themselves owe their value of Being to their motivational connection with the changing presentations within the sphere of my peculiar ownness that necessarily belong to them. That is to say, the experienced alien organism continues to manifest itself as actually an animate body, solely in its changing but incessantly harmonious behavior. This behavior has a physical side which appresentatively indicates something psychical which now must present itself in original experience by means of a process of fulfillment.

It is this kind of verifiable accessibility of what is not originally accessible which is characteristic of the existing other being. Whatever can become presented and evidently verified in the process of fulfillment originally, is *something I am,* or else it belongs to the sphere of my peculiar ownness. Whatever is experienced in a different way is *other.* The other is therefore conceivable only as an analogue of something which is included in the sphere of my peculiar ownness. Because of the way its sense is constituted it manifests itself necessarily as an intentional modification of that ego of mine which is first to be objectified, or as an intentional modification of my primordial world: the other is phenomenologically a modification of myself. It will be clear that, together with the other ego, there is appresented in the analogizing modification all that necessarily belongs to *his* primordial world and his fully concrete ego.[24]

However, what has been said does not suffice to give a really adequate explanation of the noematic complexes involved in the experience of what is alien. We must now try to reach the point where the possibility of a transcendental constitution of the objective world can become manifest and the real meaning of a transcendental-phenomenological idealism can be explained.

It will be evident that in my primordial sphere my animate body is reflexively related to itself; it originally manifests itself as occupying the central 'here'. Every other body appears in the mode 'there'. This orientation to the 'there' can be freely changed by means of my kines-

---

24. *Ibid.,* pp. 143-145 (114-116).

thesias. I can always change my position in such a way that I convert any *there* into a *here*. This implies that not only the systems of appearances that belong to my current perceiving from 'here', but also other systems of appearances, corresponding to the possible change of position which would put me 'there', belong constitutively to each physical thing.

Applying this to the experience of someone else, we see that I do not apperceive the other simply as a duplicate of myself. I do not apperceive him as having the spatial and other modes of appearance that are characteristic of me as being here; I apperceive him as having the spatial modes of appearance like those I would have, if I should go over there and be where he is. Furthermore, the other is appresentatively apperceived as the ego of a primordial world wherein his animate organism is originally constituted and experienced in the mode of the absolute here. In this appresentation, therefore, the body which presents itself in my monadic sphere in the mode 'there' concretely indicates the same body which the other ego in his monadic sphere is supposed to experience in the mode 'here'.[25]

What is *appresented* by the body over there in my primordial surrounding world, is not my psychic life. For I am bodily here as the center of a primordial world oriented around me. Consequently, the entire sphere of my peculiar ownness as primordially given has the content of the *here*. On the other hand, the other ego must be appresented as an ego now coexisting in the mode 'there', such as I should be if I were there, because his body there enters into a pairing association with my body here and, being given perceptually, becomes the core of my appresenting experience of a coexisting ego. Therefore what is appresented by the body there is appresented as an ego other than mine.

Likewise easy to understand is the manner in which, as the effective association goes on continuously, such an appresentation of someone else continuously furnishes new appresentional contents by virtue of which a constant confirmation becomes possible. The first content obviously must be formed by the understanding of the other's body and

---

25. *Ibid.,* pp. 145-146 (116-117).

its behavior, for instance, his hands functioning in pushing or his eyes functioning in seeing. Through this the ego at first is determined only as governing thus somatically.

It is also quite understandable how certain contents belonging to the higher psychic sphere arise. These contents too are indicated bodily, namely in the behavior of the body in regard to the world out there, as the behavior of someone who is angry or cheerful, which I easily understand from my own behavior under like circumstances.[26]

Constitution of the Community of Monads

But, according to Husserl, it is more important to explain the community which at various levels develops between me and the appresentatively experienced other. The first thing which is constituted in the form of a community and forms the foundation for all other intersubjectively common things, is that fact that we have the same nature in common along with the pairing of the other's body and his psycho-physical ego with my own body and psycho-physical ego.

Since the other's subjectivity, by appresentation within the sphere of my peculiar ownness which exclusively and even essentially is mine, arises with the sense of a subjectivity which is essentially someone else's, it might at first seem to be a problem how even the first communalization in regard to a common world becomes established. The other body which appears in my primordial sphere is first of all a body within the realm of my primordial nature; and this is a synthetic unity belonging to me and, therefore, included in my own essence. If that body functions appresentatively, then, in union with it, the other ego becomes an object of my consciousness appearing as there; primarily, however, the other ego with his own body is given to himself as necessarily belonging to his absolute here. How can one speak here at all of the *same* body? There seems to be an unbridgeable cleft between the two primordial spheres in question, namely mine which is for me as ego the original sphere, and his which is for me an appresented one. And if I would be able somehow to cross the cleft, this would mean, after

---

26. *Ibid.*, pp. 147-149 (117-120).

all, that I should acquire an original, and not an appresenting, experience of someone else. How can the identification come about between the body belonging to my original sphere and the body constituted quite separately in the other ego? This problem, however, appears only if the two original spheres have already been distinguished. And this does not seem to be necessary because a precise explicitation of the intentionality which is actually observable in our experience of someone else, and the discovery of the motivations which are essentially implied in that intentionality, can help us to solve the problem.

If one would follow this guiding clue and accurately discover the intentionality mentioned, together with its motivations, it would become clear how I can constitute in my monad another monad in such a way that I can experience what is constituted in me as nonetheless other than me, and how I can identify a nature constituted in me with a nature constituted by someone else, or how I can identify a nature constituted in me with one constituted in me as a nature constituted by someone else. This identification appears then to be no greater problem than any other synthetic identification.[27]

Higher Levels of Intramonadic Community. Further Problems

At any rate, it is with these considerations, Husserl informs us, that we may find a brief indication of the first and lowest level of communalization between me, the primordial monad, and the monad constituted in me as existing for itself and only appresentationally accessible to me. For the only conceivable manner in which others can have for me the sense of being others which are thus and so determined, consists in their being constituted in me as others. And if they get such a meaning from sources which yield a continuous confirmation, then they are indeed real beings which, however, exclusively have the sense with which they are constituted; they appear as monads, being for themselves precisely as I am being for myself, yet being also in communion and, therefore, in connection with me *qua* concrete ego. To be sure, they are actually separate from my monad insofar as no real connection leads from their lived experiences to mine. On the other

---

27. *Ibid.*, pp. 149-156 (120-128).

hand, however, the original communion mentioned is not just nothing. Whereas really each monad is an absolutely separate unity, the unreal intentional reaching of the other into my primordial sphere is not unreal in the sense of being dreamt only. Being is in intentional communion with being. This is an essentially unique connectedness and precisely the one that makes transcendentally possible the Being of a world of men and things.

After the first level of communalization and the first constitution of an objective world starting from the primordial world have been sufficiently explained, the higher levels offer relatively minor difficulties. There is first the community of men which must be explained, in which we find a mutual being for one another which already implies an objectifying equalization of my existence with that of all others and in which we discover that everyone, that is I and anyone else, appears as man among other men, because we find that every 'other' experiences me and everybody else as an 'other' for him. If this community is clarified, then endlessly open nature itself becomes a nature that includes an open plurality of men, as subjects of possible intercommunion. To this community there naturally corresponds a similarly open community of monads, which we designate as *transcendental intersubjectivity*.

It will be clear that for me this transcendental intersubjectivity is constituted purely within me, the meditating ego, purely by virtue of sources belonging to my intentional life; nevertheless it is constituted then *as* a community which is also constituted in every other monad as the *same* community and as necessarily bearing within itself the same objective world. We need hardly remark again that every other monad is to be taken as a monad constituted by me with the modification 'other'.

Be this as it may, every analysis and theory of transcendental phenomenology, including the theory of the transcendental constitution of an objective world, can be repeated in the realm of the natural attitude, but then we have first to put the transcendental reduction out of action. Within the realm of our naïve natural life it becomes a theory belonging to psychology. In this way it becomes clear that on the eidetic and on the empirical level a pure psychology corresponds to a transcendental phenomenology. But let us return again to our main problem.[28]

What has been said up to now does evidently not suffice to explain the constitution of that community which belongs to the full essence of mankind. On the basis, however, of our explanation of the community in the last sense mentioned, it is not too difficult to understand the possibility of specifically personal acts of the ego that have the character of social acts and by means of which all human personal communication is established. Starting from there it must be possible to explain in a transcendental way the various types of social communities with their possible hierarchical order, and among them the pre-eminent types that have the character of personalities of a higher level.

Once this would have been accomplished one would have to focus attention on the problem of the constitution of the specifically human surrounding world as a surrounding world of culture for each man and for each human community, and likewise the problem of the kind of objectivity belonging to each of them. A problem of great importance in this context also is the problem of the difference and the relation between nature and culture.

A very important point in all these descriptions is that the constitution of worlds of any kind whatever, beginning with one's own stream of lived experiences with its open and endless multiplicities, and continuing up through the objective world with its various levels of objectivation, is subject to *the law of oriented constitution,* according to which every constitution at various levels presupposes something primordially and something secondarily constituted. At each of these levels the primordially constituted world enters, with a new stratum of meaning, into the secondarily constituted world in such a way that the primordial occupies the central place because of certain oriented modes of givenness. The secondarily constituted world is as a world necessarily given as a horizon if Being that is accessible only from the primordially, constituted world.

Applying this law to the constitution of the cultural world, we find that it too, as a world of culture, is given finally on the underlying

28. *Ibid.,* pp. 156-159 (128-131).

basis of the nature common to all and on the basis of its spatio-temporal form. We see that in this way the cultural world, furthermore, is given first in relation to a 'zero member', a 'zero personality': on this level I and my culture are primordial, over against every alien culture. To me and to those who share in my culture, an alien culture is accessible only by a kind of experience of someone else, a kind of empathy, by which we project ourselves into the alien cultural community and its culture. We must abandon here a more precise exploration of the layer of meaning that gives to the world of culture as such its specific sense, and makes it a world endowed with specifically 'spiritual' predicates. For the present it must suffice that we have indicated these problems of a higher level as problems of constitution and thereby made it understandable that, with the systematic progress of transcendental phenomenological explicitation of the apodictic ego, the transcendental meaning of the world must also become disclosed to us ultimately in the full concreteness with which it is necessarily the life-world for us all. That applies likewise to all the particular formations of the surrounding world. All these matters conform to an essential style, which derives its necessity from the transcendental ego first, and then from the transcendental intersubjectivity which discloses itself in that ego.

We want to conclude these considerations with one final remark. The problems of psycho-physical, physiological and psychological genesis, and especially the problems of the child's psychic development, have here not yet been touched. They belong to a higher dimension and presuppose that the immense explicitation of the lower sphere is already realized.[29]

---

29. *Ibid.*, pp. 159-163 (131-136).

CHAPTER NINE

TRANSCENDENTAL PHENOMENOLOGY AND THE LIFE-WORLD

1. *Significance of Husserl's Last Publication*

Development of Husserl's Thought Between 1916 and 1935

When Husserl received his appointment to the chair of Philosophy in Freiburg in 1916, there was no doubt that he already had an international reputation. According to his own view, however, his thinking was just undergoing a new and very deep crisis at that time. This was why he did not dare to publish the second and third volumes of his *Ideas* and why he set to work again with the greatest possible energy in order to realize his ideal of building up a really radical philosophy. He persisted in his opinion that phenomenology had to be the fundamental and basic discipline in regard to philosophy and the different sciences, and that its method in principle was able to meet the demands of radicality. The longer he thought about the concepts of 'knowing' and 'science' the more problematic they became to him.

His conviction, however, that the realm of pure consciousness, which is to be opened up by phenomenological reduction, constitutes the domain in which every thing, every process, every movement, and every objective relationship between things has to find its origin, remained unshaken. In his attempt to answer the question of how the subjective constitution of all kinds of objects really takes place, he was led time and again to new, unexpected and very fundamental difficulties and problems. In numerous detailed analyses he tried to impress on himself the real and proper meaning of these problems in order to attempt to find a radically justified solution for the questions. Virtually nothing of these extremely valuable analyses was published during Husserl's lifetime, and even in his lectures they were seldom mentioned. The three longer publications written in Freiburg have the character of introductions which served as starting point for the analyses contained in the later manuscripts.[1]

---

1. Eugen Fink, "Die Spätphilosophie Husserls in der Freiburger Zeit", *Edmund Husserl: 1859-1959*, pp. 98-115, pp. 99-101.

Be this as it may, in these major publications Husserl returned to the fundamental problems which had occupied him since 1887 in order to try to solve them from a higher level and in a more radical way than had been possible between 1900 and 1916. In his *Formal and Transcendental Logic* (1929) it was his intention to show that traditional logic is a correlative two-in-one of a formal, apophantic logic and a formal ontology, and especially how every formal, logical *a priori* is to be radically founded in the subjective constitutions of meanings, performed by transcendental subjectivity. According to him it is in these considerations that the problems studied in *Logical Investigations* find their final solutions.

In *Cartesian Meditations* (1931) Husserl returned to the problem of how we have to question backwards, as it were, from the intramundane character of the knowable objects and the equally concealed wordlihood of the human modes of knowing, to consciousness which constitutes all sense and meaning. In a very succinct and frequently enigmatic fashion this work points to a solution for the most fundamental problems of phenomenology which despite everything had not been given an adequate answer in either *The Idea of Phenomenology* or in *Ideas*. In his last publication, *Crisis,* Husserl finally returned to the problems mentioned in his *Logos* article. After a radicalization of logic and epistemology, in *Formal and Transcendental Logic* and *Cartesian Meditations* respectively, in this work he tried to bring to light the ultimate roots of a general theory of science by means of a consistent radicalization of his initial and still naïve view on this point. In the end these three publications may be said to embody one common purpose, namely that of presenting an introduction to transcendental phenomenology by means of a typical and always more penetrating criticism of the traditional conceptions.[2]

The Meaning of 'Crisis'

The peculiarity of his work *Crisis* consists in that Husserl tries here to solve the problems involved in man's theoretical knowledge and in science with the help of a minute analysis of man's pre-scientific life

---

2. *Ibid.,* pp. 101-108 (passim).

and, therefore, by means of an accurate analysis of his daily, pre-scientific experience. In his view the *Lebenswelt,* that is, the world as we immediately experience it in our everyday life, constitutes a very complicated system of relativities, because it is the world as it is immediately given in our individual and social experiences, that in which the things appear according to their colors, their sensible qualities and their 'practical' meaning. The life-world is a vast domain of subjective phenomena which comprises all things just as they are immediately experienced. The 'worlds' of the sciences originate from and, therefore, are as such also opposite to this 'subjective', 'practical', and eternally relative world. The sciences try to transcend and conquer these 'subjective', 'practical' and 'relative' aspects of the world, not to mention the 'magical' and 'mythical' aspects, and want to understand things in a purely 'objective' way, either by using the methods of the mathematical sciences of nature or the critical methods of the sciences of mind. The 'objective' in this way becomes the ideal and the guiding clue of all theoretico-scientific thought which develops from the life-world.

True, there is no doubt about the fact that science in this way transcends the life-world, but it conceals it at the same time without noticing explicitly that it does so. And because science never became aware of this concealment of the world, it everywhere lapsed into 'objectivism', which indeed overcomes the naïve subjectivity of the life-world. On the other hand, science does not quite understand itself either, because it is no longer aware of its own origin which is to be found in certain fundamental motives of the life-world itself. That is also why science does not understand that for a radical explanation of its own foundations it requires a subjective interpretation which has its ultimate roots in the transcendental analysis of transcendental subjectivity.

Taken from this point of view, it becomes understandable why in this work Husserl's investigations range over three completely different levels: 1) the naïvely mundane phenomena of the life-world itself; 2) the realm of objectivism of the sciences which remain principally within the domain of a pre-supposed, pre-given, really existing world; 3) the subjectivity of our transcendental life of consciousness which precedes and constitutes the world, and through whose achievements the things of the life-world as well as all theoretically projectable and determinable substrates are constituted. At first glance a dialectical structure seems to manifest itself here: the immediate subjectivity of the things of the life-world is denied by the mediate objectivity of the objectivistic sciences, while their objectivism in its turn is to be denied by the transcendental subjectivism of phenomenology. However, Husserl was a stranger to such dialectics. In his estimation this book was only an introduction to the numerous detailed analyses in this realm which were already present in his manuscripts and which urged him to go in this direction.[3]

In any case, in his work *Crisis* Husserl takes his concrete starting point in the 'break-down situation of our time' which according to him was caused by the break-down of science itself.[4] He felt that only a consistently performed phenomenological philosophy would be able to overcome this fundamental crisis. In expressing this opinion Husserl harks back to ideas which were already expressed for the first time in *The Idea of a Philosophical Culture*[5] and in *Renovation: Its Problem and Its Method*[6] in 1923 and 1924.

Rejection of Objectivism

When in this context Husserl speaks about a radical crisis, he means to say that the self-understanding and the self-interpretation of man in his relation to the world and the ground of its Being (which in their main lines were normative for modern times) lost their validity and therefore could no longer offer a guiding clue to help man in determin-

---

3. *Ibid.,* pp. 106-107.
4. Edmund Husserl, *Krisis,* p. 59. See for the following also Ludwig Landgrebe, "Die Bedeutung der Phänomenologie Husserls für die Selbstbesinnung der Gegenwart", *Husserl et la pensée moderne,* pp. 216-229.
5. Edmund Husserl, "Die Idee einer philosophischen Kultur. Ihr erstes Aufkeimen in der griechischen Philosophie", *Japanisch-deutsche Zeitchhrift für Wissenschaft und Technik,* 1 (1923) 45-51. See for this also *Erste Philos.,* vol. I, pp. 203-207.
6. Edmund Husserl, "Erneuerung. Ihr Problem und ihre Methode", *The Kaizo,* 1 (1924) 84-92.

ing his place in the midst of the beings as a whole, and to decide with certainty on his attitude in the world. This break-down of man's self-understanding, therefore, means not only the break-down of the theoretical-scientific explanation of the world, but at the same time the failure of every 'practical' orientation in the world. Husserl calls the root of the break-down of man's self-understanding 'objectivism'. By this he means to indicate the conviction that the truth of the world and the coherent totality of Being consist in what is expressible in the statements of an objective-scientific context.[7] In this conviction is founded also the belief that on the basis of our objective-scientific knowledge, Being is completely and totally at man's disposal, that is to say, the conviction that man in his own reason has the capacity to put everything immediately given in experience into a conceptual context, in such a way that neither for man's knowledge nor for his 'praxis' and technology would there be left over an incomprehensible rest.[8] Human reason is to be understood here as the faculty which, indeed, does not project the world in a creative way, but is nevertheless able to reproduce the world's project with the help of its 'innate' and proper ideas, so that every intervention in its course and every change can be calculated with certainty in advance.

In this way, however, the world loses more and more the character of being that in which man always already lives, which is simply given to him as not completely available to him and which, therefore, is to be accepted by man as it is. On the contrary, the world disappears increasingly into that which is made possible and also in fact constituted by the projects of man's understanding; in this way, to an ever growing degree, it becomes an artificial world projected by the sciences in which less and less is left over which was not of its own making and work. In such a world man, too, becomes an artificial object which is nothing but a product of his own scientific project. Man's reason is no longer the faculty which learns the truth which is 'on and in itself', but is more and more conceived in terms of its instrumental significance in regard to man's scientific self-productions in a world that is first

---

7. Ludwig Landgrebe, *l.c.*, p. 217.
8. Edmund Husserl, *Krisis*, pp. 18-20.

produced by man. In its main lines this seems to be the core of what Husserl calls the phenomenon of the 'deprivation of sense', characteristic of modern mathematical natural science and its technical applicability.[9]

Husserl saw that scientific objectivism was truly a dead issue long before others generally accepted this view. And furthermore he did not content himself with an analysis of the factors by which and the situation in which such a radical crisis was caused. He also was looking for a solution to it. It was his personal conviction that the phenomenological method was the way to bring man to such a change in attitude and such an understanding of himself that this crisis could be overcome in a really radical way.[10]

Reduction to the Life-world

If one wants to evaluate the true worth of the possibilities offered to philosophy, by the phenomenological method, he has again to concentrate upon the proper meaning of the phenomenological reduction. Within this perspective this reduction evidently assumes a new form albeit without losing its original meaning inasfar as its very essence is concerned. In order to be able to bring to light Being just as it manifests itself in original and immediate experience, phenomenological reduction first puts between brackets everything which—as originating from any philosophical conceptions or scientific theories whatsoever—is explanation only. Even the horizons in which our everyday world manifests itself, are for the most part already co-determined and distorted by a preceding philosophical or scientific explanation and interpretation. To put such an explanation and interpretation between brackets means that we have to work backward from the concepts which common language offers us in order to explain Being, to those experiences from which these concepts borrow their original meaning. The term 'experience' refers here not only to watching and perceiving, but first and foremost to every concrete form of intercourse and contact with the

---

9. Ludwig Landgrebe, *Ibid.*, p. 217.
10. *Ibid.*, p. 218.

things through which we come into an immediately experiencing contact with those things. From this it is clear that our objective-scientific explanation of the world is only one determinate mode of our contact with things and that it is in no way the most fundamental mode.[11] In this sense reduction in the first place means to go back from the world as it is already explained and interpreted by the sciences to the world just as it is immediately given in experience before every science.

It is clear, however, that a methodical procedure which wants to bring to light the 'originary' experience always and everywhere must face as one of its greatest problems the fact that it always has to employ the naïve expressions of ordinary language, and that it even has to maintain these expressions because this is a necessary presupposition of the evidence of the results of its investigation. The problems which are created in consequence can be solved only in a certain kind of reflection which simultaneously maintains and purifies these expressions by comparing them with the data of our immediate experience. Only by such a reflection which rises above the naïveté of our daily life will a proper return to the life-world be possible and worthwhile, and only by such a return to the life-world will it be possible to transcend the philosophical naïveté which is implied in the so-called scientific character of traditional, objectivistic philosophy.[12]

So the return to the world of our immediate experience does not exhaust itself in naïve descriptions. For to this return to the life-world there belongs also a reflection on that which is experienced, taken just as it is experienced and, therefore, also a reflection on the subjective achievements of the experiencing itself and, finally, a reflection on the conditions of the possibility of that experience inasfar as these are found in the experiencing subject. However, if the reflection on the conditions of the possibility of experience, taken in Kant's sense, constitutes the task of transcendentally philosophical consideration, then phenomenology, too, is to be characterized as transcendental philosophy. Kant's transcendental philosophy confined itself to an investigation of the conditions of the possibility of Being just as object of our objective-scientific knowl-

---

11. Edmund Husserl, *Krisis,* p. 133.
12. *Ibid.,* pp. 59-60. Ludwig Landgrebe, *ibid.,* pp. 219-220.

edge; the consequence of this was that all the data were to be taken as referring to man purely as a theoretically knowing subject. In the same area Husserl, on the contrary, asks for the conditions of the possibility of that experience, which as the original and fundamental mode of our life in the world, precedes science as being only one of so many possible specifications of this original experience.

In other words, on this level Husserl is looking for the possibility of our 'life-worldly' experience. Therefore, the structures in which the conditions of the possibility of that experience consist, are found, not only in those structures constituted by our theoretical determination of the given data using objectifying categories, but first and foremost in those structures, which as the temporalization of temporality or as determinations of the original space constitution, refer to the subject as bodily-sensitive, and which form that which before every active, theoretical-knowing determination accounts for the typical characteristic of what is experienced, namely its being passively pre-given.[13]

It is in this way that the return from objective science to the subjective which as the condition of the possibility of every experience is at the root of this experience itself and, therefore, the return from that which is objectively determined to our transcendental life by means of the reduction, can be characterized by Husserl as the completion of the Cartesian attempt to found philosophy on the primordial experience of the *ego cogito*. On the other hand, however, taken in its radical completion this return can be proposed also as the victory over that objectivism which taken historically was the logical fruit of Descartes' view on the meaning of philosophy. In this respect the phenomenological reduction is not to be construed as the last point to which modern philosophy as the philosophy of subjectivity must lead but, rather, as the starting-point from which it could be overcome. On this level all constitution of Being within the realm of the experiencing achievements of the constituting subject is first and foremost a passive constitution; but this fact is only an indication of the fact that the constituting transcendental subjectivity, i.e., our absolute constituting transcendental life, is not at this stage of the analysis a completely autonomous *ego cogito,* but rather that the

---

13. Ludwig Landgrebe, *Ibid.*, p. 220.

constitution manifests itself here as an event which occurs to subjectivity itself. This event is, indeed, already oriented toward rationability, but it is still impossible at this point to further distinguish reason as to its being theoretical, practical, or esthetical.[14]

On this level of the analysis, reason for a phenomenologist is not therefore the totality of all the conditions which enable him 'in a thinking way' to determine the material given by the senses which in itself still is completely senseless, but rather it is that which in advance makes possible our immediate experience and its relatedness to a truth which is already given in it but is not yet at our disposal. Seen from this point of view reason is not the faculty which projects and governs, but is that faculty which learns and receives. This holds true in an absolute sense and even for every possible level if one identifies reason here with our objective-scientific reason.[15]

Negatively it follows from this conception of the reduction that the truth of the appearing Being cannot—as objectivism would have it— consist in its objective determinableness which is related to a pure theoretically knowing subject opposite to it. In other words, the true world is not the one which can be objectively determined by the sciences and as such be *completely* at our disposal. However, in this world which is not completely at our disposal, there are universal structures which can be brought to light as they are given in an original experience which can be explicitated; these are the structures of the life-world. It is in these structures that we come upon an unconditional and universally expressible *a priori*. And this seems to be the positive aspect of the reduction.[16]

The meaning of the universality of this *a priori* is evidently different from that characteristic of the statements of objective science. For the concepts in which we express this *a priori* are not 'objective' concepts but concepts 'of ourselves' which change the objects known at the same time they are bringing them to light. The further development of the

---

14. Edmund Husserl, *Krisis,* p. 84.
15. *Ibid.,* pp. 220-221.
16. *Ibid.,* pp. 221-222.

logic characteristic of such a philosophical 'speaking' is a task which is still far from being realized in an adequate way.[17]

But before returning to this theme, we shall first try to find an answer for the question of what, precisely, is to be understood by the expressions 'world', 'the world of our immediate lived experience', and 'life-world' within the context of Husserl's philosophy as a whole.

2. The World as Phenomenological Theme

Confusion Surrounding the Role of the Life-world Played in Phenomenology

Many contemporary phenomenologists are of the opinion that the life-world is one of the most important ideas which have come to light through the publication of Husserl's unpublished manuscripts. Although this idea had occupied him in one form or another at least since 1923, Husserl intended to communicate his insights concerning the life-world for the first time only about 1936 when he prepared the first part of his article *Crisis*. This conception, however, did not become generally known until Landgrebe and especially Merleau-Ponty had introduced it in their publications on the basis of their knowledge and studies of unpublished manuscripts.[18]

These publications created the impression here and there that it was Husserl's intention during his last years of life, to replace his original studies of the transcendental subjectivity with these new investigations concerning the life-world. Some interpreters of Husserl's philosophy have even suggested this. Nothing, however, is farther from the truth. On the contrary, the investigations about the life-world form only one of the four different ways in which the constituting activity of the transcendental subjectivity can be brought to the fore. The world of our daily lived experience is not the last level uncoverable by our phenomenological analyses, but it itself is also constituted, and the clarification of its constitution must precisely discover the anonymous

---

17. *Ibid.*, p. 222.
18. Herbert Spiegelberg, *op. cit.*, vol. I, p. 159.

achievements of the transcendental ego.[19] This is already evident from the fact that the title of the section of *Crisis* in which Husserl deals with the life-world speaks of the road to phenomenological transcendental philosophy starting from the life-world.[20] Thus the interest which this idea has for its own sake, as we shall see, must not make us forget the fact that it has only a very definite place and function within the context of Husserl's transcendental phenomenology as a whole.[21]

Furthermore, one must not forget that Husserl's conception of the life-world as it is found in *Crisis* is only the logical fruit of earlier investigations concerning the world in general. For, in the foregoing we have seen that already between 1900 and 1913 Husserl undertook investigations with respect to the problem of the world as such, although at that time the world itself was not yet considered as a theme in its own right. Originally these investigations were effected in two different directions: first, in connection with the problem of the phenomenological reduction; secondly, in the course of inquiries attempting to clarify the very essence of man's perception.[22] Later, trying to lay the foundations of a general theory of science and, in this way, to delineate the subject matter of psychology in particular, Husserl focussed attention on the world just as it is given to us in immediate experience.[23] Only in the latter context do we find the motives which, in the period beginning about 1920, led Husserl to the problem of the life-world as this is explained in *Crisis*. Seen from this point of view Husserl's doctrine of the life-world as it is presented in *Crisis*, appears as an harmonious synthesis of his view on the phenomenological reduction found in *First Philosophy* and *Cartesian Meditations* on the one hand, and his mundane

---

19. Walter Biemel, "Les phases décisives dans le développement de la philosophie de Husserl", *Husserl*, pp. 32-71 (passim). In particular see the discussions following the papers given by M. Kuypers ("La conception de la philosophie comme science rigoureuse et les fondements des sciences chez Husserl") and Walter Biemel ("Les phases décisives"), *Husserl*, pp. 85 and 65.

20. Edmund Husserl, *Krisis*, pp. 105-194, p. 105.

21. Herbert Spiegelberg, *op. cit.*, vol. I, p. 160.

22. Edmund Husserl, *Ideen I*, pp. 57-69 (91-100), 76-79 (105-107), 110-117 (133-139), 199-201 (218-219).

23. Edmund Husserl, *Phän. Psychol.*, pp. 64-150.

phenomenology of the world, which was briefly outlined for the first time in *Phenomenological Psychology,* on the other.

Although it is my intention in the following to focus special attention on the most important insights in regard to the life-world as Husserl has described them in his last book, *Crisis,* a brief introduction explaining the most significant results of Husserl's investigations concerning the world in general and the world of our immediate experiences in particular seems to be of some importance in this context.

The World and the Phenomenological Epoché

We have seen that Husserl generally describes the phenomenological *epoché* as a disconnection of the so-called general thesis of our natural attitude. This thesis can—as we know—be briefly characterized as follows. I find continuously present to me and standing over against me the one spatio-temporal fact-world to which I myself belong as do all other human beings found in it and related to it in the same way as I do. I find this fact-world to be out there; and I also take it always just as it gives itself to me as something that exists out there. Any doubt, negation, or rejection of certain data of the natural world does not affect the general thesis of the natural standpoint. The world is as a fact-world always there, even if it at certain spots appears to be other than I originally supposed. In order to know this fact-world more truly and comprehensively than our everyday experience is able to do, and also to solve all the problems which manifest themselves on its basis, man has to build up different sciences which, however, all remain sciences of the natural attitude.

Taken as a whole, therefore, our world as the world in which we always find ourselves consciously living, remains certain, no matter how many details become doubtful. Only particular parts of it ever undergo the correction 'not so but otherwise'. This means that every position or negation presupposes as a universal basis our belief in the reality of the world. Every positing is a positing and every cancelling is a cancelling on this basis which, within the realm of the natural attitude, we can never shake. Therefore, if the *epoché* really wants to make us transcend the domain of the natural attitude, it has to be universal and not limited to particular acts and their meant objects as meant. In other

words, by the phenomenological reduction the general thesis characteristic of the natural attitude as such must be put out of action.[24]

In this way, while developing the doctrine of the phenomenological
epoché, Husserl acquired a first definition of the world: the world is
the all-encompassing doxic basis that as a total horizon includes every
particular positing. It is true that Husserl in these analyses was primarily concerned with acts of perceiving. But since he was convinced
that perception is the primordial existence-positing act and, therefore,
constitutes the fundament of acts of every other kind, we may conclude
that the world is the horizon of our total human attitude, that is, our
intentional directedness in all our diverse acts.

Thus the general thesis as the universal fundamental doxic positing of
the world does not consist in a determinate act which, at some time or
other, is to be explicitly performed, but is rather the foundation for every
concrete act whatsoever. It is nothing but the elemental fact that, from
the very start, the ego lives in the world, is intentionally directed toward
beings which are always tacitly understood as intramundane beings.

The World as Appearing in the Phenomenological Analysis of Perception

Within the context of his investigations concerning the meaning of the
phenomenological reduction Husserl thus came to the conclusion that
by world is to be understood the all-embracing doxic basis which as a
total horizon includes every particular positing. This view was in fact
not more than a further clarification of the world as the horizon of every
perception. For, as we have seen in the foregoing, analysis of the
syntheses in which the perception of a material thing comes into being
shows that we cannot restrict ourselves to the thing-perception as an
isolated phenomenon, if we intend to uncover the concrete and full
meaning of this material thing. The perceived thing always manifests
itself in a certain horizon, in the form of a background of things which
are consciously and more or less explicit 'meant' along with the thing in
question. Every material thing manifests itself in perception as having
its outer horizon which is not only spatially but also temporally extended. Let us try to explain this again with the same example.

---

24. Edmund Husserl, *Ideen I,* pp. 57-63 (91-96).

In front of me stands this black table. I see it and touch it. This perceiving seeing and touching of the table is the full concrete experience of the table that stands here and is, in truth, given to me with a relative lack of clearness, appearing to me from this particular angle. I am turned toward the table and apprehend it as being this here and now. But because every perceived thing manifests itself as having a background in experience, my act of perception has the character of a singling out. Around and behind the table are chairs, the book-case, the television set, the wall with its window and the pictures. And these in a certain sense are also perceived, perceptually there in the field of intuition. But as long as I was turned toward the table I did not *apprehend* them, not even in a secondary sense. They appeared, but were not singled out. Every act of perception has such a zone of background 'intuitions' which together constitute my consciousness of all that as a matter of fact lies in the co-perceived background. Taken in its full concretion as correlate of our concrete perceptual life this 'spatial horizon' is our surrounding world. In this surrounding world we live in, open possibilities of further experience manifest themselves and thus refer us to ever wider horizons. That is why we experience our surrounding world as part of 'the' world, that part, namely, which is directly accessible to us.

But this world does not only possess a spatial order, it has also its temporal order in the succession of time. That is to say, the world now present to me has its temporal horizon which extends unendingly in two directions, its known and unknown past and future.[25]

After all this, we may conclude that Husserl's earlier analyses of the perception of a concrete thing uncovered to him a structure which he eventually understood as a first characterization of the world: the world, first of all, as the horizon of all our perceiving acts, then, as the horizon to which every human activity finally points.

The Essential Structures of the World of Our Immediate Experience

These ideas, only very briefly indicated, here occupied Husserl more and more after his *Ideas* appeared, and especially in the twenties when

---

25. *Ibid.*, pp. 76-79 (91-96).

he was looking for a deeper insight into the relationship between phenomenology and psychology, on the one hand, and the problem of the reduction, on the other. During that period, the world concept, which was at first defined generally as the all-embracing horizon of any experience, received a more differentiated content. According to him, however, those analyses concerning the world, as analyses belonging to a mundane phenomenology which remains within the domain of the natural attitude, have only a preliminary character; hence on this level the problem of the world can never find its final solution. A real understanding of the world can be obtained only by means of a radical explanation of its constitution by transcendental subjectivity, and such an explanation can be given, after the reduction has been performed, with the help of detailed constitutional analyses, as is explained in the foregoing chapters.

But before returning to this point, let us first try to describe a few leading traits of Husserl's mundane-phenomenological analyses concerning the world of our immediate experience, especially as we find them in his lecture course *Phenomenological Psychology*.

In this series of lectures Husserl wished to delineate subject matter, method and function of a new eidetic science, called 'phenomenological psychology' and, especially, to determine its relation to empirical psychology and transcendental phenomenology. According to him, however, it is impossible to define the pure 'psychical' as the subject matter of phenomenological psychology, if one does not take one's starting point in a general ontology of the world of our immediate experience.[26]

In his brief outline of such a general ontology of the world of our immediate experience Husserl deals first with the crucial problem created by the fact that many philosophers, influenced by Kant, explicitly deny that the world could ever be an object of any possible experience. Husserl admits that obviously only real, individual beings are immediately experienced, but it is his conviction that in these experiences which immediately refer to individual things, the world is co-perceived as their necessary horizon. If it is true that the world is experienced

---

26. Edmund Husserl, *Phän. Psychol.*, pp. 55-64.

as the necessary horizon in which the individual beings can manifest themselves, it will be clear why every intersubjectively experienced being is conceivable only as being *in* the world and why space and time are the necessary *a priori* forms in which each concrete being is to be ordered. For, originally, the world manifests itself only as a spatio-temporal horizon, as concretely filled space and concretely filled time.[27]

Furthermore, from this conception of the world as the necessary horizon of every perceived thing it follows also inasfar as method is concerned, that the descriptive and eidetic analyses of the most general structures of the world must take their starting point in the consideration of exemplary, real, individual things taken in their essential relatedness to the horizon which in fact is the world.[28]

When we, while studying those phenomena, use eidetic reduction to focus attention on the essential structure of experienced being as such, it becomes clear that this being manifests itself as concretely being there and that—within the realm of our natural attitude—we self evidently conceive it as being real in the real world. This world, however, to which our whole natural life necessarily is referred, manifests itself as not only changing in itself, but also as being subject to our always changing conceptions and ideas. This means that what we normally call 'the' world, is not the world as it is immediately experienced, but this world as always being already covered with layers of meaning which have their origin in our conceptions and opinions, themselves the results of our practical and theoretical activities.

On closer investigation it becomes then manifest that our view on 'the' world is *especially* influenced by two factors. First, our way of apprehending the world is determined by the fact that the sciences have explained the world with the help of categories which, although they undergo continuous development and correction, claim to define the world objectively as a set of given objects and relationships, existing in themselves and capable of being grasped by exact methods. Our conception of the world, therefore, involves, quite as a matter of course,

---

27. *Ibid.*, pp. 93-97.
28. *Ibid.*, pp. 98-99.

the belief that this is an objective, exactly determined and determinable world. However, to this conviction the broadening of our historical, ethnological, and sociological knowledge has added the awareness that the view of the world determined by the sciences cannot be considered as the only one. Today, as in earlier times, we find human communities whose understanding of the world has in no way been affected by the sciences. The necessary consequence of this fact is that the scientific view on the world is itself only one among many and, like all the others, it has been produced by a certain society under definite conditions. Thus, the conviction of many scientists that their view on the world is the only true one, the only one that is valid objectively, is unacceptable. We must admit a plurality and historical relativity of views of the world, none of which may claim for itself an absolute truth about 'the' world.

Accordingly, when Husserl struggled with the problem of the world, it was evident to him from the very start that the determinations due to the world thanks to the accomplishments of the sciences, cannot be considered as essential structures which belong necessarily to the world as such. On the the contrary, we must turn from the world as it always is already there for us, with its sense as explicitated by the sciences, and go back to the world as it is prior to science, the immediately lived world with its original givenness, which is the underlying basis for every scientific determination. Correlatively, we must go back from our scientific view on the world to our pre-scientific experiences.[29]

When we now perform such a reduction which obviously is to be distinguished from the transcendental reduction, 'the' world begins to manifest itself as consisting of concrete substances, all of which have their characteristic 'modes', such as size, shape, color, etc. Each individual, concrete substance manifests itself as a causal unity, which is causally related to its surroundings and, within the context of the changing causal relations, manifests itself as a substratum of fixed and causally determined properties. To the general structure that necessarily belongs to the very essence of this and every conceivable world belongs, too, the distinction between different regions of being, of which the regions of liv-

---

29. *Ibid.*, pp. 52-57.

ing and non-living beings are the most striking examples. The region of consciously living subject appears to occupy a privileged and central place in the world of our immediate experience. Although every concrete substance in the world possesses necessarily and essentially spatial, temporal, and causal aspects, the consciously living subjects manifest themselves as, in addition to these aspects, having certain characteristics all of which belong to the order of the 'psychical'.[30]

All this is obviously to be described in detail, and in many aspects to be completed also. What is said, however, may suffice as a first characterization of the world of our immediate experience. We shall return to this topic in the following section in which we shall give a brief outline of Husserl's view on the world as this is found in his last publication 'Crisis', where Husserl approaches the theme from a completely different point of view.[31]

3. The Life-World in Husserl's 'Crisis'

As was mentioned in the preceding section, Husserl introduces the question of the life-world in his last book, Crisis, as one of the four roads to transcendental phenomenology.[32] The life-world could give us a particularly interesting and revealing clue for the study of the universal and transcendental constitution of the transcendental ego. It is, however, not our intention to describe this new road to transcendental phenomenology in a complete way, but rather to explain the most important insights regarding the very nature and meaning of the life-world itself and its function within phenomenological philosophy as a whole. Therefore we shall confine ourselves here to a brief summary of some sections of Husserl's Crisis and some other important manuscripts written in 1936 and 1937. First we shall try to describe more accurately what is meant by the term 'Lebenswelt'; then we shall indicate the relation be-

30. Ibid., pp. 99-100.

31. See for the foregoing section as a whole Ludwig Landgrebe, "The World as Phenomenological Problem", Philosophy and Phenomenological Research 1 (1940-1941), 38-58, pp. 38-45.

32. See Eugen Fink, loc. cit., p. 108, and Boehm's Introduction to Edmund Husserl, Erste Philos., vol. II, pp. xxx-xxxvii.

tween the life-world and the scientific worlds. Ultimately we hope to explain the possibility of an ontology of the life-world and its significance for transcendental phenomenology. In so doing I shall be guided by the relevant sections of Gurwitsch's excellent study on *Crisis* which will be quoted below.

Description of the Life-World

Under the influence of modern science since Galileo, the life-world, as the world of our common lived experience, has been replaced by the objectively true world of science which, as modern Western scientists would have it, passes for reality in the strict sense of the word. However, it can be shown quite easily that such a view is completely unacceptable. For one thing, no objective entity of science is available to direct an immediate experience, whereas the life-world does offer itself, actually or virtually, in every perceptual experience and all its possible derivatives. Furthermore, the universe of science proves to be a network of ideal constructs, a theoretico-logical superstructure; its apprehension and conception, therefore, are of the same nature as those of any idea of the mathematical sciences. For the construction of the world of science implies, as a mental accomplishment, certain definite procedures in which idealization plays an integral role. Idealization, however, obviously implies something to be idealized. Therefore, because of its intrinsic sense as a superstructure, the world of science must have a firm basis upon which it can rest and upon which it is built. This foundational basis cannot be anything other than the life-world and the immediate evidence of our lived experiences—the term 'evidence' referring to immediate self-presentation of the objects involved. And so all theoretical truth, whether logical, mathematical, or scientific, has its final justification and roots in evidences which concern events and happenings in the life-world.

If Husserl, therefore, gives the evidences of the life-world a privileged status over those of scientific, objective theory, it is attributable to the latter's being based upon the former. The operations and procedures whose outgrowths and constituted correlates are objective theory, and, generally speaking, the objective world of science, always imply those acts of consciousness in and through which the life-world appears as always present and pre-given, as existing in its own right prior to all scientific endeavor. Therefore, for a really fundamental understanding of the world of science we must return to the life-world and elucidate the role it plays in several aspects in the constitution and development of science.[33]

Radical philosophical reflection then, must begin by making clear the universal presupposition which is at the root of our life and all our engagements. This presupposition is the doxically accepted and even naïve self-evidence of the world in which we live and with which we are always on familiar terms. At each minute of our life, we are concerned, somehow or other, with things, animals, other people, which manifest themselves as intramundane beings, and we, too, see ourselves as part of this world. None of the beings appears in isolation; each refers to a certain framework into which it is inserted; it manifests itself within an all-encompassing and ever extended horizon: the world-horizon. Unlike certain mundane beings which may occasionally show themselves and then fade away, the world itself is continously present to us as the universal field of all actual and possible activities of any conceivable kind. If the world is always there as pre-given, if to live is to be taken as living in the world, it is because the world proclaims itself simultaneously with the appearance of every particular mundane being with which we might be involved. The implicit and vague awareness of the world permeates all our comings and goings and becomes part of them as their most fundamental, though never explicitly formulated, presupposition. Correspondingly, the world, tacitly taken for granted, proves to be the ground for all our endeavors, regardless of their proper orientation.[34]

The world indeed includes nature. However, by nature is to be understood here nature as it is given in immediate experience, and not the idealized nature of the physical sciences. But the world comprises more than *mere* nature; there is also 'culture'. For among the beings

---

33. Edmund Husserl, *Krisis,* pp. 48-54, 114-116, 130-138.
34. *Ibid.,* pp. 145-146.

in the midst of which we find ourselves, there are not only natural beings, objects which may be described exhaustively by pointing to their color, shape, size, weight, etc., but also tools, instruments, books, buildings, art objects, that is, objects which have human meaning, serve human aims and needs, and satisfy human desires. Because the world has such objects at all and, therefore, provides the framework within which we live our human life, we refer to it as our life-world.[35]

Within the life-world we encounter other human beings and assume without question that they not only live in the world but are also aware of it, that they are faced with those things and objects which confront us, although to each one of us, determined by his point of view, the objects and the world in general may appear under varying perspectives. Nonetheless each of us takes it for granted that the world is one and the same for all of us, a common intersubjective world, the world of our common experience.[36]

As we encounter each other in the common world, each of us may adopt toward the other an attitude of a disinterested observer, or, conversely, we may become involved with one another and engage ourselves in the myriad relationships of mutual enterprise and cooperation. We then live not only in the same world but live, work, and actualize our potentialities in it together; we enmesh our intentions, plans, and activities with theirs in full reciprocal interaction. If because of its reference to man's life the world takes on the character of a life-world, the reference is not only to individual persons, but also, and even principally, to an historical society whose social life consists in the interrelatedness of thought and action in different modalities. The term 'life-world' has essentially an historico-social implication: a life-world is relative to a given society at a certain moment of its history. It must, therefore, be taken as it is thought of by the historical society whose world it is, as is, for instance, explained by Lucien Lévy-Bruhl in his interpretation of the mythical and magical world of primitive society.[37] Whether we act on our own or in cooperation with

35. *Ibid.*, pp. 130-133.
36. *Ibid.*, pp. 138-139.
37. Herbert Spiegelberg, *op. cit.*, vol. I, p. 161.

other people and engage in mutual endeavors, the things with which we are confronted, our own plans and projects, and finally the world in its entirety appear to us in the light of convictions, opinions, beliefs and conceptions which are prevalent in the society of which we are part. The term 'society' may be taken here in the broadest sense denoting the whole historical civilization to which we belong, or in the narrower sense of a special group within a larger community. The life-world provides the ground of our life, a basis always taken for granted, always taken as already given and existing independently of and prior to all our individual and collective activities. We meet one another as mundane being among intramundane beings on this ground which we all share.[38]

Besides being objects in the life-world, we are simultaneously subjects in relation to the life-world, insofar as it derives its meaning from our collective human life. These collective accomplishments become a part of the life-world which not only is as it is taken to be by the respective society but also comprises all its innovations. In and through the life of the society in question, its life-world undergoes changes and transformations and consequently is subject to always new re-interpretations.[39]

The Life-World and the World of Science

Reflecting upon the life-world as it immediately manifests itself to us, we were able to point to its historical character and its essential relativity to a certain living society. Now we want to focus attention on the fact that in the collective endeavors which have been referred to our scientific activities play an important role. When, for instance, Einstein refers to the investigations and results of Lorentz, the reference is obviously not to a physical or psycho-physical construction of Lorentz which would show him as he really and objectively is in himself, although both Einstein and Lorentz as well as their laboratories, the equipment involved and the books used could be investigated as 'physical'

---

38. Edmund Husserl, *Krisis*, pp. 140-142; *Phän. Phychol.*, pp. 52-57.
39. Aron Gurwitsch, "The Last Work of Edmund Husserl", *Philosophy and Phenomenological Research*, 16 (1955-1956) 370-399, pp. 370-373.

objects with the help of physical methods. But to the working physicist Einstein, Lorentz appears as a colleague who lives in the same world, has certain interest in common with him, and is engaged in analogous endeavors. Meeting Lorentz in the same life-world and finding himself in contact and harmony with him, because of their shared aims and common knowledge, Einstein tries to understand Lorentz's ideas; he uses them as they are or changes them; he uses Lorentz's results as bases for further investigation and as premises for further conclusions or employs them in some other way in his own work which he then presents to his scientific colleagues for further consideration and critique.

Science arises from and develops in such interaction of the scientific activities of the members of the scientific community. This community, of course is made up not only of contemporary scientists but also of those who worked before them and upon whose achievements present-day scientists are building. It is, moreover, an open community, in that whatever is achieved now will be carried further by future scientists. The interaction spoken of here is characterized by general discussion, constructive critiques, agreement, and, eventually the making of any necessary alterations, all this to the end of coming to a justifiable and satisfactory conclusion. Science taken in this light manifests itself as a collective cultural achievement, basically not too different from the results of other cultural accomplishments. In regard to scientific activities, Husserl significantly refers to a special type of *praxis,* namely the *praxis* of theorizing.[40]

For a better understanding of what is involved in science, one has to investigate and analyze the mental functions and operations involved in scientific pursuits, and the different modes in which mental activities come to be intersubjectively interrelated. Inasfar as the human sciences deal with man's psychical life and with the creations arising from that life, natural science as it developed since Galileo, being also a creation of the human mind, belongs within the domain of investigation of the sciences of man. Objective nature, that is, nature as it really is in itself, should not be thought of as referring to a reality underlying the appear-

---

40. Edmund Husserl, *Krisis,* p. 135 and pp. 132-138 (passim).

ances in the life-world, a hidden reality which may be uncovered by means of certain methods and techniques. Rather it implies the idea of an unlimited intersubjective achievement, an idea toward which the members of the community of scientists direct their work, and which is approximated by the results of their complementary activities. These results are actually the scientific theories which serve also to delineate the successive phases of the historical advance of science.

Just as is true for all cultural activities, the search for scientific knowledge takes place in the life-world. Scientific questions and problems come up within the life-world and refer to certain aspects of it isolated in abstraction as, for instance, the spatio-temporal or corporeal aspect. Over and over the scientist makes use of events and happenings in the life-world in which he carries out his experimentation, finds his equipment, and takes his pointer-readings. To make use of those events and happenings for and in scientific theories is, however, not the same as to conceptualize and interpret them in scientific terminology. As far as the scientist is concerned, his laboratory is for him the place of study and research; actually he sees it in its relation to the specific human pursuits it serves; he does not consider it in reference to what, taken in the context of a fully developed, universal scientific explanation of all phenomena, it would prove objectively to be in itself, no more so than he considers his colleagues as physico-chemical systems.

The aim of scientific pursuits refers to human existence in the life-world, too; it is but one of several ends which underlie collective, scientific practice and other such intersubjectively concatenated endeavors. If the goals of science are of a specific nature, so are all other goals which orient our cultural life. The specific aim under consideration is to develop to the fullest extent in scope and accuracy, the possibilities of prediction and induction going beyond those germane to pre-scientific, commonly shared experience. Or, as Husserl explains it, this aim is to replace knowledge, in the sense of the familiarity which we have of the life-world in our everyday life and which suffices for our practical needs and our orientation in the life-world, by knowledge in the strict sense of the term, understood in relationship to the ideas of objective truth and Being-in-itself.

Again, as is true for all cultural endeavors, the concrete contributions and results of our scientific projects accrue to the life-world. It is scarcely necessary to mention that the existence of science and scientific theories makes up an integral part of the historico-cultural reality of modern Western man, that is, of his life-world. This is not to be construed as meaning, in the traditional sense, that the universe built up by science is the true reality which is to take the place of the life-world. It does, however, imply that to Western man nature, as given in common experience, seems to have the character of being available for possible scientific interpretation and explanation.

The life-world appears to be the base upon which the world of science is built as a superstructure; the specific logico-mathematical evidence refers, in its very essence, to evidences involving common experience. This does not mean that the life-world is to be seen solely as a point of departure for moving to another realm of Being. Such a position could give rise to the idea of a double truth: subjective and relative truth pertaining to practical situations in the life-world, and objective and scientific truth which, notwithstanding its relation to the first, is not fundamentally affected by this relation. However, as Husserl insists, the life-world does intervene in the implementations of science; the life-world is given to us and we experience ourselves as existing in it, regardless of whether or not we are engaged in scientific projects. Over the centuries man has lived in many life-worlds before the rise of science in the modern sense of this term. Finally science is an integral part of the specific life-world of Western man. The ideas of 'objective truth' and 'Being-in-itself' through which the subjectivity and relativity of common experience is to be transcended, insofar as these ideas serve to guide and give direction to the particular human activity which Husserl calls theoretical *praxis,* are related themselves to the domain of the psychical, the subjective, and thus the relative.

Perhaps initially it seemed that the question of the life-world was considered for the sake of the philosophical elucidation of science only. Now it becomes evident that the philosophy of science, whatever its value and significance may be, deals only with a particular and partial theme.

The life-world appears here not only as an autonomous theme, but also as the more universal and, therefore, the principal theme.[41]

Ontology of the Life-World

A science of the life-world which recognizes this world's specific character and accepts it as it offers itself in immediate experience of pre-scientific life, obviously can not be a science in the sense of Galileo, that is, one in which a theoretical, logico-mathematical superstructure assumes pre-eminence over the life-world. In the first place, we must perform a reduction concerning objective science. This does not mean refusing to recognize that objective science really exists and pretending to live in a world devoid of objective science. This reduction does not mean denying or even questioning its validity. Objective science with its conclusions and achievements continues to be what it always has been, that is a cultural fact related to our life-world. There is no idea of giving up interest in objective science. However, under the reduction, we refrain from following through on certain interests; we suspend them and take them out of action. We do not allow ourselves to be involved in the procedures of objective science; we assume the attitude of disinterested spectators in regard to those procedures. Such an attitude involves not only an absence of consent to theories of objective science but also in refraining from assuming any critical position in regard to the truth or untruth of such theories; this automatically cancels out denial and doubt as specific critical attitudes. Valid theories of objective science remain so for us. However, under the reduction we hold them simply accepted as valid, without going forward ourselves on the basis of their accepted validity, which we wish neither to challenge nor to avail ourselves of. No theory, no finding, no statement of objective science will be allowed to enter into our consideration as a founded truth, starting point, premise, or argument. To be sure, the reduction deals not only with specific theories and outcomes but concerns also the very idea of objective science as such. While continuing to recognize this idea as playing

---

41. *Ibid.*, pp. 48-54, 126-138, 463-467. See also Aron Gurwitsch, *loc. cit.*, pp. 373-375.

an important role in our cultural life, we shall keep ourselves from being motivated and determined by it.[42]

This reduction enables us to take the life-world for what it is, just as we experience it as our historico-cultural reality, without referring it to, or considering it as supplanted by Being as it really is in itself. Yet the whole notion of a general science of the life-world seems plagued by an insurmountable difficulty. Such a science, though not Galilean in nature, must have a certain objectivity and validity, too; it must develop methods which will enable it to make true and founded statements, that is, assertions which appear as conclusive and convincing to everybody who employs the same methods. This, though, seems inconsistent with what has been explained concerning the essential relativity of the life-world to a certain society and even to a specific phase in the history of that society. Does not each life-world require a science for itself? Can there be such a thing as a general science of the life-world as such?[43]

Despite its relativity, the life-world shows itself to possess an invariant structure, to be more exact, an unchanging structural framework to which the relative and variable belongs. Prior to, and completely separate from objective science, the life-world manifests itself as extended in space and time. The space referred to is, needless to say, that which we experience, our lived space, and not a geometrical space; it does not contain any ideal mathematical entities, it is not divisible *ad infinitum,* it does not constitute an infinitesimal continuum, etc. This is true also for time. In the life-world we meet corporeal beings, but they are not bodies, in the sense of geometry or physics. Finally, the life-world exhibits causality, not conceived as laws of nature formulated in equations of functional dependency, but rather a certain regularity and typical uniformity. As Husserl expresses it, things have their habits of behaving in similar ways under typically similar conditions.

It should be mentioned that the categories belonging to the life-world and denoting its invariable structures are designated by the same terms as the objective categories which are developed in *a priori* sciences, such as logic and the different mathematical disciplines. The identity in ter-

---

42. Edmund Husserl, *Krisis,* pp. 138-140.
43. *Ibid.,* pp. 140-142.

minology must not be permitted to mask the distinction between the *a priori* belonging to the life-world and the objective *a priori*. What the identity in terminology does indicate is the essential reference of the objective *a priori* to the *a priori* of the life-world: founded on the *a priori* of the life-world the objective a *priori* is produced through idealization. Posing the issue of the origin of geometry, Husserl accordingly insists upon the historico-intentional investigations which have their point of departure in the invariable structure of perceptual space and spatiality as lived in pre-geometrical experience, and not in the passing apperceptions of a specific historical period, such as the mythico-magical conceptions which, as a matter of recorded history, were involved in, and to some extent certainly had an influence upon, the rise of early geometry.[44]

The general science of the life-world as conceived by Husserl, has as its subject matter the invariable general style and the unchanging formal structure of the life-world. This science does not have to restrict itself to the life-world of Western man, nor even to actual life-worlds of societies which exist or existed in past history. By moving from one actual life-world to another and determining the difference between them, we may free ourselves of all considerations of actuality. Starting from any actual life-world, we may in complete freedom vary and alter it in imagination and in this way fabricate varieties of possible life-worlds merely as possible, about which the problem of their historical actuality has no importance. The goal of the method of free variation in this concrete case is to bring to light what essentially and necessarily belongs to a life-world as such.[45]

In this way Husserl arrives at the notion of an ontology of the life-world as such, understood as a possible world of intersubjective experience. The structures uncovered by this ontology are present in every factual life-world, whatever may be its historical and accidental content. It is to be recognized, however, that an ontology of the life-world differs fundamentally from the ontologies of the modern tradition which have been strongly influenced by the notion 'Being-in-itself'. In other words, traditional ontologies have had their roots in the objective *a priori*,

---

44. *Ibid.*, pp. 144-145.
45. *Ibid.*, pp. 145-146; 146-151.

whereas the ontology which Husserl has in mind is concerned with the *a priori* of the life-world. In bringing to the fore the idea of an ontology of the life-world, even in *Crisis* Husserl does not do much more than formulate this idea. His principal interest lies also here in another direction.[46]

Ontology of the Life-World and Transcendental Phenomenology

In the natural attitude we are interested in the things themselves, their qualities and properties; we are concerned with what the objects are, whether as objects of the immediately lived world or as seen within the horizon of a specific scientific orientation interested in 'Being as it really is in itself'. We are absorbed here in our mundane projects and plans. So we do not focus attention on the modes in which intra-mundane beings and the world itself manifest themselves. The acts of consciousness through which the world and whatever is in it become accessible to us, are lived but not explicitly thematized; they remain more or less hidden. We are, however, able to sever connections with our naïve and natural attitude and to manifest a new *theoretical* interest in things, not as they are in themselves, but as they manifest themselves; more to the point, an interest in their appearances and the systematic concatenations of these appearances. At this point, our topic is no longer the world, but the fabric of our conscious life, the syntheses of acts of consciousness which result in a permanent awareness of the world as always being there. Moving steadfastly in this direction, we near the threshold of phenomenology whose general intention may be formulated as the endeavor to account for the world at large, the intramundane beings in particular and, as a matter of fact, for all objective entities whatsoever, in terms of experiences, acts, and achievements of consciousness. Doing so is tantamount to disclosing the world and the objective entities referred to as products and correlates of systematically concatenated and synthesized multiplicities of conscious acts, in which the former find the basis for their validity and existence.[47]

---

46. *Ibid.*, pp. 176-177. See also Aron Gurwitsch, *loc. cit.*, pp. 375-378.
47. *Ibid.*, pp 151-154

To implement such a program, we must perform a second reduction, this time in regard to the life-world itself. Here again reduction means rendering inactive, laying aside, purposely passing by, and suspension, and not denial or doubt. The whole of conscious life, in and through which there appear beings of every conceivable kind and the life-world as such, remains untouched by the transcendental reduction which is the second *epoché*. While living all these acts in their interwovenness, we do not permit ourselves, under the phenomenological reduction, to live *in* these acts; we no longer allow ourselves to be engaged in them. Our attitude is that of a disinterested onlooker who, rather than participating in it, just looks at the stream of conscious life, which flows on independently of the attitude we adopt, as a field of descriptive and analytical investigations. Acts which, in our naïve and natural attitude, are just lived, are now thematized and made subjects of reflexive analysis. In this way all mundane entities and also the life-world itself are transformed into phenomena referring to the acts of consciousness in and through which they are given.[48]

Conclusion

The life-world, it can be seen, is by no means immediately accessible as such, since everyone undergoes the influence of the culture of the 'world' in which he is living and Western man particularly is somehow 'seduced' by the scientific interpretation of the world. A particular reduction, a temporary suspension of culture and science is, therefore, indispensable for uncovering the life-world and its essential structures. Once we have performed this reduction, we are in a position to study the life-world in an ontology of the life-world which is already a kind of phenomenology; Husserl calls such a phenomenology a mundane phenomenology. Near the end of his life, Husserl believed this mundane phenomenology to be a necessary condition for a transcendental phenomenology. For, on the one hand, it is evident that the analyses of mundane phenomenology itself have no final meaning if they are not completed by analyses in the transcendental sphere

---

48. *Ibid.*, pp. 154-156. See also Aron Gurwitsch, *loc. cit.*, pp. 378-380.

toward which the transcendental reduction is the proper approach. But, on the other hand, Husserl saw also that only after the inquiries of the mundane phenomenology have been effected does the transcendental reduction have a sound basis and proper guide. Thus we must first return from the world of culture to the original life-world by means of a first reduction; then the transcendental reduction must lead us further back from the structures of the life-world to the hidden achievements of a 'functioning intentionality'. The discovery of these achievements then allows us to describe the original constitution of the characteristic features of the life-world and all the objectivities later based upon them.[49]

---

49. Herbert Spiegelberg, *op. cit.*, vol. I, pp. 160-162.

CHAPTER TEN

PHENOMENOLOGY AND PSYCHOLOGY

We have tried in the preceding chapters to give a brief explanation of some of the fundamental aspects of Husserl's phenomenological philosophy. We have dealt successively with Husserl's conception of the essential difference between the natural and philosophical attitude in general, with the fundamental distinction between fact and essence and with the eidetic reduction, with Husserl's famous theory concerning the phenomenological *epoché*, with his view on intentionality and intentional analysis, and finally with his conception of constitution. Ultimately we tried to describe two other points which concerned Husserl most in the last period of his life, namely, his ideas on intersubjectivity and the *Lebenswelt*.

We shall now try to illustrate the most essential elements of what was said above, briefly considering the relationship between phenomenological philosophy and psychology. For it seems that one of the most important needs toward an exact understanding of Husserl's philosophy is precisely the clarification of this relationship between phenomenology and psychology, for if it is not clearly explained then all that Husserl has told us about phenomenological philosophy remains ambiguous.[1]

Even Husserl himself in his long philosophical career did not find it easy to determine his attitude toward psychology, nor to define its exact function within the framework of his changing conception of phenomenology, as we shall see presently. It becomes possible to make a brief outline of the most important phases of Husserl's philosophical development, in fact, on the basis of his different conceptions of the relationship between philosophy and psychology.[2] Although our main intention is to determine

---

1. Herbert Spiegelberg, *op. cit.*, vol. I, p. 149. See for this Chapter as a whole: M. Drüe, *Edmund Husserls System der phänomenologischen Psychologie* (Berlin: Walter de Gruyter, 1963). Joseph J. Kockelmans, *Edmund Husserl's Phenomenological Psychology. A Historico-Critical Study* (Pittsburgh: Duquesne University Press, 1966).

2. *Ibid.*, pp. 149-152. See also Boehm's *Introduction* to Edmund Husserl's *Erste Philos.*, vol. II, pp. *xxxvi-xxxvii;* Edmund Husserl, *Cart. Med.*, pp. 168-174 (141-148); *Krisis*, pp. 194-269 (passim).

Husserl's final view on this question, nevertheless it seems to be relevant to ground this chapter in a brief historical introduction.

1. *The Genesis of the Idea of a Phenomenological Psychology*

Psychologism and Husserl's Criticism

We saw in the initial chapters of this book that Husserl had his first contact with empirical psychology in Leipzig in 1876. Husserl had begun his scientific career with a thorough study of mathematics and physics and it was only after his first years in these areas that he came to study psychology under Wundt, Paulsen, Stumpf, and Brentano. It was the latter in particular who aroused Husserl's interest in philosophy. But at this point under the influence of his studies in psychology with Stumpf and Brentano and because of his contact with the philosophy of J. Stuart Mill, Henry Spencer, John Locke, and David Hume, Husserl soon became entangled in empiricism and psychologism. Unmistakable traces to this effect are found in his first publication, *Philosophy of Arithmetic* (1891).

After 1894, however, it became clear to Husserl that psychologism is completely unacceptable. In his *Logical Investigations* (1900-1901) he subjected this particular form of positivism to a rigorous but objective criticism and showed most convincingly that psychology cannot possibly furnish a radical explanation of the foundations of logic and mathematics. This is the task of philosophy which to be distinguished from psychology. On the other hand, it cannot be denied that such a radical explanation cannot be performed without some study of the subjective acts which make possible our awareness of the objects with which these sciences deal. In combining these two ideas Husserl finally came to the conclusion that a philosophical phenomenology, viewed as a completely new descriptive psychology, could provide the radical basis and explanation for these sciences.

Later, in 1925, reflecting upon his own development between 1891 and 1913[3] Husserl writes that in the second volume of the *Logical Investigations* he intended to explain the bestowal of meaning which comes

---

3. Edmund Husserl, *Phän. Psychol.*, pp. 20-46 (passim).

about in the context of the 'achievements' of our experience, characteristic of our logical thinking.[4] As Husserl sees it, there is a question here of a special intuitive re-flection upon the logical experiences which come about during our thinking-process but which nevertheless are not consciously experienced. What the second volume of the *Logical Investigations* proposed to show was precisely how in the 'achievements' of the inner logical experiences the constitution of all logical entities is enacted, entities which manifest themselves in our predicative thinking as concepts, judgments, conclusions, etc., and receive their universally and interoubjectively valid character from the fundamental concepts and laws of formal logic.

It was already shown in the first volume of the same book that objects such as concepts, statements, conclusions, etc., are 'irreal entities' which, nevertheless, possess objectivity because of their ideal identity. These objects are 'unities of meaning' in whose meaning-content one does not encounter any psychological act or subjective experience. They refer to 'ideal' truths which do not have a bearing on the real world. From these considerations it follows, in Husserl's view, that there must exist 'irreal' objects referring to 'irreal' truths which makes it that these 'irreal' entities can have reference to ideal and also possibly real things whose factual existence, thus, is not necessarily to be presupposed. There must, then, also exist sciences of 'irreal' entities, aprioric sciences the idea of which theoretically governs a certain domain of ideal objects.[5]

The most important theme of the *Logical Investigations,* however consists in the descriptive investigations of the psychical experiences which are connected inseparably with the ideal objects of logic and mathematics. Here again we come to the central problem posed by psychologism.

A closer investigation of these ideal objects reveals them as having their own characteristic Being-for-itself and Being-in-itself to which their pure truths refer in an a priori way, and makes them be what they are regardless of their being counted or thought. On the other hand,

4. *Ibid.,* p. 20.
5. *Ibid.,* pp. 21-24.

we must realize that these objects arise only out of our subjective, psychic activities. That is why one has to ask the question of how we can explain this strange correlation between these ideal objects of pure logic and the subjective psychic experiences which allegedly 'constitute' them. And what are we to think of the hidden psychical experiences which correlate with the ideal objects and must come about as special corresponding achievements, if the subject is to get an evident knowledge of these idealities as its objects?

These questions form the main theme of the second volume of the *Logical Investigations* inasfar as it focused its attention toward the manifold achievements of the subject by means of which the mathematical and logical entities are brought out, in and by the mathematician and the logician. Thus it provides a theory of logical and mathematical knowing acts as they relate to the logical and mathematical objects. The intention of the investigations was to shed a certain reflexive intuition upon those experiences which up to then had remained hidden, and to work out an eidetic description of them.[6] That is why this part of the *Logical Investigations* was characterized by the term 'descriptive psychology'. The term 'phenomenology' was also used in this context. This latter term pointed to the attempt to radically and consistently work back from the relevant categories of objects to the corresponding modes of consciousness in which these objects become conscious.[7]

At the beginning it was not quite clear yet how to accomplish this questioning from the objects back to the subjective experiences in which they emerge as conscious. The hypothetical constructs of naturalistic psychology were of no help in this connection; what was needed was a pure intuition followed by an accurate analysis and description which would faithfully reveal the intentional relationship of the act and its corresponding object. Brentano had already done some very important work in this direction, but his descriptive psychology still was not able to solve in a radical way the problems mentioned. Although the second volume of the *Logical Investigations* can be considered a serious attempt to materialize a descriptive psychology in a consistent way, it did not succeed

---

6. *Ibid.*, pp. 24-27.
7. *Ibid.*, pp. 27-28.

in being an essential transformation of Brentano's initial idea of a pure and descriptive psychology.[8]

As far as phenomenology is concerned, there is no question in the *Logical Investigations* of a transcendental reduction and a transcendental attitude. That is why Husserl later admitted explicitly that in this book he had not yet reached a genuinely philosophical point of view and that phenomenology, understood as descriptive psychology, could not be the truly radical science he was looking for. On the other hand, Husserl always maintained that the work done in the *Logical Investigations* was of lasting importance although what had begun there remained to be completed in more radical investigations.[9] When taken from this point of view it becomes understandable why many critics claimed that in the second volume of the *Logical Investigations* Husserl had again lapsed into the psychologism which he had so rigorously discredited in the first volume of the same book.[10] At any rate, and all things taken into account, one could say that the phenomenology of the second volume of the *Logical Investigations* was certainly the forerunner of what Husserl was later to call 'phenomenological psychology'.

Be this as it may, in his *Logical Investigations* Husserl did mention a 'phenomenology' which he characterized as a descriptive psychology. Then around 1903 it became clear to him that he needed a transcendental phenomenology instead of a descriptive psychology. The first systematic treatment of Husserl's new insights into phenomenology are to be found in the lecture series *The Idea of Phenomenology* (1907). Insofar as the main lines are concerned Husserl remained true to those insights throughout his entire career. The questions of whether within the realm of this new perspective the descriptive phenomenology of the *Logical Investigations* is to be maintained as a relatively independent discipline and, if so, how we are to understand their mutual relationships in that case, are not explicitly dealt with in *The Idea of Phenomenology*.[11]

---

8. *Ibid.*, pp. 28-30 and pp. 39-42.
9. *Ibid.*, pp. 42-46.
10. Herbert Spiegelberg, *op. cit.*, vol. I, p. 101.
11. See Walter Biemel's *Introduction* in Edmund Husserl's *Die Idee*, p. vii; see also W. Biemel, *Les phases décisives*, pp. 46-52.

A First Introduction to Husserl's Phenomenology

Husserl's View on Empirical Psychology

From 1907 on we find psychology the constant pole of comparison in Husserl's explanations of the meaning of his newly found phenomenological philosophy. Practically speaking, in every work dealing with the foundations of phenomenological philosophy Husserl tries to explain his view of psychology and to describe the difference and the relationship between these two sciences. It was particularly between 1911 and 1913 that the problem concerning the relation between empirical psychology and phenomenological philosophy held Husserl's especial attention. It became clear to him gradually that it was necessary to bridge the gap between empirical psychology and transcendental phenomenology with the help of a completely new science called 'rational psychology' or also 'eidetic psychology' first, and 'phenomenological psychology' later. This view was expressed explicitly for the first time in *Ideas* (1913), but it had been prepared in his *Logos* article (1911). As it is on the basis of Husserl's radical criticism of naturalistic psychology as described in *Philosophy as Rigorous Science* that he later and for the first time gave a preliminary description of his newly discovered eidetic or phenomenological psychology in his *Ideas,* a brief summary of the most important insights proposed in the *Logos* article would seem to be desirable in this context.

We have seen in previous chapters that in the first part of the *Logos* article Husserl attempted to explain the necessity of a phenomenological *philosophy.* This new form of philosophy is described there as a science of consciousness which is to be distinguished carefully from empirical psychology as a *natural* science of consciousness. Empirical psychology is concerned with consciousness as an empirical being in the real world, whereas phenomenology is concerned with pure consciousness.[12] In view of the fact, however, that both sciences are concerned with one and the same consciousness, even though in a completely different way and according to a different orientation, it will be clear, Husserl says, that in principle there must be a strong relationship between phenomenology and psychology.

---

12. Edmund Husserl, *Philos. str. W.,* pp. 300-322 (90-122).

However, Husserl continues, what has been said here about a necessary relationship between psychology and philosophy does not apply to modern empirical psychology. For the fundamental conviction of this psychology is that pure analysis and description of the data which immediately manifest themselves in immanent intuition are to be put aside in favor of certain indirect psychologically relevant facts brought to light by observation and experiment. Psychology does not see that these facts are deprived of their real meaning without an essential analysis of conscious life. In other words, Husserl claims, although it is true that empirical psychology indeed is able to bring to light valuable psycho-physical facts and norms, it nevertheless remains deprived of a deeper understanding and a definitive scientific evaluation of these facts as long as it does not found itself in a systematic science of consciousness and conscious life which investigates the psychical as such with the help of 'immanent' intuitive reflection. By the very fact, therefore, that experimental psychology considers itself as already methodologically perfect, still it is actually unscientific wherever it wishes to penetrate to a genuine psychological understanding. On the other hand, Husserl explains, it is equally unscientific in all those cases where the lack of clarified concepts of the psychical as such leads to an obscure formulation of problems and consequently to merely apparent solutions. To be sure, the experimental method is indispensable, particularly where there is a question of fixing intersubjectively valid connections of facts. But this does not change the fact that this procedure presupposes what no experiment can accomplish, namely, the analysis of conscious life itself.[13]

Some psychologists, such as Brentano, Stumpf, and Lipps, have recognized this defect of modern empirical psychology and have tried, therefore, to undertake thorough analytical and descriptive investigations of psychical experiences. Most of the leading psychologists did not recognize the value of these investigations and claimed that 'those empty word-analyses' were meaningless. Instead one has to question things themselves and go back to experience itself which alone can give meaning to our words.[14] In Husserl's view this criticism is without foundation

---

13. *Ibid.*, pp. 302-303 (92-94).
14. *Ibid.*, pp. 303-305 (94-97).

inasfar as the psychologists mentioned take their startingpoint only in ordinary language, not deriving any judgment at all from word analyses, but rather penetrating into the phenomena themselves. Furthermore, Husserl questions what is to be understood by 'things themselves'; and what kind of experience is it to which those critics want to return in psychology? Are they perhaps the answers of the subjects of experiments or the testees? Or is the psychologist's interpretation of their answers the experience we have to look for? The experimental psychologists will say evidently that the primary experience is to be found in the subject and that the interpretation of this experience presupposes certain self-perceptions of the psychologist which—whatever they may be—are not in any case 'introspections'.[15]

Husserl goes on to say that despite some exaggeration, there is something in this latter view which is unquestionably right. But on the other hand there is also a fundamental error in this conception. For it puts the analyses of both forms of experience on the same level with the analyses characteristic of the physical sciences, believing that in so doing psychology is an experimental science of the psychical in fundamentally the same way as the physical sciences are the experimental sciences of the physical. In this way, however, it overlooks the specific character of consciousness and psychical data.

All psychologists believe they owe all their psychological knowledge to experience. Nevertheless, the description of the naïve empirical data, along with the analyses which have to go hand in hand with this description, is effected with the help of certain concepts whose scientific value will be decisive for all further methodical steps. These concepts, however, remain by the very nature of the empirical method constantly untouched, but enter nevertheless into the final scientific judgments. On the other hand, the scientific value of these concepts was not present from the very beginning, nor can it originate from the experiences of the subjects or the psychologists. Logically it cannot be obtained from any empirical determination whatsoever. Here, therefore, is the place for eidetical analyses.[16]

---

15. *Ibid.*, pp. 305-309 (97-103).
16. *Ibid.*, pp. 309-312 (103-106).

PHENOMENOLOGY AND PSYCHOLOGY

Thus recognizing the fact that all psychological knowledge presupposes the knowledge of the essence of the psychical, and that such knowledge cannot be obtained by means of physical procedures, it becomes evident that only 'phenomenological' analyses can render the correct solution for the problems mentioned above. For only a really radical and systematic phenomenology, carried out not incidentally and in isolated reflections but in exclusive dedication to the extremely complex and confused problems of consciousness and executed in an attitude free from every naturalistic prejudice, can give us a real understanding of the essence of the psychical. Only then will the plenitude of empirical facts and the interesting laws which have been discovered bear their real fruits, because only then will it be possible psychologically to interpret and critically evaluate those facts and laws in the right way.[17]

Ultimately Husserl concludes this part of his *Logos* article with a short description of this new science, phenomenology. From this description it becomes clear that he has a philosophical phenomenology in mind in the description of which he especially accentuates the possibility and function of the ideation. He touches only in passing on the phenomenological reduction and the intentional analysis.[18] In a note[19] he promises to publish soon a more complete work devoted to this new phenomenology. Undoubtedly he refers here to the publication of the *Ideas*, the first volume of which appeared in 1913.

The Necessity of an 'Eidetic Psychology'

It is quite clear that in 1911 Husserl was not yet expressly distinguishing between phenomenological psychology and phenomenological philosophy.[20] Without a doubt he refers in the above-mentioned passage to a philosophical phenomenology. This is apparent not only in the note mentioned, but becomes clear also when we consider the whole context of the article. For Husserl most certainly does not make any distinction between *two* different phenomenological disciplines; if he

---

17. *Ibid.*, pp. 312-314 (106-109) and pp. 314-322 (109-122).
18. *Ibid.*, pp. 315-319 (110-116).
19. *Ibid.*, p. 319, note 1 (116-117, note *f*).
20. *Ibid.*, pp. 314-319 (109-117).

had really intended to refer to the possibility of a phenomenological psychology only, he would have lapsed into Brentano's psychologism for the second time, a situation which after the lecture series *The Idea of Phenomenology* (1907) would seem to be unacceptable.

But even though the distinction between two different phenomenological disciplines, namely phenomenological psychology and phenomenological philosophy, seemed not to have materialized at that time, we could in consideration of another note[21] deduce that the phenomenological philosophy being defined here is to be distinguished from the descriptive psychology which is described in the second volume of the *Logical Investigations*. If we maintain this descriptive psychology as a phenomenological psychology side by side with the philosophical phenomenology indicated in the *Logos* article, then the distinction referred to could be said to be implicitly to be understood. However, notwithstanding Husserl's later remarks in this direction, this view does not seem to be entirely satisfactory because the subject matter of psychology comes up at length in the *Logos* article, and it would seem only logical that Husserl would have brought up such a distinction if he had already realized its importance in 1911.[22]

Whatever the reasoning, in the introduction to his *Ideas* (1913) Husserl complains that his treatment of psychology in the *Logos* article had given rise to misunderstanding. Many psychologists seemed to have felt indignant, whereas others did not grasp that an essential distinction was to be made between eidetic psychology and phenomenological philosophy. He states then explicitly "that the pure phenomenology . . . , the same which emerged for the first time in *Logical Investigations,* and has revealed an ever richer and deeper meaning to me in my work during the last ten years, *is not psychology* . . ."[23] Psychology is a science of experience, it is a science of facts, of matters of fact in Hume's sense. It is also a science of realities. And too, the phenomena of which one speaks in 'psychological phenomenology' are real occurrences which, together with the real subjects to which

---

21. *Ibid.,* p. 318, note 1 (115-116, note *e*).
22. *Ibid.,* pp. 319-322 (117-122).
23. Edmund Husserl, *Ideen,* vol. I, p. 4 (38).

they belong, take their place in the spatio-temporal world. In contrast to these two sciences, pure transcendental phenomenology is first of all not a science of facts but a science of essences, whereas, secondly, it is not a science of real entities but of 'irreal' phenomena. Eidetic reduction brings us forth from the realm of the factual into the domain of pure essences, whereas a transcendental reduction cuts us loose from the real, spatio-temporal world. Philosophical phenomenology, therefore, is not a study of the essences of real phenomena but of transcendentally reduced phenomena.[24]

If this paraphrasing survey of Husserl's view, which surely goes further than Husserl's literal text, should be in harmony with Husserl's intention, it will be clear that the characteristic of phenomenological psychology consists in that it, unlike empirical psychology, employs an eidetic reduction, whereas it, unlike transcendental phenomenology, does not use a transcendental reduction. That this indeed must have been Husserl's intention becomes clear in the following passages in which he discusses the general structures of consciousness.

In one passage Husserl says that these structures can be studied by psychology as well as by means of phenomenological philosophy. Consciousness as it is given in psychological experience, that is, as human and animal consciousness, is the proper subject matter for psychology; "empirical psychology studies consciousness with empirical, and eidetic psychology with eidetic methods".[25] On the other hand, however, the whole world just as correlate of transcendental consciousness falls in modified form also within the realm of transcendental phenomenology; and so also do the psychic individuals and their psychic experiences. In other words, within phenomenology itself, consciousness appears under different forms of apprehension and in different connections in different ways; first as absolute consciousness in transcendental phenomenology and, then, as psychological consciousness in eidetic psychology. That is why every transcendental phenomenological consideration of absolute consciousness can be reinterpreted in terms of eidetic psychology which, strictly speaking, is itself not phenomenological at all, if we understand the term 'phenomenology' to refer to a *transcendental* discipline only. Whatever the case, one of the most important tasks in this context consists in an adequate explanation of the essential relations between pure or transcendental phenomenology, eidetic psychology, and empirical psychology.[26]

In his book *Ideas* eidetic psychology must occupy a position between classical empirical psychology and transcendental phenomenology. The difference between eidetic and empirical psychology lies in the former's use of the eidetic reduction, whereas eidetic psychology and transcendental phenomenology differ in that only transcendental phenomenology makes use of the transcendental reduction. In this book Husserl makes occasional use of eidetic-psychological descriptions. When he does so he makes clear that he is about to start a number of explanations in which the transcendental reduction does not matter. For instance: "We start with a series of explanations within which we do not have to concern ourselves with any phenomenological *epoché*. We are oriented toward the 'real' world and, without giving up our natural attitude, we reflect psychologically on our ego and its experiences. We indulge, precisely as if we had never heard of the transcendental attitude, in the very essence of 'consciousness of something', in which we, for instance, are conscious of material things . . ."[27] In this study we must maintain the general principle that each individual occurrence has its own essence "that can be grasped in its eidetic purity, and this purity must belong to a field of possible eidetic inquiry". The results of these investigations acquire transcendental meaning only when they are re-interpreted from an entirely new point of view. This point of view is the result of the transcendental reduction.[28]

From all this it will be evident that eidetic psychology is an *eidetic* science concerned with the essence of consciousness. It is based on an original *intuition,* but moves competely within the realm of the *natural* attitude. A comparison between this eidetic psychology of the *Ideas,* which is also called there rational psychology or psychological phenomenology, with the phenomenological psychology of which Husserl speaks

---

26. *Ibid.,* pp. 175-176 (195-196).
27. *Ibid.,* p. 74 (103) and pp. 118-119 (139-141).
28. *Ibid.,* p. 74 (103).

in his later works reveals that both undoubtedly refer to the same discipline. It is curious that in the *Ideas* Husserl does not yet mention the necessity of a psychological-phenomenological reduction as distinguished from the transcendental reduction.[29] Such a distinction, however, is essential for the definition of phenomenological psychology as shall presently be made clear.

2. *Phenomenological Psychology. Its Relation to Empirical and Phenomenological Philosophy*

Between 1913 and 1923 it seems that Husserl was particularly concerned with the so-called constitutional problems. As a result of these investigations it became clear to him that his explicitation of the meaning of phenomenological psychology as presented in *Ideas* was not adequate, as the distinction between phenomenological psychology and transcendental philosophy was not yet founded in a radical way. Also it became apparent that the new science, phenomenological psychology, was of such importance for the development of the empirical psychology of his time that a radical investigation of it seemed to be indispensable. It was for this reason that he dealt with the topic in different lecture courses between 1925 and 1927. The results of these investigations were published posthumously in 1962 in a book entitled *Phenomenological Psychology*. In this book phenomenological psychology is described as an aprioric, eidetic, intuitive, purely descriptive, and intentional science of the psychical, which remains entirely within the realm of the natural attitude.[30] Husserl tries in the book to found the necessity of such a new kind of psychology by pointing to the fact that traditional empirical psychology still lacks a systematic framework of basic concepts grounded in the intuitive clarification of the psychical essences. Whatever psychology has accumulated and is still accumulating by way of measuring and experimentation concerning objective correlations is wasted as long as there is no clear grasp of what it is that is being measured and correlated. In Husserl's view, phenomenological psychology

---

29. See however for a first indication in this direction *Ibid.*, pp. 221-222 (240-241).
30. Edmund Husserl, *Phän. Psychol.*, pp. 46-51.

is destined to supply the essential insights needed to give meaning and direction to the research presented under the title 'empirical psychology'.

The same ideas are found in Husserl's *Encyclopaedia Britannica* article,[31] his *Amsterdam Lectures*,[32] and the *Cartesian Meditations*. It is in these publications that Husserl mentions for the first time the necessity of a phenomenological-psychological reduction. In his last study, *Crisis*, Husserl returns to this point and in a detailed and minute inquiry he tries there to determine the very nature of this reduction and to found its necessity in a new way.[33]

In view of the foregoing we may safely state that in the gradual process of attempting to determine the nature of phenomenological psychology as it is related to empirical psychology and transcendental phenomenology, Husserl's thinking was in a constant state of evolution until what may be called its final phase. With the probable exception of his description of the phenomenological-psychological reduction, this final phase was reached about 1928. It is for this reason that we wish first to give a brief survey of the most important ideas of Husserl's *Amsterdam Lectures* wherein for the first time he presented a terse explanation of his final view.

Phenomenological Psychology: Its Subject Matter, Method and Function

In Husserl's view present-day psychology is the science of the real, psychical events which occur in the concrete domain of the spatio-temporal world. The term 'psychical' is to be understood as referring to the ego and all its ego-centered experiences. The 'psychical' shows itself in immediate experience as a non-self-sufficient realm of being because it manifests itself only in human and animal organisms which themselves belong to a more fundamental sphere, namely the realm of the physical. This is why psychology may be considered a branch of the more concrete

---

31. Edmund Husserl, *Phenomenology*, pp. 699-702.
32. Edmund Husserl, *Phän. Psychol.*, pp. 302-349.
33. Edmund Husserl, *Krisis*, pp. 238-269.
34. Edmund Husserl, *Philos. str. W.*, pp. 314-322 (109-122).

anthropology and zoology which deal also with the physical and psycho-physical aspects of these living beings.[35]

It is an essential characteristic of the world of experience taken as a whole that it differentiates itself in an open infinity of concrete individual realities. Furthermore, it is also an essential trait of every individual reality that it, irrespective of all possible superstructures, possesses bodily-physical reality. Man has the possibility of making abstractions from everything that is non-physical in order to consider each real being and also the world as a whole merely as 'physical nature'. Already in the domain of the mere physical there is a determinate, essential, structural regularity and lawfulness. Not only does each concrete, intramundane being possess its own nature, but all mundane bodies whatsoever co-constitute an harmonious unity governed by the universal, unifying form of spatio-temporality.[36]

The question now is, as Husserl sees it, to determine to what extent, in a onesided orientation toward the psychical, a continuously consistent experience and a theoretical inquiry founded on it are possible which, proceeding from the psychical to the psychical, never take the physical as such into consideration. In other words, in how far is a pure psychology, in addition to the pure empirical physical sciences, possible? Without further investigation it is clear that the factually existing psychology as an empirical science of facts will never be able to become a pure science of merely psychical facts free from any physical datum. For no matter how far the pure psychological experience and the theory founded on it could reach, it is certain that the mere psychical about which each intends to speak possesses its spatio-temporal determinations in the real world, and in its real factualness is determinable only by means of spatio-temporal determinations. Spatio-temporality, however, originally and essentially belongs to nature taken as physical nature. Everything non-physical, such as for instance the psychical, possesses a spatio-temporal position only because of its foundation in a physical organism. Thus in principle it will be impossible within the realm of empirical psychology to delimit theoretically a pure psychological investigation from

---

35. Edmund Husserl, *Phän. Psychol.*, p. 303.
36. *Ibid.*, pp. 303-304.

a psycho-physical inquiry. In other words, within the domain of empirical psychology as an objective science of facts, it is absolutely impossible to constitute a *pure,* empirical science of the mere psychical as a separate and independent discipline.[37]

Husserl tells us that a pure psychological inquiry is not completely impossible, however; and for an empirical psychology which strives for a really and strictly scientific character, such a psychology is in fact indispensable. For without a pure psychology it seems to be impossible to obtain the strictly scientific concepts in which the very essence of the psychic phenomena can be expressed truthfully. And as the concepts which delineate the universal and necessary, essential form of the psychical as such also belong to these concepts, the necessity of an aprioric science of the essence of the psychical as such makes itself felt.[38]

Husserl points out here that it is not easy to bring aprioric truths to the fore. As really essential truths they originate in apodictical insight only from the initial source of experience. The first question which is to be asked in this context is how an experience can be performed methodically in such a way that precisely as pure experience it brings forward what is essentially characteristic of the psychical as such. The term 'pure' has a double meaning here. In the first place, this experience must be *pure* in the sense of free from all the psychophysical and the physical with which it is essentially connected. All that a physical and psychophysical experience could teach us must here thematically be left out of consideration, so that we have to restrict ourselves to a pure 'phenomenological experience' in order to try to explicitate only that which is given immediately in this experience and as such. The term 'phenomenological experience' is here to be understood thus as referring exclusively to that reflection in which the psychical as such becomes accessible to us as adequately as possible. There are evidently many problems here. For, how is a pure phenomenological experience to be performed, and how can one proceed from such an experience to a uniform and purely psychical field of experience which even *ad infinitum*

---

37 *Ibid.,* pp. 304-305.
38. *Ibid.,* p. 305.

would not imply anything non-essential to the psychical as such? Furthermore, this experience must be free also from all prejudices which spring from other scientific spheres of experience and could blind us to that which phenomenological reflection immediately offers us.[39]

The difficulties necessarily connected with these two requirements are so great that one could say paradoxically that until now in modern psychology as a whole, an intentional analysis has never been properly performed.[40] This fact has its origin in the fundamental preconception that psychology, methodologically seen, ought to imitate physics and chemistry, the necessary consequence being the 'naturalization' of the psychical. After Brentano, many psychologists have indeed come to the conclusion that a naturalistic psychology is impossible, but curiously enough most of them have remained in many respects victims of this form of naturalism. The basic error of naturalism in psychology becomes manifest only when one consistently carries through the pure psychological experience in which the proper and essential characteristics of intentional life show themselves in their all-sidedness and apodictic evidence.[41]

It is Husserl's view that the root of all this confusion consists in the equalization of immanent temporarily and objective real time. Objective time is the 'extensional' form of all objective realities and, particularly, of their structural foundation, namely, physical nature. The psychical experiences, taken individually and also in their totality, in themselves do not possess the unitary form of co-existence and succession which are characteristic of the spatio-temporal as such. Characteristic of the psychical experiences is the form of 'flowing'; according to their very essence they are flowing in the unity of the stream of consciousness as a whole; and this is evidently not a parallel form of spatio-temporality.[42]

---

39. *Ibid.*, pp. 308-309.
40. *Ibid.*, p. 309.
41. *Ibid.*, pp. 309-310.
42. *Ibid.*, pp. 310-311.

Phenomenologic-Psychological Reduction

Husserl refers us to other fundamental difficulties connected with the realization of a consequent and pure phenomenological experience. First of all we must abandon all the prejudices of tradition as well as the most general self-evidences of logic which are already too onesidedly interpreted from the viewpoint of the physical. As a result we have to restrict ourselves to that which phenomenological reflection brings to light as consciousness and to that which manifests itself there in real self-evidence. So we must adhere exclusively in this situation to the phenomenological experience without paying any attention to the factualities which actually appear in it. This experience is first of all self-experience; only in this experience are consciousness and the consciousness-ego given in their completely original self-hood. All other forms of experience of the psychical are founded in the immediacy of this self-experience; this holds good also for the pure experience of the other, the others, and society. That is why in phenomenology from the beginning the method of pure self-experience is explained as the method of a consistently performed phenomenological self-disclosure.[43]

Here one has to face the difficulty that somehow we must omit from consideration what refers to external experience, which is the original source of every physical consideration. How is this to be realized?[44] If I as a phenomenologist am to realize a pure phenomenological experience in order to make consciousness, my own conscious life, as regards its pure and proper essence, into a universal and consequent theme of investigation and, therefore, first into a domain of pure phenomenological experience, then I have thematically to eliminate as non-psychic-being the real world as a whole as it was already accepted a priori in my natural life.[45]

On the other hand, however, it is evident that all consciousness indeed is and remains consciousness of something, and that in direct experience what we are immediately conscious of, is the natural world, the real spatio-temporal world. If this is true, then it is impossible to de-

---

43. *Ibid.,* pp. 311-312.
44. *Ibid.,* p. 312.
45. *Ibid.,* p. 312.

scribe a perception and an act of memory according to their very essences without mentioning the fact that they are perception and memory of this determinate object. The consequence of this is that reflection upon consciousness as such does not yet bring to light the psychical in its own pure essence. Therefore as phenomenologists we must, as it were, be the 'disinterested onlookers' of our own conscious life. Instead of living 'in' our own conscious acts and being interested in the world given in them, we must look upon consciousness exclusively as consciousness of this or that. Otherwise precisely the non-psychic world rather than our own consciousness would be the object of our description. However, within the sphere of such an *epoché* consciousness is and remains consciousness of something, of this or that object. That in every consciousness of something the conscious datum itself as such appears is essential for consciousness as psychic datum. Within the realm of *epoché*, however, this conscious datum is taken only as such; that which is experienced in every conscious intentional act is—within the realm of the *epoché*—not a being in the real world. This being is taken here only as that toward which consciousness' intention is directed; as reality in the world this object is put between brackets. In this way the phenomenological reduction is, essentially speaking, delineated. It is important to call attention again to the fact that in this reduction not only the noetical is preserved, but also the noematical as an endlessly fruitful theme of phenomenological description. It is precisely through phenomenological reduction that for the first time intentional objects can be delivered as such, that is as essential constituents of intentional experiences.[46]

Phenomenological reduction also influences our attitude with respect to the consciousness-ego, because here, too, every *real* animal and *real* human aspect is put between brackets. Just as by means of the reduction nature is reduced to a noematic phenomenon only, so also is the real human ego in the natural attitude reduced to pure psychic life. My being-man in the real world and my mundane life is maintained only as 'meant', that is, as that toward which the intentional conscious acts remain oriented.[47]

---

46. *Ibid.*, pp. 312-314.
47. *Ibid.*, pp. 314-315.

The consistent disclosure of the noema can first shift toward a consideration and analysis of the correlative noeses. And in addition to these conscious intentional acts the ego-center as such manifests itself as something on and in itself, as the ego of every *cogito,* as an ego which in all these acts is and remains phenomenologically identical. The ego manifests itself here as the center from which all acts emanate and toward which all affects flow back. But in both these respects the phenomenological ego-center is an important and extensive phenomenological theme closely connected with every other phenomenological topic.

In these analyses concerning the pure life of the ego it becomes clear, also, that in every conscious act a typical synthesis manifests itself, making every act into a unity and connecting it with other conscious acts into the unity of *one* consciousness.[48]

Phenomenological Psychology

By way of conclusion we may posit with Husserl that a systematic construction of a phenomenological psychology requires: 1) the description of all the characteristics belonging to the essence of an intentional lived experience and of the most general law of synthesis in particular; 2) the explanation of the characteristic features and forms of the different types of lived experiences which necessarily are found in every consciousness, and all their typical syntheses; 3) the explanation and essential description of the very essence of the universal stream of consciousness; 4) an inquiry into the ego as center of the lived experiences and as pole of all actualities and potentialities of consciousness. When this static description is completed we must try to analyze and describe the genesis of the life of the personal ego with its universally eidetic laws; thus we must combine a genetic phenomenology with a static type as previously described. Our genetic phenomenology must explain the different modes of active and passive genesis, and in regard to the latter, especially the phenomenological new concept of association. The static and the genetic phenomenology of reason is a special, coherent field of inquiry of a higher level which probably is more important within the realm of transcendental phenomenology.

---

48. *Ibid.,* p. 316.

Finally we must remark again that the validity of all these investigations will obviously extend beyond the particularity of the psychologist's
own consciousness. For psychical life may be revealed to us not only in
self-consciousness but equally in our consciousness of other selves, and
this latter source of experience offers us more than a reduplication of
what we find in our self-consciousness, for it establishes the difference
between our 'own' and 'the other' which we experience, and presents us
also with the characteristics of the 'social life'. And hence the further
task becomes a matter of psychology's revealing the intentions of which
this social life consists.[49]

Phenomenological and Empirical Psychology

Husserl now invites us to suppose that via the phenomenological
reduction mentioned above we have put ourselves in the sphere of the
pure psychological, and that with the help of intentional analyses and
the method of free variation we have gained an insight into the essence
of the psychical in its diverse modalities. The aprioric concepts which
in this sphere are formed through eidetic reduction, must then express
an essentially necessary style to which every imaginable, factual, and
real psychic life is tied. All empirical psychological concepts are governed by these aprioric concepts as well as by their logical 'forms', just
as analogically such is the case with physics and the general aprioric
science of nature. It is, therefore, self-evident that the aprioric truths
founded in these aprioric concepts possess an unconditional, normative
validity in regard to the regions of being in question, and in this particular case, in regard to the empirical domain of the pure psychical.[50]

Comparing phenomenology now with the much more embracing
empirical psychology, we must say that phenomenological psychology is
the absolutely necessary fundament for the performance of an exact
empirical psychology. A comparison with the physical sciences can
clarify this statement. For, natural science, which was once also a vague,
inductive, empirical science, owes its modern character to the a priori
system of forms characteristic of nature as such; this system is con-

49. *Ibid.*, pp. 315-321.
50. *Ibid.*, pp. 321-324.

stituted by pure geometry, pure mechanics, and the pure science of time. By theoretically referring the factical in experience to the a priori of these forms the originally vague experience is able to participate in the essential necessity, which is the last root of the exactness of the physical sciences.[51]

The methods of natural science and psychology are quite different, but the latter like the former can reach exactness only by means of a rationalization of the essential. This means that in empirical psychology the exactness must be founded in the very essence of the psychical as such. For since, as we have seen, the essence of the psychical as such must be brought to light through the investigations of phenomenological psychology, phenomenological psychology has to provide us with the fundamental concepts which, describing the a priori structure of the psychical as such, must govern every possible psychological description.[52]

A typical problem manifests itself here, however. For the a priori of empirical psychology is more extensive than that which is explained by phenomenological psychology. Empirical psychology as a science of the psychical which in the given world manifests itself as belonging to nature as psycho-physical datum, is, therefore, also co-founded by the a priori of physical nature. The necessary consequence of this is that empirical psychology is based also on the empirical and aprioric sciences of nature. Ultimately it is even founded in its own a priori which belongs to the psycho-physical as such. In other words, the a priori of empirical psychology is not exclusively phenomenological, for it depends not only on the essence of the psychical but also upon the essence of the physical, and more particularly upon the essence of the psycho-physical of organic nature.[53]

Phenomenological Psychology and Transcendental Philosophy

In trying to describe the relation between phenomenological psychology and transcendental phenomenology Husserl makes clear that

51. *Ibid.*, pp. 324-325.
52. *Ibid.*, p. 325.
53. *Ibid.*, pp. 326-328.

on the one hand psychology, both as an eidetic and empirical discipline, is a 'positive' science effected within the realm of the 'natural attitude' and, therefore, accepting the world as the ground of all its statements, whereas transcendental phenomenology is completely 'unworldly'. On the other hand, however, there is a close relationship between phenomenological psychology and transcendental phenomenology inasfar as phenomenological psychology requires only a re-employment in a more stringent way of its formal mechanisms of reduction and analysis to disclose the transcendental phenomena which form the subject matter of transcendental phenomenology. In order to explain this double relationship between phenomenological psychology and transcendental phenomenology we must take our starting point in what was said previously about the meaning of the transcendental reduction.[54]

Normally man lives in the natural attitude in accordance with which the world around him is at all times known and accepted as a *real fact-world* that has its real being independent of man's consciousness. Phenomenological philosophy invites every philosopher to alter this standpoint radically. This change of attitude is to be performed by the 'transcendental reduction'. The transcendental reduction is responsible for putting the general thesis of the natural attitude out of action; whatever is included in this general thesis is placed in brackets with due respect for its nature as 'being real'. In so doing the real world is not denied; neither is it doubted; the transcendental reduction is used only in the sense of completely barring oneself from using any judgment that concerns the real spatio-temporal existence of the world out there. That is why all sciences which relate to this natural world are also disconnected in the transcendental reduction, although there is no intention here of objecting to them. No use is made of their methods and conclusions.

The necessity of such a procedure in the domain of philosophy is based in the fact that the transcendental reduction is the absolutely necessary condition for finding a realm of Being that is *apodictically evident*. For what is left over after the reduction is pure conscious-

---

54. *Ibid.*, p. 328.

ness with its pure correlates and its pure ego, insofar as all this is not affected by the transcendental reduction. Transcendental reduction, therefore, is the necessary operation which renders pure consciousness and subsequently the whole phenomenological region accessible. It opens up the absolute, apodictically evident region of Being—the region of absolute consciousness, of transcendental subjectivity, in which the totality of Being, the whole actual and possible universe is contained. After the reduction there is neither a world that *really* exists for man, nor a science which he can accept. In this new attitude the whole world is for man only something *that claims being*. From this point on the world as a whole and every intramundane being is for each one only a phenomenon instead of something that really exists out there.[55]

Comparing this brief description of the transcendental reduction with the explanation of the reduction which is characteristic of phenomenological psychology, it becomes immediately clear that there is a great similarity between the two. At first consideration this resemblance is even so striking that one could believe the two to be completely identical. On closer investigation, however, it appears that notwithstanding this similarity there are also fundamental points of difference which come to the fore immediately when we focus attention on the fact that both, transcendental phenomenology and phenomenological psychology, adopt a completely different attitude in regard to the transcendental problems. Let us consider this for a moment.

We have seen that the world with its property of 'Being in and for itself' is as it is, whether or not I happen to be conscious of it. But as soon as this world makes its appearance in consciousness as 'the' world, it appears to be related to consciousness. Then it becomes clear to me that whatever exists for me is accepted in my own conscious life. In other words, I begin to realize that every showing of truth and Being goes on wholly within myself. As soon as I carry out the transcendental reduction and attempt in a systematic self-investigation and as *pure* ego to uncover my whole field of consciousness, it becomes clear that all that exists for me as pure ego becomes constituted in myself and that every kind of Being has its own form of constitution. This means that tran-

55. Edmund Husserl, *Cart. Med.*, pp. 48-63 (7-23).

scendence is an immanent characteristic, constituted within the ego, and that every imaginable being, whether immanent or transcendent, falls within the domain of transcendental subjectivity, as the subjectivity that finally constitutes all sense and Being.[56]

From what has been said in the foregoing it is clear that phenomenological psychology is not interested in this transcendental problem and its possible solution and that it, at any rate, is powerless in the face of this problem. For the meaning of the phenomenological-psychological reduction is not to bring the transcendental subjectivity to light. Phenomenological psychology hopes to expose only the foundations of empirical psychology. It is true that it will never be able to explain these foundations if in its forward development it is interested only in the intramundane beings which manifest themselves in our lived experience. Phenomenological psychology is possible and meaningful only if one is able to perform a determinate reflection in which precisely the lived experiences themselves come to the fore as intentional. This determinate reflection is made possible by a reduction—the phenomenological-psychological reduction—through which the 'objective' human ways of behavior studied in empirical psychology are reduced to unities of meaning as given in my subjectivity as a real psychological entity in the real world. That is why phenomenological psychology remains within the realm of the natural attitude.

However, all this does not alter the fact that there is still a great similarity between the two kinds of reductions. For the transcendental reduction may be considered as a certain further purification of the psychological interest. The psychologist reduces the ordinary valid world to a subjectivity of 'souls', which as such are part of the world which they inhabit. The transcendental phenomenologist reduces the already psychologically purified to the transcendental, to that most general subjectivity which constitutes the world and its 'souls'. From this point of view it becomes clear that the phenomenological-psychological reduction in its attempt to separate the psychical in its purity from everything which is not psychical has a bearing only on the different modes of man's intentional orientation toward the world reducing them to

---

56. Edmund Husserl, *Phän. Psychol.*, pp. 331-342.

unities of meaning, but does not touch the psychologist's subjectivity itself which, therefore, is still to be understood as a real psychological entity in the real world. Transcendental subjectivity, however, is not a part of this objective world, but that subjective conscious life itself, wherein the world and all its content are constituted for me. Within the realm of the transcendal reduction I, this man, 'spiritually' and 'bodily' existing in this world, am, therefore, only an appearance for myself as transcendental ego, so that the 'I' which I apprehend here, presupposes a hidden ego to whom the former is 'present'.

On the other hand, however, transcendental self-experience may at any moment, merely by a change of attitude, be turned back into psychological self-experience. Under the more stringent reduction the psychological subjectivity is transformed into the transcendental subjectivity, and, eventually the psychological intersubjectivity into the transcental intersubjectivity. It is this last which is the ultimate concrete ground whence all that transcends consciousness, including all that is real in the world, and, therefore the phenomenological-psychological intersubjectivity, derives the meaning of its Being.[57]

3. *Phenomenological Psychology in 'Crisis'*

Husserl states in his last work, *Crisis,* that every positive science including psychology must start from the realm of the life-world.[58]

We have seen already that the domain of physics is delineated by means of an abstraction in which we focus attention exclusively on the purely bodily aspects of the objects which we meet in the life-world. This abstraction provides the necessary presuppositions and foundation for a subsequent idealization and mathematization. According to Husserl we must ask ourselves whether psychology should not follow a similar procedure, namely that of a complementary abstraction. If one thinks along these lines it will soon become clear that such a procedure implies the danger of dualism in psychology, but, on the other hand, there does not seem to be a possibility of our penetrating the realm of the psychical except with the help of such a complementary abstraction. Therefore

---

57. *Ibid.,* pp. 343-344.
58. Edmund Husserl, *Krisis,* pp. 194-276 (passim) ; H. Drüe, *Edmund Husserl's System,* pp. 181-233; Aron Gurwitsch, *loc. cit.,* pp. 380-399.

everything is going to depend upon the nature and meaning of this abstraction.

In studying the problems which are necessarily connected with this complementary abstraction, it becomes evident immediately that the subject matter of psychology will constitute the stumbling-block. For the subject matter of psychology consists in our conscious experiences and these experiences are essentially intentional.[59] That is why in this context we are inadequately served by the traditional distinction between internal and external experiences. This is not to say that there are no important differences between my experiences of stones, rivers, and flowers, and my experiences of my own feelings. Yet, both these types of acts of my consciousness are lived experiences which as such belong to the subject matter of psychology. Seen from this point of view it becomes apparent that in the complementary abstraction we must leave out of consideration everything that is not psychical, whereas on the other hand we must maintain everything which as intentional correlate essentially belongs to our conscious experiences, and this is, in principle at least, precisely 'all that is'.[60]

In all his conscious acts man maintains relationships with houses, flowers, animals, and his fellow men. Intentionality, therefore, represents a real relationship between a person and a certain intramundane reality. Every description of any person's conscious acts, therefore, necessarily transcends the domain of the psychical. Thus no such description can ever be made without some reference to worldly reality with which the person concerns himself by means of his conscious acts. Husserl felt that a phenomenological reduction is required in order to conquer the problems just mentioned, believing that only such a reduction could explain how one can leave out of consideration everything which is not psychical and, at the same time, maintain all the non-psychical as 'unities of meaning'. A brief explanation will help to clarify this point.

The person whose behavior is being studied in psychology is always and of necessity confronted with worldly realities which announce them-

---

59. Edmund Husserl, *Krisis,* pp. 219-224.
60. *Ibid.,* pp. 229-235.

selves as really existing. These realities furthermore appear as pregnant with values, possibilities, utility aspects, and so on. The psychologist may or may not have certain convictions concerning these realities, and these convictions may or may not correspond with those of the persons whom he studies. The phenomenological-psychological reduction places between brackets all the psychologist's *existential* convictions and judgments concerning the object of study. Thus he is required to assume the position of that of interested bystander and witness to the 'mental' life of his subjects. In other words, while trying to shed light on the conscious life of his subjects, the psychologist comes across conscious acts and intentional objects as their inseparable correlates. He takes these acts the way they manifest themselves immediately and maintains the intentional correlates as unities of meaning only.[61]

In *Crisis* Husserl develops this view on the meaning of the reduction along lines which remain completely parallel to those we have already met in his other publications. Also, his explanation of the difference and the relationship between empirical psychology and phenomenological psychology does not contain essentially new insights. That is why we need not dwell on these topics any longer here. However, there is one question mentioned in *Crisis* where Husserl seems to transcend his earlier view. The attempt to combine his insights concerning the life-world with this view on the meaning of the phenomenological-psychological reduction seems to entail that this reduction become identical to the transcendental reduction. If this were the case, there can no longer be any difference between phenomenological psychology and transcendental phenomenology. This we must consider now in detail.

In describing the difference between empirical and phenomenological psychology Husserl stresses the point that a consequent phenomenological-psychological reduction implies the reality of all souls, including the soul of the research psychologist himself. We have met this idea time and again up till now. In *Crisis,* however, Husserl develops it in the following way.[62]

---

61. *Ibid.,* pp. 238-240; pp. 235-237.
62. *Ibid.,* pp. 254-257.

The phenomenological-psychological reduction, when applied to ourselves as psychologists, reveals that our consciousness is of necessity still related to the conscious life of others. Within the sphere of the reduction my own Being has undergone a change: my own being-man has acquired the meaning of a lived phenomenon. Yet the psychologist cannot experience himself as a human being without experiencing himself as living in a particular historical present which, in turn, necessarily refers to a past and a future. The experience of oneself as a human being also contains references to other human beings, to an open horizon of mankind, to an intersubjectivity. The experience of myself proves inseparable from the experiences of others. As we have seen, however, the phenomenological-phychological reduction reduces all human beings to *pure* subjects of conscious life. Within the sphere of the reduction a certain historical, social group manifests itself necessarily as a community of *pure* subjects. The investigator who applies the reduction belongs himself to this group. Thus he himself also becomes a *pure* subject of intentional life.

This reference to such a community of subjects forms one of the essential and constituting components of the experience of the life-world. Although this world is reduced to a pure phenonemon, it nevertheless maintains its meaning of being one and the same world for everyone. This can be adequately understood only by conceiving of the life-world as the intentional correlate of pure intersubjectivity. One of the most important problems in this context is the question of how to explain that this life-world is constituted ultimately in intersubjective syntheses of such a pure intersubjectivity.[63]

Husserl tells us that all that which is said concerning the life-world needs further clarification and more detailed descriptions. He believes, however, that it should be quite clear from what we already know on the subject that a full treatment of these ideas necessarily leads phenomenological psychology toward transcendental phenomenology because here the phenomenological-psychological reduction necessarily turns over into a transcendental reduction.[64] For, as Husserl puts it,

63. *Ibid.*, pp. 257-259.
64. *Ibid.*, p. 259. See also H. Drüe, *op. cit.*, pp. 227-245.

the descriptive psychology of intentionality brought us already to the problem of the life-world as the intersubjective 'product' of a quasi infinite and open community of pure subjects whose lives are mutually interconnected. A logical development of this problem requires us now also to take the last step in the form of the transcendental reduction. For ultimately we want to solve the problems arising from those acts and sytems of acts by means of which the absolutely isolated pure psychologist (who by means of a radical reduction experiences himself as a pure ego), is able to experience other egos and to enter into contact with them so that in their intersubjective cooperation an intersubjective life-world can emerge. The phenomenological-psychological reduction now applies, strictly speaking, only to the subject matter of psychology, namely to all acts and to all subjects and also, ultimately, to the whole of the life-world *inasfar as it is to be considered by psychology,* and thus not to the psychologist himself. However a radical consideration of the problems connected with the life-world will in the end convince the psychologist that he himself as the subject of psychological knowledge needs to be reduced in this reduction, too. It is at this moment that the phenomenological reduction necessarily becomes transformed into the transcendental reduction.[65]

In Husserl's view the surprising results of this research can be summarized briefly as follows. A pure psychology within the realm of the natural attitude seems to be impossible; there is only a transcendental psychology and this psychology is identical to transcendental philosophy. But Husserl also adds that upon closer investigation we will see that this conclusion, although indeed containing a good deal of truth, on the other hand cannot be entirely correct.

Further explanation of this remark does not serve to bring Husserl to an unambiguous point of view. For on the one hand he defends the thesis that phenomenological psychology and transcendental phenomenology cannot be completely identical[66], whereas on the other he is not able to explain the difference between the two reductions involved.[67] But it seems to me that section 72 of *Crisis* can be brought into harmony

---

65. Edmund Husserl, *Krisis,* p. 260.
66. *Ibid.,* p. 261.
67. *Ibid.,* pp. 261-263.

with Husserl's earlier writings by adopting the following interpretation.[68]

Even though a radical and consequently executed phenomenology necessarily leads to a transcendental philosophy, nevertheless it is a mistake to equate the two sciences with each other completely. For the phenomenological reduction *as such* does not encompass the subjectivity of the psychologist himself, whereas the transcendental reduction must do so. In *Crisis* Husserl wishes only to emphasize the fact that phenomenological psychology as a theoretical science is of necessity directed toward transcendental phenomenology. The striving toward more fundamental insights which characterizes all sciences propels phenomenological psychology as the study of consciousness toward transcendental philosophy because a radical explanation of the interwovenness of intentionality and life-world necessarily requires the transcendental attitude.[69] This, however, does not mean that phenomenological psychology cannot be maintained as a 'scientia media' between empirical psychology and transcendental phenomenology.

4. Conclusion

On the basis of this explanation phenomenological psychology can be characterized as an aprioric, eidetic, intuitive, purely descriptive, and intentional science of the psychical as such, which science must remain necessarily within the realm of the natural attitude.

The expression 'aprioric' refers to the fact that this psychology is focused first of all on that without which the psychical as such cannot be thought of. Only secondarily does it strive to understand psychical facticity, to formulate theories or to find explanations, although one's natural attitude makes him primarily interested in these latter aspects. Thus phenomenological psychology is interested primarily in the necessary a priori of every possible empirical psychology.[70]

Intuition and description point to the source of this a priori. The inner intuition reveals generalities which are analyzed, and then what is seen is

---

68. Aron Gurwitsch, *l.c.*, pp. 387-396; Edmund Husserl, *Krisis*, pp. 515-516.
69. Edmund Husserl, *Krisis*, pp. 266-269.
70. Edmund Husserl, *Phän. Psychol.*, p. 46.

guided further by intuition toward general necessities of the intuited situation by means of the eidetic reduction. This method reveals the general characteristic of intentionality in the realm of the psychical. Now the double polarity involved in the conscious act, which can be expressed as *ego cogito cogitata* must be considered. Consciousness implies not only the object of conscious acts, but also the ego, the conscious person. Thus psychological investigations acquire typically a twofold aspect and a twofold teleological orientation. From this arises the necessity to investigate descriptively in two directions the systematically interwoven multiplicities of conscious acts which belong essentially to the conscious revelation of the objects of knowledge.

The phenomenological psychologist, however, remains in the natural attitude during these investigations. The transcendental attitude seeks the philosophical, radical, and apodictically evident aspects of our conscious life and in so doing leads to a radically founded philosophy. A psychologist does not wish to leave the non-philosophical, natural and dogmatic attitude. Yet phenomenological psychology can become a point of departure which will lead to philosophy ultimately, although it can never assume the character of a necessary and founding science. Sciences of the natural attitude are sciences of the world and therefore are sciences which presuppose the world. The eidetic sciences remain also sciences of the world insofar as they seek knowledge of the world.

The pure science of the essence of psychical life of man and society is *eo ipso* a science of the world. It seeks the apodictic, necessary structure of psychological facts and laws within the realm of facticity. It is only by means of, and together with an eidetic science that any empirical science can become a rigorously scientific discipline. In addition to eidetic psychology, an empirical psychology must be maintained which will concern itself with the determinations of the factual as such. The *a priori* as such provides only a formal framework within which facts insofar as they are thinkable can find a place.

Phenomenological psychology, as the eidetic and *a priori* study of the psychical, is distinguished from traditional empirical psychology insofar as phenomenological psychology is interested only in the essence of the psychical phenomena and not in factual facts, and insofar as it tries to explain these essences as unities of meaning within the realm uncovered by a typical phenomenological-psychological reduction. Phenomenological psychology is distinguishable from transcendental phenomenology since only in philosophy is a transcendental reduction performed.[71]

Concluding this chapter we want to make one more remark. In the foregoing we pointed to the fact that in the continuous process of attempting to determine the very essence of phenomenological psychology, especially inasfar as it is related to transcendental phenomenology, Husserl's thinking probably reached its final phase about 1928. A restriction was made there as regards the final description of the meaning of the phenomenological-psychological reduction. This restriction referred to the fact that in his last work, *Crisis*, Husserl came to the conclusion that, even where there is an essential distinction between phenomenological psychology and transcendental philosophy on the basis of the distinction between the two different reductions, still phenomenological psychology must necessarily fade into transcendental philosophy whence it has its ultimate foundation.[72]

Explaining this point of view Husserl there points to the fact that after the psychologist has brought to light the problem of the world as intersubjective communal product of an indefinitely open community of subjects whose conscious lives are interwoven with one another, the logic of this development necessarily implies that he performs the transcendental reduction. By means of this reduction it becomes clear how he as a pure transcendental ego apprehends alter egos as his similars with whom he enters into communication to constitute, by such intersubjective cooperation in its diverse forms, the one identical world common to all.

But, even if it is true that phenomenological psychology, developed with absolute consistency, turns into transcendental phenomenology, this does not mean that these two sciences are completely identical.[73] The

---

71. *Ibid.*, pp. 46-51.
72. Edmund Husserl, *Krisis*, pp. 238-260.
73. *Ibid.*, pp. 261-269.

meaning of this statement seems to be only that phenomenological psychology as a theoretical science necessarily strives for and, therefore, also really terminates in transcendental phenomenology. Or to put it in another way, phenomenological psychology understood as separated from a transcendental phenomenological horizon is nonsense. There is no psychology that could always remain mere psychology. The radicalizing endeavor characteristic of every science in one way or another, drives theoretical phenomenological psychology, precisely as dealing with consciousness as intentional, into the arms of transcendental phenomenology. In psychological praxis, however, every psychologist must return to the world of our immediate experience, applying there his insights into 'real' men in mundane situations.[74]

---

74. Joseph J. Kockelmans, *Husserl's Phenomenological Psychology*, Chapter VI.

CHAPTER ELEVEN

REALISM OR IDEALISM?

In the preceding chapters I have endeavored to present a brief outline of Husserl's phenomenological philosophy. Now in approaching the conclusion of this study it is appropriate to focus attention on a very fundamental problem which has been mentioned repeatedly in this investigation, but which has not as yet received its final answer. The question is, to what extent may Husserl's phenomenology be called idealistic, and further, what in the final analysis is the meaning of this kind of idealism? As a prelude to the answering of these closely allied questions, it is in order to describe briefly how Husserl himself viewed and understood his own phenomenology during the final decade of his life and work.

1. *Phenomenology as All-embracing Philosophy. Its Final Meaning*

Phenomenology and Science

If the material presented up to this point has fulfilled its intended purpose, by now it is clear that Husserl considered his own phenomenological philosophy to be "an all-embracing science grounded on an absolute foundation." Husserl believed that he had shown concretely in his various publications the possibility of such a science because he had been able to show a necessary and indubitable starting point, to give the methods to be used in this science, and to predelineate the fundamental problems to be solved. Since the preceding claims share a common point of departure in the positive sciences, it is essential here to make clear the relation between such sciences and this new conception of philosophy before proceeding to the final meaning of phenomenology.[1]

---

1. Edmund Husserl, *Cart. Med.*, pp. 178-179 (152).

A First Introduction to Husserl's Phenomenology

The consideration begins very simply. From a philosophical point of view our everyday life is naïve. We are immersed in the already given world and pay no attention to the productive intentional functions by means of which natural things are there for us. Experiencing the things in the world, we know or care nothing about the necessarily involved achieving functions. We are interested in the different kinds of objects which present themselves in and by those functions, but forget about the hidden achievements by which the objects are built up. We maintain this naïve point of view in the sciences, too. It is true that science claims to justify its theoretical steps by means of critical investigations, but such criticism, however necessary and valuable, is not an ultimate criticism of knowledge as such, and in fact no science is interested in a criticism of the original achievements nor in an uncovering of all the intentional horizons. However, only in and through such a criticism can the realm of apodictic evidences be brought to light, and correlatively, the different kinds of objectivities be evaluated in regard to their ultimate and true sense of Being.

One has only to take note of the foundational problems encountered today by all sciences to realize that notwithstanding the high level of attainment and success reached by the positive sciences, they are still naïve in a certain sense. The fundamental concepts which govern the entire domain of science and determine the sense of Being of its realm of objects as well as the ultimate meaning of its theories are products of unknown and naïvely 'lived' functions, and, therefore have still undetermined intentional horizons. Any attempt of the historically developed sciences, logic included, to attain a founded understanding of the ultimate meaning of their own achievements implies a certain self-investigation. Now, such a self-investigation is *radical* only if it is phenomenological. This is true because a radical self-investigation must be completely universal, and this is impossible without a transcendental reduction and the phenomenological method necessarily connected with it. That is to say, there must be an intentional self-explicitation of the achievements of the transcendental ego and a systematic description of the essences constituted in them, in which procedure both the self-explicitation and the description are to be performed on the basis of an immediate intuition. For a universal and eidetic self-explicitation and description must range over *all the conceivable possibilities* of the ego and the transcendental intersubjectivity.[2]

A phenomenology that really wants to proceed in a consequent and 'logical' way, therefore, must construct *a priori,* with a strict universality, and on the basis of immediate intuitions the ideal forms of every conceivable world and those worlds themselves. But such a construction is original only if phenomenology describes those worlds in correlation with the *a priori* of the intentional achievements which constitute them.

In this procedure phenomenology has no pre-given actualities or concepts of actualities, but from the start must derive its own concepts from the originary character of the constitutive achievements. Furthermore, since phenomenology must uncover all intentional horizons as completely as possible and therefore must account for all differences in range and relativities, it is clear that in this procedure phenomenology must attain on its own the systems of concepts which determine that fundamental meaning of the realms governed by the different sciences. And because the concepts which constitute those systems formally predelineate what pertains to the ideal form of any and every possible world, it is clear, too, that these concepts must be the genuine and basic ones fundamental to all science, and to each of the sciences in particular. And once the meanings and origins of concepts such as world, nature, space, time, psycho-physical being, psyche, man, society, culture, and the like are clarified in a really original and radical way via investigation of the transcendental constitution of any possible world whatsoever and every concrete world in particular, it becomes apparent finally that there can no longer be any paradoxes.

If this view is true, then it can be said that the ultimate foundation of every *a priori* science lies in transcendental phenomenology, and that they therefore belong within the realm of the all-embracing *a priori* phenomenology itself as systematically differentiated branches. In this way a new meaning is given to an old Cartesian ideal.

This universal theory of science, simultaneously a concrete logic of Being and consequently a real ontology, would be the first authentic

---

2. *Ibid.,* pp. 179-180 (152-154).

realization of a real *universe of science* grounded on an absolute foundation. It has been shown previously in more detail what can be summarized here in succinct form: the realization of such a tremendous task requires that the first and absolutely radical philosophical discipline be a solipsistic egology; then must come an intersubjective phenomenology founded on that egology, explaining first the most general and universal questions and only subsequently branching out into different regional ontologies. Finally it is in this total science of the *a priori* that the ultimate foundations for every genuine science of matters of fact must be brought to light, for the rationality of all facts lies ultimately in the *a priori*. *A priori* science is science of radical universality and necessity to which each science of matters of fact must have recourse in order to become ultimately grounded.[3]

Transcendental Idealism

Still further expanding his ideas, Husserl points out that phenomenology in all its radical foundations also excludes every form of naïve metaphysics which deals with absurd 'beings in themselves'. However, phenomenology does not reject every form of metaphysics; it is, in fact, its explicit intention to take up the fundamental problems which since Descartes' time have traditionally gone in the wrong direction via the wrong method. Phenomenology wants first to bring to light that being which is radically first and precedes and bears every worldly objectivity, namely, transcendental subjectivity. From this point phenomenology proceeds to the sphere of transcendental intersubjectivity, the universe of 'monads' which materializes its 'communion' in various ways. It is only in this realm within which everything that can have sense for us must be formulated and stated that phenomenology tries to understand the important problems of 'accidental factualness', such as the problems of death, of fate, of the possibility of authentic human life, of the meaning of history, and all ethico-religious problems.

The idea of an all-embracing philosophy, therefore, cannot be actualized in the form of an all-embracing deductive system, but as a system

---

3. *Ibid.,* pp. 180-182 (154-156).

of phenomenological disciplines which are grounded ultimately not on an axiom, but on an everything founding self-investigation. And as said, such a radical self-investigation is impossible within the realm of the natural attitude, but necessarily requires a transcendental reduction.[4]

As soon as I undertake to perform such a reduction and then attempt as a pure ego in a systematic self-investigation to uncover my own field of consciousness, it becomes apparent for me that all that is for this pure ego is constituted as that which it is in myself, and that every kind of being has its own particular form of constitution. When I try to understand the real meaning of this insight, I must come to the conclusion that transcendency, in whatever form it may manifest itself to me, is as a matter of fact an immanent characteristic constituted within the sphere of the pure ego itself. Stated in another way, every possible sense and every imaginable being, whether it manifests itself as immanent or transcendent, falls within the domain of my transcendental subjectivity which ultimately constitutes all sense and Being. Once I understand this, I see also that every attempt to conceive the universe of *true* Being as something lying outside the universe of *possible* consciousness is nonsensical because true Being and consciousness belong together essentially and inseparably, being concretely one in the only absolute concretion of transcendental subjectivity. If it is indeed true that transcendental subjectivity *is* the universe of all possible sense and Being, then an 'outside of consciousness' is certainly nonsense. As Berkeley has shown, this is true not only for my *de facto* ego and what manifests itself in fact and thanks to my own constitution as existing for me, but also for this ego as an example of the eidos 'ego', that is to say, for the transcendental ego.[5]

Following this line, it becomes evident that a genuine epistemology cannot operate any longer with inconsistent inferences leading from a supposed immanency to a supposed transcendency, which as 'Being in itself' is obviously essentially unknowable, and therefore completely meaningless. Epistemology appears to be meaningful only as a transcendental phenomenology which tries to clarify in a systematic way our

---

4. *Ibid.,* pp. 182-183 (156-157).
5. *Ibid.,* pp. 116-118 (83-85).

knowledge achievements as essentially intentional achievements constituting the intended objectivities, and thus to show that every kind of
being, real or ideal, becomes understandable only as a product of transcendental subjectivity.

From this point of view transcendental phenomenology is clearly
eo ipso transcendental idealism, but in a fundamentally and even essentially new sense. For it is not a 'psychological idealism' which tries to
derive a meaningful world from meaningless sense-data, nor is it a
Kantian idealism that still maintains, although as a limit-idea only, the
reality of a world of 'beings in themselves'. On the contrary, we have
here a kind of transcendental idealism which is nothing but a consequently performed self-explicitation in the form of a systematic, egological science, as has just been specified.[6]

Different Interpretations of the Meaning of This Transcendental Idealism

As far as I can determine, Husserl did not change his view on this
cardinal point of his philosophy in any essential way after 1907, although
it is true that he made repeated attempts to determine the final meaning of this view as accurately as possible and to found it as radically
as possible. The view itself seems to be quite clear initially; yet for over
thirty years scholars have not been able to agree on the interpretation
of Husserl's phenomenology where this point is concerned.

The question of whether his thought should be interpreted *ultimately*
in a realistic or idealistic way has proved difficult to answer. Some interpreters hold that Husserl's phenomenology is realistic in its very
essence;[7] others see his work as one or another form of idealism, the
exact nature of which they cannot determine or agree upon.[8] And in
the recent past an 'existentialistic' interpretation of Husserl's phenomen-

---

6. *Ibid.*, pp. 118-121 (85-88).
7. See for the most important older literature H. Boelaars, "De intentionaliteit
der kennis by Edmund Husserl", *Bijdragen* 3 (1940), 111-161, 221-264, pp. 112-121.
8. See for this point of view the publications of Gaston Berger, Ludwig Landgrebe, Alphonse De Waelhens, Paul Ricoeur, Pierre Thévenaz, Max Müller,
Stephan Strasser, Eugen Fink, Walter Biemel, Jean Wahl, Aron Gurwitsch,
Roman Ingarden and Quentin Lauer, quoted in this study.

ology has been proposed; here it is argued that Husserl transcends the opposition, realism-idealism.[9]

The noteworthy aspect of this situation is that none of the solutions advocated is convincing. This is obvious in that the proponents of the different positions cannot satisfy one another and that the discussion therefore is taken up time and again. Moreover, every proposed solution refers to an extensive series of clear texts convincing in themselves, but when quotations of the opposition are taken into account in connection with them, the convincing element seems to evaporate. It seems certain that Husserl recognized the problem and thought he had given a clear and convincing answer to it. But, in spite of this, the situation remains unsolved and, in order to cope with it, several authors have searched for supplementary considerations. Although their efforts contain a core of truth, the fundamental ambiguity in Husserl's texts persists.

To elaborate this point I shall give here a survey of certain idealistic interpretations of Husserl's work and also treat somewhat more extensively the opinions of Merleau-Ponty and De Waelhens. I have especially chosen from the idealistic group those authors who either for their characterization of Husserl's idealism or for the importance of the fundamental reasons they present in support of their opinions should, in my opinion, be included in this study. I hope after a certain point of development has been reached to come to a conclusion about the ambiguity insofar as this is possible.

Before starting, I might mention that the realistic interpretations of Husserl's work are no longer discussed, as contemporary authors consider them completely inadmissible from the outset. Moreover, these interpretations are dealt with implicitly in the critique presented by the various authors who have adopted an idealistic interpretation of Husserl's work.

---

9. See, for instance, Maurice Merleau-Ponty, *Phénoménologie de la perception.* (Paris: Presses Universitaires de France, 1945.), passim. See also the later publications of Alphonse De Waelhens which will be quoted in the notes 73-75 of this chapter.

2. *Idealistic Interpretation of Husserl's Phenomenology*

Gaston Berger

A first point of view to be looked into here is that of Gaston Berger as it is amply explained in his work, *Le cogito dans la philosophie de Husserl.*[10] Berger begins by pointing out that some commentators have seen Husserl as upholding a natural realism in his *Logical Investigations,* but claim that after his *Ideas* he turned more and more to some form of idealism. Berger does not agree that this is so. Although Husserl is certain to have undergone an evolution, the main ideas of his work have always remained the same, at least intentionally.[11] It is Berger's contention that Husserl never wished to deal with traditional realism but that, on the other hand, he was in violent protest against both subjective idealism and the "magic" idealism of the romanticists. What Husserl wanted was a strict rational reflection in which individual persons need no longer appear. This is an absolute demand if philosophy ever wants to grow into a 'strict science', granted that any real science is impersonal.[12] A necessary condition for this ideal is the phenomenological and transcendental reduction by means of which the world we live in is not destroyed, nor denied, but only 'bracketed'. What remains after this reduction is the transcendental ego with its transcendental life. Having penetrated into the transcendental sphere by means of reduction, it is important that one brings to light the very essence of that which manifests itself here by means of intentional and constitutive analyses.[13]

Plainly, the transcendental phenomenological reduction and the theory of constitution form the two fundamental ideas of Husserl's phenomenology.[14] The phenomenological reduction offers to the mind the possibility of discovering its own essence; formerly and as a common

---

10. Gaston Berger, *Le cogito dans la philosophie de Husserl* (Paris: Aubier, 1941).

11. *Ibid.,* pp. 12-15.

12. *Ibid.,* p. 67.

13. *Ibid.,* pp. 67-74.

14. *Ibid.,* p. 16, p. 94.

situation, lost in the world, now the mind finds itself again. And this moment of finding itself is precisely when the mind is able to take on a distinctly new task: namely, the interpretation of the world as a coherent system which was constituted by the mind itself. Thus the coherence and unity of the world are in the final analysis rooted in the unity of the ego to which all elements of the world necessarily point. The constitutive analyses have the task of showing how the ego constitutes the mundane beings and the world itself.[15]

When considering the exact meaning of the term 'constitution' in Husserl, Berger finds one thing immediately clear. Husserl uses the term to indicate the original relation between the 'I' and the world, the ego and any mundane structure. In connection with this it is important to note that every mundane being, as well as the world itself whose sense we attempt to determine in this way, necessarily point to the transcendental ego. Consequently, trying to understand the constitution of the world by means of the 'I' consists in attempting to see how the ego gives sense to anything which manifests itself to us in the world, and especially how it gives an existential meaning, a value of Being, to some aspects of the world. Whoever wishes to understand Husserl's idea of constitution accurately must transport himself to the level of meanings; in fact this advice is important for phenomenology as a whole. We must never forget that the world itself has its whole Being as a certain sense which presupposes absolute consciousness as a field of sense-giving.[16] Thus phenomenology does not deny the real existence of the world; the issue is only one of explaining the meaning of this undeniably and unquestionably real world. To be consistent, one must say the same for the ego itself; in addition, the ego in a certain way is a sense which must be explicitated, which in turn means that constitutional problems must be posed for it as well. Transcendental idealism has one goal, namely to explicitate and found in a definite manner the thesis of any being whatsoever.[17]

---

15. *Ibid.*, p. 94.
16. Edmund Husserl, *Ideen I*, p. 135 (153-154).
17. Gaston Berger, *op. cit.*, pp. 94-95.

A First Introduction to Husserl's Phenomenology

In the natural attitude it is impossible to understand a philosophy which is taken up completely with meaning. Yet Husserl wants to posit here that meaning should not only have an important place in philosophy, but precisely that problems of meaning are the only philosophical problems. Therefore it is not right that we, either implicitly or explicitly, suppose things 'below' or 'beyond' the objects 'meant', things which ought to bear certain meanings and which later on should be made intelligible by consciousness in some way or another. Such is Kant's opinion, and according to Berger many interpreters of Husserl's work have mistakenly seen a return to Kant's philosophy in Husserl's phenomenology. However, in Husserl's view transcendental subjectivity does not give sense to a pre-existing thing or to a pre-existing world; he accepts no 'thing-in-itself'. "Experience is not a hole in consciousness into which a world, which precedes all experience, sends its rays."[18] And so sense is not thrust upon matter in order to 'inform' this matter later on. Husserl finally rejects the dualism of 'matter' and 'form'; that is to say, it is his opinion that this dualism is not an irreducible and absolute datum.[19]

One is at first astounded that Husserl can speak of meanings without mentioning things that might bear these meanings. However, it should not be forgotten that phenomenology demands quite another attitude. If phenomenological reduction is properly understood, it is clear that one need not necessarily lapse into classical idealism because one rejects traditional realism. Also, one does not lose Being completely by adhering to meanings only, for the domain of meanings implies the sphere of Being. Having-sense is not a way of being, but Being is one of the ways in which something can have sense. Being does not constitute an absolute and universal basis, but sense, the idea, is the foundation of all. Changing from a philosophy of Being to a transcendental phenomenology does not narrow the perspective, but on the contrary widens it, because phenomenology furnishes the possibility of understanding metaphysics in an original way, inasmuch as it projects a theory of the constitution of Being. In transcending realism phenomenology does not reject ontology,

---

18. Edmund Husserl, *F. tr. L.,* p. 206.
19. Gaston Berger, *op. cit.,* pp. 95-06.

but serves rather to found it. Therefore it bears appropriately the name of 'concrete logic of Being'.[20]

Against this background constitution is not an 'informing' but a 'creating' act. The only question is precisely what 'creation' means here. Husserl uses different expressions in this context: to produce, to fulfill in an active way, to thematize, etc., (*produktiv schaffen, aktiv erfüllen, thematisch machen*). These terms must not be taken too literally. Strictly speaking, transcendental consciousness does not make or produce anything whatsoever. Every activity develops in the world and as such is already a constituted structure. What complicates the question here is that we have to use the language of a natural world. Be this as it may, in a constitutive analysis Husserl does not want to make anything, nor to deduce or construct anything. He wishes only to describe the possible modes of being conscious of the objects; his sole intention is to reveal the implicit intentionalities in experience itself conceived in a transcendental state.[21] Although Husserl speaks frequently of 'producing' and of 'production', constitution is neither productive nor receptive; probably the term *'Leistung'* could best be translated by 'act', because in the first instance in Husserl, this term indicates intentionality itself. *'Leistung'* now expresses the same relation; it only underlines the fact that this relation constitutes the object precisely as object.[22]

Thus the constituting *cogito* is neither active nor passive, at least when these terms are understood in a mundane way; on the other hand, however, constitution really is creative inasmuch as nothing exists before it. Furthermore, it must be noted here that the *cogito* effects a cognitive relation between the ego and the object; in other words, the cogito really is an intuition also. Nevertheless the ego is in no way a disinterested spectator who is to be completely alien to the scene unfolding before him. For this reason the term 'intuition' must be combined with the term "creation"; phenomenology is a philosophy of creative intuition in which intuition posits its objects.[23] The link be-

---

20. *Ibid.*, pp. 96-97. Edmund Husserl, *Cart. Med.*, p. 181 (155).
21. Edmund Husserl, *Cart. Med.*, p. 89 (52-53).
22. Gaston Berger, *op. cit.*, pp. 97-100.
23. *Ibid.*, p. 10.

tween intuition and creation becomes clearer when one remembers that constitutive analyses are analyses of meaning. Such analyses must be characterized through the researching of sense, by its method of explicitating implications and by linking up the constituted structures together with the constituting life of the ego.[24] The last of these three characterizations, however, cannot be expressed very well in our common natural language. Just as one cannot expect to understand the phenomenological reduction from the natural attitude, so one cannot expect to describe constitution in mundane terms, for the latter is just a theory about the genesis of the world itself.[25] In reference to this fact, therefore, we can probably best delimit constitution as Berger does: to explain the constitution of an object is to show to which intention of the transcendental ego it corresponds and how the given aspects and the potential horizons of this object are implied in the very nature of this intention.[26]

Ludwig Landgrebe

According to Landgrebe[27] it is extremely difficult to determine the exact place Husserl's phenomenology occupies in contemporary philosophy. This is not because only relatively few works of Husserl have been published as yet, nor because the majority of his published works outline an ideal program rather than realizing one. The main reason is that the analyses which Husserl made seem to do away with his ideal program and the self-interpretation implied in it, although certainly Husserl himself was not explicitly conscious of this. In virtue of the ambitious program which Husserl imposed upon himself in his philosophical life and which he has described so well in his *Ideas* and in his *Cartesian Meditations,* his philosophy must be understood as a radicalization of the Cartesian claim that all philosophical knowledge must be based on an absolutely sure and indubitable insight in order to enable philosophy to be built up as a rigorous science. His numerous and detailed analyses, however, are in several important aspects in contradic-

---

24. *Ibid.,* p. 113.
25. *Ibid.,* p. 104.
26. *Ibid.,* p. 110.
27. Ludwig Landgrebe, *Philosophie der Gegenwart* (Bonn: Athenäum-Verlag, 1952), pp. 31-40.

tion with his attempts to think through the modern subject-object problem; in the analyses referred to, this problem appears to be a false one.[28]

The reduction of our deduced knowledge to the apodictic certitude of the *cogito* is not rooted in epistemological considerations but in methodological reflections only. Referring to his considerations about positivism, Husserl argues that, "by means of the elimination of every theory and of all metaphysical conceptions which are blindly accepted from tradition, we must return to a pure and original experience in which the things themselves can appear to us immediately in an original way." Here it is very important to establish first the criteria for such an experience and then to answer the question of how we could justify such originality. Because experience is a mode of having something in a conscious way, only consciousness itself is able to distinguish an original and real experience from a supposed and even fancied one. As adult intellectuals, however, we have already determinate conceptions about things and problems; for this reason it is necessary to return by means of a certain method from our deduced knowledge and insights about the world to original experiences in which every being whatsoever is given in a completely primordial way as it is in-itself.[29]

That method is the famous intentional analysis in which we have to seek the activities of consciousness through which every being as such is given in an original way. In the application of this method phenomenological reduction is of fundamental importance because it affords the possibility of describing the phenomena purely and as they are immediately given to consciousness with the elimination of all opinions and pre-conceptions that transcend what is originally intended by consciousness. However, consciousness cannot be described and the individual acts cannot be distinguished from one another unless an initial distinction is made between consciousness and that of which one is conscious, and unless attention is paid to the way in which every act is directed to its object. This means that the analysis of our conscious life must have as its theme the different ways in which it is directed to objects through its acts, or stated another way, the

---

28. *Ibid.,* pp. 31-32.
29. *Ibid.,* pp. 32-34.

different modes which intentionality itself can assume. Accordingly, the question about the very essence of every being is reduced to the question of the modes of consciousness in which in its originality every being must manifest itself as such. Thus the essence of every being is to be determined, by means of intentional analysis, in returning from being to the activities of consciousness in which every being is constituted as a "this" or a "that". In this way Being and consciousness appear in a strict correlation; there is nothing about which we are able to say something unless there is a corresponding constituting activity of consciousness in which it, as this determinate thing, is given as such.

In the performance of these intentional analyses the essential distinction between all possible objects of consciousness must be chosen as a guiding clue in our inquiry about the corresponding modes of consciousness. In so doing the phenomenological reduction, which in the beginning manifests itself only as the elimination of all unfounded conceptions about things, appears now as a return to the last and absolute point with which all our knowledge of the world, of the things, and of their essential structures is necessarily connected; this point is the absolute certainty about me, myself, as a being who is conscious of itself and of the world. This *ego cogito,* however, is in no way a starting point for deductive reasoning; its discovery brings to light only an original field of description. The intentional analyses of phenomenology therefore move in a twofold direction; on one hand, they are noematic descriptions which have the essential characteristics of *species, genera, regions,* etc., as guiding clues; on the other, they are noetic descriptions concerning the activities of consciousness in which a being of this or that sort is always originally given as its object.[30]

Initially the ego conceives itself, too, as a mundane being, namely as this determinate ego in the midst of other egos. In a further and deeper analysis, however, it appears as a function of its own activities on the basis of an already constituted world in which it is together with other egos as this determinate man. It is also possible to push this analysis further; then the ego will find in itself a center of intentional

---

30. *Ibid.,* pp. 34-35.

activities through which every being is what it is and through which it can appear only as this determinate being. So the ego will find in itself an absolute consciousness through which in the strictest sense everything is what it is: the things, other people, and even it, itself.[31]

This methodological conviction determines from the outset the direction for seeking solutions to the main problems of metaphysics, that is the problem of Being itself, the problems concerning its original meaning, and the modes in which it manifests itself. For Husserl Being is a *priori* the correlate of consciousness; thus Being is being-object, being-object-for-consciousness, in which consciousness every being is given originally in its proper essence. It is true that the absolute constituting consciousness in the last instance is an "itself-forming-stream" of constituting activities, but it is able to understand itself and to reveal itself in its own essence only in the results of its activities, i.e., in the objective unities, in the constituted objects. This implies and reveals again the disclosure of an essential correlation between all beings whatsoever and the activities of consciousness necessarily connected with them. Here every factual being, even man himself, loses its proper signification; it manifests itself only as an example and as the model of a being of this sort; it is simply a guiding clue for answering the question concerning which activities of consciousness unconditionally, universally, and necessarily belong to a being of such a sort in general. Here Husserl shows himself to be a protagonist of idealism.[32]

It becomes apparent that the return to a *cogito* as the final starting point of philosophy involves a hidden contradiction which Husserl himself did not seem to perceive. It is Landgrebe's opinion that the chief merit of Husserl's philosophy consists in that he pushed his ideas, which as a matter of fact have been fundamental tenets of philosophy since Descartes, to their ultimate consequences where this subject-centered philosophy appears to cancel itself out. Heidegger clearly recognized this fact and subsequently steered European philosophy into completely

---

31. *Ibid.*, pp. 36-37.
32. *Ibid.*, pp. 37-38.

new channels, away from all forms of idealism. We shall return to this point later.[33]

In 1953 Landgrebe again summarized this conception of Husserl's philosophy by referring to a study by Jean Wahl dealing with several problems in the first part of Husserl's *Experience and Judgment.* (This work was edited by Landgrebe himself.) In his article Jean Wahl expresses the opinion that from the very beginning a realistic tendency predominates in *Experience and Judgment.*[34] In a letter written to Jean Wahl, Landgrebe tells him that this realistic tendency is not his alone.[35] As far as he is concerned Husserl's whole work is permeated by a divergency between his idealistic program as it is outlined in *Ideas* and in *Cartesian Meditations,* and the results of his detailed analyses in later years. Husserl seemed not to have been conscious of this divergency. Landgrebe admits that he, too, took an idealistic stand in 1939, as Husserl did, and that this divergency escaped him also at that time. Only later did it become evident to him that the historical importance of Husserl's phenomenology is the triumph of idealism over itself as the result of an effort to think through to its very end a theory which has its starting point in subjectivity.[36]

*Two Comparative Studies of the Phenomenology of
Husserl and Heidegger*

Two comparative studies by Landgrebe and Biemel on the phenomenology of Husserl and Heidegger would seem to have a special importance in this context.[37] Landgrebe begins his comparative considerations by observing that it is highly unfortunate that the documents in which both Husserl and Heidegger attempted to present their views in

---

33. *Ibid.,* pp. 38-40.

34. J. Wahl, "Notes sur la première partie de 'Erfahrung und Urteil' de Husserl", *Phénoménologie-Existence.* Recueil d'études par H. Birault, H. Van Breda, A. Gurwitsch, E. Levinas, P. Ricoeur et J. Wahl (Paris: Gallimard, 1953), pp. 77-105, p. 77.

35. *Phénoménologie-Existence,* pp. 205-206.

36. *Ibid.,* p. 205.

37. Ludwig Landgrebe, *Phänomenologie und Metaphysik,* pp. 83-100. Walter Biemel, "Husserls Encyclopaedia Britannica Artikel und Heideggers Anmerkungen dazu", *Tijdschrift voor philosophie,* 12 (1950) 246-280.

regard to each other's philosophy are not at our disposal. We know only that Husserl in his famous Epilogue (*Nachwort*) explicitly rejects Heidegger's interpretation of phenomenology[38] and the way Heidegger gives an original and new interpretation of Husserl's phenomenology in his own principal work *Being and Time*.[39] Furthermore, it is quite difficult to compare Husserl's conception of phenomenology with that of Heidegger because both philosophers were not able to survey each other's work completely, so that their critical considerations are sometimes rooted in faulty interpretations; this holds true for Husserl especially. Finally it is and remains evident that their conceptions, despite several points of agreement, differ essentially from each other.[40]

However, Husserl as well as Heidegger starts from the insight that every sort of being has its own and proper way of giving-itself to consciousness and that only on the ground of this original way of self-givenness are we able to determine our philosophical opinions about Being.[41] From the very beginning Heidegger conceives this fundamental principle in a way which was found originally in Husserl's earliest philosophical works, too, namely, as a claim for the realization of a natural concept of the world. In Husserl's view this principle was not only of importance for a description of Being which should be free from every pre-conception and theory; it had a very determinate function, also, in the whole context of his philosophy which is crowned by his theory of the phenomenological reduction. The function of this natural concept of the world is probably to be explained as follows.

The intentional analysis, as the universal uncovering of the activities of consciousness, takes its guiding clues from the objects, thus from the always varying mode of Being of the objects which demand again and again of consciousness a certain kind of activity in which beings of this region are given originally. Consequently when we wish to find a proper starting point for the question about the activities of consciousness, it becomes absolutely necessary first to get a clear insight into the structure

---

38. Edmund Husserl, *Ideen III*, p. 140.
39. Martin Heidegger, *Sein und Zeit* (Tübingen: Max Niemeyer, 1953), pp. 27-39.
40. Ludwig Landgrebe, *op. cit.*, pp. 83-84.
41. *Ibid.*, p. 85.

of the objects themselves. Only in this way is it understandable what the object of our experience properly and originally is and, correlatively, what the deepest and most primordial activities of consciousness exactly mean; and, on the other hand, what derived and constituted objects really are and, correlatively, what secondary activities of consciousness properly mean.[42]

Now without a doubt the prevailing tradition of the exact sciences imposes upon us certain prejudices in connection with our original project of experience, namely, that the object as it manifests itself in an exact determination of science should be the original form of Being. But in fact, the objects of the exact sciences are abstractions and constructions grounded on the world as it is given in original experience. Thus, when we want to discover the really original structures of the objects of the different regions of Being, so that later they may serve as guiding clues for the question about the correlative activities of consciousness, it becomes absolutely necessary to reject the pre-conceptions of the positive sciences and to penetrate into Being itself as it is immediately given in an original experience. Therefore we must return to the world as it manifests itself in pure experience: the *Lebenswelt*. Husserl himself conceives this in the following way. Before the phenomenological reduction and the constitutive analyses which must be performed in that sphere, we must try to find guiding clues by means of a new reduction which takes us from the cultural and scientific world to the original *Lebenswelt*. The link, however, between the two reductions is essential in Husserl.[43]

This reduction from the world of culture to the *Lebenswelt* is one of the most important points which Heidegger borrows from Husserl. For, according to Heidegger, Being-in-the-world is the fundamental structure of *Dasein*; it is, therefore, the main theme of "fundamental ontology" to show the original relation between *Dasein* and world, and to show how *Dasein*, properly speaking, is mundane and how it *has* a world. But, then, it is also necessary to explain the primordial con-

---

42. *Ibid.*, p. 85.
43. *Ibid.*, pp. 85-87.

cept of the natural world.[44] Heidegger, one of the most devoted disciples of Husserl, nonetheless rejects the phenomenological reduction. Like Husserl, Heidegger, too, protests against all those who instead of seeing it as a return to the very roots of subjectivity attempt to interpret phenomenology in a classically realistic way.[45]

One of the most striking points of difference between Husserl and Heidegger consists in the way each conceives of phenomena. For Heidegger a phenomenon is that which manifests itself, and more concretely speaking, "Being of the beings, their sense, their modifications and their derivatives".[46] Heidegger came to this conception of phenomenon because he started from a completely different idea of intentionality than Husserl did. In Heidegger intentionality means a relation to the beings, or better, a relation to the world; this is already clear from his definition of *Dasein* as Being-in-the-world.[47] Based on this, one can readily understand that for Heidegger an intentional analysis can never take the form of a constitutive analysis as Husserl conceives it. And in this connection Heidegger has to reject not only a phenomenological, but also and even more so, any transcendental reduction. For the same reason a transcendental subjectivity is inadmissible for Heidegger as is a theory about the *ego* as an "uninterested spectator" and a complete and universal reflection.[48] In conclusion, we may say that Heidegger rejects Husserl's method because in his opinion this method does not pay sufficient attention to the original experience *Dasein* has of itself, for in this way the very essence of *Dasein* does not come to light "in the originality of its *existence*". Husserl's method can lead only to an 'idealized subject', but never to the proper essence of *Dasein,* that is to say, to the facticity of his *ek-sistence*. Therefore this method is unable to reveal what subjectivity really is in the most proper and radical sense of this term.[49] In the final analysis, however, the difference between Heidegger and Husserl appears to be even more

---

44. *Ibid.,* p. 87. Martin Heidegger, *op. cit.,* p. 52.
45. Ludwig Landgrebe, *op. cit.,* p. 87.
46. Martin Heidegger, *op. cit.,* p. 28, p. 35.
47. *Ibid.,* pp. 52-62.
48. Ludwig Landgrebe, *op. cit.,* pp. 87-94.
49. *Ibid.,* p. 94.

fundamental. Husserl posits a *priori* that Being is identical with being-object. It is just this point which Heidegger's philosophy is dead set against.[50]

Walter Biemel, too, comes to an analogous conclusion based on a letter which Heidegger wrote to Husserl about the latter's project for an article on phenomenology to be published in the *Encyclopaedia Britannica*. According to Biemel, it is essential for Husserl's method that every being be made a problem in order to ascertain in this way that which is completely unproblematical and which therefore is the absolute basis for every being. Husserl sees this basis in the transcendental ego. If, however, this ego is the fundamental ground of all Being, then consequently all Being has to be constituted in this ego; thus all Being must be solved in consciousness so that the transcendental ego becomes Being as such. Husserl's whole method is determined by his phenomenological and transcendental reduction by means of which the totality of Being is "bracketed" in order to find a pure and transcendental ego. These reductions are not found in Heidegger in any sense. In his view the relation between *Dasein* and other beings belongs precisely to the very essence of *Dasein* itself.[51] Through his reductions Husserl tries to loosen the transcendental ego from the world in order to keep it as pure from every mundane being as possible; for Heidegger on the contrary *Dasein* is precisely that being which first discloses the world. For Heidegger, then, the relation between *Dasein* and the world is even essential, and this is the main reason why he defines *Dasein* as Being-in-the-world. Husserl's pure ego is a fallacy, an artificial abstraction, which stands in the way of our conceiving man in his concrete ek-sistence. It is Biemel's opinion, too, that the main difference between the philosophy of Husserl and Heidegger exists in a different conception of Being, although Biemel's interpretation of this difference is not identical to Landgrebe's. In other respects both interpretations evidently imply each other and both conclude that Heidegger rejects Husserl's philosophy because he believes Husserl's phenomenology to be an inadmissible form of idealism.[52]

---

50. *Ibid.*, pp. 99-100.
51. Walter Biemel, *loc. cit.*, pp. 273-276.
52. *Ibid.*, pp. 276-280.

Paul Ricoeur

Ricoeur insists that we must clearly distinguish Husserl's method, that is, his famous intentional analysis, from his idealistic doctrine which determined this method more and more profoundly from 1905 on.[53] It seems that Husserl himself did not observe this distinction which is the reason for his frequent confusing of method and doctrine, especially when he speaks about constitution.

Methodically considered, the expression 'constitutive analysis' has the same meaning as the expression 'intentional analysis'. It consists in that we start from a meaning that is already constituted in an object forming a unity continually present to consciousness, in order to analyze by means of a well-chosen guiding clue the different intentions which overlap each other in that meaning. Such a method does not yet imply a single prejudice concerning the fundamental sense of consciousness and Being. At most one could speak here of a "methodical idealism" inasmuch as through the use of the phenomenological reduction every reality is conceived as a sense for a consciousness. But this sense *for* a consciousness is interpreted by Husserl as a sense *in* and *through my* consciousness. At the moment he does so, however, he passes a metaphysical judgment concerning the fundamental sense of reality and so transcends the methodical rule that only consciousness is to be questioned.[54]

The same idea is to be found in Landgrebe, too, when he says that we must distinguish between Husserl's methodical conception of constitution and his idealistic interpretation of it. Constitution as a projecting activity of consciousness does not mean only the bringing-to-light of a being to consciousness; it means, rather, creation of the world as a creation of Being by consciousness itself.[55]

Be that as it may, as Ricoeur sees it, Husserl boldly draws all of his conclusions from this *a priori* choice. The return to the ego leads him

---

53. Paul Ricoeur, "Analyses et problèmes dans 'Ideen II' de Husserl", *Phénoménologie-Existence*, pp. 23-76.

54. *Ibid.*, pp. 24-25.

55. Ludwig Landgrebe, "Seinsregionen und regionale Ontologien in Husserl's Phänomenologie", *Studium Generale*, 9 (1956), 313-324, p. 316.

to a "monadology" according to which, in the first instance, the world is the meaning which my ego unfolds in itself. It is true indeed that later Husserl paradoxically tries to transcend this transcendental solipsism with the help of considerations about the other and about intersubjectivity; but he never actually succeeded in this. This transcendental idealism is to be found especially in his *Ideas* and his *Cartesian Meditations*.[56]

Ricoeur has repeated this view in several of his more recent publications. In an article on Husserl's *Cartesian Meditations,* for example, he writes that Husserl's transcendental idealism is quite evident, at least in the fourth meditation.[57] Sections 40 and 41 especially contain very striking formulae of this idealism. They do not constitute a mere repetition of the reduction from the world to meaning and from meaning to the *cogito* but, instead, further radicalize this original idealism in function of a *monad* which is introduced here. Ricoeur tries to explain these two sections starting from Husserl's text which follows here: "Since the monadically concrete ego includes the whole of both actual and potential conscious life, it is clear that the problem of explicitating this monadic ego phenomenologically (the problem of its constitution for itself) must include all constitutional problems without exception. Consequently the phenomenology of the self-constitution coincides with phenomenology as a whole."[58] Ricoeur concludes from this text that if transcendental reality as a whole consists in the life of the ego, then the problem of the constitution of reality coincides with the self-constitution of this ego; thus phenomenology becomes identical with a self-explicitation of the things, of body, the psychical, culture, etc. Here the ego is no longer a subject-pole opposite an object-pole, but becomes that which contains everything. Everything now is a *constructum* for and through the transcendental subjectivity, a result of its achievements. Phenomenology as a whole is in this way solely a self-explicitation of my ego as subject of all possible knowledge.[59] Hence in Husserl's final

---

56. Paul Ricoeur, *loc. cit.,* p. 25.
57. Paul Ricoeur, "Etude sur les 'Méditations Cartésiennes' de Husserl", *Revue Philosophique de Louvain,* 52 (1954) 75-109, pp. 107-109.
58. Edmund Husserl, *Cart. Med.,* pp. 102-103 (67-68).
59. *Ibid.,* p. 118.

view on the ego, phenomenology and idealism appear to be inseparably connected.

However, this idealistic view seems to be in contradiction with what Husserl proposed in the first part of this same work, so that we are forced to conclude here that Husserl's phenomenology is ambiguous on this point. "As a description devoted to the things as they manifest themselves, phenomenology is a generous attempt to respect the variety of the appearing and to restore to every form of it the weight of its strangeness, or if you prefer, its 'otherness'; as an idealistic interpretation of its own descriptive behavior, however, Husserl's phenomenology is a radical effort to reduce every 'otherness' to the monadic life of the ego, thus to ipseity."[60]

Eugen Fink

Fink also finds it inadmissible to claim that Husserl would have developed from an original realism to a subjectivistic idealism.[61] Husserl's original realism was as subjectivistic as his later idealism. For Being itself of which phenomenology speaks is not Being-in-itself, but that Being which essentially is object, thus Being-for-us. Husserl argues that the question of the tie between Being and being-object is a false problem. In fact, however, this problem seems to be the fundamental question of philosophy. Husserl evades this problem because he rejects all forms of speculation. He simply posits that Being is identical with phenomenon because a thing essentially not able to manifest itself does not have any sense; what is not able to appear as a phenomenon is simply nothing. Husserl overlooks here that the phenomenality of phenomena can be in no way a phenomenal datum, so that he makes *a priori* a decision about a point which really is to be examined.

The main fault attached to this *a priori* decision is that Husserl conceives the appearing of the things only as an appearing for a

---

60. Paul Ricoeur, "Etude sur les 'Méditations Cartésiennes'," pp. 108-109, 96-100. See also his article: "Husserl et le sens de l'histoire", *Revue de métaphysique et de morale*, 54 (1949) 280-316.

61. Eugen Fink, 'L'analyse intentionnelle et le problème de la pensée spéculative", *Problèmes actuels de la phénoménologie*, H. L. Van Breda ed. (Brugge-Paris: Desclée et Brouwers, 1952), pp. 53-87.

knowing subject, although this appearing is to be understood originally in an ontological way as an ontological relation between one being and the other. This manifesting-itself is more general than the special mode which is based on it and in which a thing manifests itself to a knowing subject. In regard to its ontological possibility, knowledge is rooted in the general Being of things for other things.[62] In modern philosophy intentionality is seen rather exclusively as an epistemological relation; this is connected with the fact that substance has been almost exclusively interpreted as a subject; in metaphysics this has even been generally accepted since the time of Descartes and Leibniz. In this view phenomena are indeed identical with the objects which are represented in and by a representing ego. It seems that unconsciously Husserl stays on the same footing as modern metaphysics without admitting this fundament explicitly, however, and without being conscious of the problems closely connected with that standpoint.

In this context it is of special importance that Husserl holds the phenomenon to be simply identical with Being and vice versa. For him a phenomenon is in every case not the mode in which one being can be in relation to other beings or to the representing ego. For Husserl Being is being-object, and that is all. Later he draws all his conclusions in a very radical way from this *a priori* decision. If the thing is principally and solely phenomenon, then it does not have any substantiality; it is what it is only in relation to a knowing subject, while this subject itself is what it is only in the representing of this represented object. This representation is fundamentally not a relation between two substantial things that could be separated from each other; it is the relation itself which is primary here. The ego and the represented object are only two dependent moments of one single relation. The subject-object-relation with all its noetico-noematical structures is now the proper theme of phenomenology. It is self-evident that one can find very important aspects in these considerations, but it is also unfortunate that Husserl never learned to see intentionality in a more fundamental way, that is, as a relation between beings.

---

62. *Ibid.*, p. 70.

However, there is still another point which must be mentioned here. Once Husserl had learned to consider the thing as a phenomenon in the sense just explained, and later to consider the phenomenon as a structural element of intentionality which cannot be separated from the other elements of that structure, he finally came to conceive intentionality as a universal process in which the opposition between subject and object is transcended by the concrete unity of intentional life.[63] Then the thing begins to appear as an index of multiple subjective achievements, as a product of these subjective activities, as a constitutive product of a transcendental subjectivity. Husserl, however, could not clear up this matter completely in his further reflection upon these data. His doctrine on the transcendental constitution continues to hesitate between sense-giving and creation. But it must be recognized that it was not possible for him to find a positive solution because he intended only to analyze; he did not understand that such problems as the above cannot be solved with that or similar methods.[64]

Van Peursen

According to Van Peursen,[65] Husserl's phenomenology developed from a pure method into first philosophy. In connection with that development the function of the phenomenological reduction has changed. But despite the change it has remained a fundamental point of his method and has consisted always in the bracketing of reality. It was Husserl's opinion that with the reduction he could escape from the epistemological difficulties which had arisen after Kant. Husserl believed that with the advent of the reduction there was no sense whatsoever in speaking about the existence of the world outside consciousness, nor in carrying on endless discussions about the question of realism or idealism. And so when Husserl speaks about things themselves, he does not intend to speak about natural, real things, about mundane beings, but about the phenomena which, divorced from

63. *Ibid.*, p. 76.
64. *Ibid.*, pp. 68-84.
65. C. Van Peursen, "Phénoménologie et ontologie" *Rencontre*. Contributions à une psychologie humaine dédiées au Professeur F.J.J. Buytendijk (Utrecht-Antwerpen: Het Spectrum, 1957), pp. 308-317.

the question of whether or not they really exist in a natural world, manifest themselves to us. Thus from the beginning, Husserl is not interested in the Being of the things but in the logical structures of the phenomena which are completely independent of their actual Being in a natural world. Even consciousness itself, essentially intentional, is not conceived as a psychical and natural reality, but as a logically undeniable structure, whatever may be thought of its factual reality.

We come in due course in these considerations to the very essence of phenomenology; it starts from the idea of meaning and not from Being. The issue is to disclose the meaning of everything which manifests itself to consciousness, and not to prove the reality of one thing or another. In the past philosophy always searched for an in-itself, an absolute Being; but phenomenology first and last seeks sense, which is never a thing-in-itself, but requires always a relational structure, a reciprocal relation between consiousness and Being. In Husserl's view consciousness and Being are not to be conceived as two distinct entities because, for one thing, Being itself is bracketed by reduction. Furthermore, both are essentially connected with each other so that one cannot be without the other. In the further evolution of Husserl's thinking a certain form of idealism begins to appear with increasing frequency, especially between the years 1907 and 1935; however there is no question here of an idealism-of-Being, but only of an idealism connected with the constitution of meaning.[66]

Meaning takes a central place in Husserl's philosophy. A question could be posed here as to whether an inquiry into the sense of the phenomena does not imply a certain conception about Being. As a matter of fact an analysis of the sense of Being is found already in Husserl's *Ideas*. There he attempts to describe the sense of the real world; the description is accomplished within the sphere of the phenomenological reduction. Husserl is not trying to prove that the natural world really exists, but wishes only to discover the logical sense of the phenomena which manifest themselves as real world. This world reveals a correlation with the experience of an actual and given ego. Thus, that a thing really exists means only that it can be constituted

---

66. *Ibid.,* pp. 308-309.

by consciousness. Moreover, the sense of the really existing things clearly implies that these things must be "transcendent" to consciousness: it appears that they do not depend on it. However, this thesis does not yet imply a metaphysical presupposition, for all that is involved is a gnoseological independence. But notwithstanding this gnoseological independence, it is quite evident that world and consciousness are correlative.

In his later works, however, Husserl goes further. There the Being of the world for a consciousness is interpreted as a Being through and in consciousness.

Finally, Husserl searches for an "absolute mind as a source of all constitution"; then an 'achievement' which is very difficult to determine becomes the fundamental and final basis of every datum.[67] According to Van Peursen this can only be interpreted in an idealistic way.[68] Husserl intends here a pure experience, which cannot exist in our human history. In this connection his final reduction leads to an a-historical experience which is correlative to an impersonal mind which would have to constitute the final sense of this original experience. In addition, Husserl's considerations on intersubjectivity cannot furnish a satisfactory solution, and thus his philosophy seems to remain within the sphere of Hegel's idealism.[69]

3. The Interpretation of Merleau-Ponty and De Waelhens

Around 1945 Merleau-Ponty proposed a wholly new interpretation of Husserl's phenomenology. He begins by distinguishing several periods in Husserl's work to which attention had already been directed by other authors. As Merleau-Ponty saw it, Husserl was in his second period, thus without a doubt between 1913 and 1931, a protagonist of transcendental idealism. It may even be said that in all his published works Husserl adhered to this point of view. In order to prove this opinion Merleau-Ponty claims that in all his works Husserl continued to admit a transcendental reduction, admitting also the pos-

---

67. *Ibid.*, pp. 309-311.
68. Paul Ricoeur, "Husserl et le sense de l'histoire", passim.
69. C. Van Peursen, *loc. cit.*, pp. 311-312.

sibility of a complete reflection, and that Husserl always had an inadmissible conception of intersubjectivity. It is indeed true that in his last period Husserl held the opinion that every reflection must begin by returning to and describing the life-world, but in his published works Husserl continued requiring a reduction by means of which the structures of this life-world are to be reduced to a transcendental stream of a universal constitution through which all problems concerning the world can be definitely solved. It seems that in this period Husserl developed in the right direction, but even in his latest writings there remained several traces of his "logical" period.[70]

In the introduction to his *Phenomenology of Perception,* however, Merleau-Ponty gives another interpretation of Husserl's phenomenology. Although this interpretation is based on texts of Husserl himself, and especially on unpublished texts of Husserl's last period, it seems that it transcends Husserl's intention in several aspects. This is true especially for the interpretation of the transcendental reduction and for the problems which are closely connected with it, namely, problems concerning the other, intersubjectivity, constitution and the theoretical possibility of a complete reflection. Merleau-Ponty sufficiently stresses that Husserl did not thrash out these problems, although the fundamental principles for the proper solution may be found in his works. In this context Merleau-Ponty mentions especially the return from an objective-scientific world to the *Lebenswelt* and also the fact that Husserl in his later works explicitly distinguished between an act-intentionality and a "functioning intentionality". According to Merleau-Ponty the originality of Husserl's philosophy consists in the fact that under the intentionality of representations Husserl has found and revealed a more profound intentionality which other philosophers have called 'ek-sistence'.[71]

In recent years Alphonse De Waelhens, who previously had interpreted Husserl's phenomenology idealistically,[72] has come to share

---

70. Maurice Merleau-Ponty, *op. cit.,* pp. 73, 281, 419, 430-431, 490.
71. *Ibid.,* p. 141, 478-479, and pp. *ii-xvi.*
72. Alphonse De Waelhens, "Phénoménologie et métaphysique", *Revue Philosophique de Louvain,* 47 (1949), 366-376. See also "Phénoménologie et Réalisme", *Revue néoscolastique de Philosophie* 39 (1936), 497-517.

Merleau-Ponty's conception. In 1954 he appeared to have accepted the interpretation of phenomenology which Merleau-Ponty advocated on the ground of Heidegger's conception of phenomenology.[73] Regarding the question of whether or not this interpretation is found in Husserl's last published works also, De Waelhens is cautious in giving his opinion; the sum and substance of it would seem to be that the interpretation is not to be found there. De Waelhens attributes the mystery in the interpretation of Husserl's work to the latter's continuous oscillation between sense and presence; depending upon which element is stressed more than the other, we come to either an idealistic or realistic interpretation. On the other hand, Husserl seems to be of the opinion that one element is to be continuously related to the other. This appears to be the main reason why Husserl's phenomenology lends itself to being described as a philosophy in which reality is defined as an encounter. But in De Waelhens' estimation, Husserl never saw the consequences of this point of view, nor did he in any one way or another try to solve the problems connected with this conception.[74]

In the colloquy on phenomenology held at Krefeld (Germany) in 1956, and also in the Royaumont (France) colloquy of 1957, De Waelhens goes even further, arguing that the existentialistic interpretation of phenomenology in its very essence can be found in all of Husserl's important texts from 1906 on. This is a point of view to be dealt with here since it seems to be of considerable importance.[75]

According to De Waelhens intentionality as it is found in Husserl's *Logical Investigations* means in the first place that mode of thinking by means of which this thinking is able to contain in an ideal way something other than that which it, itself, is. Intentionality could, for instance, be said to be that characteristic property of consciousness by reason of which it is in no way possible to identify the expressed content with the expressing act, thus, that property through which consciousness always intends that which it itself is not. Since this intending generally

---

73. Alphonse De Waelhens, "Phénoménologie husserlienne et phénoménologie hégélienne" *Revue Philosophique de Louvain*, 52 (1954), 234-249. See also "L'idée phénoménologique d'intentionnalité", *Husserl et la pensée moderne*, pp. 115-142.

74. Alphonse De Waelhens, "Phénoménologie husserlienne", p. 242.

75. Alphonse De Waelhens, "L'idée phénoménologique", pp. 116-127.

is a complex happening, that which is constituted by the intending act, namely, the constituted sense, is built up from a multiplicity of meaning-levels. As a result, the complex total sense can be analyzed into its different components of meaning which are so many intentionalities.

This description of intentionality can also be applied to another domain. For if it is essential to consciousness to constitute a sense which is different from it itself, then it is essential to consciousness, also, that it constitutes objects. Therefore intentionality means neither that there is any relation between consciousness and an external object, nor that in consciousness itself a relation originates between two psychic contents. Intentionality has nothing to do with relations between two "real" objects. Only the act of sense-giving is essential. The exteriority of the contents represents the exteriority of the thought itself, understood in its relation to thinking which intends this content. In this way, the object is an inseparable element of the meaning phenomenon itself. Thus, when Husserl admits the existence of an object this never means that he intends to be a realist. In his philosophy every object appears only as being determined by the structures of thinking itself. It is this thinking itself which has a sense and which orientates itself to a pole of identity that it itself has constituted. When Husserl speaks about transcendency, he never supposes the reality of the object in question but only the existence of a sense-concept.

But this is not yet all. This first description of intentionality is to be considered now in a wholly new direction. In the foregoing intentionality was determined only in function of a theory of meaning and expression; we must try now in a more fundamental consideration to determine what a consciousness, which is essentially intentional, really is in itself. Then we are not speaking about the intentionality of an act, but about the proper Being of intentionality itself.

When one wishes to determine the very essence of intentionality, hence the very essence of consciousness, it does not make sense to undertake an accurate analysis of the words 'consciousness' and 'intentionality'. It is not right to 'flee' from the real world into the world of words. On the contrary, one must try to reveal the real presence of myself to myself and, inseparably connected with his, my presence to the things. For it is impossible to say that the assertion, according to which the concept of intentionality indicates that all consciousness is consciousness of something else, is an original idea with Husserl; it is, in fact, a very old idea. The main difference between Husserl's conception of intentionality and Kant's, for instance, consists especially in Husserl's idea that the unity of the world is already constituted and experienced as such before it is *explicitly* posited by knowledge itself. In this event it becomes absolutely impossible that this relation-of-knowledge, alone, and in the most proper sense of the term, could be the most primary relation between consciousness and world. Thus knowledge itself is a founded relation, and its necessary orientation to something else appears then as a property that is not characteristic of knowledge alone. The constitution of an object is then rather to be considered as a tendency which is proper to knowledge only in a typical and deduced way, and which in its proper manner is realized by a mode of being-related in which consciousness itself transcends that mode of being-related. Moreover, it appears also that consciousness, and thus the ego, is nothing but openness, relatedness to the other, negation of a being-based in and on itself, and hence at least in one way or another, nothing other than negativity. Thus, consciousness appears not to be pure interiority; it has to be understood as a coming-to-light, as a being-open-to, as a going-out-of-itself, as an ek-sistence.

However, if it is true that consciousness is nothing in and through itself, and thus that the Being of consciousness consists in opening-itself and in directing-itself-to-the-other, then it is evident also that the reality of consciousness understood in this way does not consist in an inner quality, and therefore neither in an unchangeable and unexteriorized self-possession. The openness which consciousness itself is, is much better disclosed by that to which consciousness opens itself. It is impossible for the latter to be the totality of all that is because consciousness then would have to consist in one or another form of absolute reflection. So we must admit that consciousness as an openness is determined in everyone by a factual limitation, and that this fact constitutes precisely our human facticity. Human consciousness manifests itself factually only as an openness to this or to that, and never immediately as an openness to the totality of Being, although a virtual openness to the totality of Being is not excluded. A philosophy of a complete reflection, a philosophy of an absolute knowledge in the sense of Hegel, is excluded in this way, since in this conception intentionality appears to be essentially historical and temporalizing.

We have characterized consciousness through the negativity of a radical openness; we also understand that this openness intends the totality of Being only virtually, being factually and effectively always a limited and finite presence to the things. Thus it becomes evident also that consciousness is able to manifest itself to itself and to the others, and thus to possess its real negativity, only by the very fact that, and by means of the mode in which, it factually discloses its view on the things and, at the same time, impresses its shape upon them. Hence it follows also that the proper Being of consciousness, thus the proper Being of subjectivity, cannot be defined directly and in itself because it is determined by the intentionality of an essential negativity. It can be defined only by being related to a dimension of reality which has arisen from facticity itself, and which is precisely consciousness itself as existing and as presence to itself and to the other. In this way we attain the definitive meaning of intentionality. This is also the very reason why modern thinking on intentionality does not call it consciousness, but *Dasein,* ek-sistence, relation, encounter, incarnated reality and so on. In connection with this we prefer not even to speak of intentionality, but rather about 'care' (*Sorge*), in order to indicate our explicit rejection of the rationalism of bygone centuries.

De Waelhens thinks it is possible on the basis of this interpretation of Husserl's conception of intentionaliy to show that in this way Husserl has also transcended the classical alternative realism-idealism. It seems to be possible to show here, too, how Husserl's work could be interpreted in a realistic as well as idealistic way, and why Husserl had to express himself sometimes in one way, and sometimes in the other.

First, it is evident that the main problem, as it was posited by realism and idealism, is neither a fundamental nor an exactly definable problem. For it makes no sense to ask how a subject can know a reality which is transcendent to himself if this subject is in no way alien to this reality, and if it is true that this subject himself, alone, is real and so can possess only himself in a continuous interaction with the world. In other words this question is meaningless because co-existence, encounter, and Being-in-the-world belong to the very essence of subjectivity itself, and furthermore because subjectivity's knowledge is only a special mode of this co-existence, in which mode the subject says to himself what the things are, and in which mode the subject places himself at a distance in order to constitute the world, himself and the mundane beings as objects which later on can be offered to the pure glance of subjectivity.

On the other hand, it makes no sense either to ask how a thing might be able to express itself and other beings if it belongs to the very essence of this 'thing' to be related to the other, that is to say, if this 'thing' by means of its intentionality and transcendental openness is destined to give sense to everything it intends by connecting this 'thing' with the others and finally with the totality of Being. Thus through our own ek-sistence itself we constitute the sense of the things; our theoretical knowledge is but a certain, and important, mode which this original constitution of sense can assume.

Now even if it is accepted that in this view of intentionality the famous opposition between realism and idealism is transcended in principle, this still does not mean that phenomenology does not have to express itself in the language of realism as well as idealism, thereby obviously giving rise to a difficult ambiguity, which can probably best be explained as follows.

We may say that Husserl's phenomenology is realistic inasmuch as it rejects a world of images and representations and the idea of representative thinking, and inasmuch as it refutes the conception of a consciousness which would possess itself in the absolute transparency of its contents. Also, phenomenology can be said to be realistic inasmuch as it believes a 'spiritual origin' of the world to be an incomprehensible myth and holds that only intuition is the original access to the things, and also that evidence is to be defined by means of a bodily presence of the intended objects. It protests immediately, however, against a realism that speaks of an objective pre-given world of objective things with objective statutes of being wholly independent of man, conceiving truth as an objective something which "lies" in the things like pebbles in a brook, claiming that philosophy is a study of eternal essences, comparing time with the flow of a river and conceiving history as the sum of all events which have happened since the appearance of man in the world.

The expressions of phenomenology become idealistics when it argues that there is sense and meaning only when a non-human being meets a being whose essence it is to be a *lumen naturale*. According to phenomenology things, it is true, receive only the meaning which belongs to them; but it remains true also that things have sense only as a consequence of their relatedness to man with whom they are in interaction. Man, indeed, does not create meaning in the strictest sense of this term, but it is true also that encounter is the origin of all sense. It is for this reason that phenomenology protests against idealism when idealism speaks of consciousness only and tries to reduce things to consciousness. It is not right to speak of consciousness only, where one should speak of *Dasein,* ek-sistence, encounter, which we really are. Because the constitution of sense in the encounter is the very Being of man himself, only exceptionally is this constitution rooted in our reflexive thinking and in thinking in general. Man's original Being-related-to-the-world wholly is illuminating, creating-of-sense and constituting.

In Royaumont, De Waelhens returned to this conception and, on the occasion of a commentary on Husserl's *The Idea of Phenomenology* (1907), again argued that phenomenology is an attempt to transcend the classical alternative, realism-idealism.[76]

Survey and Conclusion

Ambiguity in Husserl's Texts

In summarizing all that has just been said, and reflecting on the arguments presented for all of these conceptions, it is evident that there are very difficult problems to be dealt with here. As previously mentioned, the strange element in this situation is that none of the solutions

---

76. Alphonse De Waelhens, "Commentaires sur l'Idée de la Phénoménologie", *Husserl,* pp. 79-97.

advocated seems to be cogent. That this is true may be gathered from the fact that the adherents of the various opinions cannot convince one another, and that the discussion is taken up again and again. Especially impressive in this connection is the fact that every solution may refer to an extensive series of clear texts which appear perfectly convincing, but only as long as the quotations of the opponents are not taken into consideration. And this has been the case for over thirty years.

Everyone who advocates an idealistic interpretation of Husserl's phenomenology has to concede that the arguments of the protagonists of a realistic interpretation are not offered without reason. Therefore almost every 'idealist' admits that in Husserl's work there are series of texts which can be interpreted either in an empirist-realistic way, or in an existentialistic manner, and which in any case seem to resist an 'idealistic' interpretation. Some years ago Jean Wahl composed an anthology of such quotations,[77] a few points of which we wish to underline here. Husserl often argues explicitly that phenomenology in the first place deals with 'things themselves', with Being as such. In our contact with things experience occupies an important place. Although Husserl often posits that all reality is a sense only for a consciousness, on the other hand, he argues also that every sense is founded on an act of seeing; thus according to him intuition seems to be the original approach to Being. In other places sense is proposed as a form which has to 'inform' a non-intentional matter. Sometimes it seems that sense transcends itself and intends an object which must give the final mark of reality to that sense and which has to give 'reason' to consciousness. In Husserl's doctrine on evidence, which occupies an important place in his phenomenology, evidence itself is finally defined in terms of a bodily presence of the intended objects. Also, his idea of fulfillment, which is closely connected with his conception of evidence, is probably to be interpreted in a realistic way. In many places intentionality is called the center of phenomenology; this, however, is often to be understood as a Being-in-the-world, while the subject then seems to appear as an openness to the world. The relation between *noesis* and *noema* seems to re-

---

77. J. Wahl, "Note sur quelques aspects empiristes de la pensée de Husserl", *Phénoménologie-Existence*, pp. 107-135.

quire an existentialistic context, too. In other places Husserl writes that it is important to notice explicitly that the world really exists, and that the task of phenomenology consists just in determining the final sense of this undeniable reality.[78]

On the other side of the picture, every 'realist' and 'existentialist' has to concede that there are many texts in Husserl's works which resist a non-idealistic interpretation. It seems to be true that for Husserl meaning is more important than Being. For him Being is being-object. Thus, sense and meaning alone exist; every reality is only a sense for, in, and through consciousness. In this way phenomenology seems to be a study of pure consciousness, since there is nothing outside consciousness. Husserl often argues that a complete reflection is possible. Although in several places an original giving experience seems to be of primordial importance, on the other hand, it proves still to be the affirmation of a Being which is based on consciousness itself. In many instances it is impossible that intentionality be conceived as an ontological relation; it turns out to be the experience of sense rather than an original Being-in-the-world; consciousness then is no longer proposed as an openness to the world. Husserl never speaks of *Dasein,* of encounter, openness, etc., but always of consciousness and subjectivity. Furthermore, it seems that in Husserl's phenomenology immanence prevails over transcendence; encounter is not primary, but consciousness itself. Transcendence is also defined in terms of immanence, and existence in terms of 'ratio'. Only the transcendental consciousness is absolute; the world depends on an actual consciousness both in regard to its Being and to its sense. Husserl's ideas about reduction and constitution often are only understandable in an idealistic interpretation. Phenomenological reduction is represented frequently as the 'bracketing of Being', which seems to be based on idealistic prejudices. However, in particular his considerations about the transcendental reduction seem to be incompatible with an existentialistic interpretation of intentionality. Many 'idealistic' authors find it of great importance that Heidegger and Merleau-Ponty considered Husserl's doctrine to be an inadmissible form of idealism; an essential

---

78. J. Wahl, *loc. cit.,;* see also P. Ricoeur, "Etude sur les 'Méditations Cartésiennes' ", pp. 95-96.

difference exists between the phenomenology of Husserl and that of the 'existentialists'.[79]

Valuable But Inadequate Supplementary Considerations

Obviously such ambiguity as exists in Husserl's work gives no satisfaction. In order to escape the unsatisfactory facet of this situation several authors have searched for supplementary considerations. Some have tried to solve the problems by admitting an evolution in Husserl's phenomenology in this aspect. For instance, Boelaars, and several older commentators on Husserl's work, argue that Husserl developed from a point of view which antecedes the alternative realism-idealism, via a critical period to a transcendental idealism.[80] Yet excluding the unpublished manuscripts, we may posit that such a solution to our problem is very improbable, for the problem returns in all of Husserl's work between 1907 and 1938. Since 1940, therefore, this interpretation has been generally rejected. Sharing the views of Landgrebe, Fink, Berger and Ricoeur, we must admit that such a process of growth in Husserl's thinking between 1907 and 1938 is inadmissible; thus the solution to our problem is to be found elsewhere.[81] There is however no agreement among these authors concerning their positive points of view.

According to Berger a solution could be found in the fact that the series of texts mentioned are incompatible only when considered from a natural attitude. If we really understand Husserl's view we must try to attain the transcendental sphere. The ambiguity in Husserl's texts is to be explained by the fact that even in the transcendental sphere we must use a language that is proper to our natural attitude. However, this ambiguity, and with it all the problems, will disappear immediately if we are sufficiently conscious of the fundamental analogy of the words

---

79. L. Landgrebe, *Phänomenologie und Metaphysik*, pp. 83-100. Paul Ricoeur, *loc. cit.*, pp. 77-78, 92-94, 96-100, 102, 107-109.
80. H. Boelaars, "De intentionaliteit der kennis bij Edmund Husserl", pp. 112-121, 158-161, 238-240, 254-259.
81. Gaston Berger, *Le cogito dans la philosophie de Husserl*, pp. 12-15. Eugen Fink, "Die phänomenologische Philosophie Edmund Husserl in der gegenwärtigen Kritik", *Kantstudien*, 38 (1933) 319-383; "Das Problem der Phänomenologie Edmund Husserl", *Revue internationale de philosophie*, 1 (1938-1939) 226-270. Ludwig Landgrebe, *Phänomenologie und Metaphysik*, pp. 56-100 (passim).

to be used in phenomenology; phenomenology will then prove to be a philosophy of creative intuition. Although there seems to be a certain truth in Berger's consideration, it is not completely satisfactory, however, since as Berger explicitly concedes, he cannot give a convincing explication of Husserl's conception of the relation between constitution and intuition.[82]

Landgrebe and Ricoeur attempt to find a solution for our problems by distinguishing between analyses and the most profound intention with which these analyses are written. Husserl is an idealist in regard to his intention, but an 'existentialist' with respect to his analyses, thereby refuting this basic intention.[83]

Other authors mention that Husserl will analyze only in order to avoid all unfounded constructions. In particular he will evade all metaphysical prejudices in order to describe the things which manifest themselves to us and only insofar as they manifest themselves. Now it is evident that the problem of the opposition between realism and idealism is a theoretical problem which cannot be solved by means of analyses alone. On the other hand however, it is also evident that the point of view which Husserl assumes in this way cannot be maintained in a consistent manner since, as Fink expresses it so pithily, it is impossible to say anything whatsoever about the phenomenality of phenomena by means of analyses alone; while, on the other hand, it is absolutely necessary that one have a certain point of view in regard to this question, since otherwise the series of analyses is not founded. Thus although Husserl explicitly rejects a metaphysics-a-priori, nonetheless he implictly accepts a metaphysical standpoint. It is not surprising then that this a priori view is not always the same, simply because it is always only implicitly present. Whatever the case may be, in any event Husserl conceives this a priori viewpoint sometimes in a realistic way, other times in an idealistic way, insofar as the nature and the object of the analyses require it.[84]

---

82. Gaston Berger, *Le cogito dans la philosophie de Husserl*, pp. 100-117. See also Paul Ricoeur, *loc. cit.*, pp. 96-100.

83. See notes 28, 35, 54 and 55 of this chapter.

84. Eugen Fink, "L'analyse intentionnelle", *Problèmes actuels*, pp. 68-70.

In addition to these points, Fink points out the fact that in the work of every philosopher a distinction is to be made between thematic and operational concepts. What is striking is that in Husserl's philosophy the most fundamental concepts and conceptions are only operational concepts with which he works without explicitly defining them. It follows immediately then that in his philosophy we shall not find an answer for our problem, although he himself undoubtedly (probably implicitly) had one solution or another.[85]

It is De Waelhens' opinion that since 1906 Husserl had been thinking against an existentialistic background. De Waelhens sees the opposition between realism and idealism as radically transcended. On the other hand, however, it seems to be understandable and admissible that in such a view on our problem it is always possible, and even necessary, to use realistic terminology as well as idealistic.[86]

Finally, other authors point out that in regard to this aspect of Husserl's phenomenology there is a fundamental and even essential ambiguity; it consists in this that Husserl, who certainly was aware of our problem and was conscious also of the necessity of finding a solution for it, hesitated for a long time between transcendental idealism and an existentialistic solution.[87]

Different Attitudes. Husserl's Idealism

Despite the core of truth which all of these considerations contain, none of them seems to be satisfactory because the ambiguity *in Husserl's texts* on this point is fundamentally maintained. For, on the one hand, it is certain that in Husserl's works between 1906 and 1938 there are texts which are to be interpreted in an idealistic way, but there are also texts which necessarily require a realistic or existentialistic interpretation. On the other hand, however, the authors cited, who without exception admit the ambiguity in Husserl's texts, share the opinion that his work is to be interpreted in either an idealistic or existentialistic way. But it definitely is not evident to me how the generally admitted am-

---

85. Eugen Fink, "Operative Befriffe in Husserl's Phänomenologie", pp. 321-337.
86. Alphonse De Waelhens "L'idée phénoménologique, pp. 116-127.
87. Paul Ricoeur, "Etude sur les 'Méditations Cartésiennes' ", pp. 108-109.

biguity in the texts can be combined with any certainty concerning the final characterization of Husserl's view on this point. And it is unacceptable to me also that a great philosopher, as Husserl certainly was, did not find a clear solution for one of the most important problems of modern philosophy.

Therefore we propose as a solution to this problem that one should pay special attention to the fact that Husserl does not always think and write with the same mental attitude. It seems, in this light, desirable to distinguish three attitudes and correlatively with them, three spheres:

1) "The natural attitude", in which Husserl advocates an empirical realism inasmuch as he makes a pre-given objective world prevail over consciousness which in the last resort is passive in respect to this world.[88]

2) "The phenomenological sphere", in which Husserl endorses a point of view which could be indicated by the term existentialistic insofar as in that sphere consciousness and world are perfectly correlative.[89]

3) "The transcendental sphere", in which Husserl favors a transcendental idealism because consciousness as a transcendental subjectivity appears there as the only absolute reality, while the world proves to be nothing but a product-of-achievement for, in, and through this consciousness.[90]

Because in Husserl's eyes this last sphere is the most fundamental, his phenomenology ought to be characterized as a transcendental idealism. The advantage of this interpretation is that the "other" series of texts no longer appears as heterodox because in Husserl's work no further essential development should be assumed. Also, in this point of view the ambiguity continues to inhere in accidental points of Husserl's work, but now it may be accounted for by the fact that Husserl avoids

---

88. Edmund Husserl, *Ideen I,* pp. 57-63 (91-96).

89. Edmund Husserl, *Ideen II,* pp. 1-297. Ludwig Landgrebe, *Philosophie der Gegenwart,* pp. 31-32. Paul Ricoeur, "Analyses et problèmes dans 'Ideen II' de Husserl", *Phénoménologie-Existence,* pp. 23-76, pp. 69-76.

90. See, for instance, Edmund Husserl, *Ideen I,* the sections 33, 44, 46, 47, 49, 55, 81; *Ideen II,* pp. 297-302; *Ideen III,* 149-155; *F.tr.L.,* pp. 205-206; *Cart. Med.,* pp. 30-34, 99-121 (65-88).

theory as much as he can and, in addition, slides imperceptibly from one sphere to another.

In this interpretation Husserl's phenomenology as a whole is not acceptable. His analyses of the second sphere, however, seem to be of lasting importance, provided his idea of intentionality is interpreted in an ontological way and the phenomenological reduction is understood merely as a reduction of the world of culture to the *Lebenswelt*.

BIBLIOGRAPHY

S. Bachelard, *La logique de Husserl. Etude sur logique formelle et logique transcendentale* (Paris: Presses Universitaires de France, 1957).

O. Becker, "Die Philosophie Edmund Husserls", *Kantstudien,* 35 (1929), 119-150.

G. Berger, *Le Cogito dans la philosophie de Husserl* (Paris: Aubier, 1941).

W. Biemel, "Husserls Encyclopaedia Britannica Artikel und Heideggers Anmerkungen dazu", *Tijdschrift voor Philosophie,* 12(1950), 246-280.

R. Boehm, "Husserl et l'idéalisme classique", *Revue Philosophique de Louvain,* 57(1959), 351-396.

H. Boelaars, "De intentionaliteit der kennis bij Edmund Husserl", *Bijdragen,* 3(1940), 111-161, 221-264.
"Husserls reducties en haar betekenis voor het Thomisme", *Tijdschrift voor Philosophie,* 6(1944), 333-376.

G. Brand, *Welt, Ich und Zeit.* Nach unveröffentlichten Manuskripten Edmund Husserls (The Hague: Martinus Nijhoff, 1955).

A. De Muralt, *L'idée de la phénoménologie. L'exemplarisme husserlienne* (Paris: Gallimard, 1958).

A. De Waelhens, *Existence et Signification* (Louvain: Nauwelaerts, 1958).
Phénoménologie et vérité (Paris: Presses Universitaires de France, 1953).
La philosophie et les expériences naturelles (The Hague: Martinus Nijhoff, 1961).
"Husserl", in *Les Philosophes célèbres* (Paris: Mazenot, 1956), pp. 322-329.
"Phénoménologie husserlienne et phénoménologie hégélienne", *Revue Philosophique de Louvain,* 52(1954), 110-119.
"Husserl et la Phénoménologie", *Critique,* 8(1951), 1044-1051.

"Phénoménologie et réalisme", in *Revue Néoscolastique de Philosophie*, 39(1936), 497-517.
"De la phénoménologie à l'existentialisme", *La choix - le monde - l'existence* (Paris: Arthaud, 1947), pp. 37-82.
"Phénoménologie et dialectique", *Ordre-Désordre-Lumière* (Paris: Vrin, 1952), pp. 1-23.

A. Diemer, *Edmund Husserl. Versuch einer systematischen Darstellung seiner Phänomenolgie* (Meisenheim a.Gl.: Hain, 1956).

M. Drüe, *Edmund Husserls System der phänomenologischen Psychologie* (Berlin: Walter de Gruyter, 1963).

L. Dupré, "The Concept of Truth in Husserl's Logical Investigations", *Philosophy and Phenomenological Research*, 24(1963-1964) 345-354.

M. Farber, *The Foundation of Phenomenology. Edmund Husserl and the Quest for a Rigorous Science of Philosophy* (Cambridge: Harvard University Press, 1943).
Philosophical Essays in Memory of Edmund Husserl (Cambridge: Harvard University Press, 1940).

E. Fink, "Die phänomenologische Philosophie Edmund Husserls in der gegenwärtigen Kritik", *Kantstudien*, 38(1933), 319-383.
"Was will die Phänomenologie Edmund Husserls?", *Tatwelt*, 10(1934), 14-32.
"Das Problem der Phänomenologie Edmund Husserls", *Revue Internationale de Philosophie*, 1(1938), 226-270.
"Operative Begriffe in Husserls Phänomenologie", *Zeitschrift für philosophische Forschung*, 11(1957), 321-337.

A. Gurwitsch, *The Field of Consciousness*. (Pittsburgh: Duquesne University Press, 1964).
"The Last Work of Edmund Husserl", *Philosophy and Phenomenological Research*, 11(1956), 370-399.

Martin Heidegger, *Sein und Zeit* (Tübingen: Max Niemeyer, 1953).

H. Hohl, *Lebenswelt und Geschichte. Grundzüge der Spätphilosophie E. Husserls* (Freiburg: Karl Alber, 1962).

Iso Kern, *Husserl und Kant. Eine Untersuchung über Husserls Verhältnis zu Kant und zum Neukantianismus* (The Hague: Martinus Nijhoff, 1964).

A First Introduction to Husserl's Phenomenology

Joseph J. Kockelmans, *Edmund Husserl. Een inleiding tot zijn fenomenologie* (The Hague: Lannoo, 1963).

"Realisme—Idealisme en Husserls phaenomenologie", *Tijdschrift voor Philosophie*, 20(1958), 395-442.

Husserl's Phenomenological Psychology. A Historico-Critical Study (Pittsburgh: Duquesne University Press, 1966).

Ludwig Landgrebe, *Phänomenologie und Metaphysik* (Hamburg: Schröder, 1949).

Philosophie der Gegenwart (Bonn: Athenäum-Verlag, 1952).

Der Weg der Phänomenologie (Gütersloh: Gerd Mohn, 1963).

"Husserls Phänomenologie und die Motive zu ihrer Umbildung", *Revue Internationale de Philosophie,* 1(1938), 277-316.

"Seinsregionen und regionale Ontologien in Husserls Phänomenologie", *Studium Generale,* 9(1956), 313-324.

"The World as Phenomenological Problem", *Philosophy and Phenomenoligical Research,* 1(1939-1940) 39-53.

C. Lannoy, "Phenomenologie, ontologie en psychologie in het werk van Edmund Husserl", *Tijdschrift voor Philosophie,* 11(1949), 391-416.

Q. Lauer, *Phénoménologie de Husserl. Essai sur la genèse de l'intentionnalité* (Paris: Presses Universitaires de France, 1955.)

The Triumph of Subjectivity. An Introduction to Transcendental Phenomenology (New York: Fordham University Press, 1958).

E. Levinas, *La théorie de l'intuition dans la phénoménologie de Husserl* (Paris: Vrin, 1963).

"L'oeuvre d'Edmond Husserl", *Revue Philosophique de France et de l'Etranger,* 129(1940), 33-85.

En découvrant l'existence avec Husserl et Heidegger (Paris: Gallimard, 1949).

M. Merleau-Ponty, *Phénoménologie de la Perception* (Paris: Gallimard, 1945).

A. Osborn, *The Philosophy of Edmund Husserl in Its Development from His Mathematical Interest to His First Conception of Phenomenology in 'Logical Investigations'* (New York: International Press, 1934).

G. Pedroli, *La fenomenologia di Husserl* (Torino: Taylor, 1958).

P. Ricoeur, "Analyses et problèmes dans 'Ideen II' de Husserl", *Phénoménologie—Existence*. Recueil d'études par H. Birault, H. Van Breda, A. Gurwitsch, E. Levinas, P. Ricoeur et J. Wahl (Paris: Gallimard, 1953), pp. 23-76.
"Etude sur les 'Méditations Cartésiennes' de Husserl", *Revue Philosophique de Louvain,* 52(1954), 75-109.
"Kant et Husserl", in *Kantstudien,* 46(1954), 44-67.

A. Schuetz, "Type and Eidos in Husserl's Late Philosophy", *Philosophy and Phenomenological Research,* 20(1959), 147-165.

R. Sokolowski, *The Formation of Husserl's Concept of Constitution* (The Hague: Martinus Nijhoff, 1964).

H. Spiegelberg, *The Phenomenological Movement. A Historical Introduction.* 2 vol. (The Hague: Martinus Nijhoff, 1960).
"Phenomenology of Direct Evidence", *Philosophy and Phenomenological Research,* 2(1942), 427-456.

Stephan Strasser, *Phenomenology and the Human Sciences* (Pittsburgh: Duquesne University Press, 1963).
"Beschouwingen over het vraagstuk van de apodicticiteit en de critische verantwoording van de phaenomenologie", *Tijdschrift voor Philosophie,* 8(1946), 226-270.

P. Thévenaz, *What is Phenomenology? And Other Essays,* Tr. by James M. Edie (Chicago: Quadrangle Books, 1962).

H. Van Breda, "Het 'zuivere phaenomeen' volgens Edmund Husserl", *Tijdschrift voor Philosophie,* 3(1941), 447-498.
"Het Husserl-Archief te Leuven", *Tijdschrift voor Philosophie,* 7(1945), 195-200.

C. Van Peursen, "Phénoménologie et ontologie", *Rencontre.* Contributions à une psychologie humaine dédiées au Professor F.J.J. Buytendijk (Utrecht-Antwerpen: Het Spectrum, 1957), pp. 308-317.

J. Wahl, "Notes sur la première partie de 'Erfahrung und Urteil' de Husserl", *Phénoménologie-Existence,* pp. 77-105.
"Note sur quelques aspects empiristes de la pensée de Husserl", *Phénoménologie-Existence,* pp. 107-135.
L'ouvrage posthume de Husserl: La 'Krisis'. La crise des sciences européennes et la phénoménologie transcendentale (Paris: Les Cours de Sorbone, 1957).

A First Introduction to Husserl's Phenomenology

E. Parl Welch, *The Philosophy of Edmund Husserl. The Origin and Development of his Phenomenology* (New York: Octagon Books Inc., 1965).

For Roman Ingarden. Nine Essays in Phenomenology (The Hague: Martinus Nijhoff, 1959).

Problèmes actuels de la phénoménologie. Actes du premier Colloque international de phénoménologie. Bruxelles: Avril 1951. Edités par H. L. Van Breda (Brugge-Paris: Desclée de Brouwerx, 1952).

Husserl et la pensée moderne. Actes du deuxiéme Colloque international de phénoménologie. Krefeld: 1-3 novembre 1956. Edités par H. L. Van Breda et J. Taminiaux (The Hague: Martinus Nijhoff, 1959).

Husserl. Actes du troisième Colloque international de phénoménologie. Royaumont: 23 au 30 avril 1957. Edités par M.-A. Bera (Paris: Minuit, 1959).

Edmund Husserl: 1859-1959. Recueil commémoratif publié à l'occasion du Centenaire de la naissance du philosophe. Edité par H. L. Van Breda et J. Taminiaux (The Hague: Martinus Nijhoff, 1959).

See for a more comprehensive bibliography:

H. L. Van Breda, "Bibliographie der bis zum 30. Juni 1959 veröffentlitchen Schriften Edmund Husserl", *Edmund Husserl: 1859-1959,* pp. 289-306.

L. Eley, "Husserl-Bibliographie (1945-1959), *Zeitschrift für philosophische Forschung,* 13(1959), 357-367.

J. Patocka, "Husserl-Bibliographie", *Revue Internationale de Philosophie,* 1(1939), 374-397.

J. Raes, "Supplément à la Bibliographie de Husserl", *Revue Internationale de Philosophie,* 4(1950), 469-475.

J.-D. Robert, "Elements de bibliographie Husserlienne", *Tijdschrift voor Philosophie,* 20(1958), 534-544.

INDEX OF NAMES

(A lower case *n* after a number indicates that the reference is to a footnote on the page in question.)

Berger, G., 320(*n*), 322-326, 351, 352.
Berkeley, G., 4, 61, 80, 319.
Biemel, M., *xiii*.
Biemel, W., *ii*, *xiii*, 2, 62, 320(*n*), 330-334.
Boehm, R., *viii*.
Boelaars, H., 351.
Bohr, N., 38.
Bolzano, B., *x*.
Brand, G., 205.
Brentano, F., *x*, 2, 3, 4, 14, 17, 38, 170, 171, 205, 282, 284, 285, 287, 290, 297.

Copernicus, N., 70.

Descartes, R., *xi*, 19, 21, 30, 36, 38, 40, 41, 42, 46, 64, 65, 66, 67, 68, 69, 70, 71, 72, 73, 74, 75, 76, 137, 138, 163, 165, 172, 257, 318, 329, 338.
De Waelhens, A., *ii*, 62, 63, 320(*n*), 321, 341-348, 353.
Diemer, A., *ii*, 205.
Dilthey, W., 37, 53.

Einstein, A., 39, 271, 272.
Erdmann, J., 7.
Farber, M., *ii*, 1-19 (passim).
Fichte, J., 46.
Fink, E., *ii*, *xiii*, *xiv*, *xvi*, 201, 320(*n*), 337-339, 351, 352.
Frege, G., *xi*, 6, 7, 9.

Galileo, 38, 268, 272, 275.
Geiger, M., 83.
Goethe, J., 10.
Gurwitsch, A., *ii*, 320(*n*).

Hegel, G., 46, 341, 346.
Heidegger, M. *xii*, 329, 330, 331, 332, 333, 334, 343, 350.
Hume, D., *x*, 4, 27, 61, 80, 222, 282.

Ingarden, R. 320(*n*).

Kant, I., *xi*, 2, 19, 20, 36, 42, 44, 46, 65, 68, 69, 70, 71, 73, 182, 224, 256, 257, 264, 324, 339, 345.
Königsberger, H., *x*.
Kronecker, L., *ix*, 3.
Kummer, E., *ix*.

Landgrebe, L., *ii*, *xiii*, 101, 259, 320(*n*), 326-334, 335, 351, 352.
Lauer, Q., *ii*, 166, 167, 227, 320(*n*).
Leibniz, G., 68, 338.
Lévy-Bruhl, L., 270.
Lipps, T., 7, 8, 228, 287.
Locke, J., 4, 61, 80, 282.
Lorentz, H., 38, 271, 272.
Lotze, H., *x*.

Masaryk, T., 3.
Mach, E., 1.
Merleau-Ponty M., 62, 63, 259, 321, 341-342, 350.
Mill, J. Stuart, *x*, 5, 7, 8, 61, 282.
Müller, M., 320(*n*).

Natorp, P., 7, 8.
Neo-Kantians, 7.
Newton, I., 38.

Paulsen, F., *ix*, *x*, 282.
Pfänder, A., 83.
Plato, 38, 46, 65, 71.

Reinach, A., 83.
Ricoeur, *ii*, 320(*n*), 335-337, 351, 352.
Romantics, 46.
Rutherford, E., 38.

Scheler, M., 83.
Scholastics, 46, 72, 170.
Sigwart, Chr. *v*., 7.

INDEX OF SUBJECT MATTER

Abstraction, 80, 81, 82; Ideating Abstraction: see Ideation; and natural science, 273, 306; complementary abstraction and phenomenological psychology, 306-307. See also Eidetic Abstraction.

Abstractum, 98.

Act, as intentional experience, 145.

Actuality, of intentional life, 193-195.

Analogizing apprehension, 240-241.

Analogy, assimilative analogy, 230; analogizing apprehension, 240-241.

Anticipation, 212.

Apodicticity, and evidence, 74; of transcendental subjectivity, 162-163; as goal of phenomenology, 195-196; see also Evidence, Self-Evidence, Transcendental Subjectivity.

Apperception, mundanizing, 235; objectifying, 238; assimilative, 240; of the alter ego, 242.

Apperceptive transfer, 240.

Appresentation, 229-230, 239-241, 245.

As-If Reality, 209-210.

Association, 114; as universal principle of passive genesis, 222-223, 300; is a matter of intentionality, 222; as fundamental concept of phenomenology, 222; pairing association, 244.

Attention, and intentionality, 183-184; and intuition, 202-203.

Beginning (radical), 133, 136.

Being, as consciousness and as reality, 152-156; as intelligibility, 204; is absolute only as constituted by transcendental subjectivity, 204; must be reduced to Reason, 204; consciousness and Being-in-consciousness as forms of absolute Being, 204; refers to the objects meant, 208; as the correlate of evident verification, 209-211; can be explained only through intentional constitution, 225-226; absolute Being as monadological intersubjectivity, 230-249; Being 'as it is in itse'f' and science, 272-274, 276, 277, 278, 304; Being and consciousness are one in the absolute concretion of transcendental subjectivity, 319; is Being-object, 329, 334, 335, 337, 350; is implied in the realm of meaning, 324, 335, 337.

Belief, in the reality of the world, 210-212, 261-262.

Belonging to, 126-127.

'Bracketing', see Reduction.

Category, 93-98; logical categories, 94-95; formal categories, 94; categories of signification, 95; as standing for concepts and formal essences, 95; syntactic categories, 95; substrative categories, 95, 97; regional categories, 97, 101; as consciously constituted, 192.

Clarification (process of), 210.

Classification, of the sciences, 99.

Cogitatum, 174, 196, passim; is apodictic evident after the reduction, 196.

Cogito, is apodictic evident, 172, 196; as transcendental ground of knowledge, 173-174; contains its cogitatum, 174, 179; refers to the ego, 179; see also passim.

Communalization, of intentionality, 238; in regard to the common world, 245, 247; between two monads, 246-247.

Communion, between monads, 246-247, 318.

Community, of monads, 238; constitution of the community, 245-246.

Compossibility, of actualities and potentialities in the genesis of the ego, 218-219.

Concretum, 98.

Consciousness, and attention (Descartes), 74-75; and intention (Husserl), 74-75; is essentially intentional, 169-200 (passim); as relation sui generis, 170, 345; as openness, 169-170, 345-347; as negativity, 345. Consciousness of inner time, 179-183, 193; consciousness is not informing (Kant) but 'creating', 325; and Dasein, 332-334, 346-347; and Sorge, 346.

Pure consciousness (=transcendental consciousness) as residue after the reduction, 140-143, 159; as absolute region of Being, 143; and reality, 143-157; as subject matter of phenomenology, 148, 157-164; as a self-contained system of absolute Being, 158-159, 204.

Constitution, of numbers (in *Phil. d. A.*), 3, 5; of ideal objects in general, 12-13, 281-282; in *The Idea,* 33-34, 202-203; in *Ideas* and *F. tr. L.*, 203-205; in *C.M.*, 206-207; of essences, 82-83; and intentionality, 169, 191-192, 196-197, 199, 211-213, 225, 316-317, 319, 323, 335-337, 338, 340-341; as operational concept, 201-202; of objects, 201, 203; of acts, 201; of conscious life, 201; of transcendental subjectivity, 201, 213-224; as dissolution of Being in consciousness, 202, 257; and presentation, 203; and analysis of inner time consciousness 205; primal constitution of the stream of time, 205, 257; description of, 207-208; transcendental constitution as infinite task, 213; of other ego, 242-245; of transcendental intersubjectivity, 245-247; of world-for-everybody, 248-249; of world of culture, 248-249.

Crisis, of the sciences, 66-68, 316; and Descartes, 73; and Husserl, 73; of modern science and culture, 251-255.

Criterion of truth, as the self-evidence of intuitively grasped data, 107-108, 116-119.

Deformalization, 97, 104.

Dependence, and categorial forms, 97-98.

Description, noetic and noematic, 178; static description in phenomenological psychology, 300.

Descriptive psychology, and phenomenology, 1-19, 284-285; and empirical psychology, 16-19; and phenomenological psychology, 17-18, 284; and transcendental philosophy, 18-19, 173-174, 284-285; and epistemology, 31.

Disinterested spectator, 76, 177, 299, 333.

Dogmatic attitude, 135-139; *see also* Natural attitude.

Dogmatic sciences, 118-119.

Doubt, radical and methodical (Descartes), 67-68, 73, 75, 137-138, 165.

Ego, passim; pure ego, 162-163, 178-179; psychological and transcendental ego, 163-164; doubling of ego, 177; temporal field of ego, 182; *ego—cogito—cogitatum*, 198; ego is not an empty pole of identity, 214; constitutes itself in a transcendental genesis, 214-216, 218-220; as identical substratum of ego-properties, 215-216; the *eidos* 'ego' and the *de facto* ego, 217, 225; transcendental ego, 217, 319; pure ego and *Dasein*, 332-334. *See also* Transcendental subjectivity.

Ego—community, 238.

Eidetic abstraction, 32-33; and transcendental analysis, 216-218; *see also* Eidetic reduction.

Eidetic reduction, 79-80, 82, 83, 86-88, 106, 112-116, 134, 143; and life-world, 277; and phenomenological psychology, 291, 301.

Eidetic science, *see* Science, Pure essence, and Ontology.

Eidos, as pure essence, 86, 87, 88, 106, 113. *See also* Essence, and Pure essence.

Empathy, 85, 228-230, 249; not a primordial object-giving act, 229.

Empiricism, 61, 80, 107, 108-110, 117-118.

Epistemology, 27-28; and phenomenology, 28-29; and psychology, 31: and natural science, 51-52, 135-136; as pure phenomenology of consciousness, 77-79; and transcendental phenomenology, 251, 319-320.

Epoché, as radical inhibition of every objectifying position, 18; with respect to previous philosophical views, 107-108; *see also* Reduction.

Essence, 86, 106, 113; as ideal object, 35; general essence, 78-82; ultimate substantive essence, 97; regional essence, 98; *see also* Reduction, Fact, and General.

365

172, 307; as the very essence of consciousness, 172, 183-185, 196, 344-345; as main theme of phenomenology, 172-185; and attention, 183-184; static and dynamic aspect, 184; static description of, 185-191; dynamic description of, 191-195; 'functioning intentionality', 195, 280, 342; intentionality and ek-sistence, 332-334, 342, 345, 346; is not an ontological relation according to Husserl, 350.

Intersubjectivity, 66, 225-249; problems concerning intersubjectivity, 227-228; monadological intersubjectivity as realm of transcendental Being, 230-249; constitution of, 247; psychological and transcendental intersubjectivity, 306.

Intramonadic community, 246.

Intuition, as simple 'seeing', 33, 78, 109, 125, 128-129; of essences, 78-79, 86-89, 106, 110; possible by means of ideation, 79, 106; and self-givenness, 82; as original source of scientific justification, 85; adequate and inadequate, 86-88, 128; of individual, 86-88, 106; objectifying intuition, 90; and self-evidence, 107-108; as primordial object-giving consciousness, 110; and experience, 108-110; of essences as primordial dator act, 112, is analogous to perception, 112; primordial intuition as legitimate source of knowledge and ultimate criterion of truth, 116-118, 195-196; primordial intuition, 125-128. *See also* Principle of all principles.

Judgment, about essences, 89-90; eidetic judgments, 89-90; judged content and matter judged about, 190-191.

Laws of nature, refer to essence of things, 86.

Life-world (*Lebenswelt*), 66, 71-72, 250-280 (passim). Meaning of term, 252, 268-271; constitution of life-world by transcendental subectivity, 252-253, 278-279; and phenomenology, 259-260; in *Crisis*, 267-268; and science, 268-269, 273-275, 306; as intersubjective world, 270; historico-social

implications of, 270-271; and science, 271-275; relativity of the life-world, 276; categories belonging to the life-world and scientific categories, 276-277; as possible world of intersubjective experience, 277; as intentional correlate of transcendental subjectivity, 309-310.

Logic, and philosophy, 1-19 (passim); as natural science, 27; and psychologism, 9-12, 282-285; and phenomenology, 77-81; foundation of logic and linguistic analysis, 77-79; and epistemology, 77-78; as pure science of essences, 91-92; as study of the essence of 'object-in-general' or 'meaning-in-general', 92, 94, 96, 102-103; apophantic logic and formal ontology, 251.

Logical entities, are constituted entities, 3-5, 12-13, 281-282, 284; are 'irreal', 283; as unities of meaning, 78-79, 283; refer to 'ideal' truths, 283; have a characteristic mode of Being of their own, 283-284.

Mathematics, philosophy of, 2-5; and psychologism, 5-9; pure mathematics, 91-92; and empiricism, 117-118; *see also* Ontology.

Mathematization, of nature in natural science, 306.

Mathesis universalis, 92, 93; comprises formal logic as universal analytic, arithmetic, pure analysis, and set theory, etc., 103.

Meaning, 80, 170; and object meant, 80, 170; and multiple acts of meaning, 80; as ideal entity 80; noematic meaning, 126-127; arises from the constitutive syntheses of the ego, 231-232; as the proper subject matter of phenomenology, 323-324, 339-340; implies the whole sphere of Being, 324, 340; and presence, 343.

Method of free variation, 114-116; and phenomenological psychology, 301; *see also* Eidetic Reduction.

Monad, as the ego in its full concreteness, 215; communion of monads, 246-247, 318.